But These are Written . . .

But These are Written . . .

Essays on Johannine Literature
in Honor of Professor Benny C. Aker

EDITED BY
CRAIG S. KEENER
JEREMY S. CRENSHAW
JORDAN DANIEL MAY

PICKWICK *Publications* • Eugene, Oregon

BUT THESE ARE WRITTEN . . .
Essays on Johannine Literature in Honor of Professor Benny C. Aker

Copyright © 2014 Wipf and Stock Publishers. All rights reserved. Except for brief quotations in critical publications or reviews, no part of this book may be reproduced in any manner without prior written permission from the publisher. Write: Permissions, Wipf and Stock Publishers, 199 W. 8th Ave., Suite 3, Eugene, OR 97401.

Scripture quotations taken from the New American Standard Bible®, Copyright © 1960, 1962, 1963, 1968, 1971, 1972, 1973, 1975, 1977, 1995 by The Lockman Foundation Used by permission. (www.Lockman.org)

Scriptures taken from the Holy Bible, New International Version®, NIV®. Copyright © 1973, 1978, 1984 by Biblica, Inc.™ Used by permission of Zondervan. All rights reserved worldwide.

Scripture quotations are from Common Bible: New Revised Standard Version Bible, copyright © 1989 National Council of the Churches of Christ in the United States of America. Used by permission. All rights reserved.

Pickwick Publications
An Imprint of Wipf and Stock Publishers
199 W. 8th Ave., Suite 3
Eugene, OR 97401

www.wipfandstock.com

ISBN 13: 978-1-61097-205-5

Cataloguing-in-Publication data:

"But these are written . . .": essays on Johannine literature in honor of professor Benny C. Aker / edited by Craig S. Keener, Jeremy S. Crenshaw, and Jordan Daniel May, with a foreword by Delbert Tarr.

xx + 298 pp. ; 23 cm. Includes bibliographical references.

ISBN 13: 978-1-61097-205-5

1. Bible. Johannine literature—Criticism, interpretation, etc. 2. Aker, Benny C., 1939– I. Title.

BS2601 B89 2014

Manufactured in the U.S.A.

Contents

List of Contributors | vii
Foreword by Delbert Tarr | ix
List of Abbreviations | xi

1. Biographical Sketch of Benny C. Aker | 1
   Lois E. Olena

2. He Will Guide You into All the Truth | 15
   John W. Wyckoff

3. The Role and Function of the Demonic in the Johannine Tradition | 27
   John Christopher Thomas

4. John's Doxology: The Trinitarian Passion for the Glory of God | 48
   Bruce E. Rosdahl

5. The Virgin Birth in the Fourth Gospel? A Brief Note on the Triple-Negation in John 1.13 | 59
   Jordan Daniel May

6. Master(s) of the Sea? Ephesian Fishermen, John 6.16–21, and John 21 | 65
   Warren Carter

7. Episodes of Personal Encounter: Inquiry into John's Christology | 80
   James D. Hernando

8. A New Look at an Old Problem: A Narrative Approach to John 7.37–39 | 101
   Philip L. Mayo

9   Born of God: The "Virgin Birth" of Believers in the Fourth Gospel | 121
    Michael C. McKeever

10 Seeking Peace with Justice: Toward a Christomorphic Pneumatology | 139
    Paul Alexander

11 The Love of God: An Interdisciplinary Approach to Developing and Measuring Spiritual Maturity Based on a Johannine Love Ethic | 153
    Edward W. Watson and Angela L. Watson

12 The "Antichrists" Speak: A Message to the Community of 1 John | 171
    Robert A. Berg

13 Choose Your Own Adventure: Teaching, Participatory Hermeneutics, and the Book of Revelation | 178
    Robby Waddell

14 Will the Real Church Please Stand Up? An Exegetical Examination of Revelation 11.1–13 | 194
    Jeremy S. Crenshaw

15 The Spirit of the Lamb: A Reflection on the Pneumatology of Revelation | 214
    Frank D. Macchia

16 Was John the Revelator Pentecostal? | 221
    Robert P. Menzies

17 One Thousand Two Hundred Sixty Days: A Charismatic-Prophetic Empowerment Reading of Time and God's People in the Book of Revelation | 235
    Craig S. Keener

18 The Vocabulary and Phraseology of Revelation | 247
    Timothy P. Jenney

Appendices
   1 *Tables* | 259
   2 *Graphs* | 270

Select Author Index | 295

Contributors

Paul Alexander (PhD, Baylor University)—Ronald J. Sider Professor of Christian Ethics and Public Policy, Palmer Theological Seminary, Eastern University, Wynnewood, PA.

Robert A. Berg (PhD, Drew University)—Professor of New Testament, Evangel University, Springfield, MO.

Warren Carter (PhD, Princeton Theological Seminary)—Professor of New Testament, Brite Divinity School, Texas Christian University, Fort Worth, TX.

Jeremy S. Crenshaw (PhD Student, Regent University)—Adjunct Instructor, Oral Roberts University, Tulsa, OK.

James D. Hernando (PhD, MPhil, Drew University)—Professor of New Testament, Assemblies of God Theological Seminary at Evangel University, Springfield, MO.

Timothy P. Jenney (PhD, University of Michigan)—Adjunct Professor in Religious Studies, Regent University, Virginia Beach, VA.

Craig S. Keener (PhD, Duke University)—Professor of New Testament, Asbury Theological Seminary, Wilmore, KY.

Frank D. Macchia (DTheol, University of Basel)—Professor of Theology, Vanguard University, Costa Mesa, CA.

Jordan Daniel May (ThM, MDiv, Princeton Theological Seminary)—Correctional Chaplain with the Assemblies of God.

Philip L. Mayo (PhD, Fuller Theological Seminary)—Professor of New Testament and Greek, North Central University, Minneapolis, MN.

Michael C. McKeever (PhD, Graduate Theological Union/University of California, Berkeley)—Professor of Biblical Studies, Judson University, Elgin, IL.

Contributors

Robert P. Menzies (PhD, University of Aberdeen)—Director of Synergy, a rural service organization located in Kunming, China.

Lois E. Olena (DMin, Assemblies of God Theological Seminary)—DMin Project Coordinator and Associate Professor of Practical Theology and Jewish Studies, Assemblies of God Theological Seminary at Evangel University, Springfield, MO.

Bruce E. Rosdahl (PhD, Dallas Theological Seminary)—Department Chair of Bible and Theology/Professor of Bible and Theology, Southwestern Assemblies of God University, Waxahachie, TX.

Delbert H. Tarr Jr. (PhD, University of Minnesota)—Missions Pastor of Capital Christian Center, Sacramento, CA, and Professor Emeritus and former President, Assemblies of God Theological Seminary, Springfield, MO.

John Christopher Thomas (PhD, University of Sheffield)—Clarence J. Abbott Professor of Biblical Studies, Pentecostal Theological Seminary, Cleveland, TN and Director, Centre for Pentecostal and Charismatic Studies, School of Philosophy and Religion, Bangor University, Bangor, UK.

Robby Waddell (PhD, University of Sheffield)—Professor of New Testament and Early Christian Literature, Southeastern University, Lakeland, FL.

Angela A. Watson (PhD, Oklahoma State University)—Assistant Professor, Oklahoma Wesleyan University, Bartlesville, OK.

Edward W. Watson (PhD, Baylor University)—Chair, Undergraduate Program, School of Theology and Missions, Oral Roberts University, Tulsa, OK.

John W. Wyckoff (PhD, Baylor University)—Graduate Chair of Theological Studies and Professor of Bible and Theology, Southwestern Assemblies of God University, Waxahachie, TX.

Foreword

I SIMPLY CANNOT WRITE a foreword for my friend Ben Aker's *Festschrift* without opening with an African proverb. And this one fits him well:

An old man while seated can see farther than a young man while standing.

Do not let the phrase, "old man" offend you. In Africa, old men are respected. As one matures in age, the more honor they receive! There are no "rest homes" in Africa.

We were not "old men" when Ben and I first became friends in the 70s. Yet he was always wise beyond his years. When founding a new seminary in California, or when coming home to AGTS (Assemblies of God Theological Seminary), I chose this prince of the church for many reasons, but especially one: Look at his list of articles! Over half discuss the Holy Spirit's role in the world today or the mystery of how the supernatural is available to we mortals, who so need something besides humanistic analysis, control, and selfish power—all the while operating, "In the name of God." *Call him a "spiritual" Pentecostal brother.*

The second reason I sought out this servant-leader is because I observed his behavior, even if repeatedly falsely accused (sometimes even by his brethren). Ben Aker stood for truth and ethics, yet without retaliation. He held no rancor nor sought vengeance. *Call him an obedient and irenic disciple of the Lord.*

As for academics, this professor has two seemingly opposing sides. Although the difficulty of his classes is legendary, each one of his students personally knew how much he cared for them. Ben Aker is a real mentor. And he has the largest number of deeply loyal students. They always want to talk about him. "Do you know Ben Aker?" is the most oft opening remark heard. I am frankly jealous! Might Ben not be like the apostle Jesus loved? *Call him impressionably effective.*

Foreword

Johannine literature, perhaps Ben's primary joy, is the focus of these essays. *So stand or sit beside this seated, wise, mature professor we honor. Look in the direction he is looking, and come to see what he sees!*

Del Tarr, PhD
Former president and
professor emeritus,
Assemblies of God Theological Seminary

Abbreviations

GENERAL ABBREVIATIONS

AB	Anchor Bible
ABRL	Anchor Bible Reference Library
ACNT	Augsburg Commentaries on the New Testament
A/G	Assemblies of God
AGTS	Assemblies of God Theological Seminary
AJT	*Asian Journal of Theology*
aka	Also known as
AnBib	Analecta biblica
ANF	Alexander Roberts and William Donaldson, eds. *The Ante-Nicene Fathers*, 10 vols.
ANTC	Abingdon New Testament Commentary
AThR	*Anglican Theological Review*
B.C.E.	Before Common (or Christian) Era
BDAG	W. Bauer, F. W. Danker, W. F. Arndt, and F. W. Gingrich, eds. *Greek-English Lexicon of the New Testament and other Early Christian Literature,* 3rd ed.
BECNT	Baker Exegetical Commentary on the New Testament
BETL	Bibliotheca ephemeridum theologicarum lovaniensium
Bib	*Biblica*
BJS	Brown Judaica Series

Abbreviations

BSac	*Biblica Sacra*
ca.	circa (approximately)
CBQ	*Catholic Biblical Quarterly*
C.E.	Common (or Christian) Era
cf.	confer (compare or consult)
ch./chs.	chapter/chapters
CNT	Commentaire du Nouveau Testament
CovTQ	*Covenant Theological Quarterly*
CP	*Classical Philology*
CPT	Centre for Pentecostal Theology
CTJ	*Calvin Theological Journal*
CV	*Communio viatorum*
CYOA	Choose Your Own Adventure
diss.	dissertation
EBC	Expositor's Bible Commentary
ECNT	Exegetical Commentary on the New Testament
ed.(s.)	editor(s); edition
e.g.	exempli gratia (for example)
ERT	*Evangelical Review of Theology*
esp.	especially
et al.	et alii (and others)
etc.	et cetera (and the rest)
ETS	Evangelical Theological Society
ex.	Example
ExpTim	*Expository Times*
f./ff.	and the following ones
FG	Fourth Gospel
Fig.	Figure
GNT	Greek New Testament
GPH	Gospel Publishing House
HCSC	Harper Collins Spiritual Classics

Abbreviations

IBTS	Interpreting Biblical Texts Series
ibid.	ibidem, in the same place
ICC	International Critical Commentary
idem	the same
i.e.	id est (that is)
Int	Interpretation
ITQ	Irish Theological Quarterly
IVP	InterVarsity Press
JAP	Journal of Analytical Psychology
JBL	Journal of Biblical Literature
JEPTA	Journal of the European Pentecostal Theological Association
JPT	Journal of Pentecostal Theology
JPTSup	Journal of Pentecostal Theology: Supplement Series
JSNTSup	Journal for the Study of the New Testament: Supplement Series
JSOT	Journal for the Study of the Old Testament
JSSR	Journal for the Scientific Study of Religion
JTS	Journal of Theological Studies
LXX	Septuagint
MidJT	Midwestern Journal of Theology
Mod. Theol.	Modern Theology
n./nn.	note/notes
NA^{27}	Novum Testamentum Graece, Nestle-Aland, 27th edition
NAC	New American Commentary
NCBC	New Cambridge Bible Commentary
NCBCom	New Century Bible Commentary
Neot	Neotestamentica
NIBC	New International Biblical Commentary
NICNT	New International Commentary on the New Testament

xiii

Abbreviations

NIGTC	New International Greek Testament Commentary
NIV	New International Version
NIVABC	NIV Application Bible Commentary
NovT	*Novum Testamentum*
NovTSup	Supplements to Novum Testamentum
NT	New Testament
NTL	New Testament Library
NTS	New Testament Studies
OT	Old Testament
passim	here and there
PCS	Pentecostal Commentary Series
PNTC	Pelican New Testament Commentaries
RB	*Revue biblique*
RBS	Resources for Biblical Study
repr.	reprint
rev.	revised
SBL	Society of Biblical Literature
SBLSymS	Society of Biblical Literature Symposium Series
SBS	Stuttgarter Bibelstudien
Scr	*Scripture*
SNTSMS	Society of New Testament Studies Monograph Series
SP	Sacra Pagina
SPS	Society for Pentecostal Studies
StudBL	Studies in Biblical Literature
TDNT	Kittel and Friedrich, *Theological Dictionary of the New Testament*
TPINTC	TPI New Testament Commentaries
trans.	translator, translated by
TrinJ	*Trinity Journal*
TynBul	*Tyndale Bulletin*
UBCS	Understanding the Bible Commentary Series

Abbreviations

UBS	United Bible Society
v./vv.	verse/verses
vol./vols.	volume/volumes
WBC	Word Biblical Commentary
WBT	Word Biblical Themes
WJKP	Westminster John Knox Press
ZIBBCNT	Zondervan Illustrated Bible Background Commentary: New Testament
ZNW	*Zeitschrift für die neutestamentliche Wissenschaft und die Kunde der älteren Kirche*

OLD TESTAMENT/HEBREW BIBLE

Gen	Genesis		Isa	Isaiah
Exod	Exodus		Jer	Jeremiah
Lev	Leviticus		Ezek	Ezekiel
Num	Numbers		Dan	Daniel
Deut	Deuteronomy		Hos	Hosea
1–2 Sam	1–2 Samuel		Joel	Joel
1–2 Kgs	1–2 Kings		Mic	Micah
Job	Job		Hab	Habakkuk
Ps/Pss	Psalm(s)		Zech	Zechariah
Prov	Proverbs		Mal	Malachi

NEW TESTAMENT

Matt	Matthew		1–2 Cor	1–2 Corinthians
Mark	Mark		Gal	Galatians
Luke	Luke		Eph	Ephesians
John	John		Phil	Philippians
Acts	Acts		1–2 Thess	1–2 Thessalonians
Rom	Romans		1–2 Tim	1–2 Timothy

Abbreviations

Heb	Hebrews	1–2–3 John	1–2–3 John
Jas	James	Jude	Jude
1–2 Pet	1–2 Peter	Rev	Revelation

LXX/DEUTEROCANONICAL BOOKS

Bar	Baruch	3–4 Macc	3–4 Maccabees
1–2 Esd	1–2 Esdras	Sir	Sirach
Jdt	Judith	Wis	Wisdom of Solomon
1–2 Macc	1–2 Maccabees		

OLD TESTAMENT PSEUDEPIGRAPHA

Apoc. Ab.	Apocalypse of Abraham
Apoc. Ezek.	Apocalypse of Ezekiel
Apoc. Mos.	Apocalypse of Moses
Apoc. Sedr.	Apocalypse of Sedrach
Aris. Ex.	Aristeas the Exegete
Artap.	Artapanus
Ascen. Isa.	Ascension of Isaiah
2 Bar.	2 Baruch
4 Bar.	4 Baruch
Dem.	Demetrius (the Cartographer)
1 En.	1 Enoch
2 En.	2 Enoch
4 Esd.	4 Esdras
Eup.	Eupolemus
Hist. Rech.	History of the Rechabites
Jub.	Jubilees
L.A.E.	Life of Adam and Eve
Liv. Pro.	Lives of the Prophets

Abbreviations

Odes Sol.	*Odes of Solomon*
Ord. Levi	*Ordinances of Levi*
Ps.-Phoc.	*Pseudo-Phocylides*
Ps. Sol.	*Psalm of Solomon*
Sib. Or.	*Sibylline Oracles*
T. Adam	*Testament of Adam*
T. Ash	*Testament of Asher*
T. Dan	*Testament of Dan*
T. Iss.	*Testament of Issachar*
T. Job	*Testament of Job*
T. Jud.	*Testament of Judah*
T. Naph.	*Testament of Naphtali*
T. Naph.	*Testament of Naphtali*
T. Reu.	*Testament of Reuben*
T. Sim.	*Testament of Simeon*
T. Sol.	*Testament of Solomon*
T. Zeb.	*Testament of Zebulum*

OTHER JEWISH WRITINGS

1Qap Gen^{ar}	*Genesis Apocryphon*
1QH	Hodayot (Dead Sea Scroll)
11Q13	Melch (Dead Sea Scroll)
4Q509	papPrFêtesc (Dead Sea Scroll)
A.J.	Josephus, *Antiquites judaicae*
Ant.	Josephus, *Jewish Antiquities*
b. Meg.	Megillah (Babylonian tractate)
b. Šabb.	Šabbat (Babylonian tractate)
b. Sanh.	Sanhedrin (Babylonian tractate)
b. Suk.	Sukkah (Babylonian tractate)
b. Taan.	Taanit (Babylonian tractate)

Abbreviations

C. Ap.	Josephus, *Contra Apionem*
CD	*Cairo Genizah* copy of the *Damascus Document*
J.W.	Josephus, *Jewish Wars*
m. Suk.	Sukkah (Mishnah tractate)
t. Suk.	Sukkah (Tosefta tractate)
y. Suk.	Sukkah (Yerushalmi tractate)

OTHER CHRISTIAN WRITINGS

adv. Graece	Tatian, *Address to the Greeks*
Apoc. Esd.	*Apocalypse of Esdras*
Apoc. John	*Apocalypse of John*
Apoc. John Chry.	*Apocalypse of John Chrysostom*
Apoc. Paul	*Apocalypse of Paul*
Apoc. Pet.	*Apocalypse of Peter*
1 Apol.	Justin Martyr, *1 Apology*
Apos. Con.	*Apostolic Constitutions and Canons*
Barn.	*Barnabas*
Carn. Chr.	Tertullian, *The Flesh of Christ*
1–2 Clem.	*1–2 Clement*
Dial.	Justin Martyr, *Dialogue with Trypho*
Did.	*Didache*
Ep. Apos.	*Epistle to the Apostles*
Ign. Eph.	Ignatius, *To the Ephesians*
6 Esd.	*6 Esdras*
Gos. Bart.	*Gospel of Bartholomew*
Heir.	Irenaeus, *Against Heresies*
Hist. eccl.	Eusebius, *Historia ecclesiastica*
it^b	Old Latin manuscript 4
Syr^c	Syriac Curetonian
Syr^p	Peshitta Syriac

Syr^s Sinaitic Syriac
Smyrn. Ignatius, *To the Smyrnaeans*

OTHER ANCIENT LITERATURE

3 Reg. Dio Chrysistom, De regno 3 (Or. 3)
Abr. Philo, *De Abrahamo*
Aet. Philo, *De aeternitate mundi*
Ages. Plutarch, *Agesilaus*
Ann. Tacitus, *Annales*
Ant. rom. Dionysius of Halicarnassus, *Antiquitates romanae*
Cher. Philo, *De cherubim*
Conf. Philo, *De confusion linguarum*
Congr. Philo, *De congress eruditionis*
Decal. Philo, *De decalogo*
Det. Philo, *Quod deterius potiori insidari soleat*
Deus. Philo, *Quod Deus sit immutabilis*
Dom. Suetonius, *Domitianus*
Ebr. Philo, *De ebrietate*
Ep. Symmachus, *Epistulae*
Flacc. Philo, *In Flaccum*
Fug. Philo, *De fuga et inventione*
Gig. Philo, *De gigantibus*
Her. Philo, *Quis rerum divinarium heres sit*
Hist. Herodutus, *Historiae*
Hist. Polybius, *Histories*
Hypoth. Philo, *Hypothetica*
Ios. Philo, *De Iosepho*
Lang. Varro, *On the Latin Language*
Leg. Philo, *Legum allegoriae*
Legat. Philo, *Legatio ad Gaium*

Abbreviations

Lys.	Plutarch, *Lysander*
Migr.	Philo, *De migration Abrahami*
Mos.	Philo, *De vita Mosis*
Mut.	Philo, *De mutatione nominum*
Nat.	Pliny the Elder, *Naturalis historia*
Opif.	Philo, *De opificop mundi*
Paneg.	Isocrates, *Panegyricus 50*
Plant.	Philo, *De plantatione*
Post.	Philo, *De posteritate*
Prov.	Philo, *De peovidentia*
Pyth.	Iamblichus, *Pythagoras*
QG	Philo, *Quaestiones et solutions in Genesin*
3 Reg.	Dio Chrysistom, *De regno 3 (Or. 3)*
Res Gestae.	Augustus, *Res Gestae Divi Augusti*
Sacr.	Philo, *De sacrificiis Abelis et Caini*
Sat.	Juvenal, *Satirae*
Sobr.	Philo, *De sobrietate*
Somn.	Philo, *De somniis*
Spec.	Philo, *De specialibus legibus*
Virt.	Philo, *De virtutibus*
Vit. Apoll.	Philostratus, *Vita Apollonii*

1

Biographical Sketch of Benny C. Aker[1]

Lois E. Olena

THE HUMBLE PRINCE

Family Background

BENNY AKER WAS BORN in 1939, the youngest of seven children, with a twenty-six year span between himself and his oldest sibling. His father was a farmer and rancher who had gone west from Oklahoma and landed in New Mexico, the "land of enchantment." After a brief move to California during Ben's preschool years, the family moved back to New Mexico and lived in a little town called Cuba.

Although his dad was nominally Methodist, since the family had attended a Methodist church in California, Ben's mom—a pious Baptist (or "Bapticostal")—was the true spiritual pillar and influence in his life. Because she was a praying woman, the family now has a treasure trove of miraculous stories that took place on the ranch where God often intervened for them.

All the kids worked the ranch; they would buy and sell cattle and farm the land. At one point in Cuba they also did logging, lumbering, and sawmilling to help with the groceries. Eventually two of Ben's older brothers

---

1. This biographical sketch is based on a July 21, 2010 interview with Benny Aker at the Assemblies of God Theological Seminary in Springfield, MO.

felt called to the ministry, and together with other family members, established a Baptist church in Cuba that is still going. The brothers served as lay preachers, and family members ministered in any way possible in that little congregation. There, Ben was saved and baptized at the age of nine. Eventually they contacted the Southern Baptist Convention (SBC) in Albuquerque, and the SBC ultimately sent two home missionaries to take over.

Cuba was a tough little town, but that church served as the mainstay of the community. Ben was born a couple of miles away from the Navajo reservation in an ethnically diverse area, so he knew what it was like to grow up as a minority in the midst of the various reservations, Pueblo Indians, and other local people.

After a while, Ben's father came down with heart disease, so the family moved south to Los Lunas, which had a lower elevation. There they became involved in the Los Lunas Baptist Church, then after a couple years moved to Albuquerque where they became involved at Trinity Baptist Church.

Young Love

While living in Albuquerque, Ben's family became acquainted with the family of another man, who was a hunter and carpenter. He used to come up to Ben's older brother's ranch in the high country to hunt. The two families became acquainted, and the man just happened to have a daughter named Barb. She and Ben were about eleven when they first met but had little contact until many years later.

After Ben's graduation from high school, the two began dating. At first, she did not want to get serious because Ben was Baptist and she was Assemblies of God (A/G). Barb prayed, "Lord, I've got to have him filled with the Spirit or else this isn't going to work!" She was adamant about that since she had grown up A/G.

Eventually Barb's prayers were answered, and Ben was filled with the Spirit in April 1960. "That transformed my life," Ben recalls. "It was such a radical transformation. My commitment and devotion to the Lord was very special. I couldn't understand why Pentecostal folks weren't more excited about and more in love with Jesus. My experience was powerful and personally transforming. It captured my heart forever."

Ben and Barb were married over a year later, and Ben immediately became involved at First Assembly. He served as the youth director and Sunday school superintendent. He would preach in parks and anywhere else he could, talking about the Lord. He preached in jail services and on Pueblo reservations. Barb became even more involved there too, playing piano for a home missionary working in the city. "That lady never forgave me for stealing her good helper!" Ben remembers. A faithful partner and praying woman, Barbara always served alongside Ben in complete harmony and support, and God used her greatly. Eventually, Ben and Barb became the proud parents of a son, Steven.

THE CALL OF GOD

Out of Ben's walk with the Lord came a deepening of his spiritual experiences and hungers, which eventually led to a sense of being called into pastoral ministry. He recounts:

> The Lord would do special things like dreams and such, and they were legitimate. I had no problems with those kinds of events. I could feel impressions, and the Lord would give me revelations of certain kinds; it was wonderful to be in tune with Him and have Him in a sovereign way reach down and get a hold of this kid, this backward, poor, country boy. It was a growing thing but did not take too long. This came out of what I was doing already on the reservations, in the parks, in jails, and with the youth. I was everywhere, just wanting to tell others about the Lord.

At work, Ben had become a journeyman gas fitter for Southern Union Gas Company. One day he and his helper were working on a refrigerator, and Ben was enthusiastically telling the man—one might even say *preaching*—about how good God was. The owner stood there, listening, then followed Ben to the truck and asked, "Tell me how I can get what you have." That kind of thing evolved quickly into ministry, and the Lord was beginning to impress upon Ben the sense that he had something more for him.

But Ben wrestled with the Lord about this sense of calling: "I said, 'Lord, you do not know who you're calling! This is a twenty-four hour thing you're asking me to do.'" He knew he would need to adjust from having another vocation, a job, where he could devote certain times of the week, to this—ministry that was day and night serving the Lord in a full-time capacity. "I can't handle that, Lord," Ben argued. But the Lord just seemed to speak to him and say, "Yeah, I know you're not much good, but I'm going to change that and help you."

It took several months for Ben to adjust his attitude and his frame of reference. "It was sort of like therapy," he recalls. "I worked but was constantly thinking about it. There was this sweet presence of the Lord, a nudging, a sense of urgency. Finally I gave in, and it was a relief. 'Wow, let's go!' I said." The Lord had worked him over, and he was ready.

His young bride of two years, however, was resisting. During this time of struggling over the issue, though, their house was robbed, and that robbery proved influential in changing her mind. Barb knew that the God who could allow the spoiling of goods could also show his hand on her person in motivating her toward obedience. So she yielded. The year was 1962.

1964–1970 (Central Bible College: Student/Dean/Pastor)

Ben's sense of calling was connected to his intent to leave New Mexico for Bible college. Several pastors of First Assembly had been graduates of Central Bible Institute, so that seemed the clear destination. By the time Ben and Barb arrived on campus, it was August of 1964—the year the General Council of the A/G changed the school's name to Central Bible College (CBC).

Ben graduated in 1967 and was planning to launch out as a church planter. He was in touch with various districts and was discovering that each worked differently. "Some were affirming and helpful, but others took a *go fly a kite* approach," he recollects with a smile. So he looked for available openings at churches, tried out at some, and just waited on the Lord.

During this time, a door opened for Ben to come on staff at CBC. The school had been expecting another man, who had just finished at Wheaton, to come to CBC as dorm supervisor. A week or two before the man was due to arrive, he contacted Don Johns, academic dean at the time, and said, "I can't do it. I just have too many reservations about my Christianity and about the A/G." Since CBC needed someone quickly, and Ben was in transition, Johns asked him if he would serve in this capacity.

Ben had always been a good student, graduating in three years, so it was a smooth transition for him—from being an excellent student to taking on a leadership role on campus. Immediately upon arrival at CBC he had noted the difference among teachers and began to see that he wanted to do something different. He wanted to carry as much of an academic load as he could and delve deeper into the biblical text. He remembers,

> In those days, it was in vogue to say, "Well, the Greek says," but I knew these people did not know Greek. And also many would just refer to secondary sources. I felt, well, that's helpful, that's good, but there is another level for which I need to prepare. I needed to consult the language myself. So I took Anthony Palma for first-year Greek and Larry Hurtado for my second year. I took my first and second years of Hebrew with Stan Horton. And Bill Menzies taught me Church History. In addition to these professors, Don Johns, a professor and academic dean,

also influenced my teaching methods. My life-long educational goal was to teach students—not courses. I did very well. I was on the Dean's List, had some scholarships, and even subbed a little for Stan Horton.

Ben was chosen to represent his senior class as the commencement speaker. But because of his background he felt a bit daunted by that responsibility. Dr. Stanley Horton proved to be an important influence in his life at that juncture, as Ben recalls in a letter he wrote to his professor years later:

> Coming from a ranch in New Mexico, my background did not prepare me for public life. I remember the feeling of being overwhelmed when I was chosen to represent my senior class as commencement speaker. The sermon had to be completely memorized without the aid of notes. As my trembling body mounted the steps of the platform, I looked up and you were there sitting on the platform. You gave me that wonderful Dr. Horton smile and a nod of your head—I shall never forget that moment of encouragement. Our thanks are to you for the wonderful space you have filled in our lives and to God who makes it possible.[2]

While Ben was serving as dorm supervisor, Ben and Barb also served in a little country church in nearby Strafford. Ben assisted the pastor for a while and then served as interim pastor for several years (1967–70) when that pastor moved elsewhere. In 1970, Ben was ordained with the A/G.

Eventually the dean, Donald Johns, came back to Ben and said, "I'd be interested in you staying on as a professor, but you'll have to go on for further education." During this time when many in the A/G were unsupportive of higher education, there were a unique few at CBC who had the vision for excelling academically, and Johns was one of those. These leaders saw promising students and pushed them onward, an urging that made all the difference in the world for A/G and Pentecostal scholarship in the ensuing decades. Johns told Ben he did not need to go on for further education in order to be a successful pastor in the A/G, because Ben had always proved to be gung ho for evangelism and the practical, vibrant, Spirit-filled ministry of the church. But he knew that Ben wanted both; he wanted the integration between academics and the work of the church in his life:

> Many have thought that because I was in academics that I wasn't for evangelism and such. But the *reason* I am passionate for this, first, that I want to do the academics I do, is because of my

2. L. E. Olena, *Stanley Horton: Shaper of Pentecostal History* (Springfield, MO: GPH, 2009) 287.

passion for Jesus. It's also the foundation to be successful and to endure for the Lord in whatever ministry context you're in. You need some strength out there! The fact that many in the A/G at that time were saying higher education was unimportant drove us onward to do it. Some of us had a real passion to help point the way for these young men and women of potential.

Throughout his academic career, Ben would continue to see himself in that very role—as a facilitator, to help promising young men and women along the path where God was leading them. God did the calling and empowering, but Ben wanted to help God move them along the way. This integration was something he always tried to weave into his classes—the need for the power of the Spirit along with the academics.

Ben had experienced the power of the Spirit many times during those days at CBC: "We had some wonderful times in chapel. And Don Johns was very instrumental in my life. He was the dean, he would oversee the chapel, and when the Spirit would move, and all kinds of things would arise, he would model how to do it. I think he learned it from people like D. W. Kerr and W. I. Evans and J. W. Welch. Johns was a wonderful mentor. That impact is still working today. Those were formative times for me as a young man in my late 20s."

1971–1982: Central Bible College

Ben began teaching at CBC in 1971 when he was thirty-two years old and was there eleven years, first as an instructor then as Assistant Professor in Bible and Theology. He taught Greek, Bible (book courses), Theology, and Homiletics (both beginning and advanced). The expository preaching course he had taken as a student as well as the excellent training he received from CBC president, Phil Crouch, when the faculty chose him to be the commencement speaker, had served him well. He was planning on writing a book on homiletics but got waylaid because his teaching load got spread out and was not as focused. He had learned much about preaching and loved sharing what he knew, but that was placed on the back burner when he focused more on his advanced degrees and teaching in his area of advanced concentration.

While teaching at CBC, there were particular students who came through, like Craig Keener, and others, and there was a Jewish contingency that came to CBC—both Jewish believers who were students and students interested in Jewish studies. Both groups came together and formed a club on campus. Ben was influential and had a part in encouraging students in this area—acquainting them with the literature and the ideas. Some, like Keener, took it and ran with it.

At one point at CBC there was a changing of the guard. This meant that some wanted to return to the school being an institute rather than a college. Of course Ben was not for this, and these individuals did not like his influence. "Gary McGee and I were partners in this," remembers Ben, "but Gary was smarter and more tactful than I." Part of the argument was that they wanted the students to be more involved in Christian service. But if they had looked more carefully at the situation, they would have seen that the students under Ben's influence were involved in Christian service more consistently than any others. "Craig Keener," Ben remembers, "was always *somewhere* witnessing and involved in Jewish ministries." Street ministry was just exploding because they just had to get out there and tell them about Jesus. This was what influenced Craig. He found you do not have to be an egghead, that someone can have passion for people and souls *and* for the Word.

That kind of passion continued to lead Ben on his own journey for higher education. During the summers of the years he was teaching at CBC, he worked on his graduate studies and eventually earned an MAR in NT from Concordia Seminary in St. Louis in 1974. Between 1976–82, he served in Springfield, Missouri as an Adjunct Professor of Greek and NT at the new Assemblies of God Graduate School and as an adjunct at Evangel University in 1978. His doctoral journey was right around the corner.

PhD Studies

In the late '70s Ben began his studies toward a PhD in Biblical Languages and Literature from St. Louis University. Although both Greek and Hebrew were required for the degree, Greek was Ben's primary focus. He always saw Greek as a tool, however, because "the end product was to know God. And anything I could find to know God better, and to know what He said in its inspired way, that was what I wanted." In addition to the modern research languages (French and German) he needed, Ben took a course in Ugaritic and Akkadian at Covenant with R. Laird Harris, a brilliant evangelical linguist and biblical scholar. In addition, he also taught himself Aramaic and Latin.

These language studies and earlier rabbinic studies had set the stage for Ben's dissertation, "The Merits of the Fathers: An Interpretation of John 8:31–59," which he completed in 1984. This work deals fundamentally with NT theology and the doctrine of salvation and imputation. Ben's doctoral father was a Catholic scholar who converted from being a Lutheran pastor

But These are Written . . .

while attending a Jewish seminary. From his own Jewish studies, Ben could understand this professor's journey.

Regarding the Greco-Roman and rabbinic sources Ben came in contact with during this time, he recounts:

> You can't write and read and not be aware of this vast amount of literature. But in scholarship there are these waves. So for example, at one time it was all Babylonian stuff. And that wave was over. Then it was all Hellenistic stuff. You get over that, and it's all Jewish stuff. Now scholarship has mellowed out. It's taken the whole scope of these things, and you can see how they all fit together. That's what Craig Keener did. So you put what the rabbis are saying in the Greco-Roman context, and you see what has influenced them and how the church has reacted, for example how John was reacting to all these forces, including the church and synagogue in the Greco-Roman period dealing with Roman imperialism. And as you grow, you mellow out, and you expand yourself and get smarter and hopefully wiser, and you blend the cultures a little more and learn to not put one over the other. You just see how they all have something to contribute. That's something I had to do after I finished my dissertation. I found that, with the way everything was going, I needed to broaden myself.

But all along there was a method to Ben's madness. He was passionate about an educated church reaching the lost in the power of the Spirit, and he was passionate about having better-prepared men and women for ministry. The message could not just be emotional or experiential. In the contemporary culture, the A/G had to teach people to think more. Even the early church had to do that, Ben reasoned.

But in the training of young men and women early on in the A/G, there were no mechanisms, and no schools, to do this. So Ben had to go somewhere else. However, there was an element in the A/G who did not like him going off to St. Louis University or Concordia. Other young A/G scholars had to go off to other schools. But at Dallas Theological Seminary, Southwestern Baptist Theological Seminary, or Central Baptist Theological Seminary, they did not get a Pentecostal focus. They would come back, and the Pentecostal emphasis would often have been diluted. In years to come, this situation emerged into a whole new focus on publishing as a part of Ben's life work.

Biographical Sketch of Benny C. Aker

1982–1983: Hendrickson Publishers

One of Ben's CBC students, Steve Hendrickson, was from the north shore of Boston. His dad was an A/G pastor and presbyter. Steve came to CBC as a music major but while there took hermeneutics with Ben. Steve saw Ben's passion for quality Pentecostal scholarship and appreciated the need for increased Christian publishing. Early in his time at CBC Steve had decided he was not going to work locally and make "beans" to put himself through school. He told his professor, "I'm going to have to do better." So he started Christian Book Distributors (CBD) out of his parents' garage, and that really took off.

After that, Steve wanted to start a publishing company. So he and Ben began Hendrickson Publishers. Ben reminisces about the early days of the company:

> This is how people like Roger Stronstad became so well known. We were in the early stages of Hendrickson Publishers, and Roger Stronstad had done a masters thesis, which became his book. He had sent it to Bill Menzies to try to get it to GPH, but GPH turned it down. So Bill called me and said, "Roger's got a good piece of work here, and you'll want to take a look at it." And of course we did, we asked him to revise it, and the rest is history. *That* is the reason I was doing what I was doing. We began that publishing house as a mechanism to generate dialogue and as a place to grow new ideas. And look how reputable it is today. Beginning a publishing company was indeed challenging!

Ben served as general editor for Hendrickson from 1982 to 1983 and as editorial consultant until 2005. At first, Ben did some of the editing, but he was also going after manuscript projects. He and Steve would march the aisles at Society of Biblical Literature, Evangelical Theological Society, and the Society for Pentecostal Studies and encourage writers.

This was a time of transition in Ben's life. He had experienced a number of unfortunate situations in his final years at CBC and had decided to resign from there in the spring of 1982. Some of his colleagues, it seems, were jealous, and he had felt rather excluded at that point, so he felt it best just to move on. Ben was getting ready to head to Boston with the publishing company to take the next step, to move on-site and go from there, but he never felt right about it. Fortunately things worked out so he could work from his home in Springfield. But this was a tumultuous time in Springfield.

But These are Written . . .

Missions

Beginning in 1984, Ben spent a good amount of time overseas, teaching in various missions contexts such as Lomé in Togo, West Africa (West Africa Advanced School of Theology); Manila, Philippines and Kuala Lumpur, Malaysia (Far East Advanced School of Theology—now Asia Pacific Theological Seminary); Singapore (Asia Theological Centre for Evangelism and Missions); and other places such as Capetown, South Africa and Costa Rica. In the United States, he taught or guest lectured at nine out of the A/G's eighteen schools.

California Theological Seminary

Concurrent with the time of upheaval in Springfield and Ben's departure from CBC, Bill Menzies and Del Tarr had also felt the heat and did not like the way things were going. So they got an idea to launch a Pentecostal-Charismatic seminary and headed to California—dreaming and visioning and making concrete plans. Del would be the president, and Bill would be the dean. Raleigh J. Ferrell, in the same ballpark with the then-current turmoil, would join them later. Del and Bill were putting together a faculty and so approached Ben to see if he was interested; they knew his reputation among the students. Ben knew that these men understood the language of both practitioners and academicians, that they grasped the issues, and that they knew what constituted a good seminary. So he agreed, and for the next six years served at the new California Theological Seminary as acting Academic Dean, Associate Professor of NT, and then as Professor of NT.

Assemblies of God Theological Seminary

Meanwhile, the Assemblies of God Theological Seminary (AGTS) in Springfield was struggling and by 1990, Del Tarr was asked to return to serve as president. He agreed, eventually leading the school through certain radical steps necessary to preserve the institution, including making board changes and facilitating reconciliation.

At the same time that Tarr returned to Springfield to prepare the way for the school's revitalization, Aker came on board the AGTS faculty. He served as Professor of NT/Exegesis at AGTS from 1990–2006. From 1995–97 and 2004–06 he served as chair of the AGTS Bible and Theology Department.

These years saw him also busy serving as book review editor for *Paraclete* (1993–94), adjunct teaching in Evangel's Theology Department again (1994), and continuing to serve as editorial consultant for Hendrickson (to 2005). In 2001, the General Council of the A/G presented him with the *Delta Sigma* Educator Award for twenty-five years of service, and in 2003 they awarded him with the *Delta Alpha* Distinguished Educator Award. Dr. Jim Railey, Professor of Theology at AGTS, had this to say at the awarding of the 2003 honor:

> Aker is known among his colleagues not only as an excellent teacher but also as a model of the steadfast believer. Through the several circumstances of his life, in situations of severe trial, he has maintained an unmovable faith in the ability of God to do the miraculous and to provide for the grace needed to allow His strength to be seen. With a strong prophetic voice, Aker leads the way to responsible engagement with the purposes of God among the community of faith.[3]

Part of that community of faith has included the following academic societies in which Dr. Aker has held membership: Evangelical Theological Society, Institute of Biblical Research, Society for Biblical Literature, and the Society for Pentecostal Studies.

RETIREMENT

In his retirement, besides preaching and teaching in various contexts, his publication and scholarly efforts have included writing and mentoring for Global University ("Graduate Greek III" and a course on the Gospel of John) and advising doctoral participants at AGTS. He also continues to serve the Lord at his local church, Evangel Temple in Springfield, Missouri, in a variety of ways.

PUBLICATIONS

More of Aker's academic years were spent helping other authors get discovered than they were writing his own works. When asked the question, out of all the things he had done—from pastoring to various ministries, and as far as his youth, to teaching to publishing—what did he feel was his greatest contribution for the kingdom, Dr. Aker responded that he is most

---

3. J. Railey, "Life Narrative," unpublished paper (Springfield, MO: Assemblies of God Theological Seminary) 2.

But These are Written . . .

proud to say that he was able to help develop opportunities for scholarship. "That's all some people need is a chance and a venue," he noted. Through his influence while teaching, in working with Hendrickson, or fostering scholarship through playing an integral role in the Society for Pentecostal Studies as site coordinator the year SPS came to AGTS in Springfield, Ben was all about facilitating the work of God in other people. That desire has not only helped produce scholars around the world, but also has led to his playing an important role in developing some key pastoral leaders, superintendents, missionaries, and others over the years. This too gave him great satisfaction, knowing that he has former students in so many capacities—helping to advance the kingdom in so many ways.

Even with his many efforts to facilitate the work of others, though, Dr. Aker still found time to make his own significant scholarly contributions. A list of his principal publications follows this biographical sketch.

His own book, about revisioning spiritual gifts, he has put "on the back burner" for now but hopes to finish it in a few years. A 2002 article for *Journal of Pentecostal Theology*, "Charismata: Gifts, Enablements, or Ministries?" more or less captures what that book is about. Ben provides a sneak preview:

> The way we get into the foundations of the charismata is an exegetical blunder, a linguistic blunder. Kenneth Birding came out with an article, in fact put labels to what I was thinking. I've taught this for a long time. He wrote a book on it. He later came out with a book on it, in which he referred to me. I wrote a cover recommendation for it. The idea is that when you start looking at spiritual gifts *from the biblical data*, you uncover a whole can of worms, a whole host of issues. You see that experientially, Pentecostals have it together, but they could be twice as effective. So you have to rearticulate: what is the nature of spiritual gifts? So we *ought to* rename it. And Ken Birding does it too. It's not spiritual gifts. They're not gifts. They're ministries. To sort of come with a new name, spiritual ministries, that gets into the issue, then what are they when you get them? If it's a ministry vs. a gift, then when do you get them? You have a whole series of things attached to the original idea that you have to come back and address—and probably a text at a time. So it develops into a whole thing about the theology of the church, theology of ministry, of Jesus, of the Spirit, new terms you've got to use, biblical terms.

PRINCIPAL PUBLICATIONS (LISTED CHRONOLOGICALLY)

"Graduate Greek III." Correspondence Course. Springfield, MO: Global University, 2010.

"The Healing of the Lame Man in Acts 3: The Other Side of Signs and Wonders," Enrichment (Fall 2010) 116–23.

"Fruit of the Spirit." In The New Interpreter's Dictionary of the Bible D-H, edited by Katharine Doob Sakenfeld, 2:492. Nashville: Abingdon, 2007.

"Charisma." In The New Interpreter's Dictionary of the Bible A-C, edited by Katharine Doob Sakenfeld, 1:584. Nashville: Abingdon, 2006.

"Born Again." In Encyclopedia of Pentecostal and Charismatic Christianity, edited by Stanley Burgess, 67–72. New York: Routledge, 2006.

"Streams in the Desert: Sources on the Spirit for Pentecostal Preachers." Encounter 1/1 (Summer 2004) n.p. http://www.agts.edu/encounter/articles/2004_summer/aker.htm.

"A Review of the TNIV." Published electronically by Zondervan, 2002. http://www.agts.edu/faculty/faculty_publications/book_reviews/aker_nivt.pdf.

"Charismata: Gifts, Enablements, or Ministries?" JPT 11/1 (October 2002) 53–69.

"John." In Life in the Spirit: New Testament Commentary (formerly Full Life Bible Commentary to the New Testament) edited by French L. Arrington and Roger Stronstad. Grand Rapids: Zondervan, 1999.

"Acts 2 as a Paradigmatic Narrative for Luke's Theology of the Spirit." Paper presented at the Annual Meeting of the Evangelical Theological Society 1998. http://www.agts.edu/faculty/faculty_publications/articles/aker_acts2.pdf.

"John, Gospel of." In Dictionary of Pentecostal and Charismatic Movements, edited by Stanley M. Burgess and Gary B. McGee. Grand Rapids: Zondervan, 1988.

"Matthew, Gospel of," in Dictionary of Pentecostal and Charismatic Movements, edited by Stanley M. Burgess and Gary B. McGee. Grand Rapids: Zondervan, 1988.

Signs and Wonders in Ministry Today. Edited by Benny C. Aker and Gary B. McGee. Springfield, MO: GPH, 1996.

"The Gospel in Action." In Signs and Wonders in Ministry Today, edited by Benny C. Aker and Gary B. McGee. Springfield, MO: GPH, 1996.

(With Edgar R. Lee) "Naturally Supernatural." In Signs and Wonders in Ministry Today, edited by Benny C. Aker and Gary B. McGee. Springfield, MO: GPH, 1996.

"The Gift of Tongues in I Corinthians 14:1–5." Paraclete (Winter 1995) 13–21.

"What Does the Bible Say about Signs and Wonders?" Pentecostal Evangel (May 28, 1995) 8–10.

The Old Testament Hebrew-English Dictionary: Aleph-Beth. Edited by Gregory A Lint. Springfield, MO: World Library, 1995. Contributed word studies on 24 Hebrew words.

"Seminary Education and Critical Thinking—Not?" Assemblies of God Educator 40/4 (October–December 1994) 1, 4–5.

"How Do We Know Christianity Is the Only True Religion?" Christian Education Counsel: Leader Edition (Nov 6, 1994) 1–4.

"What Does It Mean To Be Pentecostal?" Paraclete (Summer 1994) 15–17. Reprinted in Enrichment (Winter 1996) 99, 103.

But These are Written . . .

Commentary on Deuteronomy 23–34 in *The Quest Study Bible* (NIV). Grand Rapids: Zondervan, 1994.

(With James H. Railey Jr.) "Theological Foundations." In *Systematic Theology*, edited by Stanley M. Horton. Springfield, MO: GPH, 1993.

"Devotionals: June 26–July 2." In *God's Word For Today* (June–August 1993) 31–38.

"What's Happened to the Power?" *Pentecostal Evangel* (June 24, 1991) 6–7.

"New Directions in Lucan Theology: Reflections on Luke 3:21–22 and Some Implications." In *Faces of Renewal: Studies in Honor of Stanley M. Horton*, edited by Paul Elbert, 108–27. Peabody, MA: Hendrickson, 1988.

"Some Reflections on Pentecostal Hermeneutics." *Paraclete* (Spring 1985) 18–20.

"The Merits of the Fathers: An Interpretation of John 8:31–59." PhD diss., Saint Louis University, 1984.

"'Breathed': A Study on the Biblical Distinction Between Regeneration and Spirit Baptism." *Paraclete* (Summer 1983) 13–16.

Unpublished Manuscripts:

"Social Background of the New Testament" for GPH.

"Paul" for GPH.

"The Lampstand in the New Testament." Chapter in unpublished book. Springfield, MO: GPH, 2001.

2

He Will Guide You into All the Truth

JOHN W. WYCKOFF

INTRODUCTION

Need for Discussion of Spirit's Work of Illumination

IN 1990, WHEN I completed my doctoral dissertation on "The Relationship of the Holy Spirit in Biblical Hermeneutics," very little was being written on this subject. My search of the literature from the early church fathers through the 1980s revealed that, while much was written on the related areas of revelation and inspiration, there was very little written on illumination. I found that the idea of illumination was often mentioned or eluded to in the literature, but there was very little elaboration on this matter. Usually the discussion was limited to either a denial that the Spirit has anything at all to do with understanding Scripture today, on the one hand, or a strong affirmation of faith that indeed he plays some significant, but mysterious role in the process, on the other hand. Writing about illumination in 1993, Clark Pinnock notes that scholars "mention it in passing but seldom offer a proper discussion of it." He complains that "Gordon D. Fee, a Pentecostal biblical scholar, can write a book entitled *Gospel and Spirit: Issues in New Testament Hermeneutics* and say nothing about the Spirit's role in interpretation."[1]

1. C. H. Pinnock, "The Work of the Holy Spirit in Hermeneutics," *JPT* 2 (1993) 7.

Fortunately however, especially since the turn of the twenty-first century, much is now being written on this very important topic, largely thanks to the persistence of the Pentecostal movement. This is because, as Pinnock notes, with the advent of the Pentecostal movement at the beginning of the twentieth century, "a 'new hermeneutic' was born." He concludes that because of this development, "It would not be an exaggeration to say that the Pentecostal movement is the most important event in church history until now . . ."[2]

A thorough discussion of illumination is important because it is part of the process by which God reveals himself to mankind. In fact, all that we know, understand, and are certain of regarding God is the result of a special work of the Spirit. This chapter will discuss what the Fourth Gospel reveals about the idea of illumination. That is, it will discuss what John says relative to the role of the Spirit in helping us understand Scripture and helping us know the person of Jesus Christ. With regard to what Scripture says specifically about the Spirit's work of illumination, the Fourth Gospel is, perhaps, the most fruitful book of the NT. As Pinnock suggests, "Thinking about and reflecting upon Spirit-hermeneutics is evident in John's Gospel."[3] In his gospel, John speaks variously about the Spirit seventeen times. In several of these references, he may be seen as at least indirectly speaking about illumination.

Identification and Description of Important Terms

For the sake of our discussion here, I need to begin by identifying, defining, and briefly clarify four terms used herein to discuss the Spirit's work of revealing God to mankind. First, in this essay, the broad, overall process of the Spirit's work of revealing God to humanity is termed *enlightenment*. This work began the moment that God first created Adam and Eve, and it has been continuously occurring until the present time. Second, the term *revelation* refers to "new," or first-time, enlightenment. Thus, revelation is the first step in the broad, on-going process of God revealing himself. Most Christians believe that no *new* revelation is being given today. The term *special* revelation refers to enlightenment that has been preserved in special form, including Scripture (both the OT and NT) and Jesus Christ, who is the ultimate of God's self-revelation to humanity. The third term in this discussion is *inspiration*. This term comes from 2 Tim 3.16, where

---

2. C. H. Pinnock, "The Work of the Spirit in the Interpretation of Holy Scripture from the Perspective of a Charismatic Biblical Theologian," *JPT* 18 (2009) 168–69.

3. Ibid., 162.

Paul explains: "All Scripture is inspired by God (θεόπςευστος) . . ."[4] This Greek word literally means "God breathed." Simply stated, the concept of inspiration identifies and reasonably describes how the Spirit does his work of providing revelation. Fourth, *illumination* refers to the enlightenment work of the Spirit in which he enables us to gain special understanding of previously given revelation.

Questions Related to Illumination

The notion that the Spirit helps understand special revelation brings with it several significant questions. The most central and important are: (1) *What* does the Spirit help us understand? (2) *How* does the Spirit help us understand special revelation? (3) *Why* is this special work of the Spirit important? The following paragraphs will examine the Fourth Gospel to see what, if any, answers John provides for these questions.

INSIGHTS FROM THE GOSPEL OF JOHN

What the Spirit Helps Us Understand About Revelation

Regarding the first question of *what* does the Spirit help us understand, the usual, simple answer is: In illumination, the Spirit helps us understand Scripture. This answer is correct. Pinnock notes: "The Spirit loves to work with Scripture . . ."[5] And, it is a good place to start. Scripture is the appropriate starting place in answering the *what* question because right up front we need to understand that in his work of illumination, the Spirit does not show us new truth that is somehow above and beyond the truth that is already revealed in Scripture. Pinnock correctly notes that "the Spirit unfolds what has already been given in salvation history and in the Bible. We should not expect to encounter something different from that."[6] Simply stated, the Spirit is not inspiring new revelation through illumination or any other work today.

While to say that the Spirit helps us understand Scripture is a correct and good beginning answer, this is not the complete, ultimate answer to the *what* question. In times of prayer and meditation, when the Spirit helps us

---

4. Unless otherwise noted, all Scripture quotations are taken from NASB.
5. Pinnock, "Work of the Spirit in Interpretation," 162.
6. Ibid., 163.

understand something about Jesus Christ and we come to know him better, what happens there, is also properly called illumination, even if the understanding of specific Scripture is not directly involved. Therefore, rather than simply saying that illumination is the work of the Spirit in helping us understand Scripture, it is more correct to say that illumination is the work of the Spirit in helping us understand and know special revelation.

Furthermore, the claim that the Spirit helps us understand Scripture logically suggests that he helps us understand or know something from or about Scripture, and ultimately something about Jesus Christ, that we could not otherwise understand or know. Thus, the real, eventual question is: What is that something from or about Scripture and about Jesus Christ that the Spirit helps us understand and know? Upon thoughtful consideration of this, we realize that in a sense, there is not much any of us can say regarding that something. This is because, being a work of the Spirit, illumination is miraculous. And, a miracle, by definition, is supernatural—beyond human ability to understand.

However, we find that John at least takes us one step closer to realizing what that something is. And, this one step is very important. In John 15.26, he quotes Jesus as saying: "When the Helper comes, whom I will send to you from the Father, that is the Spirit of truth who proceeds from the Father, He will *testify about me*" (emphasis mine). Thus, *what* the Spirit does in his work of illumination is enable individuals to understand the person of Jesus Christ and the significance of his work to them personally.

Although this answer is not very specific and, therefore, possibly not very satisfying to some, nevertheless, it is obviously very important because it keeps the focus of the Spirit and his work where it must always be. Biblical theologians commonly contend that Scripture is ultimately christocentric; that is, Jesus Christ is the ultimate, central focus of Scripture.[7] John clearly makes this point in his gospel. First, he records Jesus' observation: "It is they [Scriptures] that testify on my behalf" (John 5.39).[8] Then, he records Jesus' declaration: "I am the way, the truth and the life" (John 14.6). Finally, he also records Jesus referring to the Spirit as the "Spirit of truth" (John 15.26; 16.13). Since Jesus is the personification of truth, this is John's equivalent to Luke's (Acts 8.39) "Spirit of the Lord" and Paul's (Rom 8.9; Phil 1.19) and

---

7. See G. Hasel, *Old Testament Theology: Basic Issues in the Current Debate* (Grand Rapids: Eerdmans, 1989) 142, where Hasel makes a case for the OT being theocentric. Jesus himself declares that the OT "bear witness to Me" (John 5.39) which means that ultimately, in the broad, general sense, the OT is christocentric. Also, see G. Hasel, *New Testament Theology: Basic Issues in the Current Debate* (Grand Rapids: Eerdmans, 1987) 155, 161–64, where Hasel makes a case for the NT being christocentric.

8. Also, see Luke 24.27.

Peter's (1 Pet 1.11) "Spirit of Christ." Such terminology signifies not only a special relationship of the Spirit to Jesus Christ, but it also focuses attention upon the work of the Spirit in revealing Jesus Christ.

Therefore, as the message of Scripture is christocentric, likewise, the Spirit's work of illumination is appropriately christocentric. As Brown states, what he "makes known are the things of Christ."[9] He does not have a purpose that is separate from that of Jesus Christ; so, he does not have a message that is different from that of Jesus Christ. This is what Jesus means when he says, "when He, the Spirit of Truth, comes . . . He will not speak on His own initiative." Further, Jesus says the Spirit will only speak "whatever He hears" (John 16.13). As we will see in the later section on the importance of illumination, this christocentric purpose and message of the Spirit's work is absolutely essential to the completion or God's plan of redemption in and through Jesus Christ.

Also, a proper recognition of the christocentric purpose and message of the Spirit's work of illumination helps us understand a phrase in John 16.13 that might otherwise be misunderstood. In this verse John records Jesus saying, "when He, the Spirit of Truth comes, He will guide you into *all* the truth" (emphasis mine). If this *all* is taken in an absolute, all-inclusive sense, I suppose we would expect the Spirit to help us understand truth in all areas of life, such scientific truth and mathematics. Certainly, if God the Father wanted him to do so, the Spirit is certainly capable of helping us understand any and *all* the truth. But, this is not what he is sent for, because he has a much more important focus. Jesus himself qualifies and clarifies this "all truth" according to John's record in the previous chapter. In John 15.26, he records Jesus saying, "He [the Spirit] will testify about Me." Thus, "all the truth" in John 16.13 refers to all the truth that is necessary for us to understand about Jesus Christ and redemption in and through him.

How the Spirit Helps Understand Revelation

Regarding the *second* question of *how* does the Spirit help us understand special revelation, as in the case of the *what* question, there is a sense in which there is not much that any of us can say specifically concerning *how* the Spirit does this work. Again, this is because illumination is a miraculous work and thus beyond human ability to explain. Pinnock concludes: "One cannot demonstrate the Spirit's illumination but only point to where

---

9. P. E. Brown, *The Holy Spirit: The Spirit's Interpretative Role in Relation to Biblical Hermeneutics* (Bristol: Christian Focus, 2002) 70.

it seems to be happening."[10] Therefore, the best possible answer to this question, even with insights from Scripture, will leave much to mystery. Nevertheless, upon close consideration, we find that in the Fourth Gospel, John reveals three important things concerning *how* the Spirit helps us understand special revelation.

One, the Spirit *teaches* all things and *guides* into all the truth. Specifically, John quotes Jesus as saying that, as the helper, "the Holy Spirit will teach you all things" (John 14.26) and "guide you into all the truth" (John 16.13). One who teaches and guides is not one who only imparts information. Rather, one who teaches and guides; clarifies, explains, elaborates and otherwise helps the student understand something that would be very difficult to understand without the teacher's help. In this case, however, the student understands something that would not just be very difficult, but rather impossible, to understand without the teacher's (Spirit's) help.

Since Jesus was speaking to his apostles when he made this statement, some suggest that this special work of teaching and guiding applies only to the apostles who actually heard Jesus' teaching. However, Brown believes that when the whole context is considered, it is difficult to restrict this to the apostles. He concludes: "these passages indicate that the coming and ministry of the Spirit applies to all disciples, but has particular relevance and application to the Apostles."[11] If the Spirit could and did give the apostles special explanation and understanding of Jesus' teaching after he returned to heaven, then it is reasonable to conclude that he can and does provide special explanation and understanding to those who study and hear Scripture today.

The suggestion that the Spirit functions as a *teacher* is possibly the best model to picture *how* the he does his work of illumination.[12] The Spirit, who is the author of the textbook (Scripture) is also the teacher and guide, standing over or setting beside the student who is seeking to understand. Taking what the student is reading or hearing in Scripture, the Spirit "teaches"—he elaborates in order to explain, not only more clearly, but also more fully, the meaning and significance of the truth about the person and work of Jesus Christ. He "guides" his students into the truth.

Two, in his teaching and guiding, the Spirit enables individuals to remember the teachings of Jesus. Specifically, John quotes Jesus as saying, "He will . . . bring to your remembrance all that I said to you" (John 14.26). Obviously, Jesus is talking about the Spirit supernaturally enhancing memory

---

10. Pinnock, "Work of the Holy Spirit in Hermeneutics," 20.

11. Brown, *Holy Spirit*, 66.

12. See J. W. Wyckoff, *Pneuma and Logos: The Role of the Spirit in Biblical Hermeneutics* (Eugene, OR: Wipf and Stock, 2010) 97–122.

above and beyond one's normal memory ability. This would possibly include: enablement to remember things that would otherwise be forgotten; providing superior quality of recall; and, at critical times, bringing to mind important things that have special significance relative to specific occasions.

Again, some suggest that Jesus' promise that the Spirit will enhance ability to remember his teachings only applies to the apostles who personally heard Jesus' teachings. But, again, Brown concludes that the whole context makes it difficult to restrict this ministry of bringing to remembrance to the apostles.[13] Also, likewise again, if the Spirit could and did help the apostles remember the things that he taught them personally, then, it is reasonable to conclude that he can and does help us remember the things that we have learned when reading, studying and hearing divine truth in Scripture. Many Christians testify to having these kinds of distinctive recall experiences which they considered to be special, divine moments.

Also, interestingly, it is reasonable to think that, all during the time that John was being inspired for writing his gospel account, the Spirit was helping him in these exact same ways. That is, in his work of inspiring John to write his gospel: (1) the Spirit was enhancing John's memory of the things he had heard Jesus teach; and, (2) the Spirit was teaching and guiding John into a better understanding of all of the truth concerning Jesus Christ. Thus, what the Spirit now does in his work of illumination, he also did in his work of inspiration when he breathed upon John, supernaturally enabling him to write the divinely authoritative Fourth Gospel.[14]

Third, *convincing* and/or *convicting* is also an important aspect of *how* the Spirit does his work of illumination. John records Jesus declaring the following when speaking about the Spirit's ministry: "And He, when He comes, will convict [or convince] the world concerning sin and righteousness and judgment" (John 16.8). It is important to realize that being convicted or convinced concerning something is a unique kind of understanding and/or knowing something. One who is convinced or convicted concerning something, understands and/or knows that something in a uniquely particular way. Now, since *only* the Spirit can convict or convince on this level, this is a clear area in which he helps us understand and/or know something that we would not otherwise understand and/or know on our own. As Morris notes:

---

13. Brown, *Holy Spirit*, 66.

14. I think Pinnock is correct when he suggests that inspiration and illumination are really the same kind of work of the Spirit. See Pinnock, "Work of the Holy Spirit in Hermeneutics," 3–5. The nature of these two works is the same. The difference is in their purpose and results.

But These are Written . . .

"Apart from the Holy Spirit men do not really know the truth about sin or righteousness or judgment."[15]

However, there is question as to what exactly Jesus means here. This is because the Greek word ελεγχω, that is here translated "convict" in the NASB, can also be translated "convince."[16] The meanings conveyed in these two possible translations, while related, are not exactly the same. That is, "convince" and "convict" are not exactly equal synonymous terms. Convince means to persuade or assure. Convict means to sentence, condemn, or find guilty.[17] On the one hand, a person who is found guilty of a crime and condemned and sentenced, might not be convinced that he or she is guilty. On the other hand, a person who is convinced of something, even of sin, might not be worthy of being convicted. He or she might simply be convinced of some truth or reality, including the truth or reality about sin and God's attitude regarding it.

Then, which meaning is intended here—convince or convict? On the one hand, in favor of convince, of the three things that John records Jesus saying about *how* the Spirit does his work of illumination (bring to remembrance, teach, and convict or convince) the first two seem to be directed especially towards the apostles and other believers. If Jesus is also speaking of the Spirit's work in the apostles and other believers, when he is speaking about convincing or convicting, perhaps convince is the best choice, since these persons are forgiven and therefore not to be condemned and sentenced to judgment.

On the other hand, in favor of convict, Morris points out: "This is the one place in scripture where the Spirit is spoken of as performing a work in 'the world.'"[18] Thus, in this case, Jesus seems to be saying that this particular work of the Spirit is directed especially toward the unredeemed, rather than toward the apostles and other believers. Therefore, this part of the context indicates that perhaps convict is the best choice, since the world is guilty of sin and therefore, worthy of being condemned and sentenced to judgment. Hence, Morris agrees with Brown who concludes that "'convict' seems better than 'convince.'"[19]

However, the Spirit is certainly capable of both convincing and convicting, and logically there are obviously occasions for both. In fact, since

---

15. L. Morris, *The Gospel According to John* (Grand Rapids: Eerdmans, 1981) 697–98.

16. Brown, *Holy Spirit*, 68.

17. See M. C. Tenney, *The Gospel of John* (Grand Rapids: Zondervan, 1981) 157.

18. Morris, *John*, 697.

19. Brown, *Holy Spirit*, 68.

God does not want any to perish, it seems reasonable that especially since this work is said to be directed towards the world, the Holy Spirit does both. That is, before he convicts, condemns, and sentences the world to judgment, he surely first convinces them concerning the reality of sin and righteousness, thus giving them an opportunity to respond to his grace for their salvation. Finally, there is no logical reason why Jesus could not intend both of these possible meanings here. The apostles and all other believers, before their conversion, are "of the world." And, at some point or points these are all convinced concerning the truths of Jesus Christ and also convicted about sin, righteousness and judgment. Thus, perhaps the best translation would be: "And He, when He comes, will convince/convict the world concerning sin and righteousness and judgment" (John 16.8).

Why the Spirit Helps Us Understand Revelation

The topic of convincing and convicting naturally brings us to the third significant question brought forward by the notion that the Spirit helps in understanding special revelation. That question is: *Why* is the Spirit's work of illumination important? Fortunately, as in the case of the *what* and *how* questions, in the Fourth Gospel John provides some helpful insights regarding this third question.

Discussion of *why* does the Spirit do the work of illumination is important because this work is not an end in itself. Rather, it is a means to an end.[20] Pinnock observes: "Interpretation is about more than retrieving information—it is also about the effects on readers that texts can set in motion."[21] Writing about the "teleological work of the Spirit," Nebeker understands the importance of the Spirit's work of illumination lies in the fact that the focus and purpose of this work is *christological* and *transformational*. That is, "the role of the Holy Spirit in hermeneutics is (1) aiding our understanding of who Christ is, and (2) effecting our transformation into Christ's image."[22]

Interestingly, when we study all of what John says about the Spirit in the Fourth Gospel closely, we learn that he understands the ultimate work of the Spirit to be that of producing eternal life in believers. By producing eternal life we mean both initial salvation, including regeneration, justification, and initial sanctification and also the on-going work of transforming believers into the image of Christ, commonly termed progressive sanctification.

20. Ibid., 72.
21. Pinnock, "Work of the Holy Spirit," 13.
22. G. L. Nebeker, "The Holy Spirit, Hermeneutics, and Transformation: From Present to Future Glory," *ERT* 27/1 (2003) 49, 53.

John identifies this ultimate work of Spirit early in his gospel, in his record of Jesus' conversation with Nicodemus (John 3.1–21). Jesus tells Nicodemus that, in order to "see the kingdom of God," he must be "born again" (John 3.3). That is, he must be "born of . . . the Spirit" in order to "enter into the kingdom of God" (John 3.5–6). In this conversation, Jesus equates "seeing" or "entering" the kingdom of God with receiving "eternal life" (John 3.16).[23] And, in his very next reference to a work of the Spirit in his gospel, John records Jesus' declaration: "It is the Spirit who gives life" (John 6.63). Then, near the end of his account, John reveals his main purpose in writing his gospel. He says these things "have been written so that you may believe that Jesus is the Christ, the Son of God; and, that believing you may have life in His name" (John 20.31). Thus, John directly relates his main purpose for writing his gospel to what he understands to be the ultimate work of the Spirit in the world since Jesus' return to the Father.

John's statement of purpose (John 20.31) also indicates the specific role that he expects his gospel account to play in the Spirit's work of redemption. He expects his gospel to be (1) read, (2) understood, and (3) believed, with the result being that the reader will (4) receive eternal life (beginning at new birth and continuing until glorification) through Jesus Christ. Certainly, receiving eternal life is a supernatural, miraculous work of the Spirit, as John makes abundantly clear in his record of Jesus' conversation with Nicodemus. Jesus says to Nicodemus, "Truly, truly, I say unto you, unless one is born of water and the Spirit he cannot enter into the kingdom of God. That which is born of the flesh is flesh, and that which is born of the Spirit is spirit. Do not be amazed that I said to you, 'You must be born again'" (John 3.5–7).

However, John also knows that in this process of reading, understanding, believing, and receiving, only the reading part is "natural." He knows that like being born again (receiving eternal life) both understanding and believing are also supernatural, miraculous works of the Spirit, as we have discussed above. We can now recognize and truly appreciate the importance of the Spirit's work of illumination. Without it, individuals would never receive eternal life. This is because to receive eternal life, obviously, individuals must not only read or hear the gospel, they must also understand and believe (be convinced of the truth of) that message. And, this is precisely what the Spirit does in his work of illumination. Thus, the ultimate purpose of the Spirit's work of illumination is directly related to the purpose of the

---

23. See G. E. Ladd, *A Theology of the New Testament*, rev. ed. (Grand Rapids: Eerdmans, 1993) 295, 338–39.

gospel—producing eternal life, which includes the transformation of the believer into the image of Christ.

Earlier in this essay we emphasized the christological focus of *what* the Spirit helps us understand. There we suggested that this christological focus on the purpose and message of the Spirit's work of illumination would be found to be absolutely essential to God's plan of redemption in and through Jesus Christ. We now see that indeed this is the case because now we not only understand the exclusive role of the Spirit in generating new birth (John 3.16) we also understand his essential and exclusive role leading up to and following that experience. Only the Spirit can provide the understanding of the person and work of Jesus Christ that is necessary to being born again and being transformed into his image. Nebeker concurs: "This transformation, we maintain, is attainable only through the Spirit working in conjunction with our hearing and reflection upon the scriptures."[24] In summary, and plainly stated: Without the Spirit's miraculous work of helping us understand special revelation, there would be no salvation, no transforming into the image of Christ, and no eternal life.

CONCLUSION

More than any other book in the canon of Scripture, the Gospel of John offers useful insights into the Spirit's work of helping us understand Scripture. Being a miraculous work, aspects of illumination will always remain a mystery. However, the Fourth Gospel provides some especially helpful insights about this special work of the Spirit.

One, while the Spirit certainly illuminates Scripture, further, and more importantly, John reveals that *what* the Spirit ultimately helps readers and hearers understand is the person and work of Jesus Christ (John 14.6; 15.26; 16.13). Scripture is his primary source (John 5.39) and he reveals nothing that is above or beyond the truth found in Scripture.

Two, with regard to *how* the Spirit does this miraculous work, John tells us that he supernaturally enhances memory of Jesus' teachings (John 14.26); he teaches (makes clear, explains, and elaborates upon) all the truth about Jesus Christ that is necessary to redemption (John 14.26; 16.13); and, he convinces and convicts all persons concerning sin, righteousness, and judgment as these are revealed in Jesus Christ (John 16.8–11).

Third, John provides insights that allow us to realize *why* the Spirit's work of illumination is important. It is here in the Fourth Gospel that we most clearly see, on the one hand, the direct relationship between the Spirit's

---

24. Nebeker, "The Holy Spirit, Hermeneutics, and Transformation," 52.

work of illumination; and, on the other hand, the main, ultimate reason for which the Father and Son have sent him into the world—to produce eternal life in believers. John shows that illumination is essential in the process of salvation because a supernatural understanding of the person and work of Jesus Christ is absolutely necessary in order to be able to respond to God's grace through Jesus Christ and thereby receive eternal life (John 14.26; 16.8–13; 20.31).

No other book in the NT provides these kinds of important insights into the Spirit's work of illumination. These insights should motivate us to be constantly open to this work of the Spirit. Every time we read and study Scripture, every time we hear a biblical sermon or an exposition on Scripture, we should be consciously aware of and responsive to the Spirit's desire to do this marvelous work in us.

3

The Role and Function of the Demonic in the Johannine Tradition

JOHN CHRISTOPHER THOMAS

IT IS A SINGULAR honor to be invited to contribute to this *Festschrift* in honor of my good friend Benny C. Aker. I first met Benny in the early 1980s, an exciting time for Pentecostals working in biblical studies. Both of us were in the midst of PhD studies and, as I recall, we were both trying to find our way with regard to the integration of biblical studies and Pentecostal theology, though I am not certain that "Pentecostal theology" as a discipline was on either of our radar screens at the time. A teacher of longstanding in the A/G tradition, Benny had recently signed on with Hendrickson Publishers to assist in the development of an entire line of books designed to push Pentecostal scholarship forward. Heady days indeed! My interaction with Benny over the years revealed him to be a thoughtful, discerning, and warm brother and friend, someone whose company I always enjoyed and from whom I always learned; our friendship has made me all the richer. I am happy to contribute this piece in his honor, a study that incorporates a topic and biblical corpus in which he has shown interest over the years.

Most previous studies of this topic have been motivated by a desire to explain the omission of exorcism accounts in this literature and/or to propose a new definition of Johannine exorcism. Normally such enquiries take as their starting point the fact that since Jesus is known as an exorcist in the synoptic tradition, consequently, the absence of this emphasis in the

Johannine literature calls for explanation. On this view, the Johannine literature is then examined with a view to making it fit with the evidence of the Synoptics in order for it to "make sense." Such enquiries rather clearly are historical investigations that privilege the historical critical methodological approach, with the implicit, or explicit, goal being an explanation of the development of Johannine thought from the original activity of Jesus. However, such an approach begs a number of literary and theological questions, if not a few historical ones as well.

Rather than approaching the Johannine literature through the lens of the Synoptics, or privileging the historical critical method as the most hermeneutically appropriate tool for the task, this essay comes at the topic from more of a literary and theological perspective. In this approach the text is given a place of privilege and engaged on its own terms first in order to discern the shape and scope of Johannine thought on this topic to ensure that this understanding is not unduly shaped by outside concerns, whether they be the synoptic tradition or the so-called historical context of the first century. Thus, after a brief overview of some of the previous studies devoted to this topic, a literary reading or hearing is offered of the relevant Johannine texts as found in the Fourth Gospel, 1–2 John, and the Apocalypse. While historical arguments can be offered to support the order in which these documents are encountered, I am becoming more and more convinced of the wisdom of engaging these documents within their canonical context and thus will utilize that approach here. In a following section I seek to hear the distinct contributions of the Johannine voice(s) on this topic in the broader "Black Gospel Choir of Scripture."[1] Finally, I offer some concluding reflections on the implications of these findings for Pentecostal theology and ministry.

HEARING THE VOICES OF SCHOLARSHIP ON THIS TOPIC

In order to illustrate the scholarly concerns and interests of those who have devoted previous attention to this topic, the work of three scholars are briefly surveyed.

Despite the fact that, in contrast to the Synoptics, the Fourth Gospel contains no accounts of exorcisms, Edwin K. Broadhead argues that even

---

1. On this metaphor for Scripture, see J. C. Thomas, "'What the Spirit Is Saying to the Church'—The Testimony of a Pentecostal in New Testament Studies," in *Spirit and Scripture: Examining a Pneumatic Hermeneutic*, eds. K. L. Spawn and A. T. Wright (London: T. & T. Clark, 2012) 122–29.

the Fourth Gospel is not without echoes of exorcism.² According to Broadhead, an examination of John 6.66–71 reveals several "novel traits" that point to a mixed ancestry of this passage. Among these pointers are the appearance of "The Twelve" (6.67, 70, 71), the description of Jesus as "the Holy One of God" (6.69), the occurrence of "to choose" (ἐκλέγομαι) in conjunction with "The Twelve" in 6.70, the occurrence of "devil" (διάβολος) in 6.70, and the anomaly of the name of Judas Simon of Iscariot (6.71).³ All of these, it is argued, carry echoes of the synoptic exorcism tradition. In order to account for such an anomaly Broadhead offers a stage-by-stage analysis of the development of the exorcism tradition. In Stage One, exorcism stories functioned as traditional stories; in Stage Two exorcisms served as christological paradigms; in Stage Three they support the development of discipleship in relation to christological claims; in Stage Four the demonic images are transferred or omitted as discipleship takes priority over Christology. According to Broadhead, by the time of the Fourth Gospel none of the references to the demonic is attached to an exorcism scene but deals exclusively with failed discipleship. Exorcism has fallen victim to the Johannine hermeneutic.

Eric Plumer has also given his attention to "The Absence of Exorcisms in the FG," in a study that seeks to explain this striking omission.⁴ After dispensing with explanations that prove inadequate (i.e., the Fourth Evangelist simply did not know of "the relevant traditions") Plumer develops the idea that the absence may be owing to John's theological interests. Arguing that exorcisms do not radically enough differentiate Jesus from other miracle-workers, and that exorcisms may well have been omitted owing to their magical connotations, Plumer settles on the idea that John's familiarity with the Beelzebul charges by the Jewish authorities fatally undermines the ability to recount his exorcisms. Sensing that the exorcism stories were inadequate vehicles for his message of salvation, which took on an increasingly interiorized characteristic (i.e., "the conflict between truth and lies," the shift from the kingdom of God to the majestic "I am"), John thus develops the traditions in a way that addresses the vulnerability of the community to the attacks of the Jewish synagogue. Thus, the Jesus traditions have been so remarkably recast that they are hardly recognizable.

The most impressive attempt to answer the question about the absence of exorcisms stories in the Fourth Gospel to date comes from Graham H. Twelftree as part of his study of exorcism among early Christians in a chapter

2. E. K. Broadhead, "Echoes of an Exorcism in the FG," *ZNW* 86 (1995) 111–19.
3. All Scripture translations are my own.
4. E. Plumer, "The Absence of Exorcisms in the FG," *Bib* 78 (1997) 350–51.

devoted to Johannine Christianity.[5] After dismissing inadequate solutions, Twelftree seeks to ground his proposal historically by describing Johannine purpose and audience. Arguing that Johannine miracles are astounding and unambiguously performed by a divine being, Twelftree goes on to describe exorcisms as common and unspectacular, ambiguous in significance and origin, while Johannine miracles serve as signs. Owing to the fact that Jesus' entire ministry is seen as in battle with Satan and that the charge of demon possession against Jesus has reference to belief and unbelief, truth and lies, ultimately the readers would see in his ministry a cosmic exorcism, where instead of individual exorcisms, knowing Jesus is the way in which the demon possession of unbelief is combated. This emphasis Twelftree sees played out in 1 John and the Apocalypse as well.

HEARING THE TEXT OF THE FOURTH GOSPEL

This hearing of Johannine texts begins with the Gospel according to John, a narrative normally divided into the following major sections: the Prologue (1.1–18), the Book of Signs (1.19—12.50), the Book of Glory (13.1—20.31), and the Epilogue (21.1-25). Significantly, the three texts that touch directly upon this topic all occur in a section of the Book of Signs that is devoted specifically to hostility toward Jesus (5.1—12.50). Unlike Mark, where the hostility to Jesus steadily grows from unspoken opposition (2.1-12) to a decision to kill Jesus (3.1-6), in the Fourth Gospel the hostile opposition to Jesus immediately morphs into an attempt to kill Jesus, a desire of his opponents that is sustained throughout the Fourth Gospel. Equally important is the fact that no texts that have reference to the demonic occur in the Book of Glory, a large portion of which is devoted to the farewell materials where Jesus prepares his disciples for his departure (13.1—17.26).

John 7.20

Set in the context of the Feast of Tabernacles, the first text of relevance for this study is found in John 7.20. Rejecting his unbelieving brothers' challenge to go up to Jerusalem for the feast in order to display his signs publicly (7.3-5), Jesus goes up after them secretly (7.10). At this time "the Jews" are seeking him saying, "Where is that one?" (7.11) while the crowds seem split in their assessment saying on the one hand, "This one is good," and others, on

---

5. G. H. Twelftree, *In the Name of Jesus: Exorcism among the Early Christians* (Grand Rapids: Baker, 2007) 183–205.

the other hand, were saying, "No, but he deceives the crowd" (7.12). In any case, no one was speaking openly about him owing to "the fear of the Jews" (7.13), but Jesus, it seems, was already teaching in the temple. Such teaching astonished "the Jews" for Jesus had no rabbinical training (7.15). If, Jesus responds, his teaching does not originate with himself but with the one who sent him, one whom he seeks to glorify, and if conversely, his opponents, though being given the law by Moses, "do not do the law," "why," he asks, "do you seek to kill me" (7.16–19). Such teaching causes the crowd to answer, "You have a demon; who is seeking to kill you?" (7.20). The emphasis of this charge in the Greek text is placed upon the word "demon" (Δαιμόνιον) as it stands first in the sentence. Unmistakably, the charge is made that Jesus has a demon. But what sense would such a charge make?

In 7.20, the accusation seems to be closely connected to Jesus' claim that they are seeking to kill him, an assertion they dismiss, retorting, "who is seeking to kill you?" On first glance, it appears the accusation that Jesus has a demon is directly connected to the fact that in their view he is a liar for they, in effect, accuse him of lying when he charges that they are seeking to kill him—a claim which they deny. There even may be an accusation that Jesus is delusional,[6] owing to the fact that, as they see it, no one is seeking to take his life. Such may be a valid understanding as far as it goes, but their accusation may go deeper still. An earlier assessment of Jesus' identity is that he deceives the crowd (7.12). This first appearance of the πλανάω word family in the Fourth Gospel might go so far as to imply that the charge leveled at Jesus of having a demon, ostensibly because he is "lying" or delusional when he claims that they are seeking to kill him, points to a deeper charge that includes deception of the crowds, which would suggest his "lying" or delusion is even more sinister.

In response to the crowd's accusation, Jesus picks back up on the charge that his opponents do not keep the law. How precisely? By circumcising an infant on a Sabbath, Jesus implies that they actually override Sabbath observance, breaking the law, in order not to break the law (7.21–23a)![7] How then, Jesus asks, can you be angry with me for making a "whole" (ὅλον) man "whole" (ὑγιῆ) on the Sabbath? This question reminds the readers of two things. First, it reminds them of the healing of the man at the pool in John 5.1–18, a healing that included the forgiveness of the man's sins (cf. the command in 5.14 to "stop sinning lest something worse come upon you").[8]

6. D. A. Carson, *The Gospel According to John* (Grand Rapids: Eerdmans, 1991) 314.

7. On this whole question, cf. J. C. Thomas, "The FG and Rabbinic Judaism," in *The Spirit of the New Testament* (Blandford Forum, UK: Deo, 2005) 146–47.

8. On this text, cf. the discussion in J. C. Thomas, *The Devil, Disease, and Deliverance: The Origins of Illness in New Testament Thought* (Cleveland, TN: CPT, 2011)

Second, this reference to the healing of the man at the pool in John 5 would remind the readers that Jesus is neither delusional nor a liar for his claims that his opponents are seeking to kill him, for they would now remember that it was on the occasion of his healing of this man on the Sabbath that "the Jews" began to seek to kill him (5.18). Jesus makes clear that his opponents are lacking in discernment and judgment, for he instructs them, "Do not judge according to sight, but judge right judgment" (7.24).

John 8.48–52

The next text of relevance occurs near the end of a long and particularly contentious dialogue between Jesus and "the Jews," some who seem to have believed in him (8.31). Specifically, Jesus a) proclaims that some of his Jewish opponents will die in their sins, b) keeps the charge before them that they are seeking to kill him, and c) denies that they are children of Abraham despite their claims, calling them "children of the Devil," who is a liar and murderer from the beginning. At this point, "The Jews answered and said to him, 'Do we not say well that a Samaritan you are and a demon you have?'" While it is not altogether clear how these charges are to be understood, there are hints that assist the readers in making sense of them.

First, it is clear that the charge that Jesus is a Samaritan is meant as a slanderous allegation. For a variety of reasons there were historic hostilities between the Jews and the Samaritans—John 4.9b simply notes enigmatically that "Jews and Samaritans do not use together with"[9]—which included Jewish accusations that the Samaritans were impure racially, owing to the fact that the Assyrians brought in a variety of peoples to live in the midst of the people of the northern tribes (2 Kgs 17)[10] and were theologically corrupt, owing to their distinctive brand of monotheism, which included adherence to the Pentateuch, worship on Mount Gerizim, a no-nonsense approach to Sabbath observance, and the expectation of the Prophet like Moses. Readers of the Fourth Gospel know that Jesus has quite an extended conversation with a woman from Samaria who acknowledges to her village, in question form, that Jesus is the Christ (4.30) a proclamation that results in the conversion of the village, which includes the confession, "We know that you are truly the Savior of the world" (4.42). The fact that Jesus stayed with them two days (4.40) as well as his enthusiastic Samaritan reception, implies a very close relationship between Jesus and the Samaritans. In the light of all

---

81–98.

9. On this, see J. C. Thomas, "The FG and Rabbinic Judaism," 137–41.

10. J. Marsh, *Saint John* (New York: Penguin, 1968) 368.

this, the reader of the Fourth Gospel might well conclude that the charge the Jews bring of Jesus being a Samaritan might have reference at least to Jesus' own alleged "unorthodox" beliefs—that he is sent by the Father and speaks on the Father's behalf—by which he might deceive the crowds. At the same time, it is at least theoretically possible that this accusation raises the question of Jesus' parentage with regard to his claims about the one who sent him. It might possibly even include a subtle reference to the unconventional nature of his birth,[11] though it should be noted that the Fourth Gospel offers no other hints as to knowledge of the details about Jesus' birth. Second, the now familiar charge that Jesus has a demon would, for the readers of the Fourth Gospel, again seem to be tied to Jesus' continued reference to the fact that they are seeking to kill him. While the charge of delusion is not explicit in their words, it might easily be imagined his words could be taken as the delusional ravings of a mad man.

Jesus' response to these accusations is even more revealing, for while he explicitly denies the charge that he has a demon, he does not explicitly deny the allegation that he is a Samaritan! Rather, he speaks of honoring his Father, even as his opponents dishonor him. Though Jesus does not seek his own glory, there is one who seeks and judges, words reminiscent of the judgment language found in 7.24 in the context of the first accusation that Jesus has a demon. Building on his words from 8.31, Jesus here states, "Amen, amen, I say unto you, if any keep my words, that one will never ever see death" (8.51). These words prove to be too much for "the Jews" who retort, "Now we know that you have a demon" for though you claim that anyone who keeps your word will never see death, both Abraham and the prophets died (8.52). Again the charge of Jesus having a demon seems to be tied to the idea that Jesus is lying, and by this means seeks to deceive the people. Jesus' words with regard to his own special relationship to Abraham (8.54–56, 58) do little to dispel the hostility of his opponents, who pick up stones to cast them at Jesus, an indication that they regard his words as blasphemous (8.59a).

John 10.20–21

The third text from the Fourth Gospel relevant for this study occurs near the conclusion of Jesus' good shepherd discourse in which Jesus claims to be "the door," "the good shepherd" (as opposed to hirelings) who has the authority to lay aside his life and take it up again—the one whom the Father

---

11. R. E. Brown, *The Gospel According to John I–XII* (Garden City, NY: Doubleday, 1966) 366.

loves (10.7–18). Again there was a schism amongst the Jews owing to his words (10.19) "And many were saying of him, 'A demon he has and he is out of his mind; who is able to hear him?' Others were saying, 'These words are not those of one having a demon; is a demon able to open blind eyes?'"

Again the accusation that Jesus has a demon seems to be tied to his claims about the nature of his relationship with God, which includes his claim about the Father's love for him and the way in which he offers unique access to the Father. While the accusation of having a demon on this occasion is not tied explicitly to the language of lying as on earlier occasions, the implication appears to be clear. He would not make such claims if he were not lying. However, in this passage the idea that Jesus is delusional, perhaps even out of his mind, is made explicit by the appearance of the term μαίνεται, a term which carries with it the idea of "raging" to the point of madness.[12] Jesus' claims, it appears, result in the view that his opponents believe he must be delusional. In response to these accusations made by many of the Jews, others point out the incongruity of attributing his words to the demonic ("these words are not those of one who has a demon") as his actions ("opening blind eyes") do not bear out such a conclusion: "Is a demon able to open blind eyes?"

THE ROLE OF THE DEMONIC IN THE FOURTH GOSPEL

Several things might be concluded from this brief survey of the Fourth Gospel. First, it is quite significant that in the Fourth Gospel the only person ever accused of having a demon is Jesus. No one is brought to Jesus for exorcism, nor is he said to be confronted by demons in the course of his ministry. In this Johannine narrative, there is no exorcism sought or performed. If the claims that Jesus has a demon are false, as revealed in John's narrative, there is a sense in which it is accurate to observe that in the Fourth Gospel there are no demons. Second, on each occasion Jesus is accused of having a demon, the accusation comes from his "Jewish" opponents. Thus, in John the conflict about the demonic has to do with Jesus' person and work, indicating the extent of the opposition offered to Jesus by his opponents. Rather than responding in faith to the fullest revelation of the Father and the offer of salvation they encounter, these opponents choose to attribute him and his words to the realm of the demonic. Third, the accusation that Jesus has a demon is often tied either explicitly or implicitly to the charge that Jesus is lying. The rich irony present in this aspect of the accusation is that it is

---

12. H. Preisker, "μαίνομαι," *TDNT* 4.360–61.

the one who is (identified as) the "Truth" that is, in this charge, accused of lying![13] While demons play no role in the Fourth Gospel, it might be fair to infer that if lies are tied to the idea of the demonic in Johannine thought it is the opponents of Jesus, "the Jews," those who make such accusations, who are liars and speak the language of their father the Devil! Fourth, in the Fourth Gospel the accusation that Jesus has a demon is closely related to the idea that Jesus deceives the people through his claims. Clearly, the deception here inferred has to do with the judgment that Jesus' teaching, rather than containing the truth of salvation, is leading people away from the truth. Again, the rich irony of course is that the one whom they accuse of such deception has already been identified in the narrative as "the Truth." Still, it would appear that in the narrative world of the Fourth Gospel there is a tacit identification between the demonic and deception. Fifth, the charge that Jesus has a demon is also closely tied to the idea that Jesus is deemed to be delusional—his claims reveal that he is out of his mind! Such an association may well imply that in the Johannine world such delusions were at least partially self-induced.

HEARING THE TEXT OF 1–2 JOHN

While the word demon occurs nowhere in 1–3 John, there are texts in these documents of relevance to this investigation. This survey will begin with a couple of interrelated texts and move to the one of strategic importance. Each text will be briefly surveyed.

2 John 7

The first text to be examined occurs in 2 John, an epistle that appears to follow 3 John chronologically, while preceding 1 John.[14] Standing at the heart of this little epistle, 2 John 7 conveys some important information for the purposes of this study and in some ways sets the stage for an examination of the other texts. The Elder writes, "Many deceivers (πλάνοι) have gone out into the world, not confessing Jesus Christ coming in the flesh; this is the deceiver (ὁ πλάνος) and the antichrist (ὁ ἀντίχριστος)."

Already in the Fourth Gospel the accusation that Jesus has a demon was connected to the idea that he deceives the crowds (John 7.12) and

13. On this major theme in the Fourth Gospel, cf. A. T. Lincoln, *Truth on Trial: The Lawsuit Motif in the Fourth Gospel* (Peabody, MA: Hendrickson, 2000).

14. Cf. J. C. Thomas, "The Order of the Composition of the Johannine Epistles," in *The Spirit of the New Testament* (Blandford Forum, UK: Deo, 2005) 248–54.

Nicodemus too (7.47). In 2 John 7, the Elder warns his readers, who appear to be located at some distance from him geographically, that deceivers have gone out as missionaries intent on carrying a message that is at odds with "the teaching of the Christ of God" (v. 9) by "not confessing Jesus Christ coming in the flesh." Though difficult to know for certain, it appears that the deceivers were appealing to Jesus' words about the *Paraclete*, who will lead and guide into all truth, as the basis for their theological innovations. Thus, the charge that they "go beyond and do not remain in the teaching of Jesus Christ of God" (v. 9) is a response to such claims about the origins of their theological deviations. Significantly, the deceivers who go out are equated with the antichrists, indicating that both are closely connected to false teaching.

1 John 2.18–27

In this passage, a number of terms familiar from the Fourth Gospel and 2 John converge, developing various themes and preparing the readers for the text of most significance for this study in 1 John. Amongst the significant developments in 1 John 2.18–27 is the reappearance of the term antichrist, only in this case the word appears in the plural. With the acknowledgement that many antichrists have come, the future possibility of 2 John is now spoken of as a past reality in 1 John 2.18. The language of "liar" also reappears in this passage with the reminder that every liar is not out of the truth. But the language of 2 John which describes the deceiver and antichrist by what they are not confessing has changed in 1 John 2.22 to what the liar denies, "Jesus is not the Christ," which is quickly identified as "the antichrist" the one who denies the father and the son. The admonitions to remain in that which they have heard from the beginning (v. 24) and to remember the anointing which they have received and consequently know all things (v. 20) are written owing to those who are deceiving "you" (v. 26). Thus, in this passage there is an equation between "the liar," "the antichrists," and "those who deceive you." This equation is important in helping to understand the meaning of the next text considered.

1 John 4.1–6

Following fast on the words of 3.24b, "and in this we know that he remains in us, out of the Spirit which he has given to us," occurs the text of greatest relevance for this enquiry, 1 John 4.1–6. A number of important aspects of this text should be underscored. The first verse alone introduces a variety of significant issues, "Beloved, do not believe every spirit, but test the spirits to see if they are of God, because many false prophets have gone out into the world."

With these words the community is called to the process of discernment. The impression left is that there is a great deal of spirit activity in the community that must be evaluated and discerned.[15] Not only this, but for the first time the work of human spokespersons is cast explicitly in pneumatic terms, implying that such spokespersons do not simply speak on their own but are pneumatically inspired, either by God or by some other spirit source. In point of fact, the deceivers and antichrists here appear to be labeled as false prophets who have gone out into the world (as missionaries?). The introduction of prophetic language reveals the conviction that the work of the deceivers and antichrists is coterminous with false prophecy, which is inspired by a spirit other than God. Thus, the call to discernment is essential for the community. On this occasion it appears that a first step in the discernment process, to determine whether a spirit is of God, is connected to the content of one's confession, especially as it relates to the confession "Jesus Christ has come in the flesh." As a reading of the Fourth Gospel and 1 John reveals, this confession is shorthand for belief in the person of Jesus Christ (1 John 3.23) which includes:

> that fellowship with the Father includes fellowship with the Son (1.3); that cleansing from sin is accomplished through Jesus' blood (1.7); that the righteous Jesus acts as an Advocate for the believer (2.1) based on his Atoning Sacrifice (2.2); that he is a model for the believer's walk (2.6); that forgiveness of sin comes through his name (2.12); that he remains in the believer (2.14); that this righteous one will be manifest at his appearing (2.28–29); that his mode of existence and purity are the model for the believer (3.2–3); that he came to take away sin and is himself without sin (3.5–6); that he came to destroy the works of the Devil (3.7); and that he laid aside his life on behalf of the believers.[16]

Obviously this confession is not simply a narrow doctrinal point to be affirmed in these precise words, but rather is an affirmation and acknowledgement of experiences in which the believers are participants with Jesus in various ways. As such, if a spirit's words concur with this broad theological confession, it indicates that the Spirit has inspired such speech

---

15. G. Strecker, *The Johannine Epistles*, trans. L. M. Maloney; ed. H. Attridge (Minneapolis: Fortress, 1996) 132.

16. J. C. Thomas, *1 John, 2 John, 3 John* (Blandford Forum, UK: Deo, 2011) 192–93.

and actions. These words appear to suggest that the Spirit validates them as well. Conversely, if a spirit inspired prophetic figure does not embrace and confess this Johannine understanding of Jesus it reveals that such a spirit does not originate from God, but rather is literally "that of the antichrist." The fact that in the Greek text the word "spirit" does not appear, but has to be supplied, is a subtle way of underscoring that "the spirit of antichrist" is not to be regarded as comparable to the Spirit of God but is rather that which inspires the deceivers, antichrists, and false prophets. The last verse of this passage makes clear that standing in diametric opposition to "the Spirit of Truth" is "the spirit of deception," a title that occurs only here in the NT. Though sometimes translated "the spirit of error," such a translation obscures the fact that the Greek term translated in that fashion (πλάνης) is actually from the same word family as the verb "deceive" (πλανάω, 1 John 1.8; 2.26; 3.7) and the noun "deceivers" (πλάνοι, 2 John 7). As "the deceiver" is synonymous with "the antichrist" in 2 John 7, so here in 1 John 4.6 "the 'spirit' of the antichrist" is synonymous with "the spirit of deception."[17] Thus, in this section's final statement it becomes clear that "the spirit of deception" is responsible for the many "deceivers" who have gone out into the world to "deceive" as many as possible, including members of the Johannine community.[18] It is this spirit, "that of the antichrist," that is manifest in the "spirits" that do not confess Jesus. However, the community has nothing to fear for it knows the difference between "the Spirit of Truth" (God) and "the spirit of deception" (the evil one) and is capable of testing the "spirits" present in their context for they have received the Spirit (3.24).[19]

THE ROLE OF THE DEMONIC IN 1-2 JOHN

What are the implications of this brief survey for the topic at hand? First, it is significant that despite a number of similarities with the teaching of the Fourth Gospel on this point the word demon does not ever occur, nor is anyone (even Jesus!) accused of having a demon. Second, as in the Fourth Gospel there is a considerable presence of deception language. However, in 1 and 2 John the accusations of deception are not directed to Jesus or his followers but to those who are now deemed to be opponents of the community. Specifically, these opponents are called deceivers and antichrists, those who do not confess Jesus coming in the flesh—shorthand it seems

17. For this definition, cf. J. P Louw and E. A. Nida, *Greek-English Lexicon of the New Testament Based on Semantic Domains*, 2 vols. (New York: UBS, 1988) 1:367.

18. D. Rensberger, *1 John, 2 John, 3 John* (Nashville: Abingdon, 1997) 114.

19. Cf. Thomas, *1 John, 2 John, 3 John*, 211–12.

The Role and Function of the Demonic in the Johannine Tradition

for the entire matrix of Johannine beliefs about Jesus and participation in his salvific work. Third, pneumatic and prophetic language is employed to describe the work of such opponents. Their prophetic utterances are treated as spirit inspired, false though they may be. Among other things such language reveals the extent to which Spirit activity is present in the community. Fourth, unlike the letters of Ignatius that give pride of place to the Bishop or the teaching of the *Didache* (11.1; 12.1) where rules governing the behavior of itinerate prophets, teachers, and apostles were already being formulated, in 1 John the community is called to corporate discernment assessing the confession of and participation in the salvific work of Jesus in all its fullness. Fifth, the spirit inspiration of the false prophets with which the community is familiar is attributed to "that of the antichrist," which in turn is attributed to "the spirit of deception" in contrast to "the Spirit of Truth." Sixth, the relationship between the charges of having a demon in the Fourth Gospel and the role of "the spirit of deception," deceivers, antichrists, and false prophets in 1 and 2 John are remarkably similar, bringing some greater clarity as to the role of the demonic in Johannine thought.

HEARING THE TEXT OF THE APOCALYPSE

Three passages in the Apocalypse have direct reference to the demonic and quite obviously have a bearing on this investigation. The texts are treated in their narrative order.

Revelation 9.20

Revelation 9.20 reads, "the rest of the men, those who were not killed by these plagues, did not repent of the works of their hands, in order that they not worship the demons and the idols of gold and silver and bronze and stone and wood, which are not able to see nor hear nor walk." Owing to the fact that there appears to be little interest in demons or the demonic in the Johannine literature to this point, the mention of demons here in the Apocalypse might come as a bit of a surprise to the hearers. The appearance of demons in 9.20, apparently in connection with idolatry, would seem to suggest some relationship between their worship and idolatry. While it is possible that the hearers of the Apocalypse would take this mention to indicate that the worship of demons is to be equated with the worship of idols, the rest of the verse, which makes clear that idols are impotent, suggests otherwise. Rather it seems to indicate that the relationship between demons and idols is that the former inspires the worship of the latter. For the first time in the Apocalypse the hearers encounter the word worship in connection with one other than God and/or his people (Rev 3.9; 4.10; 5.14; 7.11). In this way, the theme of false worship is introduced into the book, a theme that will function prominently and gain significance as the book unfolds. On this occasion, its appearance makes the choice between the worship of God and the worship of demons and idols all the clearer for the hearers. The description of the idols, which sits nicely with the phrase "the works of their hands," could not help but evoke for the hearers the biting words of numerous OT writers with regard to the foolishness and futility of idolatry (Isa 40.18–20; 41.6–7; 44.9–20; Jer 10; Ps 115.3–8).[20] Despite their composition, whether of gold, silver, bronze, stone, or wood, they are unable to act, to see, or hear, or walk. And yet, these impotent idols and the demons that inspire their worship are tenaciously grasped by those who, ironically enough, have seen firsthand the activity of "the living God" in the form of the plagues and judgments wrought upon the earth and its inhabitants! Significantly, repentance, not exorcism, seems to be called for by those who worship the demons and the idols they inspire.

Revelation 16.13–14

For the first time since 15.5, the hearers are told of something John saw, "And I saw out of the mouth of the dragon and out of the mouth of the beast and out of the mouth of the false prophet three unclean spirits as frogs." For the hearers the emphasis of these words would be clear as the phrase "out of the mouth of" not only stands in a position of emphasis, but also occurs three times in this verse! Such an emphasis upon what comes from the mouths of this triumvirate of evil, mentioned here together for the first time in the book,[21] would no doubt remind the hearers of the things that have been said to come from their mouths previously, including the river which came from the mouth of the ancient serpent to drown the rest of the seed of the woman clothed with the sun (12.15) and the great and blasphemous things that come from the mouth of the beast (13.5–6). At the same time, these would likely be thought of in contrast to the double-edged sword that comes from the mouth of Jesus (1.16; 2.16) the fire and smoke of God that come from the mouths of the horses when the sixth angel trumpets (9.17–19) and the fire that comes from the mouth of the two witnesses (11.5).[22] But perhaps

---

20. F. J. Murphy, *Fallen Is Babylon: The Revelation to John* (Harrisburg, PA: Trinity, 1998) 249.

21. G. Osborne, *Revelation* (Grand Rapids: Baker, 2008) 591.

22. J. Sweet, *Revelation* (London: SCM, 1979) 249.

The Role and Function of the Demonic in the Johannine Tradition

most poignantly they would be reminded of the fact that in the mouths of the 144,000 were found no lies (14.5). If the hearers earlier suspected that the beast from the earth functioned as a false prophet (13.11–16) their suspicions are confirmed in 16.13 for he is here explicitly identified as the "false prophet." In fact, what comes from the mouths of these figures are "unclean spirits, as frogs." Both the words "unclean spirits" and "as frogs" would perhaps give the hearers pause when first encountered, for this is the first mention of "unclean spirits" in the entire Johannine tradition, not to mention frogs! What would the hearers of the Apocalypse make of this unique phrase? The first hint is the adjective "unclean," which will come to be identified with the sexual immorality of the Great Whore (17.4) and with the fallen Babylon (18.2). Whatever else they might be, these spirits are "unclean" in the latter Johannine sense. The second hint comes in the form of the somewhat enigmatic words that these unclean spirits came out of the mouths of this triumvirate "as frogs." On one level, this designation continues the juxtaposition of the previous verse in that while God send a plague of frogs upon the Egyptians (8.15) here the enemies of God send the frogs. But at another level, it would be clear to the hearers that the phrase "as frogs" too conveys that these spirits are unclean for frogs were deemed to be unclean in the Torah (Lev 11.9–12, 41–47) contact from which necessitates ritual cleansing.[23] It is even possible that mention of the frogs would conjure up images of magicians and sorcerers.[24] This much is clear at this point: these unclean spirits are closely identified with the triumvirate of evil and as such would share their unclean nature.

The hearers do not have to wait long to learn a bit more about these unclean spirits for they soon are told, "For they are spirits of demons (demonic spirits) who do signs, which are sent out to the kings of the whole inhabited world to gather them together into the war of the great day of God the All Powerful One." The identification of these unclean spirits as demonic spirits may assist the hearers in assessing the nature of the worship of demons that the rest of humankind refused to turn from and repent of in Rev 9.20–21. Though not stated as such on that occasion, it now becomes clear that their worship was closely associated with the dragon, the beast, and the false prophet. Such an understanding makes sense in a community where the only person to be accused of being demon possessed is Jesus (John 7.20; 8.48, 49, 52; 10.20, 21). In Rev 16.14 these demonic spirits do signs, like the beast from the earth, the false prophet, did earlier to deceive the inhabitants of the earth (13.13–14) bearing a striking resemblance to the spirits that

---

23. S. S. Smalley, *The Revelation to John* (Downers Grove, IL: IVP, 2005) 409.
24. So P. Prigent, *L'Apocalypse de Saint Jean* (Geneva: Labor et Fides, 2000) 366.

must be tested to determine whether they be from the Spirit of Truth or the spirit of deception (1 John 4.1–6). A similar agenda seems to be at work here, as the signs performed by these demonic spirits appear to be linked to their ability to gather the kings together.[25] Ironically, the activity of the evil triumvirate takes place in tandem with the activity of God, for at the very time the sixth bowl of his wrath is being poured out, demonic spirits go forth from the triumvirate to gather together all the kings of the inhabited world for the war to end all wars, the war of the great day of God the All Powerful One! It appears that just as with other images previously, "the kings from the east" have morphed into "all the kings of the inhabited world," as the focus moves from a single compass point to that of the whole world.[26] With regard to the identity of this war, it apparently is well known to the hearers owing to the articular form of the word "the war" (τὸν πόλεμον).[27] Could it be other than the final cataclysmic war to end all wars, the Day of the Lord, the day on which John writes?

Revelation 18.2

In this passage the hearers encounter the following words:

> And he cried with a strong voice saying,
> "Fallen, fallen is Babylon the Great,
> and she has become a habitation of demons
> and a prison of every unclean spirit
> and a prison of every unclean and hateful bird."

The first words to come from this angel's mouth, "Fallen, fallen is Babylon the Great," could not help but take the hearers back to Rev 14.8 where this exact phrase occurs, when Babylon the Great is mentioned for the first time in the Apocalypse. It would also likely remind them of the fact that these same words were spoken about the Babylon the Great of old, as this same phrase is used to describe that previous event in Isa 21.9, perhaps underscoring the fact that this Babylon the Great will fall under the judgment of God as surely as did that Babylon the Great. It is not insignificant that this future event is described with a past tense verb (aorist) underscoring the certainty of the future judgment, a grammatical technique sometimes known as the prophetic perfect.[28] The fallen state of Babylon the Great re-

---

25. Murphy, *Fallen Is Babylon*, 343.
26. Smalley, *The Revelation to John*, 410.
27. D. E. Aune, *Revelation 6–16* (Nashville: Thomas Nelson, 1998) 896.
28. D. E. Aune, *Revelation 17–22* (Nashville: Thomas Nelson, 1998) 985. The Greek

sults in its transformation from a city of opulent splendor into a place of unclean creatures of every description. In point of fact, each of the three lines that describe Babylon the Great in her fallen state underscores the unclean nature of the place. The first line, "she has become a habitation of demons," would convey at least two ideas to the hearers. This first and only appearance of the noun "habitation" (κατοικητήριον) to this point in the Apocalypse would remind the hearers of the numerous occurrences of the verb "inhabit" or "dwell" (κατοικέω) which has often appeared in the book in association with those who oppose God and or his people (Rev 3.10; 6.10; 8.13; 11.10; 13.8, 12, 14; 17.2, 8) especially those who enter into the idolatrous worship of the beast (13.8, 12, 14; 17.2, 8). Thus, this very term would convey to the hearers the idea that Babylon the Great has become, as she was, a place of idolatrous worship. The fact that she is now called "a habitation of demons" pushes this association further as has been seen, in the Apocalypse demons have been intimately associated with the deception of false prophecy that leads to idolatrous worship (9.20; 16.13–14). Babylon the Great in her fallenness is what she was before, a place of demonic deception that leads to idolatrous worship. The second line, "a prison of every unclean spirit," reinforces the first. While it is possible to take the term "prison" (φυλακὴ) as "haunt" or a general word for "habitation" or "domain" its use elsewhere in the Johannine literature (John 3.24) and the Apocalypse in particular (Rev 2.10) suggests that it would likely be taken to mean "prison" here rather than understood more generally as reference to domain.[29] The hearers would likely see in this term the idea that Babylon the Great, who has imprisoned many by her domination, "sitting upon many waters," has now become a prison where every unclean spirit is captive. Neither would the discerning hearers be unaware that in the Johannine worldview unclean spirits are themselves closely associated with deception (1 John 4.1–6) and idolatrous worship (Rev 16.13–14). The third line, "and a prison of every unclean and hateful bird," not only continues the emphasis upon the unclean nature of Babylon the Great, but may also remind the hearers of Isaiah's words with regard to the fall of Edom and the unclean birds that take it over (Isa 34.11–15). At the same time, the fact that these birds are described as "hateful" (μεμισημένου) may suggest to the hearers that even these unclean birds may somehow be the instruments of God's activity, as to this point in the Apocalypse the term hate has been identified with the church in Ephesus who hates the works of the Nicolaitans (Rev 2.6)

---

of Rev 18.2 follows the Hebrew text of Isa 21.9, not the LXX.

29. As, e.g., R. H. Mounce, *The Book of Revelation* (Grand Rapids: Eerdmans, 1977) 323, and others argue.

as does the resurrected Jesus himself, and identified with the ten kings who hate the whore, devour her flesh and burn it in fire, a purpose which God has put into their hearts (17.16–17). Perhaps the hearers would wonder if these birds too have a similar role to play?

THE ROLE OF THE DEMONIC IN THE APOCALYPSE

What are the implications of this brief examination of the Apocalypse for the topic at hand? First, as with the other Johannine documents, there appears to be a tight connection between demons and deception. In the case of the Apocalypse such deception results in idolatrous worship and open rebellion against God and his people. Second, for the first time in the Johannine literature reference is made to "unclean spirits" underscoring their nature and the nature of their work. Such demonic unclean spirits are even signified by the image of frogs, a ceremonially unclean animal, coming from the mouth of the trinity of evil. Third, while 1 John makes clear the connection between the spirits that do not confess Jesus, i.e., the false prophets and the spirit of deception, the Apocalypse makes the origins of demonic spirits even more explicit by pointing out the extremely tight connection that exists between demons/unclean spirits and the triumvirate of evil! Fourth, significantly the idolatrous worship inspired by demons is, in the Apocalypse, something for which men and women should (be able to) repent—no exorcism appears to be necessary nor is its possibility even mentioned.

HEARING THE BLACK GOSPEL CHOIR OF SCRIPTURE

What then is the role of the demonic in Johannine thought and what is the contribution of such a view to the Scripture choir?

First, it is significant that the only person actually accused of having a demon in the whole of the Johannine literature is Jesus. While it is theoretically possible, by means of a reverse reading of these texts, to argue that it is actually the ones who make these accusations that have a demon, such a charge is never made in this family of writings, suggesting that such an approach may be flawed. Rather, the accusation that Jesus has a demon reveals the extent of the opposition of "the Jews" to Jesus and his message of salvation. Second, there is a clear association in all the Johannine documents examined between demons/spirits/unclean spirits and deception. Not only does this association figure into the charges made against Jesus, but they are also connected to the deception of the deceivers, antichrists, and false prophets in 1–2 John, as well as the deception which results in idolatrous worship and open rebellion to God in the Apocalypse. Thus, it would appear that one of the fundamental roles played by the demonic in the Johannine literature is its association with the work of deception (including lying) at various levels. Third, while it is clear that the Johannine literature takes seriously and has a place for the activity of the spirit world, both good and evil, the directives given to the believing community are to discern between the prophetic activity and words of the spirits and to offer faithful witness in the face of false prophecy and, in turn, the spirit of deception. Fourth, the Johannine literature consistently links "demonic" activity to its origins, either explicitly or implicitly; origins that include the Devil (in the Fourth Gospel), the spirit of deception (in 1 John), and the triumvirate of evil—the dragon, the beast, and the false prophet (in the Apocalypse). Such attributions make clear in no uncertain terms that such spirit-inspired prophetic deception is no benign activity but derives from very malevolent sources. Fifth, despite such sinister activity the appropriate response of those affected by such demonic influences is repentance. In point of fact, it appears that such deception is something that the deceived individuals should be able to recognize and to which they should be able to respond with repentance, both for their own deception and the work of their own hands resulting from such a deceived state. There is absolutely no notion of demon possession to the point that one is in need of exorcism. In fact, such an understanding does not even seem to appear on the Johannine radar screen.

What contribution does such a distinct voice make to the "Black Gospel Choir of Scripture"? It would seem that based on a reading of the Johannine literature on its own terms, not via the lens of the Synoptic Gospels, Acts, and Paul, an understanding of the role of the demonic in the Johannine literature has gifts to give both to the academy and the church. Heard alongside other canonical voices on this topic, the Johannine literature may help to enable a more nuanced understanding of the role of the demonic in Scripture, which to this point seems to have been dominated by a view of Jesus and his followers as exorcists, whose work is a concrete example of the in-breaking of the kingdom of God. While such an understanding is correct as far as it goes, its error seems to be the attempt to make all the other biblical voices conform to this particular emphasis without giving due regard to the diversity of the Scripture choir. One by-product of such a one-dimensional understanding is seen by the way in which the Johannine literature has been approached on this topic, with the assumption that John's presentation must be made to conform in some way to the other Scripture voices. When this is the starting point, paradigms and language that John has not employed, such as exorcism, are superimposed upon the Johannine texts in a way that ultimately obscures the Johannine teaching on the topic rather than explicating it.

Though any number of things might be cited, two contributions of the Johannine voice to the Scripture choir on this topic are here offered. First, in contrast to demonic activity described in the Synoptic Gospels and Acts, where demon possession is often viewed as a hostile takeover of an individual with little indication of the culpability of the demon possessed individual, in the Johannine literature deception of various kinds are attributed to demons, perhaps being their essential work. The fact that deception is rarely attributed to demons outside the Johannine literature expands significantly the scriptural view of the demonic. Second, the Johannine testimony on this topic also expands the understanding of the demonic that, while acknowledging the reality of demonic spirits and their origins, sees Jesus' person and message as powerful enough to liberate those deceived by such false prophets and their message—a liberation brought by repentance that includes repenting for the works of their own hands wrought by such deceptive teaching and prophesying. The implications of this study could also be explored by placing the distinctive Johannine voice alongside other NT voices, allowing hearers the opportunity to discern the new theological sounds generated by the combination of notes not normally heard together.

HEARING WHAT THE SPIRIT IS SAYING TO THE CHURCHES

The results of this study not only have implications for a better understanding of this topic within the world of Scripture but also have a variety of implications for Pentecostal ministry. One such example is offered here. When the Johannine voice on the role of the demonic is allowed to become part of those biblical texts from which a model of ministry is constructed with regard to the spirit world, it broadens one's horizon in dramatic ways. Specifically, this understanding offers some needed critique for those who see ministry exclusively through the somewhat narrow confines of "deliverance," which often assumes that the only biblical paradigm in matters demonic is the spiritual warfare model that tends to define all ministry in terms of the expansion of the kingdom of God in conflict with the kingdom of Satan. The fact that not all biblical voices fit within such a paradigm has not sufficiently been taken on board and integrated into a more holistic model of ministry. One of the implications of such ministry reflection might well lead to the discovery that not everyone needs "deliverance" as such, but are able to respond to Jesus and his message in faith offering repentance, despite their deception. When such a ministry model is allowed a place is made for the reclamation of the volitional in responding to the work of demonic spirits instead of conceiving all of life in the dualistic terms of God and the devil. Such a move would no doubt necessitate a reconsideration of sanctification in the life of the believer.

My hope is that this essay will make a small contribution to the theology and ministry practice of our tradition and in some way bring a degree of honor to the recipient of this *Festschrift*, my friend Benny Aker.

4

John's Doxology
The Trinitarian Passion for the Glory of God
BRUCE E. ROSDAHL

IT IS A PRIVILEGE to present this essay in honor of Ben Aker, whose love and respect for the Word of God left an enduring legacy among his students at AGTS. I never had the privilege to take one of his courses, but witnessed his influence as students conversed about this favorite professor who infused in them a passion for God's Word.

The Prologue of the Fourth Gospel opens with the wondrous declaration that God has manifested his glory to the world. The Word of God became flesh and dwelt among us and "we have seen his glory" (John 1.14).[1] Scholars point to a parallel of God's manifested glory in John and Exodus 33–34.[2] Moses asks God "to show me your glory" (כבד Exod 33.18) and God reveals himself in a remarkable way to his servant. In John's gospel, the revelation of the glory of God occurs in a most miraculous manner. The glory of the eternal Son, who was with God in the beginning and who is God, appeared in the wonder of the incarnation. His glory would be further on display in his life, ministry, and redeeming work on the cross. The latter receiving the most emphasis, as Köstenberger notes, "identification of the

---

1. All translations from the Greek or Hebrew texts are by the author unless otherwise noted.

2. See C. S. Keener, *Gospel of John: A Commentary*, 2 vols. (Peabody, MA: Hendrickson, 2003) 1:410.

theology of glory with the theology of the cross is at the very heart of John's Gospel ... Indeed, as mentioned, it is emphatically not only the second half of John's Gospel that is a 'Book of Glory'; rather, John's entire Gospel was written to show that God's glory was continually on display through Jesus' ministry, from its inception all the way to the cross and beyond."[3]

This theophany, however, was not only for the glory of the Second Person of the Trinity. The glory on display was the glory of the triune God. This trinitarian emphasis in John's theology is seen as each member of the Godhead works to the glory of God. It is true that the greatest emphasis is placed on God's glory revealed in the redeeming work of his Son. But, as Barrett notes, in the Fourth Gospel "his very Christocentricity is theocentric."[4] Consequently, John's doxology, his theology of glory, does have a christocentric emphasis, but it must be placed within his larger trinitarian theology. Köstenberger concurs, concluding that John's theology of glory is "both trinitarian in nature and serves as an all-encompassing paradigmatic component of the Johannine worldview."[5] Thompson describes the relationship of the christocentric and theocentric character of John's theology in terms of concentric circles, "in which the Christological circle lies within and shares its center with the larger theological circle."[6]

In order to see this trinitarian emphasis in John's doxology, this synopsis will highlight four themes within the gospel: the Father glorifies his name, the Father glorifies the Son, the Son glorifies the Father, and the Spirit glorifies the Son. In addition, no study of John's theology of glory would be complete without including an excursus on the glory of God in the believer.

GLORY IN JOHN'S GOSPEL

A prominent feature of the Fourth Gospel is the use of "glory" (δόξα). The NT use of the word does not follow classical etymology. In classical literature the word denotes honor, reputation, or a favorable human opinion. The NT does employ this meaning in certain contexts, even within John (12.43) but the primary use derives from the LXX, which finds its meaning in the manifestation of the glory of God. "In reality, the term always speaks of one thing. God's power is an expression of the 'divine nature,' and the honour

---

3. A. J. Köstenberger, *A Theology of John's Gospel and Letters* (Grand Rapids: Zondervan, 2009) 294.

4. C. K. Barrett, *Essays on John* (Philadelphia: Westminster, 1982) 32.

5. Ibid., 295.

6. M. M. Thompson, *The God of the Gospel of John* (Grand Rapids: Eerdmans, 2001) 239.

ascribed to God by man is finally no other than an affirmation of this nature. The δόξα θεοῦ is the 'divine glory' which reveals the nature of God in creation and in His acts, which fill both heaven and earth."[7]

The LXX takes on the semantic value from the OT meaning of "Glory of YHWH" (כבוד יהוה). God's glory could be displayed through various means, whether it was the vision of Isaiah, the shaking of Sinai, or God's handiwork in creation. In the Targums, the Rabbis labeled God's manifestation as the shekinah glory of God, drawing upon the meaning of the verb בשׁכן, which means "to dwell."[8] In John's gospel, God's shekinah glory is manifested in the incarnation of his Son (1.14). The Evangelist testifies, "We have seen his glory, glory as of the only Son from the Father" (1.14).

In some cases, the Fourth Gospel employs a nuanced meaning of the verb δοξάζω, which denotes the death, resurrection, and ascension of Christ. In John 7.38–39, Jesus prophesied of the coming of the Spirit as "living water," but the Spirit would not come until Jesus was glorified. On the eve of his crucifixion, he repeatedly declared that now the hour had come for the Son to be glorified. In Johannine contexts, these terms have specific theological nuance. Ensor explains, "The 'hour' of Jesus' departure to the Father, which is the 'now' of his 'glorification,' thus includes *both* his death *and* subsequent exaltation to the Father's presence to enjoy the glory he had with the Father before the world was made (17:5). Both aspects of this climatic 'glorification' are encapsulated in the word ὑψόω, which alludes both to the 'lifting up' of Jesus on the cross and his being exalted thereafter (implied in 8:28; 12:32)."[9]

The redeeming work of the cross becomes the apex when the Son is glorified and the Father is glorified through him (7.39; 12.16, 23, 28; 13.31–32; 17.1). In essence, the glory of God is on grand display in the saving work of his Son. The Fourth Gospel places the death of Christ as the key event where "one sees the ultimate revelation of the Son of Man who is the visible glory of YHWH."[10] As will be seen, however, it is not only the Son who glorifies the Father, but each member of the Trinity seeks to bring glory to God, whereby God as Redeemer is proclaimed to the world.

---

7. G. Kittel, "δόξα in the LXX and Hellenistic Apocrypha," *TDNT* 2.244.

8. E.g., Exod 24.16 where the glory of God dwells on Mount Sinai. See also R. E. Brown, *Gospel According to John I–XII* (Garden City, NY: Doubleday, 1966) 32–34.

9. P. Ensor, "The Glorification of the Son of Man: An Analysis of John 13:31–32," *TynBul* 58 (2007) 233–34. For John's employment of "glorify" and "lifted up" from Isa 52.13, see R. Bauckham, *God Crucified: Monotheism and Christology in the New Testament* (Grand Rapids: Eerdmans, 1998) 63–68.

10. C. A. Gieschen, "The Death of Jesus in the Gospel of John: Atonement for Sin?" *CovTQ* 72 (2008) 246.

John's Doxology

THE FATHER GLORIFIES HIS NAME

In one sense, the panorama of John's theology of glory is subsumed under this category. From the incarnation in the opening Prologue to the climax of the crucifixion, resurrection, and ascension, God's glory is manifested to the world. On the other hand, John 12 contains the one dialogue where the Father specifically declares his purpose to glorify his name. Some Greeks approached Andrew with a desire to speak to Jesus and Phillip relayed the message to the Master. Jesus responds to the news by proclaiming that his hour has come. The "hour" is a Johannine idiom pointing to the crucifixion of Jesus.[11] It identifies his crucifixion, resurrection, and ascension as the climax of the unfolding redemptive story. Calvary becomes the crowning moment when God is glorified.

For John, Jesus not only knows the hour, but also controls the hour. His crucifixion was not the happenstance of a fickle crowd, the dominance of a Roman procurator, nor the scheming of religious leaders; the crucifixion of Christ was the *telos* of his incarnation (12.27). It was the declared purpose for which God sent his Son into the world (3.16). This sovereign control is apparent in a feature only John includes in the betrayal narrative. John 18 shows Jesus in control even at the moment when it seems he would be broadsided by one of his own. When Judas leads the Roman cohort to the garden of Gethsemane, it is Jesus, "knowing all that would happen to him," who approaches his arresters. It is Jesus who asks, "Whom do you seek?" Only John records that when Jesus identifies himself as "I am he," the cohort falls to the ground.[12] The narrative is a powerful reminder that Christ was not the victim of circumstances gone awry. He was not arrested until he allowed himself to be. The narrative exemplifies his earlier pronouncement that no one takes his life, "I lay it down of my accord" (10.18).

The desire of the Greeks to meet with Jesus also resulted in his petition to the Father that he would "glorify his name." Such a petition for God to glorify his name is common in prayers of the day, as seen in the Kaddish and echoed in the Lord's Prayer. In the context of John's gospel, however, Keener observes, "this prayer for 'glory' is a prayer for the hastening of the cross (7:39; 12:23-24)."[13] The Father's response from heaven was "I have

---

11. E.g., John's use of "hour" (ἡ ὥρα) as denoting the time of the crucifixion (e.g., John 2.4; 4.21; 8.20; 12.23, 27; 13.1; 16.32; 17.1). See also D. M. Smith, "The Theology of the Gospel of John," in *New Testament Theology*, edited by J. D. G. Dunn (Cambridge: Cambridge University Press, 1995) 119–20.

12. For John's use of "I am" (ἐγώ εἰμι) see John 4.26; 6.35; 8.12, 58; 9.5; 10.11; 11.25; 14.6; 15.1; 18.5.

13. Keener, *Gospel of John*, 2:876.

glorified it and will glorify it again." The use of the aorist and future tenses is intriguing. The declaration that God will glorify his name (future) certainly is a reference to the coming crucifixion and a direct answer to Jesus' prayer. The Father not only states he will glorify his name, but also that he has glorified it (aorist). The declaration is a reminder that while the crucifixion is an apex for the glorification of God in the Fourth Gospel, it is not the only way God glorifies his name. Borchert's sense that this refers to Jesus' "life and work as a whole on earth up to the cross" seems accurate.[14] John records that God's glory is manifested in the incarnation (1.14) in the miracles that Jesus performed (2.11) and the work God sent him to do (17.4). Thus, one aspect of John's doxology is that God will glorify his name.

THE FATHER GLORIFIES THE SON

A second expression of John's theology of glory is the Father's desire to glorify the Son. Four accounts in the gospel illustrate that God is glorified as the Father seeks to glorify the Son. In John 8, Jesus is teaching in the temple and the crowd challenges his messianic claims. They question the legitimacy of his birth, the validity of his teaching, and accuse him of being possessed by a demon. When Jesus asserts that he is both greater than and before Abraham, his interlocutors had enough and desired to stone him. Jesus responds that he is not seeking his own glory, which serves as a rebuke of the religious leaders. In contrast, he lives in submission to the Father and can claim twice that "it is my Father who glorifies me" (8.50, 54).

The same claim occurs in the narrative of the raising of Lazarus (11.1–44). Mary and Martha send word that their brother is sick and Jesus declares a divine purpose in the request. God will be glorified through the resurrecting of Lazarus from the dead. The glory given to God, however, is not for the Father alone, it is also to glorify the Son. Jesus interprets the purpose, "It is for the glory of God, so that the Son of God may be glorified through it" (11.4). Here, the Fourth Gospel makes a clear declaration that God the Father sought to glorify the Son. As Lazarus miraculously walked out of the tomb, the world saw the glory of the Son on display. In the same way, the world would see the glory of God hanging on the cross on Calvary and God would be glorified through him.

John 13 also asserts the same symbiotic relationship of the glory of God and the glory the Son. On the eve of his crucifixion, Jesus declares that the time of his glorification was at hand and God would be glorified in him. The Father, however, is not a passive observer. The Father will "glorify

---

14. G. L. Borchert, *John* (Nashville: Broadman and Holman, 1996) 57.

[Jesus] in himself, and will glorify him at once" (13.32).[15] The prevalence of the symbiotic relationship in John prompts Keener to conclude that God's glory "is inseparable from the glory of Son."[16] As noted earlier, much of the emphasis on the glory of God in John centers on the redemptive work of Christ. The point here is that part of the drama also includes the Father actively seeking to glorify the Son.

The final narrative illustrating that the Father glorifies the Son occurs in Jesus' high priestly prayer in John 17. The prayer commences with Jesus asking the Father to "glorify the Son in order that the Son may glorify you" (17.1). The request relates to his impending death as Jesus affirms that "the hour" has come. The theme of glory continues throughout Jesus' prayer. In v. 5, he petitions the Father to "glorify me now in your presence with the glory I had with you before the world existed." The request is a clear declaration of the glory of the preincarnate Son and harkens back to the opening of the gospel (1.1). Note, as well, that it is the Father who will glorify the Son. Jesus acknowledges two more times that he received his glory from the Father (17.22, 24). This fact becomes crucial in the context of this intercessory prayer, as Jesus desires to take the glory he received from the Father and give it to his followers (17.22).[17]

THE SON GLORIFIES THE FATHER

A third expression of John's theology of glory is that the Son seeks to glorify the Father. Jesus is emphatic, "I do not seek my own glory" (8.50). The passion of the Son is to glorify the Father in his life and death. The Son's submission to the Father is prominent in the Fourth Gospel. Keener observes this theme and its function, "Johannine Christology is among the most exalted in the NT, but its portrayal of Christ's subordination to the Father is equally sharp. Taken together, the emphasis of these various strands suggests their polemical function: one could not deny Jesus' Lordship while truly following God the Father, as the synagogue leadership claimed to do."[18] Thus, Jesus subordination stands in contrast to the self-seeking religious leaders who rejected Jesus as Messiah. Jesus confronts their rebellion and arrogance by

---

15. The textual variant in v. 32 that includes a possible homoioteleuton, "If God is glorified in him," does not change the meaning of the following clause that the Father will glorify the Son.

16. Keener, *Gospel of John*, 2:921.

17. For this theme in John's theology, see "Believers and the Glory of God" later in this work.

18. Keener, *Gospel of John*, 1:320.

demonstrating true authority and honor (i.e., glory) come from being in submission to God. Jesus did not speak from his own authority or seek his own honor; he sought the glory of the One who sent him (7.18). The Fourth Gospel describes the work of the Spirit in the same fashion, as he is sent by the Father and the Son and will speak only what he has heard (16.13).

Jesus also seeks to glorify the Father by answering the prayers of his disciples. In his farewell address, Jesus tells his disciples that whatever they ask in his name, he will do. He follows this promise with a qualifying purpose, "in order that the Father will be glorified in the Son" (14.13). The future answered prayers of the disciples will bring glory to God. Even as he speaks of his pending ascension, his return to the former glory does not change this purpose to glorify the Father in what he does.

The most prevalent expression of the Son's desire to glorify the Father centers on his work of redemption. Jesus told his disciples, "Now is the Son of Man glorified and God is glorified in him" (13.1). Judas had just exited to enact his plan of betrayal and it prompted the announcement that the time of his glorification was at hand. This "glorification" referenced his impending death on the cross where he would glorify God. Later that evening, the theme reoccurs in Jesus' prayer. The time had come for the Father to glorify the Son so that the Son could glorify the Father (17.1). With his death so near, Jesus could now say, "I have glorified you on the earth, having completed the work you gave me to do" (17.4). The work the Son completed speaks to the purpose of the incarnation. The mission of the Son was his sacrificial death on behalf of the world. This mission was in clear focus throughout his life and ministry. Jesus told his disciples that his "food" was to accomplish the will of the One who sent him (4.34) and that this mission testified he was sent by the Father (5.36). Thus, the mission of the Son includes glorifying God through his redeeming work.

THE SPIRIT GLORIFIES THE SON

The final expression of John's theology of glory is that the Spirit glorifies the Son. The work of the Holy Spirit features prominently in Jesus' farewell address (14–16) as his presence assures the disciples they will not be orphaned. The Father will send the promised *Paraclete* at the request of the Son. "Jesus is thus a Paraclete," explains Burge, "who is now sending a second Paraclete. This means that the ongoing work of the Spirit will be a continuation of the work of Jesus during the disciples' lifetime."[19] He bears witness to Christ and places the world on trial; he convicts the world of sin, righteousness, and

---

19. G. M. Burge, *John* (Grand Rapids: Zondervan, 2000) 396.

judgment. He is the Spirit of Truth who will guide, teach, and remind the disciples what they heard Jesus say. Finally, Jesus concludes that the Spirit "will glorify me" (John 16.14).[20]

Throughout Johannine theology is a christocentric emphasis that includes its pneumatology. One key work of the Spirit is to glorify the Son. Recognizing the christocentric emphasis, however, is a partial but inadequate description of Johannine pneumatology. Neither can the statement be used to suggest any sense of inferiority to the work of the Spirit. The Spirit glorifying the Son is only part of a larger drama in John. From the Prologue to finale, the manifestation of God's glory is on display, particularly as it is manifested in God's redeeming work of the Son. The Fourth Gospel shows each member of the Godhead working to glorify God. Consequently, the Father seeks to glorify the Son, the Son seeks to glorify the Father, and the Spirit seeks to glorify the Son. It is within the broader context of Johannine theology that the glorifying work of the Spirit must be understood.

In the same way the gospel speaks of the Father glorifying the Son and the Son glorifying the Father, Jesus now declares the ministry of the Spirit is to exalt his ministry. The Spirit is not sent to proclaim a new message or establish a new ministry; his work is inextricably tied to the work that preceded him. As the Father sent the Son as Savior of the world, now the Father and Son send the Spirit to continue the proclamation of the good news. Even at the end of the gospel, the Son breathes upon the disciples that they might receive the Spirit and proclaim the message of forgiveness in his name (20.19–23).

As noted, it would be a mistake to interpret the Spirit's work of glorifying the Son as minimizing the Spirit's significance. Even the Father is described as glorifying the Son, which implies no inequality. On the contrary, the Son-exalting work of the Spirit reflects John's trinitarian theology.[21] "John's theology is uncompromisingly theocentric," writes Borchert, "because Jesus has received his mission from the Father, and it is the Spirit's task to communicate what comes from Jesus to the disciples."[22] Consequently, the Father, Son, and Spirit together seek to bring glory to God. The Spirit glorifying the Son contributes towards this broader emphasis in Johannine theology that the triune God be glorified.

---

20. ἐκεῖνος ἐμὲ δοξάσει.

21. Gruenler provides a thematic analysis of the social relationship of the Trinity in Johannine theology, which affirms that any subordination language in the gospel does not imply any ontological subordination. See R. G. Gruenler, *The Trinity in the Gospel of John: A Thematic Commentary on the Fourth Gospel* (Grand Rapids: Baker, 1986).

22. Borchert, *John*, 171.

But These are Written . . .

BELIEVERS AND THE GLORY OF GOD

This study focused on how the Father, Son, and Spirit work to glorify God's name in the Fourth Gospel. John's theology of glory includes another expression that must not be overlooked. Believers in some measure can share in and bring glory to God. In the farewell address, Jesus told his disciples, "By this my Father is glorified, that you bear much fruit, and so prove to be my disciples" (15.8). He describes his relationship with his followers as vine and branches and the Father as the vinedresser. The metaphor accentuates believers' dependence upon the Father and Son for vitality and fruitfulness. If the branches are to bear fruit, they must abide in the vine. The primary expression of this fruit is the disciples' love for one another. Thus, the command follows for the disciples to demonstrate they are genuine followers by emulating the love of Christ, a theme common to Johannine writings.

Jesus repeats the theme of love expressed in unity among believers as he intercedes for believers in John 17. After he prays that the Father be glorified in his imminent death (vv. 1–5) Jesus turns to pray for his present disciples (vv. 6–19). Jesus proclaims that he is "glorified in them" (v. 10) and prays "that they may be one" (v. 11). The frequency of the unity theme in the Fourth Gospel demonstrates John's concern that his readers comprehend the supreme value the Messiah placed on unity (13.34–35; 15.12, 17; 17.11, 22). The necessity of unity went beyond mere pragmatics of getting along; love and unity served a missional function to the world. A body of believers characterized by love proclaimed to the world that they were the people of God. It was a sanctifying mark as belonging to Christ, but also a testimonial to a fractured world of the love of God. Unity becomes paramount for the followers of Christ to glorify God to the world. Keener captures the application power of how unity is a miracle witness to the world.

> The Fourth Gospel equipped John's audience with an apologetic approach from Scripture but most of all summoned them to invite the open-minded to "come and see" (1:39, 46; 4:29, 39–42) which in their day must have included the questioning to experience the presence of Jesus living among his followers by the Spirit. This presence of Jesus would be experienced through prophetic proclamation (16:7–11) but also through the mutual love of the disciples, who thus revealed Jesus' character (13:34–35; 15:8–12). The way believers treat one another is an essential component of proclaiming Jesus to the world. Indeed, if one compares this prayer with Jesus' earlier prayer in 11:42, one finds that the unity of believers provides the same kind of

witness concerning Jesus' origin as Jesus' raising of Lazarus (ὅτι σύ με ἀπέστειλας 11:42, 17:23).[23]

Jesus not only prayed for his present disciples but also for those who would come to believe through their witness (vv. 20–26). The goal of his prayer remained the same, nonetheless: "that they may be one" (v. 21) even "perfectly one" (v. 23). Jesus was glorified in his present disciples through their fruitfulness (15.8) love for another (13.35) and unity (17.11). In the same way, Jesus will give glory to these future disciples "that they may be one" (v. 22). The essence of Jesus' intercession was the same for his present and future followers. He prayed for love and unity so that the world would come to believe in the Son and have eternal life (v. 21). For the Evangelist's audience, such a message would speak to the heart of their world. If they desired to glorify God by following the footsteps of the Master, they must love one another.

The final statement of the way believers can glorify God comes as Jesus predicts the manner of Peter's death (21.18–19). In focus here is not whether the text predicts crucifixion as the manner of his death. What is clear is that John's parenthetical explanation identifies Peter's martyrdom as a means to bring glory to God, "(This he said to show by what kind of death he was to glorify God)" (v. 19). Jesus warned his disciples that if unbelievers persecuted him, they would also persecute his followers (15.20). Peter would be one of many disciples throughout the church's history who would be called upon to glorify God by dying for their faith.

CONCLUSION

Saint Augustine spent nearly thirty years composing his *De Trinitate* (400–428 C.E.). One proposition he had to counter argued that the Father is greater than the Son. Proponents appealed to the Fourth Gospel's assertion that the Father glorifies the Son, which they contended made him greater than the Son. Augustine reminds his opponents that the gospel also states that the Spirit glorifies the Son. He turned their argument on them in defense of the Trinity, "If he who glorifies is greater than the one he glorifies, let them at least grant that those who glorify each other are equal."[24]

Augustine's instincts were correct. John's doxology is a trinitarian theology of glory. Each member of the Godhead works to glory of God. This

---

23. Keener, *Gospel of John*, 2:1061.

24. Saint Augustine, *The Trinity* in *The Works of Augustine*, trans. E. Hill, ed. J. E. Rotelle (New York: New York City Press, 1991) 100–1.

theology of glory finds particular expression in the theology of the cross. John points the reader not to Mount Sinai, but to a hill called Golgotha to see the manifestation of the shekinah glory. Thus, the Son plays a central role via his incarnation, death, and resurrection. Such an emphasis fits the evangelistic thrust of the gospel as it calls on the world to believe in the Son and have eternal life. Nonetheless, this christocentric message must be placed in the midst of John's trinitarian theology of glory. Here the Father, Son, and Spirit all work to glorify God as Redeemer. The onus now falls upon his followers to continue this doxology through the proclamation of the gospel, transformed lives, and a community characterized by love. Jesus prayed to the Father that it would be so, and the Father and Son sent the Spirit to make it a reality. *Soli Deo gloria!*

5

The Virgin Birth in the Fourth Gospel?
A Brief Note on the Triple-Negation in John 1.13
By Jordan Daniel May

IT IS A GREAT privilege contributing to this volume, which honors such a prominent figure in the Assemblies of God as Ben Aker. I remember with delight reading his scholarship on Johannine Literature, noting both his reasoned approach in examining Scripture and the passionate presentation of his arguments. Thank you, Dr. Aker, for your devotion to the academy and commitment to Pentecostal scholarship.

A BRIEF NOTE ON THE TRIPLE-NEGATION IN JOHN 1.13

The earliest patristic witnesses from the second century support the recording of a singular verb in John 1.13 ("who was born" ὅς . . . ἐγεννήθη as opposed to the current plural, "who were born" οἳ . . . ἐγεννήθησαν[1]) therefore alluding to the virgin birth of Christ.[2] Yet all available Greek manuscripts

---

1. The translation is my own, based upon the Greek text of NA[27].

2. With the exception of Tatian's *Diatessaron*, the earliest patristic witnesses from the second century support strongly the singular verb in John 1.13 (e.g., *Ep. Apos.* 3.2; Ignatius, *Smyrn.* 1.1; Irenaeus, *Haer.* 3.16.2, 3.19.2; Tertullian, *Carn. Chr.* 19; and possibly Justin Martyr, *1 Apol.* 21.1; 23.2; 32.9; *Dial.* 54.2; 63.2). Yet there is also some evidence for Tatian's support of the singular as well (i.e. *adv. Graece.* 5.2). The only English

record the present plural.³ Scholars will surely continue to debate the textual and patristic issues,⁴ but my question is simply whether we can see any fingerprints from an original singular verb within the present text itself. Thus in the course of this note I will examine John 1.13, specifically the emphasis within the triple-negation as relating to either the spiritual birth of believers or to the virgin birth of Christ.

To begin, the stress within the triple-negation in v. 13 rules out a natural birth. Perhaps the author's purpose here is to counter those within Israel who viewed their covenant identity as dependent upon their national or ethnic status (cf. John 8.37–41).⁵ This argument seems conceivable at first glance, but would the author have to make an emphatic point that believers are not spiritually born from natural means? It would be one thing to express a simple contrast between physical and spiritual birth (e.g., John 3.6; cf. 1 Pet 1.23) but why do so ardently by highlighting three negatives? The triple-negation emphasizes the point that natural means had nothing to do with this supernatural birth, yet why would the author feel it necessary to use these specific idioms? The author's use of "not of bloods, nor of the will of the flesh, nor the will of man" (οὐκ ἐξ αἱμάτων οὐδὲ ἐκ θελήματος σαρκὸς οὐδὲ ἐκ θελήματος ἀνδρὸς) has an obvious polemical overtone to it. Many commentators have noted the unusualness of the plural "bloods" (αἱμάτων) in this verse.⁶ Why does the author use the plural αἱμάτων as opposed to the normal use of the singular "blood" (αἷμα)?

---

translation to accept the singular is the Jerusalem Bible (1966). The New Jerusalem Bible (1985) however, accepts the plural.

3. With few exceptions, all other mss outside of the Greek corpus include the plural, i.e., the Latin, Syriac, Coptic, Armenian, and Ethiopic versions. But one fourth-century Latin text (it^b) the Syriac Curetonian (Syr^c) the Syriac Sinaiticus (Syr^s) and six manuscripts of the Syriac Peshitta (Syr^p) include the singular verb. Although the verb in the Syriac is singular, the relative pronoun remains plural. This is a common occurrence in Syriac translations, however. So J. M. Lagrange, *Évangile selon Saint Jean* (Paris: Gabalda, 1948) 714.

4. See, e.g., J. Galot, *Etre né de Dieu: Jean 1,13* (Rome: Biblical Institute, 1969) 41–49; T. F. Torrance, "The Doctrine of the Virgin Birth," *Scottish Bulletin of Evangelical Theology* 12.1 (Spring 1994) 8–25; M. Vellanickal, *The Divine Sonship of Christians in the Johannine Writings* (Rome: Biblical Institute, 1972) 114–15 (thanks to the staff of *Harvard Theological Review* for bringing this source to my attention); A. Von Harnack, *Studien zur Geschichte des Neuen Testaments und der Alten Kirche* (Berlin: de Gruyter, 1931) 115–27.

5. So J. W. Pryor, "Of the Virgin Birth or the Birth of Christians? The Text of John 1:13 Once More," *NT* 28 (1985) 302.

6. E.g., C. S. Keener, *The Gospel of John* (Peabody, MA: Hendrickson, 2003) 1:404; F. J. Moloney, *The Gospel of John* (Collegeville, MN: Liturgical, 1998) 45; J. R. Michaels, *The Gospel of John* (Grand Rapids: Eerdmans, 2010) 72.

The Virgin Birth in the Fourth Gospel?

Some maintain the possibility that the plural here denotes the "commingling of male and female strains in ordinary generation."[7] The author, with his use of the plural, may be implying that only one parent was involved in procreation, thus referencing the virginal conception of Christ (cf. Justin Martyr, *1 Apol.* 32.9; *Dial.* 54.2; 63.2).[8] Likewise, the author's use of "nor of the will of the flesh" (οὐδὲ ἐκ θελήματος σαρκὸς) counters any idea of sexual desire in procreation (cf. *1 Apol.* 21.1) and the use of "nor of the will of man" (οὐδὲ ἐκ θελήματος ἀνδρὸς) counters any thought of male, or possibly a husband's, initiative in procreation (cf. *1 Apol.* 23.2).[9] Would the author need to emphasize that believers are not born spiritually from either sexual desire or the will of a male or husband? In contrast, if the author applied this polemical argument to the virgin birth of Christ, especially in light of possible charges of illegitimacy (John 8.41; cf. Mark 6.3) the triple-negation would make more sense, seeing that it rules out a natural birth.[10]

Furthermore, if this passage refers to the spiritual birth of believers, why would the author negate the natural birth with his use of the triple-negation when all believers are first born naturally (cf. John 3.6)? In other words, the spiritual birth of believers does not negate the natural birth as the triple-negation maintains forcefully, but instead presupposes it.[11] In his conversation with Nicodemus, Jesus does not exclude the natural birth, but distinguishes between the birth of the flesh and the birth of the Spirit (John 3.1–5). Jesus does not deny the natural birth of Nicodemus, but rather expounds on the need for his second or spiritual birth from above. While John 1.13 distinguishes between two births, it does not distinguish between two births *for believers*. Rather, it distinguishes between two births for two separate categories of humanity—one category born naturally and the other *super*naturally. In fact, this passage would effectively deny the believers' natural birth in the process of affirming their spiritual birth. This passage would thus distinguish sharply between two human classes: 1) those born naturally, and 2) those born *solely* of God. But the greater theology of the Fourth Gospel and the

---

7. So E. F. Harrison, *A Short Life of Christ* (Grand Rapids: Eerdmans, 1968) 44. To be fair, however, Harrison eventually concludes to the contrary. See also Moloney, *Gospel of John*, 45.

8. For an opposing argument, see H. J. Cadbury, "The Ancient Physiological Notions Underlying John I:13 and Heb XI:11," *The Expositor* 9 (1924) 430–39.

9. So G. R. Beasley-Murray, *John* (Nashville: Thomas Nelson, 1999) 13; Michaels, *Gospel of John*, 72.

10. For a detailed analysis of the charge of Christ's illegitimacy, see R. B. Brown, *The Birth of the Messiah: A Commentary on the Infancy Narratives in Matthew and Luke* (Garden City, NY: Image, 1979) 534–42.

11. So Vellanickal, *Divine Sonship*, 117.

Johannine corpus teaches that the two categories *within* humanity are 1) those born naturally, and 2) those born naturally and then reborn spiritually by faith in the name of Christ (cf. John 1.12; 3.1–5; 3.16–18; 1 John 5.1; 5.13 *passim*). As a result, if this passage refers to the spiritual birth of believers, then it is logical to conclude that believers are a special class or race of humanity which are only born spiritually, but not naturally (cf. *Odes Sol.* 41.8–10).[12] On the contrary, if John 1.13 refers to the virgin birth of Christ, then the forceful triple-negation would make more sense, seeing that Jesus was born only once (that is, Jesus *was not* born naturally, *but was* born *super*naturally).[13]

Then again, one could make the argument that John 1.13 only expounds further the theological truth posed already in v. 12: "But to as many who did receive him to them he gave authority to become sons of God—to those believing in his name" (ὅσοι δὲ ἔλαβον αὐτόν, ἔδωκεν αὐτοῖς ἐξουσίαν τέκνα θεοῦ γενέσθαι, τοῖς πιστεύουσιν εἰς τὸ ὄνομα αὐτοῦ). The passage would not distinguish between two classes of humanity, but would only describe the spiritual birth of those who were given the authority to become children of God. Although this interpretation appears logical at first glance,[14] a closer reading of the text indicates otherwise. The idea that v. 13 expounds on v. 12 makes little sense in that it raises the question: how

---

12. This is the reason Tertullian offers for the Valentinians altering the text: "What, then, is the meaning of this passage, 'Born not of blood, nor of the will of the flesh, nor of the will of man, but of God?' I shall make more use of this passage after I have confuted [the Valentinians] who have tampered with it. They maintain that it was written thus (in the plural) 'Who were born, not of blood, nor of the will of the flesh, nor of the will of man, but of God,' as if designating those who were before mentioned as 'believing in his name,' in order to point out the existence of that mysterious seed of the elect and spiritual which they appropriate to themselves. But how can this be, when all who believe in the name of the Lord are, by reason of the common principle of the human race, born of blood, and of the will of the flesh, and of man, as indeed is Valentinus himself? The expression is in the singular number, as referring to the Lord, 'He was born of God'" (*Carn. Chr.*, 19, in *ANF* 3:537).

13. Support for the singular verb in John 1.13 is also found in the specific language used for supernatural birth within the Fourth Gospel and the Johannine corpus. The author speaks of the τέκνα θεοῦ (John 1.12; 11.52; 1 John 3.1–2, 10; 5.2) and γεννηθῆναι ἐκ τοῦ θεοῦ (1 John 2.29; 3.9; 4.7; 5.1–4, 18) frequently within his writings. And when speaking of believers, the author always speaks of the τέκνα θεοῦ in the plural and γεννηθῆναι ἐκ τοῦ θεοῦ in the singular, even when both expressions follow each other closely (e.g., 1 John 5.1–2). Thus if John 1.13 expounds v. 12 and refers to the spiritual birth of believers, it would be the only exception to the Johannine usage of supernatural birth language. So Vellanickal, *Divine Sonship*, 121.

14. This is the majority reading of John 1.12–13. See, e.g., R. E. Brown, *The Gospel According to John I–XXII* (Garden City, NY: Doubleday, 1966) 12; R. K. Bultmann, *The Gospel of John* (Louisville, KY: WJKP, 1971) 59–60; E. Haenchen, *John 1: A Commentary on the Gospel of John* (Philadelphia: Augsburg Fortress, 1984) 118; R. Schnackenburg, *The Gospel According to S. John* (New York: Crossroad, 1972) 1:263.

can those who are *already* born of God, as v. 13 maintains, receive the authority to become children of God. Renowned Johannine scholar Raymond Brown states that to ask such a question "is to impose too exact a logic on the sequence" of the passage.[15] Yet the grammar of v. 12 indicates otherwise. The use of the aorist infinitive "to become" (γενέσθαι) in v. 12 implies that those who have received this authority must maintain their identity as God's children through continual faith and commitment.[16] Similarly, the present participle "believe" (πιστεύουσιν) in v. 12 points to the continual life of faith for those who believe in "his name" (ὄνομα αὐτοῦ). Thus v. 12 presents the idea of the "children of God" (τέκνα θεοῦ) as those who have received the authority to become such by a continual life of faith (cf. John 20.31). In contrast, v. 13, with its use of the aorist "were born" (ἐγεννήθησαν) presents an event that took place at a definite moment in time. The sharp difference here between a group who has the authority to become the "children of God" (τέκνα θεοῦ) and a group who has been "born of God" (ἐκ θεοῦ ἐγεννήθησαν) further supports the notion that v. 13 originally referred to the virgin birth of Christ. If this reading of the passage is accepted, it affirms that Christ has given those who believe in his name the authority to become children of God, just as he himself was born of God.[17]

CONCLUSION

In this note, I argued that the stress within the triple-negation in John 1.13 is rather unusual, at least in regard to the spiritual birth of believers. The reality that the author chose to employ three negatives, if applied to the spiritual birth of believers, seems unnecessary. In fact, the emphasis that believers are not spiritually born through natural means appears excessive. Yet the triple-negation, with its strong polemical overtone, would be more effective if applied to Christ's virgin birth, specifically in view of possible charges of

---

15. Brown, *John*, 12.
16. Moloney, *The Gospel of John*, 44.
17. The καὶ in the beginning of v. 14 may also demand that the singular verb is accepted. In the Prologue of the Fourth Gospel (John 1.1–18) the author uses the conjunction καὶ to combine related thoughts sixteen times. And the author has not introduced new thoughts with the use of the conjunction καὶ in the Prologue. Thus, the most natural reading of this text would connect vv. 13 and 14, thus understanding v. 14 as a continuation of v. 13 (i.e., ". . . was born of God, and the Word became flesh . . ."). Vellanickal makes this point. He claims, "the use of καὶ in the beginning of the phrase in Jn always recalls an idea that preceded" (*Divine Sonship*, 118). Though this is true most of the time, and is true in the Prologue (if v. 14 is accepted as connecting with v. 13) it is not always true in the Fourth Gospel (i.e., John 2.1, 13; 7.1).

But These are Written . . .

illegitimacy. The author's use of "not of bloods, nor of the will of the flesh, nor the will of man" would essentially counter any challenge leveled against the virgin birth of Christ.

6

Master(s) of the Sea?
Ephesian Fishermen, John 6.16–21, and John 21
WARREN CARTER

IN AN IMPORTANT STUDY, G. H. R. Horsley has drawn attention to a mid-first-century inscription from Ephesus (*I.Eph* 1a.20)[1] in which a fishing association in first century C.E. Ephesus dedicates a toll-collection and fish-market building at the harbor.[2] I propose to put this inscriptional text into conversation with two passages in John's gospel, namely Jesus walking on the sea (6.16–21) and Jesus' resurrection appearance to the fishing disciples at the Sea of Tiberias (21.1–23). My focus concerns the three texts' assertions of control over the sea and the battle for thalassic sovereignty created by this intertextuality. My argument is that in asserting God's thalassic control, the scenes in John's gospel mimic yet contest assertions of imperial control. John's scenes participate in the gospel's "rhetoric of distance" by calling disciples to distance themselves from imperial socioeconomic involvements such as those in which fishing and trade associations are enmeshed.[3]

---

1. H. Wankel, *Die Inschriften von Ephesos*, vol. 1a—8.2 (Bonn: Habelt, 1970–84).

2. G. H. R. Horsley, "A Fishing Cartel in First-Century Ephesos," in *New Documents Illustrating Early Christianity: Linguistic Essays with Cumulative Indexes to Vols. 1–5* (North Ryde: Macquarie University, 1989) 5:95–114.

3. Once at a Central States SBL meeting, Benny Aker insightfully and collegially participated in a panel reviewing my book *Matthew and Empire*. I appreciated his careful and respectful engagement. This article is offered with appreciation and best wishes.

But These are Written . . .

My argument develops the thesis of my recent study, *John and Empire*, in which I argue that John constructs a rhetoric of distance to persuade followers of Jesus to retreat from what the gospel author regards as compromised involvement with structures of Rome's empire.[4] I locate this engagement with John's gospel in Ephesus. I am not thereby claiming that John was written in Ephesus or written specifically for Jesus-believers in the city. Rather I am interested in imagining something of the intertextuality that occurs when the gospel was read or heard there as part of the larger socio-economic and cultural networks—including fishcatchers and sellers—that comprised this urban center in the Roman province of Asia.

The argument proceeds in three steps. Section one locates the fishing inscription in the doxic and euergetistic context of first-century Ephesus. Section two examines various traditions evoked by Jesus' walking on the sea. Section three argues that the call to discipleship in ch. 21 distances Jesus' disciples from socioeconomic involvements.

1. THE EMPEROR NERO AS MASTER OF THE SEA

According to *I.Eph* 1a.20, the association of "fishermen and fishmongers" (οἱ ἁλιεῖς καὶ ὀψαριοπῶλαι) of fishcatchers and sellers, has constructed a customs building near the harbor in Ephesus.[5] The dedicatory inscription lists the names of some ninety-nine to one hundred males,[6] in order of the amount they contributed to the building, from the greatest to the least. The first named, Publius Hordeonius Lollianus, along with his (unnamed) wife and children, paid for four columns (lines 12–14). The second, Publius Cornelius Alexandros, paved "the open area with Phokaian stone, 100 cubits" (lines 15–18). The third, Tiberius Claudius Metrodoros, along with his (unnamed) wife and children, contributed three columns and paved "the colonnade that is beside the stele with Phokaian stone" (lines 19–24). The list continues through those who contributed one column, to those who donated various sums of money from fifty denarii down to five denarii. The total amount of money is close to one thousand denarii, an average of about

---

4. W. Carter, *John and Empire: Initial Explorations* (New York: T. & T. Clark, 2008).

5. There are several clues to the building's type and scope. The inscription identifies eighteen columns (lines 14–44, 70), a paved open area (line 16) and colonnade (line 22), four thousand bricks (lines 30–35), a stoa (line 37), and three hundred tiles (line 39). The presence of the stoa (plural) suggests to Horsley ("A Fishing Cartel," 104) "more than one colonnaded portico; and it would not be unusual for shops to have opened on to them."

6. One woman is named: "P. Cornelius Felix, with Cornelia Ision, 1 column" (lines 40–41).

Master(s) of the Sea?

twenty-five denarii per household. The double-columned sequence is broken at lines 67–71 to honor Lucius Fabricius Vitalis for being "the works superintendent and deviser of the construction" as well as for donating two columns.

Horsley particularly examines what the names indicate about social status. He concludes that about 50 percent are Roman citizens, up to 46 percent have non-servile status (they are Greeks and citizens of Ephesus) and at least 3 percent are slaves. Horsley emphasizes the "considerable spread in formal civic rank and wealth" and suggests that this "mix [is] closely akin to that represented in the Pauline congregations."[7] He also suggests that the range in status and wealth of those associated with the fishing industry indicates different roles in the association, that some "of the larger donations may have come from men in whose boats and shops hirelings and slaves actually did the physical work."[8]

Horsley poses the interesting question as to why this association of fishcatchers and marketers should construct this building for the collection of taxes at their own expense (ἐκ τῶν ἰδίων, line 10).[9] He rules out "altruism" as "the primary motive," and argues that the "provision of this building . . . must have been intended to ensure that those who were not members of the group at Ephesos were barred from bringing their catch ashore there and marketing it in the city." The issue for Horsley is not just a monopoly on supply of fish but also "self-interest" in terms of financial return on tax-farming leases for fish as well as for other imports and exports moving through the harbor. Horsley offers two factors in support of this explanation. First, he notes the "general, undifferentiating self-description" of the association in line 7 ("fishermen and fishmongers," οἱ ἁλιεῖς καὶ ὀψαριοπῶλαι). And second he appeals to a "fragmentary papyrus" of unknown provenance, dating from the second or third century C.E. referring "to the illegal sale of fish in an Egyptian town-market."

The explanation that the association was controlling competition and maximizing its financial interest seems reasonable. The inscription does provide a public list of members of the association, and the custom house is strategically located. The explanation, though, is not exhaustive. The inscription offers no evidence for, nor signs of, competition, opponents, or even the existence of another group against which its identity needs to be established and boundaries set in place. In fact, the "general, undifferentiating

---

7. Horsley, "A Fishing Cartel," 110.

8. Ibid., 110. Horsley suggests that "Phorbos" and "Secundus" are "watchmen" (lines 31–34) who are "responsible for keeping safe the customs house and the shops . . . [that] adjoin it."

9. Ibid., 103.

self-description" of the association in line 7 ("fishermen and fishmongers") is blandly inclusive. The association does not distinctively identify itself nor define itself against any other group. It does, though, locate itself clearly within its civic context. Its act of construction has proceeded under the city's sanction (lines 9–10). Set in this civic context, it presents itself as representing the fishing enterprise in establishing this facility, not as defining itself over against other illegitimate practices. Horsley's appeal to a later Egyptian papyrus adds little to the argument except to indicate that illegal sales were possible. The Ephesian inscription makes no reference to policing legal sales.

Unnoticed by Horsley, the inscription's opening lines position the association's act of construction carefully with respect to civic context. The inscription dedicates (ἀνέθηκαν) the custom house "To Nero Claudius Caesar Augustus Germanicus the Imperator, and to Julia Agrippina Augusta his mother, and to Octavia the wife of the Imperator, and the *demos* of the Romans and the *demos* of the Ephesians..." (lines 4–6). More than controlling competition, the inscription constructs the association as a loyal participant in imperial Ephesus with its act of constructing the custom house as honoring the emperor. The inscription participates in the common civic practice of recognizing Roman rule and honoring the person and presence of the emperor.[10]

Such doxic activity increasingly pervaded Ephesus through the first century C.E. Guy Rogers comments on this Romanization of Ephesus, claiming that by century's end Roman citizens, including imperial agents from Rome, Latin-speaking immigrants, Greeks who were Roman citizens from other cities, and Ephesians, had:

> transformed the upper city architecturally and spatially, changed the calendar of the city, [taken] control over the celebration of major festivals, and celebrated the cult of the new god—the emperor. In short it is extremely difficult to find even one area of Ephesian institutional or social life documented in the huge epigraphical corpus of the city in which Roman presence ... was not pervasive or persistent by the end of the first century AD.[11]

---

10. For associations and Roman Asia, P. Harland, *Associations, Synagogues, and Congregations* (Minneapolis: Fortress, 2003) 1–173; also J. N. Kraybill, *Imperial Cult and Commerce in John's Apocalypse* (Sheffield: Sheffield Academic, 1996).

11. G. Rogers, *The Sacred Identity of Ephesos* (New York: Routledge, 1991) 141; S. Friesen, *Twice Neokoros: Ephesus, Asia, and the Cult of the Flavian Imperial* (Leiden: Brill, 1993); P. Scherrer, "The City of Ephesos: From the Roman Period to Late Antiquity," in *Ephesos Metropolis of Asia: An Interdisciplinary Approach to its Archaeology, Religion, and Culture*, ed. H. Koester (Valley Forge, PA: Trinity, 1995) 1–26.

Master(s) of the Sea?

The epigraphical corpus itself promoted this Romanizing identity. By the time of John's gospel in the late first century C.E., Ephesus' residents, especially its elite, had long recognized Rome's unassailable power and engaged in the practices and behaviors of "Romanization" that marked elites elsewhere in the empire.[12] They actively participated in civic patronage, euergetism, trade, political leadership, rhetoric, and priesthoods. They built buildings and monuments as material and tangible signs of Roman power and presence, often dedicating them to the emperor, demonstrating their loyalty, wealth, and civic status.[13] They promoted Ephesus' identity, seeking to outdo other Asian cities in exhibiting imperial allegiance. They thereby negotiated Roman power, recognizing, honoring, and integrating it into their civic space, while simultaneously experiencing the benefits and rewards of status, power, and wealth that loyalty and assimilation into imperial political, societal, and economic networks produced.

This process had been continuous through the first century C.E. With the reign of Augustus, the instability and public strife of the first century B.C.E. increasingly gave way to greater stability and to the considerable integration of Ephesus into Rome's world. Under Augustus, the "small plateau between (the slopes of) Bülbüldag and Panayirdag was chosen as the new center of the Roman city," dominated by the construction of the two largest buildings, the temple for Divus Julius and the Sebasteion (for Augustus) both of which focused attention on Rome.[14] In addition,[15] a leading member of Ephesus' elite, G. Sextilius Pollio, his wife Ofillia Bassa, and their children dedicated between 4 and 14 C.E. a three-aisled Basilika Stoa to Artemis, Augustus, Tiberius, and the city of Ephesos (*I.Eph* 2.404). At the eastern end of the stoa were large statues of the emperor Augustus and his wife Livia, as well as other members of the imperial family such as Germanicus. There

---

12. P. Brunt, "The Romanization of the Local Ruling Classes in the Roman Empire," in *Roman Imperial Themes* (Oxford: Clarendon, 1990) 267–81; A. D. Macro, "The Cities of Asia Minor under the Roman Imperium," in *Aufsteig und Niedergang der romischen Welt*, eds. H. Temporini and W. Haase (New York: de Gruyter, 1989) 2:658–97, esp. 660–63, 678–89 (civic administration and magistracies) 682–84 (intercity rivalry) 684–85 (elite wealth and civic euergetism) 692–93 (rhetoric); R. MacMullen, "Notes on Romanization," in *Changes in the Roman Empire: Essays on the Ordinary* (Princeton, NJ: Princeton University Press, 1990) 55–66.

13. Rogers (*Sacred Identity*, 127–35) lists sixty constructions, location, date, and inscriptional references prior to Trajan.

14. Scherrer, "Ephesos," 4; Rogers, *Sacred Identity*, 91; S. Friesen, *Imperial Cults and the Apocalypse of John: Reading John in the Ruins* (Oxford: Oxford University Press, 2001) 99–101.

15. I am largely following Scherrer, "Ephesos," 4–7; see also Rogers, *Sacred Identity*, 128–35; S. van Tilborg, *Reading John in Ephesus* (New York: Brill, 1996) 174–212.

were also statues of the donors. Sextilius Pollio was subsequently buried on the western side of the Agora. His tomb, dedicated by his son Proculus, was visible to Curetes Street, honoring him and demonstrating to passersby the honor of civic investment.

To the west, where the sacred way intersected with the processional way to the sacred site of Ortygia, two imperial freedmen Mazaeus and Mithridates dedicated the impressive monumental or triumphal gates between 4–2 B.C.E.[16] The complex included statues of Augustus, his designated heirs Gaius and Lucius Caesar, and another son of Augustus' brother-in-law, Agrippa (*I.Eph* 2.253). A triumphal arch for Augustus was constructed on the south side of the agora in 3 B.C.E. (*I.Eph* 7.1.3006/7). Aqueducts were built by Augustus (*I.Eph* 2.401) and by Sextilius Pollio along with a fountain at the temple for Divus Julius (*I.Eph* 2.404). Augustus' name is also associated with road-building (*I.Eph* 2.459).

During the reign of the emperor Tiberius (14–37 C.E.) additions were made to the agora. An equestrian statue of Claudius was dedicated by Roman citizens in 43 C.E., and a hall forming the eastern upper story dedicated to Artemis, the god Claudius, Nero, Agrippina, and the people of Ephesus (*I.Eph* 7.3003). During Nero's reign (54–68 C.E.) the theater was enlarged, and the stadium reconstructed, funded in part by Stertinus Orpex (*I.Eph* 2.411). Claudia Metrodora and her husband dedicated the rebuilt southern wall of the agora to Artemis, the god Claudius, Nero, Agrippina (Nero's mother) and the people of Ephesus (*I.Eph* 7.1.3003).[17] In addition to the custom house dedicated to Nero, the harbor was dredged by the proconsul Barea Soranus to relieve the silting from the Kaystros River, and the customs of Asia were reorganized (Tacitus, *Ann.* 16.23).[18]

Under the Flavian emperors Vespasian, Titus, and Domitian (69–96 C.E.) the upper agora area was developed. Most prominent was the temple of the Flavian Sebastoi dedicated in 89–90, honoring Ephesus as a neokorate city, a term that signified Ephesus' privileged identity as "warden" or "keeper" of the imperial temple.[19] It was funded by T. Claudius Aristion, its first high priest, who with his wife Julia Lydia Laterane "were the most important couple in the city at the end of the first century and the beginning of the second."[20] The proconsul Calvisius Ruso expanded the monument to

16. *I.Eph* 7.3006, 3007.

17. Van Tilborg, *Reading John*, 184.

18. On the continual struggle with silting in the harbors, D. Crouch, *Geology and Settlements: Greco-Roman Patterns* (New York: Oxford University Press, 2003) 221, 236–40.

19. Van Tilborg, *Reading John*, 199–200 n. 57.

20. Ibid., 102–3.

Sextillius Pollio in 92–93 C.E. to include a fountain dedicated to Domitian (*I.Eph* 2.413, 419). Near the harbor, a gymnasium was finished in 92–93 C.E. (*I.Eph* 3. 621, 633, 661) and T. Claudius Aristion completed baths before 92–93 C.E. (*I.Eph* 2.508; 4.1104). The very powerful T. Claudius Aristion (and friends) was imperial high priest and held the prestigious civic offices of prytany[21] in 92 C.E. and scribe of the demos or assembly in 93 (*I.Eph* 2.427, 461, 508).

Other activities proclaimed by inscriptions honored emperors and the imperial family. Apollonios Passalas erected a statue of Augustus in 19/18 B.C.E. (*I.Eph* 3.902). A wealthy freedman of Augustus, G. Nepos Nikephoros, funded the annual Roman games with a sacrifice to Roma, Augustus, and Artemis (*I.Eph* 3.859A). This combination linked Ephesus and Rome, goddess and god, old and new. It located Ephesus in the Roman order and Rome in Ephesian antiquity. During Claudius' reign, when Alexander Memnon was leader of "the games of the emperor" and "secretariat of the city," he erected a statue of Claudius' wife (*I.Eph* 2.261).[22] Also during Claudius' reign, the heirs of Tiberius Kl. Damonikos followed his testamentary wishes and erected a statue for the emperor (*I.Eph* 2.259B).[23] Hymn singers honored not only the deified Augustus, Tiberius, and Claudius, but also in 44 C.E. hymn singers honored the deified Julia, wife of Augustus with hymns, sacrifices, and meals (*I.Eph* 1.17–19; also 7.2.3801.2 for Tiberius).[24]

The dedication of the custom house to the emperor Nero belongs in the context of this civic doxic activity. By honoring Nero, the association of "fishermen and fishmongers" locates itself in Rome's world as loyal citizens. It aligns itself with Roman power and presence, and in collecting tolls, shows itself in its Ephesian civic context to be an agent and beneficiary of that power. In return for this building, the collection of tolls, and the sale of fish, the association can expect to be recognized for its loyalty; its euergetism should result in civic honor and economic well-being. The large inscription of named donors should help accomplish these ends.

But the question as to why Nero and his family are honored needs to be pressed further. Horsley suggests, reasonably, that the fishing association had leased the rights to fish the ponds and sections of the Kaystros River

---

21. Friesen (*Imperial Cults*, 97–98) identifies four functions for the prytanis: 1) to maintain the cult of Hestia and the city's eternal flame; 2) to welcome official city guests including hosting dinners at the prytaneion; 3) to exercise oversight with the Kouretes of the mysteries of Artemis; and 4) to have oversight of an official cycle of 365 sacrifices for various deities in the city.

22. Van Tilborg, *Reading John*, 177–78.

23. Ibid., 181.

24. Ibid., 186–87.

that were dedicated to Ephesus' leading deity Artemis, and that the tariffs collected at the custom house were paid to the temple of Artemis.[25] Such leasing, he argues, does not preclude fishing in other areas nor collection of other harbor tolls. If he is right, Artemis has a significant claim on the activities and funds of the association. Why, then, is the toll house not dedicated to Artemis, at least in a shared dedication with Nero?

Historical silence is always difficult to fill, but at least two factors involving imperial power perhaps offer some explanation. The first factor concerns taxes. As John Kautsky expresses it, "To rule in aristocratic empires is, above all, to tax."[26] Taxes enact what Gerhard Lenski calls the "proprietary theory" of the Roman Empire in which control over land, resources, people, and production was exerted through "the collection of taxes, tribute money, rents, and services" for the benefit of the ruling elite.[27] The imposition of taxes on fish products expressed this proprietary view of empire. Tolls on fish products were, according to Horsley, farmed out to *publicani* who collected the contracted amount.[28] The custom house thus negotiated imperial power and sovereignty by complying with its demands in the gathering of tolls, while simultaneously gaining societal and financial benefit from the interaction.

Second, the custom house and dedicatory inscription to Nero recognized the reach of Roman power by evoking its mastery over the sea. The proprietary theory of empire embraced not only land but also sea. References across a range of ancient literatures attest a widespread recognition of Rome and its emperors as rulers of the sea.

Philo, for example, complains that King Agrippa was subjected in Alexandria to an indignity unparalleled "ever since the Augustan house assumed the sovereignty of land and sea" (*Flacc.* 1.104). In *Legatio ad Gaium*, Philo recognizes that while Gaius Caligula causes misery, Augustus "the best of the emperors . . . he who first received the title of Augustus . . . disseminated peace everywhere over sea and land . . ." (*Legat.* 1.309). Philo employs the metaphor of Augustus calming political storms: "Europe and Asia . . . [were] waging grievous war all over all sea and land" which would have destroyed "the whole human race . . . had it not been for one man and leader, Augustus . . . This is the Caesar who calmed the torrential storms . . ." But then Philo returns to Augustus' literal control of the seas: "This is he who cleared the sea of pirate ships and filled it with merchant vessels"

---

25. Horsley, "A Fishing Cartel," 105.

26. J. H. Kautsky, *Politics of Aristocratic Empires* (Chapel Hill: University of North Carolina Press, 1984) 150.

27. G. Lenski, *Power and Privilege: A Theory of Social Stratification* (New York: McGraw-Hill, 1984) 214–17.

28. Horsley, "A Fishing Cartel," 103.

(*Legat.* 1.144–46). Augustus himself takes up the same theme in asserting that he "freed the sea from pirates" (*Res Gestae.* 25).

Philo similarly acknowledges the Emperor Tiberius' mastery of the sea: "What of Gaius' predecessor Tiberius, from whom he derived his sovereignty, who for twenty-three years was invested with dominion over land and sea?" (*Legat.* 1.141). And predictably, Philo identifies Gaius Caligula as "the sovereign of earth and sea . . ." (*Legat.* 1.44). Josephus develops this link, acknowledging Gaius to "triumph over land and sea" (*Ant.* 19.81). He declares that Gaius "not only manifested the madness of his insolence in relation to the Jews who dwelt in Jerusalem . . . but he also sent it forth to spread over every land and sea which was subject to the Romans . . ." (*Ant.* 19.1). He gives an example of Gaius' excess and power:

> . . . it was insufferable, he thought, to cross the bay from the city of Dicaearchia . . . to Misenum . . . in a trireme. Then, too, he considered it his privilege as lord of the sea to require the same service from the sea as he received from the land. [He constructs a bridge with pontoons] and over this bridge he drove in his chariot. That way of travelling, said he, befitted his godhead. (*Ant.* 19.5–6)

After being captured in the war of 66–70 C.E., Josephus predicts Vespasian and his son will become emperors. Josephus declares "for you, Caesar, are master not of me only, but of land and sea and the whole human race" (*J.W.* 3.401–2). And Josephus presents Vespasian's son, the future Emperor Titus, reminding his troops before their assault on the tower of Antonia in Jerusalem that their identity as Roman soldiers means they are "masters of well nigh every land and sea . . ." (*J.W.* 6.43).

The same epithet describes the emperor Domitian. The satirist Juvenal narrates the inevitable fate of an enormous turbot fish in becoming dinner for the Emperor Domitian, mocking two lawyers Palfurius and Armillatus who, he claims, will argue that "every rare and beautiful thing in the wide ocean, in whatever sea it swims, belongs to the imperial treasury" (*Sat.* 4.37-55). Subsequently Juvenal describes Domitian as "ruler of lands and seas and nations" (*Sat.* 4.83). Philostratus has Apollonius confront the powerful tyrant Domitian (whom he regards as worse than Nero) describing him as "master both of sea and land" (*Vit. Apoll.* 7.3).[29] And Pliny celebrates

---

29. Various other figures and peoples are identified as masters of the sea: Polycrates the first Greek (Herodotus, *Hist.* 3.122); the Carthaginians (Polybius, *Hist.* 1.7.6); the Spartans (Plutarch, *Lys.* 6.2); the Persians (Plutarch, *Ages.* 23.1); Xerxes who "sailed upon the sea, and walked upon the sea, and could not be contained by the seas" (so Josephus, *J.W.* 2.358); Apollonius of Tyana (Philostratus, *Vit. Apoll.* 4.13); Rome (Josephus, *J.W.* 2.366–67); unspecified "mighty rulers . . . who with their arms have subdued

that Trajan guides the ship of state (*Pan.* 6.2) and "gives thanks to our ruler" because in sending Domitian's informers away in boats on stormy seas he "had entrusted [their] punishment to the gods of the sea" (34.5—35.1), a claim that assumes an alliance between emperor and gods in directing the sea's purposes.[30]

The fishcatchers' and fishmongers' dedication to Nero participates in this imperial world, enhancing Roman prestige, recognizing its power even over the sea, and benefitting from involvement in it. By its connection to toll-collection and the attendant imperial claims about the sea, the inscription proclaims Roman sovereignty over the sea and those who utilized its resources.

2. READING JOHN'S GOSPEL IN EPHESUS: GOD AS MASTER OF THE SEA (JOHN 6.16–21)[31]

John 6.16–21 also asserts control over the sea. The disciples are crossing the sea to Capernaum.[32] A strong wind develops and Jesus approaches walking on the sea. They are frightened by Jesus' appearance (not the storm), Jesus reveals himself to them ("I am"), they want him to join them in the boat, and immediately they reach the shore. John does not present the disciples as being in danger,[33] nor does Jesus clearly join the disciples in the boat, nor does Jesus clearly calm the storm.[34] That is, the scene is not about Jesus using his power for the benefit of disciples,[35] nor is it a rescue scene.[36]

---

sea and land," (Philo, *Ebr.* 1.113); a person who has "sovereignty over land and sea" (Philo, *Her.* 1.7). God controls the sea in Josephus, *C. Ap.* 22.121; *J.W.* 5.218; *Ant.* 1.282; Philo, *Flacc.* 1.123.

30. For discussion, see E. Manolaraki, "Political and Rhetorical Seascapes in Pliny's Panegyricus," *CP* 103 (2008) 374–94.

31. All Scripture translations are my own unless noted otherwise.

32. On this scene, see J. P. Heil, *Jesus Walking on the Water: Meaning and Gospel Functions of Matthew 14:22–23, Mark 6:45–52 and John 6:15B–21* (Rome: Biblical Institute, 1981); P. J. Madden, *Jesus' Walking on the Sea: An Investigation of the Origin of the Narrative Account* (Berlin: de Gruyter, 1997); R. Nicholls, *Walking on the Water: Reading Matthew 14:22–33 in the Light of its Wirkungsgeschichte* (Leiden: Brill, 2008).

33. So E. Haenchen, *John*, 2 vols. (Philadelphia: Fortress, 1984) 1:282.

34. So C. K. Bernard, *The Gospel According to St. John* (London: SPCK, 1955) 185, "no miracle whatsoever." I do not explore the intertextuality with various figures who calm storms. See, e.g., C. S. Keener, *The Gospel of John: A Commentary*, 2 vols. (Peabody, MA: Hendrickson, 2003) 1:672.

35. Contra Keener, *Gospel of John*, 1:673.

36. Contra B. Lindars, *The Gospel of John* (Grand Rapids: Eerdmans, 1972) 247, who claims that Jesus' "I am" brings "Jesus to the center of thought as Saviour." Heil,

Rather, at the heart of John's scene is Jesus' walking on the sea and revealing himself to the disciples with the words "I am."[37] The key question comprises what constitutes the revelation. John-Paul Heil argues for a threefold revelation, namely a christological revelation of Jesus' "divine sonship," a soteriological revelation of Jesus' life-giving power rescuing the disciples from the dangerous storm, and an ecclesiological revelation of the disciples' solidarity with Jesus.[38] The narrative's silence, though, on stilling a storm and on Jesus getting into the boat casts doubt on Heil's soteriological and ecclesial claims. There are also problems with the claim of a christological revelation.

The most obvious is Jesus' declaration, "I am" (ἐγώ εἰμι) (6.20). This is the formula of divine self-disclosure that God speaks to Moses in Exod 3.14, and to the people in Babylonian exile through (Deutero-) Isaiah (Isa 41.4, 10). These are God's words, the language of theological revelation. John's Jesus speaks theocentric, not christocentric, language.

Second, prior to this walking-on-the-sea scene, the gospel has made it clear that Jesus does not reveal himself but reveals God. He makes the Father known (1.18). The Son does only what he sees the Father doing (5.19). The Son can do nothing except the Father's will (5.30). The Son cannot testify about himself because that constitutes false testimony (5.31). The narrative frames this walking-on-the-sea scene as a revelation of God.

Consistent with this context, the biblical tradition presents God walking on or through the sea.[39] Job describes God walking on or through the sea among other activities:

> he who removes mountains, and they do not know it, when he overturns them in his anger;
> who shakes the earth out of its place, and its pillars tremble;
> who commands the sun, and it does not rise; who seals up the stars;
> who alone stretched out the heavens and trampled the waves of the Sea;
> (Job 9.5–8 NRSV)

Jesus Walking on the Water, 173, claims that "Jesus' act means "the disciples' rescue from the sea-storm . . .""

37. R. E. Brown (*Gospel According to John I–XII* [Garden City, New York: Doubleday] 1:252) claims initially that this is "a borderline case where one cannot be certain if a divine formula is meant," but on pp. 254–55 he takes it as a divine epiphany.

38. Heil, *Jesus Walking on the Water*, 172–73.

39. I do not explore here intertextuality with other traditions of those who walk on water. See E. Boring et al, *Hellenistic Commentary to the New Testament* (Nashville: Abingdon, 1995) 99–100. They mention Xerxes (Isocrates, *Paneg.* 88–89; Dio Chrysostom, *3 Regn.* 30) and Pythagoras (Iamblichus, *Pyth.* 91). Note also the Seleucid king Antiochus IV Epiphanes in 2 Macc 5.21; 9.8.

But These are Written...

This sequence strongly asserts God's powerful control over creation. God can sovereignly move mountains, shake the earth, command the sun, stretch out the heavens, and subdue the sea. The language of Job 9.8b in the LXX closely resembles John's language for Jesus:

περιπατῶν ὡς ἐπ' ἐδάφους ἐπὶ θαλάσσης "walking on the sea/water as if on the ground"
τὸν Ἰησοῦν περιπατοῦντα ἐπὶ τῆς θαλάσσης "Jesus walking on the sea/water" (John 6.19)

In Hab 3.15, the image again appears. God "trampled the sea with your horses churning the mighty waters." This declaration follows the prophet's petition for God to "revive" his work in bringing control and justice to the earth by overcoming the wicked (especially Babylon; 3.2). The rest of the chapter depicts God's action in terms similar to Job 9. God shakes the earth and shatters mountains (3.6) overcoming the waters (3.8) stopping the moon in the heavens (3.11) trampling the nations (3.12) and saving the people (3.13). God's control and reign are total.

The presentation of God walking on or trampling the sea also recalls Psalm 77.19: "Through the sea was your way, and your paths were through many waters, and your footprints will not be known" (translation of LXX Ps 76.20).[40] This lament psalm initially wrestles with God's apparent absence (77.1–10) before recalling God's previous "mighty deeds" (77.12). Verses 16–20 concern the rescue of the Israelites at the Red Sea from the pursuing Egyptians. The exodus narrative of God enabling Moses to part the waters becomes here in v. 20 a depiction of God walking through the sea leading the people to safety though without leaving any footprints. God's control of the sea simultaneously asserts God's reign over the nations.[41]

In these scenes of God walking on or through the sea, God's control extends to both material creation and human affairs. In the context of this tradition, John's scene of Jesus walking on the sea imitates God. He does the Father's will in a God-like action, revealing God's control over the material world and over human affairs.

The intertextuality between this gospel story and the Ephesian fish-catcher and fishmonger inscription is powerful. Both accounts make similar claims of control over the physical world and over human affairs which

---

40. Ἐν τῇ θαλάσσῃ ἡ ὁδός σου καὶ αἱ τρίβοι σου ἐν ὕδασι πολλοῖς καὶ τὰ ἴχνη σου οὐ γνωσθήσονται (Ps 76.20 LXX). For similar emphases, Isa 43.16; 51.10.

41. Also to be noted are Mic 1.3 where "the Lord...will...tread upon (ἐπιβήσεται) the high places of the earth," and Amos 4.13, "For lo, the one who...treads on (ἐπιβαίνων) the heights of the earth—the Lord, the God of hosts, is his name!" Both assert God's control not only over material creation but also over humans.

require human recognition. They present figures with cosmic reach (Nero, God) who claim human allegiance. Yet the claims clash—to whom do the seas in fact belong? The intertextuality shows that the seas are not neutral but contested space where competing claims for control of the elements and human allegiances collide.

But while these claims collide, can they be accommodated or are they exclusive and excluding?

3. DISTANCE FROM IMPERIAL SEAS (JOHN 21)

The scene opens with the disciples gathered at the Sea named Tiberias (21.1).[42] John has identified this sea in 6.1 as "the Sea of Galilee also called the Sea of Tiberias," equating the two names. Interestingly, most commentators neglect to notice that the narrative in 21.1 presents the sea not primarily by geographical location (Galilee) but in terms of imperial control.[43] The name Tiberias evokes the Emperor Tiberius; the sea belongs to him. The gospel audience does not need to know that the puppet king, Herod Agrippa, had named this newly built city near the lake in 19/20 C.E. to honor the emperor (Josephus, *Ant.* 18.36–38) or that the imperially honoring city had spread its influence to rename the lake. What matters is that the sea where the disciples gather is presented as belonging to and under the power of an emperor. Naming the Sea of Tiberias contributes an important dimension to the scene. They participate in the emperor's domain.

Peter announces "I am going fishing" (ὑπάγω ἁλιεύειν, 21.3) using the cognate verb of the noun that identifies the fishermen in the inscription (*I.Eph* 1a.20, line 7). Other disciples declare, "we also are coming with you." This act of going fishing has puzzled interpreters. Is it symbolic of the apostolic mission to catch people,[44] "aimless activity undertaken in desperation,"[45] narrative staging,[46] or a return to their previous way of life?[47] The latter is closer to the mark, but with one significant emphasis. In fishing on the sea of Tiberias, they inhabit the realm of imperial authority. Their

---

42. Josephus, *J.W.* 4.456 contrasts it with the Dead Sea.

43. R. Bultmann, *Gospel of John: A Commentary*, trans. G. R. Beasley-Murray (Philadelphia: Wesminster, 1971) 706; and Haenchen, *John*, 2:222, e.g., refer to it as the Sea of Galilee.

44. C. K. Barrett, *The Gospel According to St. John* (London: SPCK, 1955) 482.

45. Brown, *Gospel of John*, 2:1096.

46. Haenchen, *John*, 2:222; F. Moloney, *Gospel of John* (Collegeville, MN: Liturgical, 1998) 549.

47. Brown, *Gospel of John*, 2:1069, even though the gospel does not previously present them as fishermen.

fishing is not recreational. Rather, as the Ephesian inscription indicates, and as K. C. Hanson and Douglas Oakman have shown, fishing was a carefully regulated, licensed, and taxed industry.[48] To fish was to participate in the imperial economy. It was to submit to and cooperate with imperial authority, recognizing that "every rare and beautiful thing in the wide ocean, in whatever sea it swims, belongs to the imperial treasury" (Juvenal, *Sat.* 4.37–55). It was to know that the emperor was master of the sea.

We might posit that the disciples' failure to catch anything is a literary means of exposing the emptiness, the bankruptcy, of imperial claims (21.3b, 5b). We might also posit that their subsequent abundant catch at Jesus' command reflects the efficaciousness of his alternative assertion of sovereignty over both the sea and human lives (21.6, 8, 10–11, 13). Abundance often represents God's gracious eschatological blessing of fertility that reverses present impotencies and deprivations (2 *Bar.* 29.5; 4 Ezra 7.121–24; 8.52–54; John 6.1–14). But what is significant is that they occupy imperial space.

John's Jesus, though, does not sanction their activity in the Sea of Tiberias. He summons them to abandon it. With a double command, he calls the leader Peter to "follow me" (21.19b, 22b). Jesus' command to "follow me" directly challenges Peter's declaration to "go fishing." The subsequent reference in v. 19 to "the kind of death" he might suffer indicates that this command to follow is a life-and-death matter. Abandoning the sea and fishing means conflict. Jesus' call to abandon fishing and to leave the sea of Tiberias requires Peter and the disciples to end their participation in the imperial economy that fishing involves. The parallel assertions of claims to sovereignty over sea and people (Tiberius/Nero; Jesus/God) appear now to be clearly competitive and conflictual. The scene sets out allegiance to God's ways revealed by Jesus as a clear alternative to imperial participation.

CONCLUSION

The name of Peter or of his seven companions does not of course appear on the list of the one hundred or so names on the Ephesian fishing inscription. The intertextuality between this scene in John 21 and the inscription would not permit it. That is, Jesus' call to follow in John 21 allows no place for Jesus-believers in fishing industries such as the association of fishcatchers and fishmongers. If any Jesus-believers belong to this association, Jesus' repeated call to fishermen to follow him requires them to withdraw, like Peter, and not go fishing. This repeated and insistent call suggests that fishing activities

---

48. K. C. Hanson and D. E. Oakman, *Palestine in the Time of Jesus: Social Structures and Social Conflicts* (Minneapolis: Fortress, 2008) 106–10.

are, for the author of John, too imperially compromised, too involved in the imperial economy. The intertextuality functions to distance Jesus-believers from such involvement.

If this is so for the association of fishcatchers and sellers, it would be so for any association in Ephesus that participates in the city's economy under Roman rule and that honors the emperor in any way. Withdrawal, retreat, and distance are the name of the game for Jesus-believers according to John's gospel's construction of discipleship. These scenes offer further instances of John's "rhetoric of distance" that urges Jesus-believers to distance themselves from civic and imperial involvements.[49] What they do not offer is any indication as to whether anyone lived accordingly.

49. Carter, *John and Empire*.

7

Episodes of Personal Encounter
Inquiry into John's Christology
JAMES D. HERNANDO

INTRODUCTION

RECENTLY, I HAVE COMPLETED a small book that I originally envisioned as the primary text for a thirteen-week Sunday school quarterly. The title of the book is *They Came to Jesus: Personal Encounters in the Fourth Gospel*. During my study one feature stood out: the distinctiveness of John's material from the Synoptic Gospels. When we examine the style and structure of the gospel, the distinctiveness of John becomes evident. Some obvious differences are the lack of movement, owing to a minimum of narrative and a preponderance of material devoted to the discourses of Jesus. Even so, John contains no parables. Moreover, in contrast to the Synoptics, there are very few miracles recorded.[1] Some scholars have calculated that approximately ninety percent of John's material is unique to his gospel.[2] This does

---

1. John records only seven miracles (five in common with the other gospels) but prefers the term "signs" (σημεῖα). See 2.11, 23; 3.2; 4.48; 6.2, 26; 7.31; 9.16; 11.47; 12.37; 20.30. Cf. "sign" (σημεῖον) 2.18; 4.54; 6.14, 30; 10.41; 12.18.

2. E.g., M. Unger places the figure at 92 percent. See M. F. Unger, *Unger's Bible Handbook* (Chicago: Moody, 1974) 544. Such estimates include material found in the Synoptic Gospels but not found in John: the infancy narratives, virgin birth, the baptism

Episodes of Personal Encounter

not suggest that the apostolic author did not know the other gospels.³ That proposition, given John's traditional late first-century dating, is unlikely. Nevertheless, for his purpose, John does not appear to rely on them.⁴

Another outstanding feature of John's gospel is the attention the author gives to personal encounters. This is evidenced by the numerous personal interviews or exchanges that he records. This noteworthy feature, while not unique to John, is disproportionate. When we tally the episodes they number twenty-seven!⁵ To be sure, some of these are too brief in the exchange

---

(though implied) wilderness temptation, transfiguration of Jesus, exorcisms, Jesus' table fellowship with sinners, institution of the Lord's supper, parables, Jesus' agony in the garden and cry of dereliction from the cross, and the ascension. John also includes material found nowhere in the gospels: John's Prologue (1.1-18) Jesus' early Judean ministry, the miracle of Cana, encounter with Nicodemus, the Samaritan woman, the cripple at the Pool of Bethesda and the blind man in Jerusalem, the resurrection of Lazarus, the washing of the disciples' feet, the "I am" sayings plus some long discourses. E.g., most of the material found in chs. 7-11 and 14-17 are found only in John.

3. I am here declaring my position that the author of the Fourth Gospel is the Apostle John. While this issue has been debated critically for nearly a century and a half, the evidence against the traditional view of apostolic authorship is inconclusive, and in this author's opinion unconvincing. For a full discussion of Johannine authorship of the gospel, see D. Guthrie, *Introduction to the New Testament* (Downers Grove, IL: IVP, 1970) 241-71.

4. L. Morris, *The Gospel According to John* (Grand Rapids: Eerdmans, 1971) 50-51. C. K. Barrett makes a plausible case for John's dependence on the Synoptics by alluding to a ten-point chronological outline that is sequenced the same in both John and Mark's gospel. To this he adds a list of impressive verbal similarities in the two gospels. However, Morris points out that much of the chronological order is of logical necessity and does not support the view that John was following Mark's order. Moreover, the verbal correspondence upon closer scrutiny turns out to be only twelve passages, "most of which are single verses." He further notes that Mark's gospel is composed of some twelve thousand words making this verbal correspondence very meager. See Morris, *John*, 52.

5. The exact number will depend upon if one counts only single person interviews/exchanges or include exchanges with multiple persons as well. This author's list included both but focused mainly on single individuals where there was two-way discourse or when groups are treated as a single party in that discourse: Two of John's disciples (1.35-39; one is Andrew in v. 40); Peter/Simon (1.40-42); Philip (1.43); Nathaniel (1.45-51); Mary his mother (2.3-4); Nicodemus (3.1-21); Samaritan woman (4.1-42); Royal official (4.46-54); Cripple by the Pool of Bethesda (5.1-9, 14-15); Philip (6.5-14); Grumbling Jews (6.41-59); Peter and the Twelve (6.67-71); Woman caught in adultery (7.53-8.11); the healed blind man (9.35-38); Martha (11.17-38); Mary (11.17-38); Judas Iscariot (12.4-8); Greeks at the feast (12.20-28); Peter—Last supper; Judas—not Iscariot (14.22-24); Philip (14.8-14); those who came to arrest him in the garden (18.1-9); the High Priest Annas (18.19-23); Pilate (18.28-38; 19.5-12); Mary Magdalen (20.11-17); Thomas (20.26-29); Peter/post-resurrection Galilee (21.15-23). Personal discourse with groups would expand this number. See Jesus' brothers (7.2-9); Jews at the feast of the Jews (7.11-24); Pharisees/Jews in the temple (8.13-47); Pharisees

to invite useful analysis. Nevertheless, a significant number yield sufficient discourse. This raises the issue of what to include in our analysis. Some encounter episodes contain a dialogue between Jesus and individuals, while others do not. On occasion, an encounter precipitates a didactic discourse where Jesus addresses or answers issues raised in the initial encounter.

The present author, after close scrutiny, became engrossed in an emerging hypothesis that called for further investigation. It surfaced through a series of preliminary questions: Do these personal encounters represent more than a literary interest of John, or do they reflect and pursue a theological agenda? In particular, do these encounters constitute a kind of narrative theology in a gospel noted for its sparse narrative content? Does John present a Christology through the numerous personal encounters he records? Of particular interest to this author was what was spoken by those Jesus encountered regarding his identity. Did John use their recorded words to promote his Christology? Moreover, what did Jesus himself say during these encounters that reveals his own self-awareness or identity?

Content analysis of the entire Gospel of John is a daunting and intimidating task given the fact that, as J. R. Michaels points out, almost anything one might say about John's theology or Christology has been said many times before.[6] This coupled with the prescribed brevity of this assignment limits this project to a modest goal and restricted focus. The present chapter begins with a content analysis placed in chart form. The chart will identify the various passages that contain personal encounters. In addition, the chart will contain annotation that provides context and identifies any christological import. After charting John's gospel, we will identify any perceived patterns and posit their theological significance. Finally, we will attempt to lay out tentative conclusions which invite further investigation and elaboration.

This inductive approach is necessary to ensure that John's gospel is comprehensively surveyed for the pertinent data to support our hypothesis. The present author envisions this project as foundational for a christological survey of John's gospel, one that can be modified and expanded, inviting exegetical and theological critique.

(9.40—10.18); Jews at the Feast of Dedication (10.22–39); the disciples (12.8–16); the multitude in Jerusalem (12.29–36).

6. J. R. Michaels, *The Gospel of John* (Grand Rapids: Eerdmans, 2010) 39.

Episodes of Personal Encounter

PERSONAL ENCOUNTERS (FOCUS ON INDIVIDUALS)[7]

Passage and Person(s) Encountered	Title/Name or Descriptor of Jesus	Commentary and Theological Significance
(1.19–29) John the Baptist and priests and Levites sent by the Jews to question him as to his (John's) own identity. Was he Christ? Elijah? Or "the Prophet?"	"The Christ," an identity some wish to identify with John the Baptist, but which he emphatically denies. John the Baptist announces Jesus is the "Lamb of God who takes away the sin of the world."	On the heels of his emphatic denial, John the Baptist proclaims Jesus' identity in messianic terms.
(1.35–42) Two disciples, one is Andrew, brother of Simon Peter.	Andrew refers to the Messiah, which translated means "Christ."	
(1.45–51) Philip invites Nathanael to meet "[Jesus] whom Moses in the Law and also the Prophets wrote." Philip identifies Jesus as being from Nazareth, the "son of Joseph."	Nathanael responds to Jesus' prophetic foreknowledge with, "Rabbi, you are the Son of God; you are the King of Israel." Jesus says that Nathanael will see the heavens open and angels ascending and descending upon the Son of Man.	Philip alludes to messianic prophecy in Moses (cf. Deut 18.15) and the Prophets. "The Son of God" is a messianic title, which carries an implicit claim to deity (cf. John 5.18; Ps 2.7; 45.6; Heb 1.8). "The King of Israel" is a messianic title expressing Jewish political and apocalyptic hope in the Davidic Messiah King (cf. 2 Sam 7.14ff.; Jer 33.5) whose coming would restore Israel's national autonomy under a messianic ruler (cf. Acts 1.6). "The Son of Man" is an enigmatic figure with a number of associations, one of which is a transcendent heavenly figure depicted prophetically in Dan 7.13, and one which Jesus also identified himself (cf. Matt 23.64; Mark 14.62).

---

7. All Scripture translations are my own.

But These are Written . . .

Passage and Person(s) Encountered	Title/Name or Descriptor of Jesus	Commentary and Theological Significance
(3.1–21) Nicodemus and Jesus	Jesus is the Son of Man who has descended from heaven. He is the Father's "only begotten Son." He is "the Son," the "only begotten Son."	Transcendent Son of Man (cf. Dan 2) emphasis on the unique, familial relationship between Jesus and his Father.
(4.1–42) Samaritan woman	Samaritan woman declares, "I know that Messiah is coming . . . (he who is called Christ); when that One comes he will declare all things to us." Jesus says, "I am (ἐγώ εἰμι) the one who is speaking to you." She informs those in her city, "Is this not the Christ?" After those from the city hear for themselves, they declare, "For we have heard for ourselves and know that this one is indeed the Savior of the world."	This is arguably the clearest statement of Jesus' messianic identity. It is hard to miss both the identity of Jesus as the Jewish Messiah and his identity as the universal Savior. The irony is that his identity is revealed to this despised Samaritan woman.
(4.46–54) Capernaum Official	Jesus is the One who could accomplish signs. The official declares, "Lord" (κύριος)" which here means "sir," "come before my son dies."	One capable of doing miracles, which attests to the presence and power of God. "So the Father knew that it was at that hour in which Jesus said to him, 'Your son lives' and he himself believed, and his whole house hold." Believed what? That he was the Messiah and thus capable of commanding healing at his word.
(5.5–15) Paralytic by the Pool of Bethsaida.	No special identification except, "the one who made me well" . . . and said, "take up your pallet and walk."	An implicit theological statement, namely that Jesus again could command healing at his word.

Episodes of Personal Encounter

Passage and Person(s) Encountered	Title/Name or Descriptor of Jesus	Commentary and Theological Significance
(5.19–47) Jews at the Feast of the Jews	The Son shares in the divine work of the Father, including raising the dead at the Son's will and discretion. He is loved of the Father and shown all things that he is doing. He is delegated as the eternal "Judge" whose word determines whether they will be resurrected to eternal life or not. The Son has life in himself, even as the Father. God has given him divine authority to execute eternal judgment because he is the Son of Man.	One who does the work of God, his Father ("My Father") thus making himself equal with God. The exchange with the Jews expounds the uniqueness of Jesus' relationship to the Father and his equality with God.
(6.22–40) The multitude by the Sea of Galilee and at Capernaum.	They address him as "Rabbi." Jesus gives the bread that endures to "eternal life which the Son of Man shall give to you . . . the one whom the Father, God has set his seal." Jesus is the "bread of God that comes down out of heaven," whom if one eats shall not hunger, and will not thirst if he believes. The Son who provides eternal life to those who believe. Jesus himself will raise believers on the last day.	The multitudes are confronted by one who has an unprecedented sense of divine authority. His message is centered on himself and what God is and will do through him. The work of God is to believe in him whom God has sent, to partake/eat the true bread of heaven that gives life to the world. The one who has come to accomplish the will of his Father, namely to lose none that the Father has given him, but raise him up on the last day.
(6.67–71) Jesus addresses the Twelve after many of the Jews withdraw from following him. Jesus initiates discourse by asking them if they wanted to leave as well.	Simon Peter asks, "Lord, to whom shall we go? You have the words of eternal life. We have believed and come to know that you are the Holy One of God."	The context and connection with the Isaianic title indicates that "Lord" here is intended as a reference to Jesus' exalted or divine status.

85

But These are Written . . .

Passage and Person(s) Encountered	Title/Name or Descriptor of Jesus	Commentary and Theological Significance
(7.53—8.11) Jesus and the woman caught in adultery.[1]	The scribes and Pharisees address Jesus as "Teacher" (Διδάσκαλε). The woman answers Jesus' question with, "No one, Lord."	Interesting that the scribes and Pharisees do not acknowledge Jesus as "Rabbi." There seems to be no exalted sense to the title "Lord" here.
(9.35–38) Jesus speaks to the blind man he had earlier healed.	Jesus asks, "Do you believe in the Son of Man?" The man responds, "Lord, I believe" (note v. 17—The healed blind man, at first questioning, states that Jesus "is a prophet.").	Since the questioning of the man and his parents were directed at finding evidence to discredit Jesus' identity as the Christ (cf. v. 22) the title "the Son of Man" is understood as messianic.
(11.17–39) Martha, Mary, and Jesus after the death of Lazarus.	Martha addresses him as "Lord." Jesus says, "I am the resurrection and the life." Martha replies, "Yes, Lord; I have believed that you are the Christ, the Son of God, even he who comes into the world."[2] Martha states, "The Teacher is here and is calling for you." Mary and Martha both address him as "Lord."[2]	Coupled with Jesus' declaration of self-identity, Martha's admission is one of the clearest messianic confessions in John's gospel.

1. The inclusion of this "encounter narrative" is at first blush problematic as the overwhelming judgment of textual critics is that this passage was not part of the original Gospel of John. This is because it is missing in nearly all of the early Greek manuscripts. Nevertheless, I have included it for two reasons. First, it was held as true in the ancient church. It was known by the first-century apostolic father, Papias (cf. Eusebius' *Hist. eccl.* 3.39.17) and mentioned in the *Apos. Con.* (2.24). As Metzger wrote, "Although the Committee was unanimous that the pericope was originally not part of the Fourth Gospel, in deference to the evident antiquity of the passage a majority decided to print it . . ." See B. M. Metzger, *A Textual Commentary on the Greek New Testament, Second Edition a Companion Volume to the United Bible Societies' Greek New Testament* (New York: UBS, 1994) 189. A second reason, as Leon Morris observes, is it "is true to the character of Jesus," which may suggest why ancient sources continued to include the story. See L. Morris, *John*, 883.

2. The identification of the one who "comes into the world" has clear messianic import in John (e.g., 4.25) and is linked to the purpose for which he is sent by the Father. See 1.9 (to bring light into the world; cf. 3.19—that light precipitates God's judgment of those who love the darkness); 3.17 (to save the world through the Son whom He sent); 6.14 (the prophet—see Deut 18.15ff.).

Episodes of Personal Encounter

Passage and Person(s) Encountered	Title/Name or Descriptor of Jesus	Commentary and Theological Significance
(12.4–8) An exchange between Jesus and Judas Iscariot that was prompted by Judas' objection to Mary using expensive ointment to anoint Jesus' feet.	None	Jesus interprets Mary's action as a prophetic foreshadowing of his burial anointing.
(12.20–28) Jesus speaks to Andrew and Philip when the Greeks request to see him at the feast.	Jesus refers to himself as the "Son of Man."	Jesus enigmatically refers to his death as the means or occasion in which the Son of Man will be glorified, by which the Father will glorify his name.
(13.6–11) Jesus Speaks to Peter at the "Last Supper."	Peter addresses Jesus as "Lord" and objects to having Jesus wash his feet.	Peter's objection seems based on the incongruity of Jesus' dignified status as Messiah in contrast to the menial service of a slave.
(14.8–14) Jesus speaks to Philip at his request, "Show us the Father."	Jesus affirms his unique filial relationship with the Father, implicitly affirms his identity as the Son of God.	Jesus states that there is a mutual indwelling between himself and the Father, so that his words and works can be equated with those of the Father. Thus, those who witness the words of Jesus have the works of God, the Father.
(18.1–9) Those that come to arrest Jesus in the Garden of Gethsemane.	Jesus, the Nazarene; Jesus identifies himself three times as the "I am" (ἐγώ εἰμι).	In view of John's "I am" sayings, these self-identifications must be understood as referencing Yahweh of the OT (cf. 8.58).
(18.19–23) Jesus before Annas, the High Priest who questions him about his disciples and his teaching.	None	Jesus gives no answer except to say what he taught in the synagogues is not a secret, but was spoken of openly.

But These are Written . . .

Passage and Person(s) Encountered	Title/Name or Descriptor of Jesus	Commentary and Theological Significance
(18.28–38; 19.5–12) Jesus before Pilate	Pilate asks, "Are you the King of the Jews?"[3] Pilate offers the release of "the King of the Jews." Soldiers declare, "Hail, King of the Jews."	Jesus asks, "Are you saying this on your own initiative or did others tell you about me?" Later, Pilate would place a multilingual sign declaring, "Jesus of Nazareth, King of the Jews."
(20.11–17) Jesus speaks to Mary Magdalene, after his resurrection.	Mary cries, "My Lord, Rabboni," "The Lord."	Jesus tells Mary, ". . . I ascend to my Father and your Father,[4] and my God and your God."
(20.26–29) Jesus speaks to Thomas, eight days after his first post-resurrection appearance to the disciples.	Thomas declares, "My Lord and my God."	Here is unequivocal testimony to John's high Christology, one that posits deity to Jesus, the Messiah.
(21.15–23) Jesus and Peter at the Sea of Galilee.	Peter addresses him as "Lord" five times.	The title "Lord" is consistent with faith in Jesus as the Christ and resurrected Lord.

   3. Pilate's query concerns whether Jesus claimed to be the Jewish Messiah. The Jews expected a Davidic Messiah-King prophesied in Ps 118.25 and Zech 9.9. The former passage is shouted by the crowds at Jesus' triumphal entry and the latter is John's elaboration that confirms this identity (12.13–14).

   4. This is the first and only time in John's gospel where this phrase is used of the believers' relationship with God.

GROUP ENCOUNTERS (CORPORATE FOCUS)

Passage and Person(s) Encountered	Title/Name or Descriptor of Jesus	Commentary and Theological Significance
(6.41–59) The (grumbling) Jews near or at Capernaum.	Jesus is the bread that came down from heaven. He declares, "I am the bread of life"; "the living bread that came down from heaven"; "Unless you eat the flesh of the Son of Man and drink His blood, you have no life in yourselves."	Jesus teaches unequivocally that he is the source and substance of eternal life . . . That eternal life hinges on their belief in him.

Episodes of Personal Encounter

Passage and Person(s) Encountered	Title/Name or Descriptor of Jesus	Commentary and Theological Significance
(7.2–9) Jesus and his unbelieving brothers.	None	Jesus does indicate that he is operating under a divinely orchestrated plan and the time of revealing himself publicly ("my time") was not yet.
(7.11–24; cf. 7.2) Jesus and the Jews at the Feast of the Jews.	None	Jesus responds to their astonishment over his teaching. His teaching is not his own nor given at his own initiative, nor given to seek his own glory, but the One who sent him.
(8.13–47) Jesus speaks to the Pharisees and Jews in the temple.	Jesus says, "I am he who bears witness of myself," which is corroborated by the "Father who bears witness of Me." Jesus says, "I am from above . . . I am not of this world . . ."; "Unless you believe that I am, you will die in your sins." Jesus refers to himself as the Son who brings freedom, and he describes himself as one who "proceeded forth and has come from God," yet not on his own initiative, "but He sent me."	The Pharisees are offended at what they perceive as improper self-witness, but Jesus defends the legitimacy of that witness because it is corroborated by the Father. The validity of Jesus' witness hinges on his origin and the fact that he speaks and does nothing on his own initiative, but only what he has seen and heard from the Father and what the Father teaches. In vv. 18, 23, 24, "I am" appears in the emphatic form. Identification with the OT designation of Yahweh seems probable, especially as it constitutes the confession that saves the believer in v. 24.
(9.40—10.18) Jesus and the Pharisees in the wake of his healing of the man born blind.	Jesus refers to himself, "I am the door of the sheep" or "the door"; "I am the good shepherd," the one who lays down his life on his own initiative, having the authority to lay it down and take it back again, an authority he received from the Father.	The issue at hand is the legitimacy of Jesus' messianic identity as the good Shepherd, an oft-used metaphor to describe Yahweh's relationship to his people in the OT and later a messianic metaphor (cf. Jer 23.1–5; Ezek 34.23ff.; Zech 13.7).

89

But These are Written . . .

Passage and Person(s) Encountered	Title/Name or Descriptor of Jesus	Commentary and Theological Significance
(10.22–39) Jesus speaks to the Jews at the Feast of Dedication.	The Jews ask Jesus to plainly declare if he is the Christ. Jesus declares that he works "in [his] Father's name," which testify of him. Jesus gives eternal life to his sheep and they will never perish, and no one will snatch them out of his hand. Jesus says, "My Father . . . has given (his sheep) to me," and "no one is able to snatch them out of my Father's hand." Jesus says, "I and the Father are one." Jesus questions the Jews' charge of blasphemy based on his claim, "I am the Son of God." Jesus does the works of his Father so that they may know that the Father is in him and he is in the Father.	Jesus indirectly answers their question by inferring that God has already answered their question by revealing his works in his name through Jesus. The unity of divine action between Jesus and the Father confirms Jesus' declaration that he and the Father are one. What can be said of the Father can be said of his son, Jesus. Moreover, the works of Jesus demonstrate the abiding unity and mutual indwelling of the Father and the Son.
(11.3–16) Jesus speaks to his Disciples on the eve of the resurrection of Lazarus.	Mary and Martha send word, "Lord . . . he whom you love is sick." Jesus declares that the sickness is not unto death, but "for the glory of God" and "that the Son of God may be glorified." Here, the disciples address Jesus as "Rabbi" and "Lord."	Note the parallelism in this anticipated miracle. It is equally for the glory of God and that the Son of God may be glorified.
(12.27–36) Jesus to the multitude in Jerusalem after his teaching on the arrival of "the hour" that has come "for the Son of Man to be glorified."	In prayer, Jesus twice addresses God as "Father," which is followed by a voice from heaven. The multitude asks him about the permanence of the Christ who the Law says is to remain forever. Jesus referred to himself as "the Son of Man" who "must be lifted up." They ask, "Who is this Son of Man?"	Note the multitude's reference to the "Law" in the broad sense of Scripture. The reference to the Law's witness to the permanence of the Christ has possible antecedents (cf. Ps 110.4; Isa 9.7; Ezek 37.25; Dan 7.14).

THE QUESTION OF JESUS' MESSIANIC IDENTITY

The words of John 20.31 provide a convenient purpose statement of John's gospel: "but these have been written that you may believe that Jesus is the Christ, the Son of God; and that believing you may have life in His name." It also reveals that faith and Christology are the main focus of the author-narrator in John's gospel.[8] Consequently, it behooves us to ask what Jesus said or declared about himself according to John. In accord with our analytical lens, moreover, we ask, "What did others say to and about him?" Together these two perspectives allow us to test our hypothesis that John has used personal encounters as a literary vehicle to transport his Christology. If so, what is revealed about Christ through this strategy?

What do the selected encounters reveal about Jesus' self-awareness? The question is intriguing and relevant to the entire debate over whether Jesus possessed a messianic self-consciousness. Many doubt he did, claiming that what is reflected in the gospels is the creation of the post-resurrection church imposed on the text.[9] This hypothesis is hard to maintain from our analysis. Postponing momentarily what Jesus is reported to have said about himself, it is clear that among those whom Jesus encountered the issue was very much in the forefront of their minds. This is to be expected as the so-called first quest for the historical Jesus made it clear that the first-century world of Palestinian Judaism was thoroughly apocalyptic in its eschatology with a strong sense of expectant messianism.[10] Our inductive study supports this conclusion. Those who come to Jesus will either express faith in him as the Messiah, or pose a question regarding his messianic identity. Even the priests and Levites who came to the Baptist did so to ascertain whether he claimed to be "the Christ." The Baptist's denials are juxtaposed to a shocking messianic declaration. Jesus is "the Lamb of God who takes away the sin of the world."[11] But consider who came to Jesus with such questions or predispositions:

---

8. A. Barus, "The Structure of the Fourth Gospel," *AJT* 21/1 (April 2007) 99.

9. L. Strobel's interview with B. Witherington III presents a helpful synopsis of this issue. See *The Case for Christ* (Grand Rapids: Zondervan) 132–42. Witherington also critiques the position of those who believe that Jesus' messianic self-consciousness is an invention of the early church and not reflective of the historical Jesus.

10. See G. A. Boyd's discussion of the Quest as pursued by Reimarus, Lessing, and Schweitzer, in *Cynic, Sage, or Son of God?* (Wheaton, IL: Victor, 1995) 20–24.

11. This declaration seems to combine the imagery of the Passover Lamb and messianic prophecy of Isa 53.7. The high priestly ministry of the Messiah is depicted by Joshua in Zech 3.3–5, who is then connected to another messianic figure, the Servant of the Lord, the Branch (v. 8) who will remove the iniquity of the land in one day. It is hard not to see in this Branch metaphor prophesies of Jeremiah concerning the

But These are Written . . .

THE PERCEPTION OF SEEKERS, DISCIPLES AND DETRACTORS

1. Those who specifically use the titles "Christ" or "Messiah" in their exchange with Jesus: Andrew (1.41); The Samaritan woman (4.25, 29); Martha (in a confession of faith—11.17–39); Jews at the Feast of Dedication (10.24); and the multitude in Jerusalem (12.34).

2. Those who use other messianic titles or descriptions: John the Baptist—"The lamb of God who takes away the sin of the world" (1.29); Philip—"the one whom Moses in the Law and also the prophets wrote" (1.45); Nathaniel—"'the Son of God' . . . the king of Israel" (1.49); Simon (Peter)—"the Holy One of God" (6.68); Martha—"the Son of God," even "he who comes into the world"[12] (12.27); Pilate (asks of his identity) and the Roman soldiers (in mockery)—"the king of the Jews" (18.39; 19.3).

What is fascinating to observe is that John places messianic titles and descriptors not only on the lips of those who were disciples and soon-to-be disciples, but on those who were not, and even those who stood in staunch opposition to Jesus. This indicates that the question of Jesus' messianic identity was certainly a prominent concern that prompted their questions and motivated them to seek him out. Those who deny Jesus a messianic consciousness claim the church edited not only his words, but the words of all those who interacted with him, creating the illusion that the people he interacted with were concerned with his messianic identity, a concern that was never there to begin with.[13]

Messiah, whom he identifies as "the righteous branch of David" who executes justice and righteousness (33.5; cf. 23.5). Moreover, his coming appears as part and parcel with the New Covenant promise (31.27–34) which culminates with a definitive and permanent remedy to the sin problem.

12. This description falls into the motif of Jesus as the "one sent by the Father," which P. Anderson argues is a major motif in John's gospel that legitimates the Johannine Jesus as the messianic agent who speaks and acts for God. See P. N. Anderson, "The Having-Sent-Me Father: Aspects of Agency, Encounter and Irony in the Johannine Father-Son Relationship," *Semeia* 85 (1999) 34–36.

13. This degree of "creative redaction" strains all limits of credulity when we witness the historical evidence of the suffering and persecution the church was, in very short order, willing to endure to propagate their own mythological creation!

THE SELF-PERCEPTION OF JESUS

To be sure, most of what we learn of John's Christology in these encounter episodes comes from the words of Jesus himself. His messianic self-consciousness is evident both by the titles he accepts, or those he gives to himself, and what he says descriptively about himself.

Son of Man

The "Son of Man" is a title that has drawn considerable attention of scholars, especially as it is used in the Synoptic Gospels.[14] The historical authenticity of these sayings in John can be defended, but that issue is secondary to our purpose. Our primary goal is to analyze how John uses the title and to determine if his use carries messianic import. We should note that like the Synoptic authors, the title is used almost exclusively by Jesus.[15] A summary of our findings are as follows:

1. The messianic import of the title is beyond dispute in 1.51, as Jesus is responding to Nathaniel's declaration that Jesus is the "Son of God" and "the King of Israel." In his response, Jesus uses the title with language that invokes the transcendent heavenly "Son of Man" figure of Dan 7.13ff. Using enigmatic language he asserts that Nathaniel will witness a theophanic revelation where angels ascend and descend upon "the Son of Man."

2. In his encounter with Nicodemus, Jesus identifies himself as "the Son of Man" who has descended from heaven (3.13). This again evokes images of the transcendent "Son of Man" portrayed in Dan 7.13ff., which found ample messianic use in the apocalyptic Jewish literature as well as in the NT (cf. Matt 10.23; 16.28; 19.28; Mark 8.38; 13.26; 14.62; Luke 12.8, 40; 17.30; 22.67, 69).

---

14. As early as the 1960s, there was enough written on the topic to warrant scholarly surveys. See I. H. Marshall, "The Synoptic Son of Man Sayings in Recent Discussion," *NTS* 12 (1966) 327–51; R. Marlow, "The Son of Man in Recent Journal Literature," *CBQ* 28 (1966) 20–39; a later and helpful survey of the literature appeared in F. F. Bruce, "The Background to the Son of Man of Sayings," in *Christ the Lord*, ed. H. H. Rowdon (Downers Grove, IL: IVP, 1982) 50–69.

15. The title appears twelve times in John and always by Jesus of himself with the one exception of the Jerusalem Jews in (12.34) who are parroting his words in a question. It is interesting to note that the title is not used by the early church as a title of Jesus, a fact that supports its authenticity if the redaction criticism criterion of dissimilarity be accepted.

But These are Written . . .

3. To the Jews at the feast, Jesus asserts his delegated authority from the Father to execute a final and eschatological judgment "because he is 'the Son of Man'" (6.40).

4. To the multitude by the Sea of Galilee, Jesus declares that "the Son of Man" provides bread that endures to eternal life (6.27).

5. In his exchange with the blind man, now healed, Jesus asks him if he believes in "the Son of Man" (9.35) the messianic import of which is provided by the immediate context (esp. v. 22).

6. To Andrew and Philip (12.23)[16] Jesus says that it is the hour for "the Son of Man" to be glorified, speaking of his death, by which the Father would glorify his name.

7. Jesus is understood by the multitude to say that "'the Son of Man' must be lifted up" (12.34). In context this is a conflation of vv. 23 and 32. Their question regarding "the Christ" shows that this use of "Son of Man" is messianic.

JESUS: THE SENT ONE FROM THE FATHER

P. N. Anderson has argued convincingly that Deut 18.15–22 is critical to understanding the Johannine Father-Son relationship in his gospel.[17] This dominant theme which appears in all major parts of John including narrative, controversy dialogues, and discourse supports his case. The influence of the Deuteronomic passage is demonstrated by what he calls "associative links and parallels to every part of its thematic outline."[18] While his treatment of the subject extends beyond the present analysis, it identifies Jesus as that prophet-like Moses whose ministry can only be rightly understood if Jesus fulfills the role of God's divine agent sent to speak and act for God. Anderson draws eight comparisons between Deut 18.18–22, five of which are found prominently in the encounter episodes in John.

1. That God will raise up for himself a prophet like me (Deut 18.15a, 18a)—Jesus closely identifies with Moses in five of our episodes: John 1.17, 45; 3.14; 5.45; 6.32. Our episodes reveal that Jesus was readily identified as a prophet—by Jesus himself (4.44) the Samaritan woman

---

16. It is not possible to say with certainty that the words of 12.23 were spoken to Andrew and Philip alone, or that his words reached the ears of the Greeks who had come to see him (v. 21).

17. See Anderson, "The Having Sent Me Father," 36–40.

18. Ibid., 36.

(4.19) the Jews (7.40) and the blind man (9.17). However, he is not only called "a prophet," but as "the prophet" (1.25) and "the prophet who is to come into the world" (6.14–15) a clear reference to the Deut 18 promise.

2. That this prophet must be heeded/listened to (Deut 15b)—because the Son is "the Son of Man" descended from heaven (John 3.13) comes from above and is above all (3.31) and bears witness to what he has seen and heard from the Father (3.36). Anyone who rejects his witness is rejecting the witness of the Father and will receive judgment (5.24; cf. 12.46–48).

3. Yahweh will put words into this prophet's mouth (Deut 18b)—Jesus declares that the words that he speaks come from God or are the words of the Father: John 3.32, 34; 7.16–18; 8.28; 12.48–50; cf. 5.19, 30. All but one of these references appears in the encounter episodes.

4. This prophet will speak all that Yahweh commands (Deut 18c)—Jesus, as we have seen, does nothing of his own initiative, and does only what he sees and hears from the Father (John 5.19; 8.28; 12.49). But also Jesus' obedience is complete. His words are the vehicle that brings eternal life, "therefore the things I speak, I speak just as the Father has told me" (12.50).

5. This prophet comes and speaks in the name of the Lord (Deut 19a) and those who reject his word, the Lord will hold accountable. Likewise, Jesus comes in the name of the Father (John 5.43) and the Lord (12.13) seeking to glorify the name of the Father (12.28). Therefore, those who reject his word are subject to judgment (5.24; 12.46–48).

Given the above parallels and comparisons, it is difficult not to conclude that Jesus in John laid claim to the fulfillment of the messianic prophet like-unto Moses. This identity was not simply co-opted but declared, recognized by others and demonstrated in both his words and works.

THE QUESTION OF JESUS' DIVINITY

John's gospel arguably evinces the highest Christology among all the gospels, and many contend, in all the NT. Synonymous with high Christology is the deity of Christ. Did Jesus claim to be divine, and if so, in what sense? Certainly no one who reads the Prologue of John's gospel (1.1–18) can deny that its author thought of Jesus as the divine Logos (1.1) the incarnate Word (1.14) the Son of God and the unique and unprecedented revelation of God (1.18).

But These are Written . . .

In our study of personal encounters there is evidence that John used occasions of encounter to declare his faith in Jesus, the divine Son of God. The evidence is multifaceted, coming not only from the mouth of his disciples, but from Jesus' teaching discourses in response to those he encountered.

The Perspective of Disciples

The title of address most often spoken in John is κύριος, κύριε in the vocative.[19] This title in John is overwhelmingly christological not secular, meaning something akin to "sir."[20] What stands out is that when directed at Jesus, the term is found overwhelmingly on the lips of his disciples or those who have come to *believe* in him in some special sense.[21] Remarkably, with regard to our present study, nearly ninety percent of such uses appear in the encounter passages or their immediate context.[22]

What did this address signify? Given its prevalence in the Greco-Roman world in referring to deities (or deified rulers) and its use in the LXX when referring to Yahweh, its application to Jesus elevates him above the status of human beings.[23] This seems evident when we examine what John records. Shortly after the Prologue we encounter the testimony of John the Baptist (1.32–34) who relates his observation of the descent of the Holy Spirit upon Jesus at his baptism. John relates that God had told him that "he upon whom you see the Spirit descending and remaining upon him, this is the one who baptizes in the Holy Spirit" (1.33). It is hard to miss the messianic association with Isaianic passages like 11.2–5; 32.15–20; 42.1–4; 44.3–4; 61.1–3. However, John concludes from his witness of Jesus' Spirit-anointing that "this is the Son of God" (John 1.34). This Messiah as Son of God connection was apparently well established as the very next witness, Nathaniel, identifies Jesus as the "Son of God" and "the King of Israel." Nathanael's titles may be viewed as programmatic for John who records Jesus'

---

19. It is found fifty-one times in John, applied to God (five times) to Jesus (forty-five times) and to Philip (one time).

20. Of the forty-five times it is used to refer to Jesus, only seven times could it be understood in the secular sense of "sir." When it is so used it is spoken to Jesus by people who are not yet believers (the Samaritan woman—4.1, 15, 19; the Capernaum official—4.49; the lame man at the Pool of Bethesda—5.7; the adulterous woman—8.11; the blind man who had not yet believed—9.36, [cf. 4.53]; the Greeks who asked to see Jesus—12.21 and by Mary Magdalene to the Lord, but thinking he was a garden keeper—20.15).

21. Thirty-eight of forty-five.

22. Thirty-nine of forty-five.

23. See BDAG, 576–77.

use of the Son-Father metaphor with a clear implication of deity throughout his gospel. Peter's reference to Jesus as the "Lord" who has "the words of eternal life" is elaborated by referring to him as "the Holy One of Israel" (6.68). This title appears twenty-seven times in Isaiah, and is often connected with the LORD, the *Tetragrammaton* for Yahweh in Second Isaiah.[24] Martha is another disciple who combines titles with messianic import that implies deity. She addresses Jesus as "Lord," and confesses her faith in him as "the Christ" and "the Son of God . . . who comes into the world" (John 11.21, 27). The climatic confession of Thomas in 20.28, "My Lord and my God," provides a declaration parallel to Nathanael's.[25] Finally, we have John's own confession embedded in his declared literary purpose: "but these have been written that you may believe that Jesus is the Christ, the Son of God; and that believing you may have life in his name" (John 20.31).

The Perspective of Jesus Himself

The preponderance of evidence for John's portrayal of the divine Christ comes from Jesus himself. It stems not only from the titles he appropriates, but also the descriptions of himself in relation to the Father, both in relationship and divine action and prerogative. Earlier, the connection was drawn between the "agency motif" of Jesus and the Father who sent him. The association with the messianic prophecy of Deut 18.15–22 was established, indicating that John was identifying Jesus as "the prophet-like-unto-Moses" whom God prophetically promised. But John portrays Jesus as much more than a prophet in his gospel.

THE FATHER-SON RELATIONSHIP

Jesus refers to himself as "Son" twenty-two times in John's gospel, always in regard to his relationship with the Father, whether stated or implied.[26] Twice in the encounter with Nicodemus Jesus refers to himself as the "only begotten Son." The use of the descriptor *monogenēs* sets Jesus apart as the *unique* Son of God, not rivaled by or compared with any other. The uniqueness of this relationship is soon developed by Jesus in several discourses. The unity

---

24. See 1.4; 5.19, 24; 10.20; 17.7; 29.19, 23; 30.11, 12, 15; 31.1; 37.23; 40.25; 41.14, 16, 20; 43.3, 14; 45.1; 47.4; 48.17; 49.7; 54.5; 55.5; 60.9, 14.

25. It seems possible that John has utilized a verbal conceptual *inclusio* that for the most part brackets his entire gospel.

26. See 3.16, 17, 18, 35, 36 (twice); 5.19 (twice); 20, 21, 22, 23 (twice) 25, 26; 8.36; 10.36; 11.4, 27; 14.13; 17.1 (twice).

of divine action is tied inextricably to the Son's unique relationship to the Father. He shares in the divine work—work that can only be thought of as the prerogative of deity. In 5.17 he says, "my Father is working until now, and I *myself* am working." The Jews did not miss the significance of this emphatic statement. They immediately sought to kill him because by calling God his Father; he was "making himself equal with God" (v. 18). The shared work between the Father and the Son includes "raising the dead" (5.20) made possible because both the Son and Father have life in themselves (5.26). Of course this is dramatically demonstrated in the raising of Lazarus. While every Jew understood that eschatological judgment was God's prerogative, the Father has delegated that role to the Son (5.25–27; cf. 6.40). The Son's words are the words of the Father, to accept him is to accept the Father. But what hinges on one's response places Jesus in a unique category. He is the "bread of God that comes down from heaven" and to eat (receive him and his teaching) results in eternal life, confirmed by being raised up on the last day (6.33–40). Peter confessed that no one but Jesus possessed "the words of eternal life" (6.68). Jesus would later confirm the validity of Peter's words to Martha when he stated, "I am the resurrection and the life" (11.25). It is hard to imagine a clearer declaration of divine authority that calls for an equation: Jesus did and will do what only God can do because he *is* God.

The above equation is a difficult one to place within the context of Judaism, so committed to monotheism (Deut 6.4). John gives us evidence that the doctrine of the Trinity needed to begin with the divine status of the Son. The trajectory from the church's Jewish roots needed to begin somewhere and John records the starting point—Jesus' own statements that indicate a unity of divine action that infers an equality of functional authority (5.20). Moreover, John goes even further as he chronicles Jesus' words that suggest an almost ontological union between the Father and the Son. To Philip's request, "show us the Father" (14.8) Jesus rebuffed him for his failure to realize that "he was in the Father and the Father was in him" (14.10). Moreover, his works indicated that the Father was abiding in him (14.11). Along these same lines, Jesus declared unambiguously, "I and the Father are one" (10.30). Some might respond that Jesus meant no more than that he and the Father are in agreement, but the context indicates otherwise. The Jews' objection to his words led them to take up stones for stoning. When Jesus asked for an explanation, they responded, ". . . because you, being a man, make yourself out *to be* God" (John 10.33).

JESUS—THE "I AM"

It is little wonder that scholars skeptical of John's Christology want to posit the "I am sayings" of John as an ecclesiastical redaction. A quick survey of these sayings demonstrates that Jesus is laying claim to deity in association with Yahweh of the OT. Keep in mind that the emphatic form is conspicuously reminiscent of Yahweh's disclosure of the divine name in Exod 3.14. In addition, the emphatic form is used in contexts that recall divine action or nature in the OT.

Divine Metaphors

1. "I am the bread of life . . . which came down from heaven" (John 6.34, 35; cf. Exod 16.4ff.).
2. "I am the light of the world" (John 8.12; cf. Ps 27.1).
3. "I am the door/gate of the sheep" (John 10.7, 8; cf. Pss 118–19).
4. "I am the good shepherd" (John 10.11, 14; cf. Ps 23).
5. "I am the resurrection and the life" (John 11.25; cf. Dan 12.2).
6. "I am the way, the truth and the life" (John 14.6; cf. Isa 40.3; Ps 31.5; Ps 42.8).
7. "I am the true vine/the vine" (John 15.1, 5; cf. Isa 5.1ff.).

"I Am" Statements of Identity:

1. "I am *he*" (i.e., the Messiah, who is called Christ; John 4.25–26).
2. "Unless you believe I am *he* you will die in your sins" (8.24).
3. "When you lift up the Son of Man (i.e., the Messiah) then you will know that I am *he*" (8.28).
4. "Truly, truly, I say to you, before Abraham was born, I am" (8.48).[27]
5. "From now on I am telling you before *it* comes to pass, so that when it does occur, you may believe that I am *He* (13.19).

---

27. The context of this saying indicates that Jesus is responding to a complaint concerning his having seen Abraham. Jesus response implies preexistence and was understood as implying a divine status, which was blasphemous to the Jews who again sought to stone him (v. 59).

But These are Written . . .

Again we note that all of the above "I am sayings" appear in our encounter episode passages or their immediate context of discourse.

CONCLUSION

Our preliminary investigation of the narrative discourses of John that include personal encounters suggests that he has constructed much of his gospel around these encounters. Despite various configurations offered, they feature prominently in John's christocentric introduction (1.1—2.11) his "Book of Signs" (2.1—12.50) the "Book of Glory" (11.1—20.29) and the Epilogue and conclusion (21.1–25).[28] Every significant christological title or description of Jesus is found in these encounter episodes. In them we find Jesus presented, portrayed and proclaimed as the eschatological prophet-like-unto-Moses, the Messiah, the Christ, the messianic Son of Man, the Son of God, the only begotten Son, the Savior of the World, the King of Israel, the Holy One of God and the *exalted* Lord. It is difficult to conceive that John did not intentionally employ personal encounter as the literary medium in which to advance his Christology, a Christology that is supreme in the NT.

---

28. For this breakdown and others, see Barus, "Structure of the Fourth Gospel," 96–99.

8

A New Look at an Old Problem
A Narrative Approach to John 7.37-39
PHILIP L. MAYO

I WOULD LIKE TO congratulate Ben Aker on his illustrious and extensive career as a NT scholar and professor. His contributions to the guild, the church, and the academic community worldwide are evidenced through his extensive publications and the personal testimonies of students who have been privileged to sit under his tutelage. I appreciate the opportunity to participate in honoring him through this celebration writing.

John 7.37-39 is one of the more perplexing passages in the Gospel of John and a plethora of scholarly articles has been written in an attempt to solve its rather enigmatic problems with little consensus.[1] One might ask, then, why bother to study a passage so thoroughly investigated? The primary approach of most articles and commentaries has been through the more traditional methods of textual and historical criticism. While these approaches have proven of some value in sorting out the issues of this text, the insights they have provided have been largely exhausted.

---

1. Note, e.g., the titles of the following articles, J. B. Cortés, "Yet Another Look at Jn 7.37-38," *CBQ* 29 (1967) 75-86; G. D. Fee, "Once More—John 7.37-39," *ExpTim* 89 (1978) 116-18. See also discussions in the following commentaries, C. K. Barrett, *The Gospel According to St. John: An Introduction with Commentary and Notes on the Greek Text*, 2nd ed. (Philadelphia: Westminster, 1978) 326-29; R. Schnackenburg, *The Gospel According to John*, 2 vols. (New York: Seabury, 1980) 2:152-57; C. S. Keener, *The Gospel of John: A Commentary*, 2 vols. (Peabody, MA: Hendrickson, 2003) 1:722-30.

But These are Written . . .

In the past fifty years of biblical studies several postmodern methodologies have been introduced into the discipline which have shed new light on these ancient texts. One of these methodologies that has yielded some very positive results for gospel studies has been narrative criticism. Unlike the historical critic who views the gospels as "windows" into history, the narrative critic regards the gospels as "mirrors"[2] that reflect a literary world in which meaning is found in front of the text, between the reader and the narrative.[3] This approach, however, does not imply indifference toward history. On the contrary, the narrative critic is concerned, especially in the case of ancient literature such as the gospels, with the culture and history of the original audience.[4] The narrative critic sees the gospels as pieces of literature whose authors have constructed a world in which plot, characters, irony, and symbolism all combine to usher the implied reader into the world of the implied author, and encourages the reader to adopt the perspective of the author, who leads the reader to a purposeful conclusion. In the case of the Gospel of John, the author's stated purpose can be found in 20.31, and the entire narrative marches toward this end.

Although John 7.37–39 has garnered considerable attention because of its complex textual and historical issues, what seems often ignored is the important role this text plays in the development of the Johannine narrative. In this one passage the author reaches a crescendo in his development of key narrative themes, symbolic imagery, and the revelation of Jesus as Messiah. It is the proposal of this essay that a narrative critical approach to John 7.37–39 will provide insight into the role of this passage in the narrative of the Fourth Gospel and, in turn, will offer an alternate way forward to finding a solution to the perplexing problems it presents.

---

2. R. A. Culpepper, *Anatomy of the Fourth Gospel: A Study in Literary Design* (Philadelphia: Fortress, 1983) 4, 236–37. Culpepper cites Krieger as the one who offers the metaphor of the text as a "mirror." See M. Krieger, *A Window to Criticism: Shakespeare's Sonnets and Poetics* (Princeton, NJ: Princeton University Press, 1964).

3. Culpepper, *Anatomy*, 4.

4. Mark Stibbe criticizes Culpepper and others for the "novelizing of the gospels," which he charges anachronistically foists on the gospels modern literary techniques. Stibbe tries to bring balance by pursuing narrative criticism with an eye toward history. This is what he calls "practical criticism," which takes into account the "natural background" of the gospels such as Jewish and Greek narrative forms. He weds historical and narrative criticisms in an attempt to view the texts as both mirrors and windows. M. W. G. Stibbe, *John as Storyteller: Narrative Criticism and the Fourth Gospel* (Cambridge: Cambridge University Press, 1992) 22–23, 75. Culpepper, *Anatomy*, 11, acknowledges that history and culture are still the concern of the narrative critic, but perhaps not as extensively as Stibbe would like.

STATEMENT OF PROBLEM

It is helpful to state at the outset the traditional exegetical issues John 7.37–39 presents and the proposed solutions that frequently come to the fore in commentaries and scholarly journals. There are essentially three exegetical questions[5] that have emerged and can be outlined as follows:

A. How should the text be punctuated? Should a full stop be placed after "let him/her drink" (πινέτω) or after "the one who believes in me" (ὁ πιστεύων εἰς ἐμέ)?[6]

B. Who is the referent of "his/her" (αὐτοῦ) in v. 38—Jesus or the believer?

C. What is the source of the OT quotation or allusion in v. 38?

Scholarly responses to these questions can essentially be divided into two camps. The first, which has gained in popularity among modern scholars,[7] is often called the Western interpretation, because of its support among Western church fathers. Those who support this view argue for punctuation that places a full stop after "the one who believes in me" (ὁ πιστεύων εἰς ἐμέ). This latter phrase, it is argued, forms a parallel expression (albeit awkward) with the previous "anyone is thirsty" (τις διψᾷ); such parallel expressions would be characteristic of an Aramaic style of teaching. The translation might read as follows, "If anyone is thirsty (τις διψᾷ) let that one come to me and let that one drink, the one who believes in me (ὁ πιστεύων εἰς ἐμέ)" (7.37; translation mine). Jesus is, thus, the referent of "his/her" (αὐτοῦ) in 7.38 and the source of the living water. The proponents of this view, then, search for an OT source text that reinforces such an image.

---

5. The issues with this passage certainly are not limited to these three questions but these are the major concerns that emerge in the majority of scholarly discussions. One additional question that may bear mentioning is where the writer understands Jesus' quotation to end, with 7.37 or 38? In other words, is the Scripture reference in 7.38 intended to be on the lips of Jesus? Most of the scholarly discussion seems to assume that it is part of Jesus' proclamation. G. Fee addresses this issue and persuasively argues through grammatical and stylistic points that 7.38 is intended to be part of Jesus' proclamation. See Fee, "Once More," 116–18.

6. Unless otherwise noted, all Scripture quotations are taken from NRSV.

7. E.g., Keener, *Gospel of John*, 1:728–30; G. R. Beasley-Murray, *John* (Mexico City: Thomas Nelson, 2000) 115–16; G. D. Kilpatrick, "The Punctuation of John VII.37–38," *JTS* 11 (1960) 340–42; Schnackenburg, *John*, 2:153–54, who observes this gain in popularity among "modern exegetes." Note too the translation change between the RSV and the NRSV the latter of which adopts the Western punctuation but retains the Eastern reading.

But These are Written...

Primary OT texts cited are Ezek 47.1–12 and Zech 14.1–9 (particularly 14.8 which references "living water").[8]

The second position is sometimes called the "traditional punctuation"[9] but it might equally be called the Eastern interpretation, since it is supported by a majority of Greek church fathers.[10] Those who support this interpretation place a full stop after "let him/her drink" (πινέτω) and they posit "the one who believes in me" (ὁ πιστεύων εἰς ἐμέ) as the referent for "his/her" (αὐτοῦ) which implies that it is out of the believer, rather than Jesus, that the living water flows. They too seek out an OT passage that might support the imagery of the text.

In the final analysis, both sides of this debate have persuasive arguments principally built on manuscript evidence, the testimony of the church fathers, and grammatical arguments. However, none of these has proven decisive and, therefore, a fresh approach is warranted. Narrative criticism offers this fresh approach. Through careful consideration of the narrative plot and the development of symbolism, particularly the water symbolism of the Fourth Gospel, one can arrive at a possible response to the interpretive questions that have plagued this text, and also will be able to see the role of this text in ushering the reader toward adopting the point of view of the author that Jesus is the Messiah, the Son of God (20.31).

THE PLOT THICKENS

Much of the chronology in the Fourth Gospel centers on the Jewish calendar (e.g., 2.23; 5.1; 6.4; 7.2; 10.22; 12.1, 12; 13.1) and it is the only canonical gospel that records Jesus' attendance at all major Jewish feasts except Purim. John's centering of Jesus' activities around the Jewish festivals serves his theological agenda, revealing Jesus as the fulfillment of the faith and hope of

---

8. Many other OT texts have been brought into the discussion as well as texts from the Dead Sea Scrolls and the Aramaic Targumim; however, the two texts above seem to be the primary texts cited and are supported by later rabbinic sources (e.g., *t. Suk.* 3.1–18). See Keener, *Gospel of John*, 1:725–26, for a full discussion. For an argument in favor of an Aramaic source see M. E. Boismard, "De son ventre couleront des fleuves d'eau (Jo., VII, 38)" *RB* 65 (1958) 524 ; cf. C. C. Torrey, *The Four Gospels: A New Translation* (London: Hodder and Stoughton, 1947) 323.

9. So called by G. Balfour and G. Fee. See G. Balfour, "The Jewishness of John's Use of the Scriptures in John 6:31 and 7:37–38," *TynBul* 46/2 (Nov 1995) 369; Fee, "Once More," 116.

10. It is recognized, however, that the geographical lines for either interpretation are not rigid. E.g., Schackenburg, *John*, 2:153, notes that some Western fathers adopted the Eastern interpretation (e.g., Ambrose, Jerome, Augustine).

Israel.¹¹ In fact, as Gail O'Day demonstrates, the entire Johannine narrative is designed as a revelatory vehicle for the person of Jesus.¹² This is clear from the purpose outlined in 20.31 and demonstrated through the presentation of Jesus' miracles as "signs," the lengthy discourses with the "Jews,"¹³ and the creative use of irony and symbolism.

Chronological time, however, is not nearly as important as narrative time. Culpepper, in his analysis of the Fourth Gospel, distinguishes between "story time" and "narrative time."¹⁴ Story time corresponds approximately to chronological time or "the duration of Jesus' ministry as John records it."¹⁵ "Narrative time, on the other hand, is determined by the order, duration, and frequency of the events in the narrative."¹⁶ With regard to duration, narrative time can pass very quickly or slowly and methodically. This kind of time variation is purposeful and creates an effect on the reader. The speed of time is generally marked by how closely narrative length corresponds to the passage of story time. For example, speeches and monologues, which occupy a large portion of the narrative, tend to correspond to an equal amount of story time, while summary statements can cover a large amount of story time in brief narrative space. Culpepper observes that the Johannine narra-

---

11. For a fuller discussion of the significance of the Jewish feasts in John, see G. R. Beasley-Murray, *John* (Dallas: Word, 1989) 69–85.

12. G. O'Day makes a cogent argument that the Evangelist has constructed the narrative in such a way as to make it a vehicle of revelation. She argues this in contradiction to Bultmann's existential approach to the revelation of Jesus in John. Bultmann, she argues, believes that Jesus is revealed, not through his words or actions (the *Was* of the narrative) but when characters come into a personal encounter with Jesus (the *Dass* of the revelation). O'Day rejects this dichotomy and argues for the "how" (*Wie*) of the revelation. G. R. O'Day, "Narrative Mode and Theological Claim: A Study in the Fourth Gospel," *JBL* 105 (1986) 668. See also her more extensive discussion in *Revelation in the Fourth Gospel: Narrative Mode and Theological Claim* (Philadelphia: Fortress, 1986).

13. The "Jews," as the narrator and the author of the Fourth Gospel refer to them, is a somewhat mysterious group who serve as a foil or protagonist for Jesus' ministry. There are seventy references to them in the gospel and considerable scholarly discussion has ensued over whom the historical counterpart might be for the "Jews." It seems multiple characters in the narrative adopt the role of the "Jews," who appear, at times, to be the crowd and at other times the Jewish authorities, and more specifically the Pharisees. Regardless of the historical referent, as Culpepper notes, from a narrative point of view this group is associated with "the world" of unbelief in John. Therefore, the designation cannot represent all Jews, since John clearly demonstrates that some Jews believe (e.g., 8.41; 11.45).

14. Culpepper, *Anatomy*, 53–54. Culpepper credits G. Genette, *Narrative Discourse: An Essay in Method*, trans. J. E. Lewin (Ithaca, NY: Cornell University Press, 1980) with this terminology.

15. Culpepper, *Anatomy*, 53.

16. Ibid., 54.

tive tends to slow down as one approaches Jesus' hour, defined in John as Jesus' crucifixion.[17]

John's gospel includes the mention of three Passover feasts (2.13—3.21; 6.4–65; 13.1—19.42). Allowing for some time before and after the first and last feasts, the gospel narrative covers approximately two and one half years of Jesus' ministry. The first year of story time, marked by the mention of the first Passover in 2.13 and the second in 6.4, passes fairly rapidly. Only brief episodes are recounted, which generally occur over perhaps a few days. There is the night encounter with Nicodemus in 3.1-15, and in 3.22 the reader is only told that "some time" has passed in Judea before Jesus returns to Galilee. There is the two to three day visit to Sychar in Samaria (4.3–42) and in 5.1 the reader learns that Jesus has returned to Judea and spends perhaps a week at an unnamed feast in Jerusalem (5.1-47).

Year two, marked by the mention of the second Passover (6.4) occupies a much larger portion of the narrative (6.1—12.50)[18] than the previous year, and provides the reader with greater detail. One can follow Jesus from Passover two (6.1-70) through the Feast of Tabernacles (7.1—10.21) in the fall of the year, and to the Feast of Dedication in the winter (10.22–42). John 11 covers events that lead up to the third Passover, first mentioned in 12.1, and which arrives in 13.1. While most of the events of the second year take place over a few days or a week, these events take on greater significance because they fill more narrative time.[19]

By the time the reader reaches the beginning of ch. 12, story time, as well as narrative time, begin to slow considerably. John 12–20 covers a period of about one week while chs. 13–19 are dedicated to approximately a twenty-four hour period. Clearly the events surrounding Jesus' death and resurrection are the climax of the narrative, and the adjustment in narrative time creates this dramatic emphasis. Since the Prologue of ch. 1, this climactic conclusion has been intimated. The entire narrative looks toward Jesus' "hour" (first mentioned in 2.4) when he will be "glorified" (first mentioned in 7.39).

Next to the Passover scenes, the Feast of Tabernacles' events are the most important of the narrative. The events of the Feast, in the second year of Jesus' ministry, begin in 7.2 and continue without interruption in

---

17. Ibid., 71–72.

18. Ibid., 72, Culpepper delineates the narrative's second year as beginning at 6.66 and concluding with 12.50, thus, he remarks that the second narrative year is comprised of 295 verses. It is not clear why he begins the second year at 6.66 since the second Passover is mentioned in 6.4 and there seems to be a clear narrative time break in 6.1.

19. The preceding outline of years one and two is based on Culpepper's discussion with some modification. See Culpepper, *Anatomy*, 71–72.

narrative time through 10.21.[20] Thus, outside of the final Passover of chs. 13–19, the Feast of Tabernacles occupies the largest single portion of the Johannine narrative, making the Tabernacles narrative highly significant. The Tabernacles narrative continues to develop the plot of the Fourth Gospel along two important lines. First, conflict between Jesus and his opponents[21] continues to augment. In fact, the narrator helps the conflict motif along by stating at the outset of the Tabernacles narrative that "after this Jesus went about in Galilee. He did not wish to go about in Judea because the Jews were looking for an opportunity to kill him" (7.1). Unfortunately, the nearness of the Feast of Tabernacles forces Jesus to go up to Jerusalem. The gospel has consistently portrayed Jesus as a law-abiding Jew and attendance at the various festivals is not only his duty but also is an integral part of his self-revelation. While the conflict between Jesus and his opponents grows intense at the Feast, since it is not yet his "hour" (7.30) Jesus will not meet his demise. Such will not be the case at the forthcoming Passover.

The second line of development in the Tabernacles narrative is the continued revelation of Jesus. This revelation becomes more detailed as narrative time has already begun to slow. Long dialogues with the crowd leave many divided as to who Jesus is. Some believe, while others refuse. This division among the crowd only continues that begun among Jesus' closest followers in ch. 6. Even the Twelve, whom Jesus has chosen, are challenged (6.67). Ironically in this crucible of conflict, abandonment, and doubt, comes on the lips of Peter, the confession of the Fourth Gospel's idyllic believer, "We have come to believe and know that you are the Holy One of God" (6.69; cf. 20.31).

Chapter 6 leaves the reader with the near abandonment of Jesus by his closest followers while ch. 7 commences with the disbelief of his own brothers. Jesus is goaded by his brothers to go up to the Feast because "no one who wants to be widely *known* acts in secret . . . *show* yourself to the world" (7.4; emphasis mine). Jesus promptly tells them he is not "going up" (ἀναβαίνω) to the Feast because "my time is not yet come" (7.6, 8). This statement is laced with double entendre characteristic of the Johannine narrative. While on the surface Jesus and his brothers discuss the right moment for him to go up to the Feast, Jesus speaks cryptically of the moment when he will be "lifted up" (3.14; 8.28; 12.32) on the cross after which he will "go up" (ἀναβαίνοντα) "to where he was before" (6.62).

---

20. The *pericopae adulterae* which occupies 7.53–8.11 is excluded from consideration, since it is not likely original to the Gospel of John.

21. These opponents are variously identified as the "Jews," Pharisees, or simply as the crowd.

But These are Written . . .

This brief dialogue between Jesus and his brothers continues a dichotomy that runs through the Fourth Gospel narrative and sets the scene for the running conflict of the Tabernacles narrative. This dichotomy, first intimated in the Prologue (1.10) is the distinction between those who are from below and the one who is from above (3.31; 8.23). Those who are from the earth do not understand the one who is from above. The dichotomy in the narrative is often developed through the author's use of irony. Jesus' brothers have goaded him to go up to the Feast in order to make himself "*known*" and to "*show*" himself to the world (7.4). Ironically, this is exactly Jesus' mission and what he accomplishes later at the Feast.

This use of irony continues in Jesus' dialogue with the crowd in ch. 7. The crowd is divided over whether Jesus is the Messiah. "We know where this man is from" they say, "but when the Messiah comes, no one will know where he is from" (7.27). This remark prompts an outcry[22] from Jesus, "You know me, and you know where I am from. I have not come on my own. But the one who sent me is true, and you do not know him" (7.28). Jesus, of course, speaks of his heavenly origins and will later speak of his return to the Father (7.33–34). The crowd, however, continues to fixate on his earthly existence. Jesus' heavenly origin and Godly mission are completely lost on them. The crowd further speculates, "Surely the Messiah does not come from Galilee, does he? Has not the Scripture said that the Messiah is descended from David and comes from Bethlehem, the village where David lived" (7.41–42)? Ironically, this is Jesus' earthly heritage but even the crowd is ignorant of that. While the Johannine narrative never speaks elsewhere of Jesus as a descendent of David or his birth in Bethlehem, this irony is not likely lost on the implied reader as both the implied reader and implied author probably share this knowledge.

In the midst of this tense exchange between Jesus and the crowd comes the self-revelatory passage of John 7.37–38. This is a central passage in the Tabernacles narrative, indeed, in the entire gospel. There are several reasons for suggesting its centrality. First, this declaration is one of only four "call or cry out" (κράζω) statements in the gospel and the second within the Tabernacles narrative. Already mentioned above is the κράζω statement of 7.28 in which Jesus cries out in the temple area concerning his origin. The first and fourth κράζω statements are found on the lips of John the Baptist (1.15) and Jesus respectively (12.44). What is interesting about these last two is that they seem to form an inclusio for the ministry portion of the gospel narrative (chs. 2–12).[23]

---

22. This is the second of four "call or cry out" (κράζω) statements in the gospel which are discussed later.

23. Dodd refers to this section as the Book of Signs. See C. H. Dodd, *The*

The paucity of the verb κράζω in the gospel and its use in addition to the standard Greek verbs of direct speech[24] seem to advance these declarations to a higher level of significance. Schnackenburg writes that the use of κράζω here "draws attention to the revelatory character of [Jesus'] words, to be heard throughout all the ages."[25] Perhaps these moments of declaration serve to strengthen the testimony motif[26] of the gospel and subtly remind the reader of the OT personification of Wisdom, who "call[s]," who "raise[s] her voice" (Prov 8.1) and who invites all who will to heed her message and to come and "eat of me" and "drink of me" (Sir 24.21; John 6.35, 54-55).[27] Clearly, Jesus' declaration of John 7.37-38 is an important revelatory moment in the narrative of which the reader needs to take note.

A second indication of the significance of 7.37-38 can be found in the time marker inserted by the narrator at 7.37. The narrator informs the reader that Jesus stood up in the temple courts and made his declaration "on the last day, the greatest of the Feast" (7.37; translation mine). The significance of Jesus making his declaration as this point in the Feast likely has a symbolic relationship to the water libation associated with the Feast (discussed more fully later) and, in addition, may take advantage of the Feast's eschatological overtones. It is possible that the narrator attempts to reinforce the eschatological significance through use of the phrase "on the last day" (Ἐν δὲ τῇ ἐσχάτῃ ἡμέρᾳ) but this is uncertain. As noted earlier, the author has a propensity for double meaning and it is possible that this phrase is intended to add emphasis to a declaration already full of eschatological nuance.[28]

The final two reasons that speak to the significance of 7.37-38 will be seen through an examination of the water symbolism developed throughout the Johannine narrative and the narrator's commentary of 7.39. Water

---

Interpretation of the Fourth Gospel (Cambridge: Cambridge University Press, 1953) 383-89.

24. In the first three instances of the use of κράζω it is also accompanied by the participle "saying" (λέγων, 1.15; 7.28; 7.38) and in the final instance by the aorist of "said" (λέγω, εἶπεν, 12.44).

25. Schnackenburg, *John*, 2:146.

26. A number of scholars have recognized a testimony motif in the Fourth Gospel. See the rather extensive treatment in A. T. Lincoln, *Truth on Trial: The Lawsuit Motif in the Fourth Gospel* (Peabody, MA: Hendrickson, 2000).

27. See Keener, *Gospel of John*, 1:724. Also note Keener's remarks concerning wisdom offering "to pour out her spirit on those who prove receptive (Prov 1:23)." Keener proposes that such language may have brought to the mind of early believers the promise in Joel 2.28-29. See also J. Blenkinsopp, "The Quenching of the Thirst: Reflections on the Utterance in the Temple, John 7:37-9," *Scr* 12 (1960) 39-48, who views Jesus' outcry like that of personified wisdom.

28. See the comments in Keener, *Gospel of John*, 1:727.

is used as a vibrant symbol in a variety of ways throughout the gospel and its uses seem to coalesce in this passage. The importance of this symbol to the Johannine narrative will be discussed at length in the following section; however, it is sufficient at this point to say that the water symbolism holds a key to resolving some of the interpretive difficulties regarding this passage. This will become evident after studying the development of this symbol in the gospel and will be verified by the narrator's interpretation of Jesus' declaration in 7.39.

LIVING WATER FROM WITHIN

It is generally recognized that the Feast of Tabernacles has had historically a close association with the symbolic use of water.[29] The Feast was a great time of celebration marked by considerable ritual at which Israel celebrated God's blessings through the harvest and a time to seek God for abundant rains for the coming season.[30] The Feast looked back to the wilderness wanderings but it also looked ahead to the eschatological day of the Lord. The Scriptures read on the opening day of the Feast, Lev 23 and Zech 14, demonstrate this twofold perspective.[31] It is Zech 14.8 that offers the closest verbal parallel to Jesus' proclamation in John 7.37–38, since the prophet uses a similar expression concerning "living water" (ὕδωρ ζῶν) which flows out of eschatological Jerusalem.[32]

Each morning of the first seven days of the Feast a procession would descend to the pool of Siloam on the southeast side of the temple mount. A priest filled a golden flask with water from the pool while the choir recited Isa 12.3. He then led the processional back up to the holocaust altar through the Water Gate[33] while they sang the *Hallel* Psalms (113–18). When the procession reached the Water Gate a long blast was blown on the ram's horn. Once the procession reached the altar, they would circle the altar once and on the seventh day seven times. Those in the procession and the observing

---

29. Most scholarly commentaries as well as a number of journal articles discuss this close association, some of which are cited in this essay. See also J. L. Rubenstein, *The History of the Sukkot in the Second Temple and Rabbinic Periods* (Atlanta: Scholars, 1995) 47–49, 82.

30. *b. Taan.* 1.1; *t. Suk.* 3.18; cf. Zech 14.17.

31. *b. Meg.* 31a.

32. See *t. Suk.* 3.1–18 for an eschatological interpretation of the Feast's water libation based on Zech 14 and Ezek 47.

33. *t. Suk.* 3.3 notes that this gate received its name due to the libation ritual. Rubenstein suggests that this points to the prominence of this feast for the Jews. Rubenstein, *History of the Sukkot*, 120.

crowd held in their right hands the *lulab* and in their left hands the *ethrog*. While circling and reciting Ps 118.25, those in the procession would shake the *lulab* and throw them on the sides of the altar. The priest would then ascend on the south side of the altar in order to pour out the libation into one of two silver bowls prepared for the occasion.[34] After the priest had poured out the libation, the crowd would cry out, "lift up your hand," in order to affirm that the ritual was complete.[35]

It is likely that this water libation ceremony stands behind the moment of Jesus' invitation on "the last day, the greatest of the Feast."[36] The readers of the Fourth Gospel may have been aware of this background to the Feast but it is difficult to know.[37] On one hand the gospel's narrative, which is organized around the Jewish feasts, seems to require that the reader know something about these feasts. However, each time the feasts are mentioned they are identified with the qualifying phrase "of the Jews" (2.13; 6.4; 7.2; 11.55) or similar epigraph, suggesting that either the audience is not Jewish or that the writer is attempting to distance himself and the readers from the Jews. In addition, terms such as "Rabbi" (1.38) and "Messiah" (1.41) need to be interpreted, however, the title "Son of Man" (1.51) does not. The reader is also told that the Jewish Feast of Dedication takes place in the winter—something a Jew would not need to be told. On the other hand, the "day of Preparation" before the Passover (19.14), Sabbath regulations, and the expectation of a "prophet who is to come into the world" (6.14; cf. 1.21, 1.25) need no explanation.

---

34. R. Jehudah (Judah) states that they were actually plaster bowls that had been darkened by wine. See *m. Suk.* 4.9; *y. Suk.* 4.6.

35. For the preceding information see *m. Suk.* 4.9; *b. Suk.* 48a–b; *y. Suk.* 3.8—4.6. Although generally accepted, there is no extant source that unequivocally states that the water ceremony was practiced in the first century. The earliest references are rabbinic sources that date to the second century. However, these sources likely speak of a ritual that had long been in practice. Zechariah 14 may indicate that the libation was practiced in the post-exilic period and Josephus's comments concerning Alexander Jannaeus before the temple altar during the Feast may indirectly reference the libation ceremony (*A.J.* 13.372). See also, Rubenstein, *History of the Sukkot*, 160.

36. Which day the writer is referencing has been a matter of some debate. The Feast is known to have been an eight day festival (see Deut 16.13,15; Ezek 45.25; and *Jub.* 16.20–31 for a seven day festival, an eighth day is added in Lev 23.34–36; Num 29.12–39; 2 Macc 10.6; cf. Josephus, *A.J.* 3.245); however, the water libation was practiced only during the first seven days. The seventh day climaxed with the circumlocution of the altar seven times. The eighth day, which was a Sabbath, is acknowledged by the rabbis to be a day unto itself (*b. Suk.* 47a; 48a; cf. 4.1, 8–9). Jesus' invitation would be appropriate on either day but the seventh day seems more likely, since it is the day on which the water libation climaxes.

37. Culpepper, *Anatomy*, 220–22.

But These are Written . . .

Making sense of this diverse evidence is challenging. It may be that the audience for which the narrative was originally intended was quite familiar with Jewish customs and the narrator's explanations were added by a later redactor for a wider audience.[38] More than likely, however, the recipients of the Fourth Gospel were a heterogeneous audience of Jewish and Gentile believers still worshipping together.[39] This audience would have had a diverse understanding of both Jewish festivals and customs with some needing the narrator's insights. In the case of 7.37–38, whether or not the reader is familiar with the water libation of the Feast of Tabernacles does not hinder the reader from grasping the significance. The narrator's interpretive comment in 7.39 applies the text to all believers subsequent to Jesus' death and resurrection and is not for the purpose of clarifying some aspect of Jewish religious custom. In addition, central to the passage is the water symbolism, which has been extensively developed throughout the narrative and has prepared the reader for the passage's import.

Water as a religious symbol has a long and rich heritage. It is a symbol for cleansing in many faiths and in Jewish thought is also a symbol of creation, life, Torah, wisdom, and the Holy Spirit.[40] The symbol of water in John, as Culpepper writes, occurs "surprisingly frequently and with the most varied associations of any of John's symbols."[41] Like most symbols in the narrative, but perhaps more so the symbol of water, it tends to expand and become varied in meaning as the narrative progresses. The result is that by the time the reader reaches the latter half of the narrative any mention of the symbol affects the reader and sends them searching for a deeper meaning.[42]

While the symbol of water expands as the narrative develops, it should still be studied as a "connected whole,"[43] for its uses throughout the narrative are not unrelated. The water symbol first appears in ch. 1 in the baptism ministry of John who, as the eschatological forerunner of the Messiah, offers a cleansing rite that foreshadows the purification from sin that will

---

38. Mark Stibbe proposes this possibility as part of a three stage process in the construction of the gospel. Stibbe, who is himself a narrative critic, suggests the Fourth Gospel's Evangelist has constructed a narrative complete with symbolism, number patterns, irony and dualism, which is based on written and oral traditions passed down by the Beloved Disciple and later redacted and supplemented by another hand. See Stibbe, *John as Storyteller*, 5–22.

39. Although not his conclusion, Culpepper, *Anatomy*, 221, raises this possibility.

40. Dodd, *Interpretation*, 138.

41. Culpepper, *Anatomy*, 192.

42. Ibid., 192–95; W. Ng, *Water Symbolism in John: An Eschatological Interpretation* (New York: Peter Lang, 2001) 7–9.

43. Ng, *Water Symbolism*, 55.

ultimately be worked out in the ministry and death of Jesus. When John is questioned as to why he has come baptizing, he replies that it is so the Redeemer of Israel might be revealed (1.31). However, this Redeemer will not baptize with water but "baptizes with the Holy Spirit" (1.33). Thus, through the metaphor of water baptism a first link is made between the symbol of water and the Holy Spirit.

In ch. 2, water is again juxtaposed to the notion of purification. This time Jesus turns water, drawn from Jewish purification jars, into a better wine than any tasted thus far. Would space allow, much could be said about the significance of this entire pericope, both for the gospel narrative and for Jewish expectation. The narrator certainly wishes the reader to grasp its significance, when he remarks that Jesus thus "revealed his glory; and his disciples believed in him" (2.11).

In ch. 3, water appears in Jesus' dialogue with Nicodemus, a Jewish leader, who comes to Jesus at night to inquire of him. Jesus' response to his inquiry is to tell him that he cannot "see the kingdom of God without being born from above" (3.3). Nicodemus finds Jesus' statement incomprehensible and Jesus' response to him seems just as obscure. Jesus tells him that he must "be born of water and Spirit" (3.5).[44] Here, as in ch. 1, the water and the Spirit are once again closely associated. Thus far, water has been associated with the purification rite of baptism, which John the Baptist has said will be superseded by Spirit-baptism. In ch. 2, it was associated with the purification rites of the Jews and now once again with the Spirit. It is, in fact, this dialogue with Nicodemus that is pulling together (albeit in a rather

---

44. Interpreting the relationship between the water and the Spirit in this text has been a matter of considerable debate. There are essentially three possible interpretations. The first argues that water refers to natural birth. One must be birthed by natural and then spiritual means. Nicodemus comment in 3.4 reinforces this possibility. However, it seems an unlikely interpretation given that water is rarely associated with natural birth in ancient sources. In addition, Jesus' statement seems somewhat absurd, since Nicodemus would clearly recognize that a person would have to experience natural birth to have any chance to enter God's kingdom. A second, and rather popular interpretation, is that it is a reference to baptism. Nicodemus could have possibly understood this kind of ritual cleansing as a starting step, but a sacramental reading of Christian baptism would be anachronistic. A third possibility is that this phrase is epexegetical. This interpretation has to its advantage that it is consistent with the symbolism of the gospel. If this interpretation is correct, John 3.5 takes one more step in uniting water symbolism with the Spirit that finds its culmination in 7.37–39. See L. Belleville, "'Born of Water and Spirit': John 3:5," *TrinJ* 2 (1980) 140–41, who does not adopt the epexegetical interpretation but does observe that such "syntactical parallels" do occur in John, e.g., "Spirit and truth" (4.23) and "spirit and life" (6.63). See also G. T. Manning Jr., *Echoes of a Prophet: The Use of Ezekiel in the Gospel of John and in Literature of the Second Temple Period* (New York: T. & T. Clark, 2004) 186–87, who argues for an epexegetical view without excluding baptism as a secondary interpretation.

unusual way) these two concepts, Spirit renewal and purification, into a new birth that will be accomplished through the work of Jesus (3.14–15).

Following Jesus' dialogue with Nicodemus is a transition passage located in 3.22—4.2. Before recounting Jesus' dialogue with the woman at the well in ch. 4, the reader is updated on the baptism ministry of both John and Jesus. This return to the topic of baptism offers a seam that weaves together the events of the preceding chapters and provides transition to the following events. The reader is told in 3.25 that a dispute has erupted between John's disciples and a Jew[45] over the matter of Jewish purification. However, the reader is not told the reason for the debate or the resolution. What this brief statement does accomplish for the narrative, however, is to link the topic of baptism and purification together, thus reuniting these two topics first introduced in chs. 1 and 2. More important, this seam passage provides for the narrative a transition from the ministry of John the Baptist to that of Jesus. The reader is told that both are baptizing, but that "all are going" (3.26) to Jesus, and that he is "making and baptizing more disciples than John" (4.1). Although John's ministry continues to draw adherents (3.23) the author wants the reader to know that there is a clear shift in favor of Jesus, which John the Baptist affirms is proper (3.27–30).

The topic of Jesus' baptismal ministry creates a transition to the dialogue scene of ch. 4. The reader is told that the Pharisees have heard that Jesus is gaining and baptizing more disciples than John (4.1) which results in Jesus leaving Judea for Galilee. His return to Galilee necessitates (according to the narrator) that he pass through Samaria where he meets the woman of Sychar at Jacob's well. Despite the language of the seam passage, which states that Jesus was baptizing (3.22, 26) with water,[46] the narrator is careful to tell the reader (4.2) that Jesus actually did not baptize anyone, but it was his disciples who performed this water rite. The historical verisimilitude of the narrator's comment is not necessary to debate at this point; however, what is important is that the reader understands that Jesus' ministry is superior to that of John's (3.27–30) and perhaps more important, that Jesus' does not baptize with water because he "baptizes with the Holy Spirit" (1.33).

The association of the Spirit with water unites once again in Jesus' exchange with the woman at the well. In this setting the woman comes to the well in Sychar to draw water where she meets Jesus who, using the symbol of water, turns the conversation to matters of eternal significance. He tells her that he has "living water" (ὕδωρ ζῶν, 4.10; cf. Zech 14.8) to give that

---

45. Some ancient manuscripts contain the plural "Jews."

46. Note the use of the third person singular of the imperfect and present tenses in these two verses.

will become in the recipient "a spring of water gushing up to eternal life" (4.14). The woman fails, at first, to see the spiritual significance of what Jesus is saying and interprets his words on an earthly level. Like Nicodemus, she reasons like one from below and not like one from above. However, unlike Nicodemus, this story ends with the woman and many in her village believing in Jesus (4.39-42).

In chs. 5 and 6, water continues to appear in the narrative but in a less overtly symbolic way. As Ng observes, the water symbol seems to go underground only to return in a dramatic way in 7.37-38.[47] The dominant symbol in ch. 6 is bread, where the Passover feast provides the backdrop for Jesus' messianic claims. Reminiscent of Moses, Jesus not only demonstrates power over water by walking on it, but he also provides bread in the wilderness for God's people. This provision of bread, which in itself is a sign of his messianic claim, provides the setting for one of Jesus' extensive discourses with the "Jews." In this discourse, Jesus makes one of several "I am" (ἐγώ εἰμι) statements of the Gospel. "I am the bread of life" he proclaims. "Whoever comes to me will never be hungry, and whoever believes in me *will never be thirsty*" (6.35; emphasis mine). Even though the dominant symbol in this dialogue is bread, note here the subtle reintroduction of water as a symbol through the metaphor of thirst. This passage looks back to similar language used in the dialogue with the Samaritan woman, "those who drink of the water that I will give them *will never be thirsty*"[48] (4.14; emphasis mine) and looks ahead to the invitation to the thirsty of 7.37-38.

Jesus' declaration in 7.37-38 forms the climax of the water motif in the Fourth Gospel narrative. While it is not the final appearance of water in the gospel, it is here that the earlier and varied associations of water with the new life promised through the Spirit are brought together with the aid of the narrator's commentary in 7.39. The narrator's comment assures that the reader does not miss this significant narrative moment by providing the necessary interpretation of the water symbolism. Thus, it would seem that the water symbolism, which has already been developed since ch. 1, provides the interpretive key[49] for understanding Jesus' declaration and its meaning for the gospel narrative.

---

47. Ng, *Water Symbolism*, 66.

48. The Greek expression of 4.14 (οὐ μὴ διψήσει εἰς τὸν αἰῶνα) and 6.35 (οὐ μὴ διψήσει πώποτε) are not as identical as they appear in the English of the NRSV, however, the meaning is not seriously affected. It may be that εἰς τὸν αἰῶνα was used in 4.14a to provide a parallel expression with 4.14b "a spring of water gushing up to eternal life (εἰς ζωὴν αἰώνιον)" (translation mine).

49. G. Fee makes a similar assertion, although not from a particularly narrative approach. He writes concerning a solution to the interpretive issues of 7.37-38,

But These are Written . . .

It was observed earlier that at this point in the plot narrative time has slowed and conflict between Jesus and his opponents has stiffened. It is no accident that the setting of this conflict is the temple courts, the seat of Jewish religious authority and pride. The reader has already witnessed conflict between Jesus and the "Jews" within the temple courts in ch. 2, at which time Jesus drove out the money changers and merchants. This cleansing of the temple anticipates the conflict that develops later in the Johannine narrative and the ultimate glorification of Jesus. What is particularly important for the reader is that in foretelling his passion and resurrection Jesus likens his body to the temple of God when he says, "Destroy this temple, and in three days I will raise it up" (2.18). The crowd completely misunderstands the double entendre, but the narrator makes sure the reader does not (1.22). By likening his body to the Jewish temple, Jesus declares himself to be the presence of God incarnate in the midst of his people. This replacement of the temple in the work of Jesus is later reinforced in the dialogue with the woman at the well in which Jesus ultimately dismisses temple worship among either the Jews or Samaritans, for the true worshipper will worship God in "spirit and truth" (4.21–24).

The replacement of the temple with Jesus' presence and ministry forms the backdrop for his claims in 7.37–38. Those readers familiar with the eschatological implications of the Feast will understand Jesus' declaration not only within the narrative context but within the additional historical context of the water libation and the prophetic tradition of Zech 14.8 and Ezek 47.1–12. However, as observed earlier, lack of knowledge of this historical background does not limit the reader in gathering the import of this moment. The setting in the temple courts, the "call or cry out" (κράζω) statement, the increased tension developed in the extensive dialogue between Jesus and the crowd (and the crowd among themselves) and above all the water symbolism point to the declaration as a climactic moment in the Tabernacles narrative.

The narrator's comment of 7.39 delivers the explanation for understanding Jesus' invitation. It is as if the narrator pulls back the veil that partially obscures water as a narrative symbol for the Spirit. All of the references to water earlier in the gospel coalesce in this one comment. The reader has learned thus far that Jesus does not baptize with water, like John (4.2) but baptizes with the Holy Spirit (1.33). The reader has also come to recognize that water is equated with purification through its connection with the baptism of John (3.25); yet, it is the changing of the water in the Jewish purification jars into

---

"Therefore, since all other arguments are stalemated, and are usually resolved by what one thinks is more in accord with Johannine theology . . . The solution lies in verse 39" (Fee, "Once More," 117).

wine that also announces that Jesus has come to do something new and better (2.11).[50] In Jesus' exchange with Nicodemus, water is connected with spiritual birth from above (3.5) and at the well in Sychar it is the "gift of God" (4.10) given to all who come to Jesus. This gift is "living water" that will become in all who ask a "spring of water gushing up to eternal life" (4.14). In 7.39, the narrator reveals this water is the Holy Spirit.

Of course, this revelation of water as a symbol for the Holy Spirit has already been intimated in 1.33, but is most boldly anticipated in ch. 4, where the reader learns that spiritual deprivation is likened to physical thirst; yet this thirst can only be quenched by embracing who Jesus is (4.13–14). As the water motif develops beyond ch. 4, it becomes clear that both hunger and thirst are symbols of spiritual need (6.35; cf. 4.14a). By the time the readers reach Jesus' invitation of 7.37–38, they have come to understand that thirst is a metaphor for spiritual need which only Jesus can quench. Thus, the invitation in 7.38 goes out to all who are thirsty to come and drink. For the one who does drink, who accepts this gift from God (4.10) is the same as the one who believes, and within that believer "'shall flow rivers of living water'" (7.38; cf. 4.10, 14b). This "living water," first promised to the Samaritan woman and now promised to all who will come, is the fulfillment of Jewish expectation (7.38) and is symbolic of the Spirit that Jesus has come to offer (7.39). Lest this symbolism should be lost on the reader, the narrator is careful to interpret this living water as the Spirit who would be given to every believer after Jesus' glorification. It is the Spirit who will become the subject of much of the Farewell Discourse (John 14–16) later in the narrative, the reception of which is anticipated in John 20.22.

The water motif continues through the end of the gospel narrative with the blind man of ch. 9 washing in the pool of Siloam, Jesus' washing the disciples' feet in ch. 13, and the water and blood which pours from Jesus' side in ch. 19. It is not clear whether water in chs. 9 and 13 is intended to be symbolic. For example, the symbolism of ch. 9 is derived less from the water in the pool of Siloam and more from the pool's name, which the narrator translates for the reader as "sent." In a similar fashion, Jesus' symbolic act of washing the disciples' feet in ch. 13 is more about servant leadership than the presence of water in the narrative (13.12–20). The reference to water flowing from Jesus' side in 19.34 is perhaps more symbolic than these latter references. The narrator's comment in 19.35, as in 7.39, highlights the significance of this event by affirming the veracity of the testimony given and the historicity of Jesus' death, so that the readers "may believe." Some see in 19.34 the use of water as

---

50. L. P. Jones, *The Symbol of Water in the Gospel of John* (Sheffield: Sheffield Academic Press, 1997) 64–65. Ng, *Water Symbolism*, 68–70, says that water in ch. 2 is an eschatological symbol (Isa 25.6) of the coming kingdom.

a symbol that brings Jesus' invitation of 7.37–38 full circle, verifying in a very physical way Jesus as the source of living water.[51]

CONCLUSION

At the beginning of this essay, three interpretive difficulties associated with 7.37–39 were outlined that have been most often the subject of numerous articles and commentaries. As was noted, most of these treatments have approached these issues from a text critical, grammatical, and historical critical method. The result has been little consensus. What this writer proposed and has undertaken is a narrative critical approach to this passage in order to shed some new light on an old problem. While there is no attempt here to propose that a narrative approach is a "magic bullet" that will end all debate, such an approach helps move the debate along by attempting a fresh look at these interpretive issues.

Among the traditional approaches, the question of how the text should be punctuated seems to be the fountainhead for the resolution to the remaining two questions. Whether one places a full stop after "let him/her drink" (πινέτω) as in the Eastern interpretation, or after "the one who believes in me" (ὁ πιστεύων εἰς ἐμέ) as in the Western interpretation, appears to determine who the referent of "his/her" (αὐτοῦ) is in v. 38 (Jesus or the believer) which in turn affects where one searches for the source of the OT text referenced by the author. This flow of argumentation, however, has often established a false dichotomy between the two sides. A central issue becomes whether the water, spoken of in the passage, flows from Jesus or from the believer. This in turn leads to the inference that one must choose between either Jesus or the believer as the source of living water. For example, if one chooses the Eastern interpretation, then the believer *must* be the source of living water and the resulting complication is finding an OT text that supports such an idea.

If one enters the world of the narrative, some of these complications are avoided. From the outset, the narrative has demonstrated, which is affirmed by the narrator, that the key to interpreting Jesus' temple proclamation is the water symbolism. The slowing of narrative time, the extensive dialogue of the Tabernacles narrative, and the space it occupies speak to the

---

51. See Schnackenburg, *John*, 2:294, who sees the blood representing Jesus' atoning death and the water representing Spirit and life (4.14; 7.38). Ng, *Water Symbolism*, 84–86, sees all water references after 7.37–38 as "subtly" connected with Jesus' death, although she admits the ch. 9 reference is more challenging to work out. She writes, "The water symbol here [in 19.31–37] tells us that all the eschatological blessings, symbolized by water, find fulfillment in the death of Christ."

A New Look at an Old Problem

importance of Jesus' temple proclamation. This proclamation made "on the last day, the greatest of the Feast" is a climactic proclamation for the narrative. It is indeed the "greatest day" of the Feast for Jesus reveals himself to Israel as the source of life-giving water. This image of life-giving water is developed from the beginning of the narrative as a symbol for purification and for the Spirit, who is the "gift of God" (4.14). The reader has been informed that Jesus is the one who gives this "gift of God" and that he is the one who "baptizes with the Holy Spirit" (1.33). It is 4.14 that lays the foundation for understanding Jesus' climactic declaration at Tabernacles and it is the narrator's interpretation that provides the finishing touch. One must ask of Jesus and he will give this living water that will become in the believer "a spring of water gushing up to eternal life" (4.14; cf. 7.38).

Jesus, then, is the source of the living water. Despite one's grammatical or punctuation choices, the narrative clearly portrays Jesus as the source of this life-giving spring. However, as Jesus told the woman in Sychar and as the narrator affirms, this living water becomes the possession of all who believe in Jesus. This possession, the narrator says, is the Holy Spirit "which believers in him were to receive" (7.39) after Jesus' glorification. The narrator's comment anticipates the lengthy discussion of the Spirit present in the Farewell Discourse,[52] where Jesus tells his disciples that when he returns to the Father he will send them another "helper/advocate" (παράκλητον) to be with them forever (14.16). He is the "Spirit of truth" who will guide them into all truth and who will be with them forever (4.17; 16.13). The Spirit will continue to testify concerning the Father and the Son (15.26–27; 16.13–15) and will bring to their remembrance all that Jesus has taught them. The Spirit, then, is the "gift of God" (4.14) promised by Jesus who initiates birth from above (3.5; cf. 20.22) and whose presence in the disciples will be verification that Jesus has returned to the Father (14.20). The overflow of the living water of the Spirit is manifest in believers through, among other ways, their testimony concerning Jesus (15.27).

What, then, is the source of the OT reference in 7.38 and to whom does it refer? At least one area of consensus in the discussion of this passage is that there is no extant OT or Targumic quotation for this passage. Barrett points out that the use of the singular "Scripture" (γραφή) seems to imply a particular OT quotation is in mind but "this quotation cannot be located with confidence."[53] Glen Balfour is probably correct that the author

---

52. Culpepper, *Anatomy*, 38–39, observes that while the narrator tends not to intrude in a significant way into the farewell discourse (with the exception of perhaps 16.17, 19; see also 13.31; 17.1; 17.3), themes anticipated in the discourse are dealt with throughout the narrative, in particular, through explanatory statements such as 7.39.

53. Barrett, *Gospel of John*, 326.

119

But These are Written . . .

is conflating a range of texts and adapting the citation to fit the narrative.[54] This use of the OT is not unprecedented in John and is similar to 6.31, another problematic passage. Balfour argues that this method of handling the Hebrew Scriptures is similar to Jewish exegetical practices detected in late-second-century rabbinic sources.[55]

Certainly two OT passages the writer likely has in mind have already been cited and they are Zech 14.8 and Ezek 47.1–12. It was observed earlier that the author has already likened Jesus' presence and ministry to that of the temple (2.19–22) and as the source of living water he is likened to the eschatological temple prophesied by the prophets. Yet, Jesus seems to extend this fulfillment to the believer as well through the gift of the Spirit.[56] The development of the water symbolism through 4.14 and 7.37–39 affirm this notion. Thus, the scriptural allusion of 7.38 would read, "Out of [the believer's] (αὐτοῦ) belly will flow living water" (translation mine). As Barrett writes, "Christ is himself the fountain of living water, but it is a valid inference that the believer, being joined to him, is also, in a secondary way, a source of living water."[57]

So, then, through developing the water symbolism in the narrative the writer comes to the climactic moment at the Feast of Tabernacles in which Jesus invites all to come and drink from him, the fountain of life, and to receive within themselves this life-giving flow. John 19.34 may be an analeptic affirmation that Jesus is the source of this life-giving flow, which is initiated by his death on the cross. While this interpretation is possible, it is not this narrative moment at which the narrator chooses to establish this point but, rather, at the Feast of Tabernacles in John 7. The gift of the Spirit promised to the disciples in the Farewell Discourse and anticipated after the resurrection in 20.22, is the possession of all who are thirsty and answer the invitation to come and believe "that Jesus is the Messiah, the Son of God, and that through believing [they] may have life in his name" (20.31).

---

54. Balfour, "John's Use," 372–74; cf. Keener, *Gospel of John*, 1:728, who would agree with Balfour and cites others.

55. Balfour, "John's Use," 357–68.

56. One might note here the presence of the idea early in the church that both the believer and the community of believers are metaphorically the temple of the Holy Spirit (1 Cor 3.16–17; 6.19; 1 Pet 2.5).

57. Barrett, *Gospel of John*, 328; cf. Balfour, "John's Use," 374, who posits the possibility that the writer is once again engaging in double entendre leaving the referent of αὐτοῦ ambiguous as to whether it is Christ or the believer.

9

Born of God
The "Virgin Birth" of Believers in the Fourth Gospel

MICHAEL C. MCKEEVER

The hint half guessed, the gift half understood, is Incarnation.
Here the impossible union
Of spheres of existence is actual,
Here the past and future
Are conquered, and reconciled . . .

T. S. ELIOTT "THE DRY SALVAGES"[1]

I REMEMBER WITH PROFOUND appreciation sitting in Ben Aker's John class and witnessing the relish he took at the prospect of opening the Fourth Gospel and leading us through that magnificent narrative. If memory serves,

---

1. "The fullness of Christian revelation resides in the essential fact of the Incarnation." Eliot quoted in P. Murray, *T. S. Eliot and Mysticism: The Secret History of "Four Quartets"* (Basingstoke: Macmillan, 1991) 84. Even prior to his conversion, T. S. Eliot was a poet known for his intertextual mode and skillful biblical allusion. In addition to proclaiming the preeminence of the incarnation, "The Dry Salvages" embodies something of a "realized eschatology" akin to John's Prologue and gospel as it weaves together diverse themes as a gesture toward the reconciliation of past and future, God, and humanity.

he spoke of it with images of a festive meal, of digging in and allowing the juices to run down our arms like someone eating the choicest part of a ripe watermelon. As he said this he raised his arms, enacting the feast that was to come. In so doing, he whet an appetite in me for the Fourth Gospel that continues to this day. His enthusiasm proved infectious as he led us into an experience with the most experiential of gospels. In that sense, he embodied the role of the Beloved Disciple who, from a place of intimate experience, models for others the possibility of entering into a living encounter with the Word Incarnate.

The present study considers how the Prologue, the "choicest part" of the Fourth Gospel, serves as a carefully constructed and reliable guide for reading John and discerning his thematic emphases.[2] Specifically, we shall focus on the center of the Prologue's chiastic structure and explore an allusion to the virgin birth and its theological implications for John's concept of what it means for believers to be called "children of God." Though, unlike Matthew and Luke, John does not overtly reference Jesus' virgin birth, there is evidence at the heart of the Prologue that he alludes to and adopts the theological significance of this event to illuminate what it means for believers to be "born of God."[3]

Our focus shall be the center of John's Prologue or what Alan Culpepper has termed in his study by the same name, "The Pivot of John's Prologue." One of the contributions of Culpepper's influential study is his meticulous structural argument that the center point of John's Prologue is v. 12b, "he gave them authority to become the children of God" (ἔδωκεν αὐτοῖς ἐχουσίαν τέκνα θεοῦ γενέσθαι) rather than the statements in v. 14 concerning the incarnation and witness of the community.[4] The second half of Culpepper's study considered the meaning of the phrase "children of God" (τέκνα θεοῦ) in John's thought, particularly in terms of its importance for the Johannine community in its debate with the synagogue concerning the true children of God. Much of this portion of his study focused on the conceptual background of the term τέκνα θεοῦ in the OT, Jewish wisdom traditions, and earlier Pauline and Jesus traditions. Several pages at the end

---

2. This may be affirmed whether one conceives of the Prologue as a carefully crafted introduction intrinsic to its composition or a distillation of Johannine themes appended later from another hand.

3. All Scripture translations are my own.

4. R. A. Culpepper, "The Pivot of John's Prologue," NTS 27 (1980–81) 1–31. Culpepper's concludes that the Prologue bears the following structure: A vv. 1–2, A'; B v. 3, B' v. 17; C vv. 4–5, C' v. 16; D vv. 6–8, D' v. 15; E vv. 9–10, E' v. 14; F v. 11, F' v. 13; G v. 12a, G' v. 12c; H v. 12b.

of the article are devoted to the thematic development of these ideas within John's narrative, especially John 8.31–47 and 11.51–52.

Given the careful focus on literary structure in the first half of the study, it is interesting to consider what alternative avenues Culpepper might have pursued if he had written several years later, after his seminal work on John's literary design in *The Anatomy of the Fourth Gospel*.[5] Though the present study derives from such contemplations, I wish to heed Culpepper's admonition concerning attempts to say anything additional about the Prologue. "The prudent course may, therefore, be to refine an already established position with the hope of being able to say something true, even if it is not altogether new."[6] What is offered here may be considered a mere afterthought to the provocative insights of earlier meticulous scholarship on a central emphasis of John's Prologue.

FATHERS PREGNANT WITH MEANING

Manuscript variations and quotations from the church fathers provide a significant record of how early readers interpreted the Fourth Gospel, not least John's Prologue. Textual variants for a singular reading at 1.13 are not overwhelming. With minor deviations, all of the Greek manuscripts include the plural reading "those not . . . born" (οἳ οὐκ . . . ἐγεννήθησας). The Fourth Edition of the UBS Greek NT has granted an "A" rating to the traditional plural reading on the strength of such evidence.[7] Indeed, the manuscript support for the plural reading is persuasive. Nevertheless, the variations one finds in patristic sources regarding the subject of v. 13 are of interest. Irenaeus, Tertullian, and possibly Justin and Ignatius give evidence of a singular reading of this verse. This implies that the statements modifying "born of God," "not of blood, nor of the will of the flesh, nor of the will of man" (οὐκ ἐξ αἱμάτων οὐδὲ ἐκ θελήματος σαρκὸς οὐδὲ ἐκ θελήματος ἀνδρὸς) refer to Jesus' birth rather than the new birth of believers. The common motivation for changes from the plural to the singular is thought to be the appeal of an explicit reference to the virgin birth in John rather

---

5. R. A. Culpepper, *Anatomy of the Fourth Gospel: A Study in Literary Design* (Philadelphia: Fortress, 1983).

6. Culpepper, "Pivot," 1.

7. B. M. Metzger, *A Textual Commentary on the Greek New Testament, Second Edition a Companion Volume to the United Bible Societies' Greek New Testament* (New York: UBS, 1994) 168–69.

than the divine origin of believers' new birth.[8] This is a sound conclusion, particularly in the evolving, polemical environment of the second century.

But let us consider Tertullian and Irenaeus more closely. Tertullian does not merely argue for a singular reading but assumes this to be the case. He accuses the Valentinian Gnostics of changing the text to support their own heretical beliefs and to refer to their own births. "They maintain that it was written thus in the plural '*Who were born*, not of blood, nor of the will of the flesh, nor of the will of man, but of God' as if designating those who were before mentioned as 'believing in His name,' in order to point out the existence of that mysterious seed of the elect and spiritual which they appropriate to themselves" (*Carn. Chr.* 19).

Tertullian argues that this must be understood as referring to Jesus' virgin birth because of its specific denial of human fatherhood yet allowance for human motherhood, and makes a similar argument several chapters later (*Carn. Chr.* 24).[9] Irenaeus also appears to quote John 1.13 in the singular when arguing for the uniqueness of Jesus, given that his origins were from God and he was born of a virgin (*Haer.* 3.16.2; 3.19.2). Finally, the earlier Coptic Version of *Epistola Apostolorum* also uses the singular to support the virgin birth of Jesus (7.10). In light of these findings, E. C. Hoskyns concludes, "it would not seem unreasonable to assume that, at the beginning of the second century, phrases such as *not by the will of man, but by the will of God* were actually current or at least wholly natural with reference to the Virgin Birth of Jesus, and that the Evangelist and his readers were familiar with such language or that it would possess an obvious application to the birth of the Lord."[10]

Apparently, several church fathers found the language and qualifying statements of John 1.13 as acceptable or even expected to describe the virgin birth of Jesus. Nevertheless, in light of the overwhelming Greek manuscript evidence, the plural appears to reflect the original reading. Yet the corruption of the text in the church fathers is not entirely peculiar. Rather, it seems to reflect a certain sensitivity to the presence of Johannine allusion to the virgin birth that, in a polemically charged environment, is taken in an overly literal or christological direction. The allusion to the virgin birth was prominent enough that it was easily susceptible for emendation to become an explicit reference to Jesus' birth in a polemically charged environment. The

---

8. Ibid., 168.

9. E. Hoskyns, *The Fourth Gospel* (London: Faber and Faber, 1947) 163; cf. B. D. Ehrman, *The Orthodox Corruption of Scripture: The Effect of Early Christological Controversies on the Text of the New Testament* (New York: Oxford University Press, 1993) 59.

10. Hoskyns, *Gospel*, 165.

corruptions are meaningful, but most likely signify an allusion concerning the virgin birth at the very heart of John's Prologue.[11] Yet, according to the manuscript evidence, this echo of the virgin birth is not referring to the birth of Jesus. Rather, it has already been reappropriated by John to characterize what it means to be "children of God" or "born of God" (vv. 12–13).

More recently, several twentieth-century scholars, including Loisy, Boismard, Dupont, Galot, Hofrichter, and Harnack, also argued for a singular reading of v. 13; though, again, unsuccessfully in light of the manuscript evidence.[12] In short, critical readers, both ancient and modern, have discerned echoes of the virgin birth at the center of John's Prologue. Yet the overwhelming evidence indicates that this allusion to miraculous birth is intended to characterize the birth of believers.

TEXTUAL RELATIONS

This kind of evidence raises questions concerning the relationship between John and earlier Christian tradition. What all could John and his readers be presumed to have known? The debate concerning John's sources is dynamic but without consensus. Opinion regarding the relationship between the Fourth Gospel and the Synoptics, for example, continues in a state of flux. Last century witnessed the pendulum swing toward a majority of scholars agreeing with the position of P. Gardner-Smith that John was composed completely independent of the Synoptics. Later the pendulum swung back toward the posture of earlier positions like that of E. C. Hoskyns and the more recent work of F. J. Neirynck, which maintain that John was well aware of synoptic sources.[13] Other theories that impinge upon the possibility of

---

11. Ibid., 166.

12. Harnack, arguing for the original presence of the singular as a marginal gloss, says "what Christian, when he reads 'not of blood ... but of God' would not think of the birth of Christ?" (quoted in J. W. Pryor, "Of the Virgin Birth or the Birth of Christians? The Text of John 1:13 Once More," *NovT* 27 [1985] 299). For a careful critique of recent arguments for a singular reading, see R. A. Culpepper, "review of M. Vellanickal, *Divine Sonship of Christians in the Johannine Writings*," *JBL* 98/3 (1979) 447–49 and Pryor, "Virgin Birth," 296–318. Pryor concludes his examination of Harnack, Galot, and Hofrichter as follows: "It has been shown that there are insufficient grounds to overthrow the plural reading, on the basis either external attestation or internal considerations of style and theology. Puzzles remain, particularly over the certainty of Irenaeus and Tertullian in their witness to a single text, but the problems in accepting the singular far outweigh those in staying with the plural" (Pryor, "Virgin Birth," 318).

13. P. Gardner-Smith, *Saint John and the Synoptic Gospels* (Cambridge: Cambridge University Press, 1938); Hoskyns, *Gospel*; F. J. Neirynck, "John and the Synoptics," in *John and the Synoptics*, ed. A. Denaux (Leuven: Leuven University Press, 1992) 3–62.

John's familiarity with synoptic sources have been proposed. For example, Richard Bauckham has argued for a rapid circulation and broad intended audience for the gospels.[14] Working independently, Thomas Brodie has drawn similar conclusions regarding John.[15]

One need not agree entirely with either Bauckham's or Brodie's proposals to recognize how they have fostered profitable discussion on the potential for greater familiarity with the synoptic tradition on the part of John and his audience.[16] As Beasley-Murray characterizes it, "while the Fourth Evangelist did not use any of the Synoptics as his sources, neither did his gospel take shape in isolation from them."[17] Statements such as Beasley-Murray's accu-

---

Numerous alternative versions of each position continue to be explored. However, on the growing influence of Neirynck's position that John was familiar with the Synoptics, see also G. R. Beasley-Murray, *John* (Dallas: Word, 2002) cxl.

14. R. Bauckham, *The Gospel for All Christian: Rethinking the Gospel Audiences* (Grand Rapids: Eerdmans, 1998) 9–48, 147–72.

15. "The simplest explanation for the relationship between Mark and John is that John, an acknowledged thinker and literary artist, knew Mark and adapted it to his own purposes" (T. L. Brodie, *The Birthing of the New Testament: The Intertextual Development of the New Testament Writings* [Sheffield: Phoenix, 2004] 257). Brody maintains that attempts to navigate the labyrinth world of hypothetical oral or written pre-gospel traditions is unnecessary and is detrimental to the exploration of fruitful intertextual gospel connections because it "obscures the one thing that is certain—the finished Gospels." On the complex yet self-evident nature of such evidence, see H. W. Attridge, "Genre Bending in the Fourth Gospel," *JBL* 121/1 (2002) 3–21. On John's knowledge of the story of Jesus as well as early Christian tradition, see D. M. Smith, "Prolegomena to a Canonical Reading of the Fourth Gospel," in *"What is John?" Readers and Readings of the Fourth Gospel*, ed. F. F. Segovia (Atlanta: Scholars, 1996) 169–82, esp. 173.

16. Minimally, one may infer a familiarity with the broad outlines of earlier gospel tradition and creative engagement with the general shape of Jesus' ministry. One may also be in good company if deducing the presence of meaningful and interpretative engagement with the synoptic tradition. Josef Blinzler mentions numerous passages implying familiarity on the part of John's readers with details not contained in the Fourth Gospel yet found in the Synoptic Gospels. "These include the baptismal activity of John (Jn 1.25) Jesus' baptism by John (Jn 1.32–33) Jesus' extensive activity as a miracle-worker (Jn 2.23; 3.2; 4.45, 47; 6.2) the arrest of the Baptist (Jn 3.24) the institution of the Eucharist (Jn 6.53–54) the selection of the 12 (Jn 6.67–71; 20.24) borrowing of the donkey by the disciples (Jn 12.14, 16) the Gethsemane scene (Jn 12.27; 18.11) the process before Caiaphas (Jn 18.24, 28) Barabbas as an amnesty candidate (18.40) the closing of Jesus' sepulchre with a stone (20.1) and the presence of women at the tomb (20.2)" (J. Blinzler, *Johannes und die Synoptiker: Ein Forschungsbericht* in J. Nissen and S. Pedersen eds., *New Readings in John: Literary and Theological Perspectives: Essays from the Scandinavian Conference on the Fourth Gospel* [Sheffield: Sheffield Academic Press, 1999] 108–21).

17. Beasley-Murray, *John*, xxxvii. Cf. also, R. E. Brown and F. J. Moloney, *An Introduction to the Gospel of John* (New York: Doubleday, 2003) 94–103; C. K. Barrett, *The Gospel According to John* (Philadelphia: Westminster, 1978) 45. I would align myself with those who recognize significant yet creative engagement with the synoptic tradition on the part of John, though the current study primarily need only depend

rately characterize the relationship between John and the synoptic tradition while also highlighting the need to move beyond an exclusive reliance on source criticism as a framework for understanding this relationship.

INTERTEXTUAL RELATIONS

For our present focus, it will be more accurate and productive to speak of such tradition as an *intertext* that informs an audience or reading of the Fourth Gospel rather than a *source* taken up into its composition. This is especially true when that tradition is elliptical, allusive, or merely presupposed information, as is so often the case in the Fourth Gospel. Hence, approaching John within the broader framework of intertextuality will prove helpful. Since discussions of intertextuality entail their own complex and varied phenomena, a brief, working definition of intertextuality sufficient for our present focus may be appropriate. Intertextuality is "the phenomenon that all texts are involved in an interplay with other texts, which results in the interpretive principle that no text can be viewed as isolated and independent. This interplay is particularly true of biblical literature, since each document, or text, is self-consciously part of a stream of tradition. The study of intertextuality pays attention to the fragments, or 'echoes,' of earlier texts that appear in later texts, examining texts that share words and themes."[18]

Though approaches to biblical intertextuality have typically focused on the functional presence of the Hebrew Scriptures in the NT, Robert Wall has underscored the likelihood that *interbiblical* exegesis, common to OT, may already have been emerging within the NT era. Indeed, Wall suggests that interpreters of the NT "should listen for echoes of an emerging *traditium* of Christian texts as a sacred complement to those inherited from Judaism."[19] Given John's elliptical and allusive nature in regard to the syn-

---

on the more broadly acknowledged contact with the gospel tradition. Moreover, while acknowledging the momentous scholarship on the prehistory of the text and remaining traces of a possible redactional history, the present study largely focuses on the final form of John for its meaning and significance.

18. A. G. Patzia and A. J. Petrotta, "Intertextuality," in *Pocket Dictionary of Biblical Studies* (Downers Grove, IL: IVP, 2002) 63. See also, e.g., D. Boyarin, *Intertextuality and the Reading of Midrash* (Bloomington: Indiana University Press, 1990).

19. R. W. Wall, "Intertextuality," in *Dictionary of New Testament Backgrounds* (Downers Grove, IL: IVP, 2000) 544. Regarding a broader framework, e.g., W. Iser, *The Implied Reader: Patterns of Communication in Prose Fiction from Bunyan to Beckett* (Baltimore: Johns Hopkins University Press: 1974) xii–xiii, 34, 183. For a recent discussion of intertextuality in John, see J. Zumstein, "Intratextuality and Intertextuality in the Gospel of John," in *Anatomies of Narrative Criticism: The Past, Present, and Future of the Fourth Gospel as Literature*, eds. S. D. Moore and T. Thatcher (Atlanta: SBL, 2008)

optic tradition, a typical source criticism paradigm will prove inadequate. "The type of intertextual process brought into motion here is not that of source criticism, that is, the careful and word-for-word revision of a written source. Rather . . . a process should be envisioned that can be described in terms of hypertextuality, meaning that John's reception of the Synoptic Gospels was distanced and free."[20]

Though placing John after the Synoptics in the NT was a later, canonical decision, it may be one that not only highlights later readers' perceptions of the relation between these streams of tradition, but a principle inscribed in John's narrative itself. As we have seen, some of John's earliest readers such as the church fathers discerned familiar gospel tradition within the narrative of the Fourth Gospel.

PARATEXT: THE GENESIS OF EXPECTATION

Since Bultmann it has been commonplace to refer to the Prologue as an overture, sounding themes that will be woven into the orchestration of the narrative. Even scholars who do not work in an explicit literary framework have underscored the import of these chapters for approaching Johannine theology in general. Most scholars recognize its distinct nature as well as its integral function in shaping expectations for a proper understanding of the entire narrative.[21] Given the advances in narrative approaches to biblical studies, however, it may be more productive to move beyond musical

---

121–36. R. L. Brawley, "An Absent Complement and Intertextuality in John 19:28–29," *JBL* 112/3 (1993) 427–43, esp. 428–30.

20. Zumstein, "Intratextuality," 130. A frequent example of this sense of hypertextuality in John would be the influence of relocating the cleansing of the temple from the end of Jesus' ministry to the beginning. "[I]t was precisely because of its specific association with the passion that the authorial authorities placed it at the beginning of the Gospel. This intertextual relationship creates a meaning effect: the shadow of the cross hangs over the narrative from its inception" (Zumstein, "Intratextuality," 131).

21. "So much of the vocabulary and so many of its themes introduced strands of thought that will be important for the body of the gospel, it is significant that some elements of the prologue do not recur later . . . Furthermore, the poetic quality of the prologue is not equaled anywhere else in the gospel" (Culpepper, *Anatomy*, 119. Cf. also, Beasley-Murray, *John*, 5). "The authoritative voice of the narrator, the privileged information that is conveyed in the prologue, the scriptural allusions, the 'primacy effect' of this perspective on Jesus—all these powerfully conditioned the way in which the reader will respond to the rest of the narrative. The reader is drawn to the narrator's confession that the divine logos was incarnate in Jesus. All that follows in the Gospel's account of what Jesus does and says serves to confirm the Prologue's declaration that "the Word became flesh and lived among us (1:14)" (R. A. Culpepper, *The Gospel and Letters of John* [Nashville: Abingdon, 1998] 120).

metaphors and draw upon the descriptive language of narrative theory. One constructive approach for capturing these dynamics of the genre of prologue is in terms of *narrative frames, paratexts*, or those portions of a narrative which stand out from the text and invite an interpretive focus. In her study, *Reading Frames*, Mary Ann Caws has observed that "often, in the most widely read and enduring narratives, certain passages stand out in relief from the flow of the prose and create, in so standing, different expectations and different effects. We perceive borders as if signaled by alterations of pattern and architectural, verbal, or diegetic clues . . . These larger-than-life situations seem to hold the essence of the work, and not infrequently is it remembered by them, each as a metonymy for the larger picture."[22]

Framing, in this particular sense, proves conceptually advantageous for how the Prologue provides interpretive cues for reading John's narrative. Through the redundancy, repetitions, and parallelisms present in the Prologue, the amount of information is reduced yet amplified. The text simultaneously sustains "deictic condensation" and "predictive expansion," evoking, in a sense, the "global system" of the narrative as a whole.[23] Similarly, a paratext may be defined as "the sum of various signs that introduce, frame, present, interrupt or conclude an existing text . . . The paratext generally carries out the function of accompanying or framing another text."[24]

This is particularly fitting for a prologue since, as a paratext, a prologue "contains as much the reading's retrospective of its writing as the writing's anticipation of its reading. A foreword (also known as a prologue) can aim at setting the work's significance . . . The foreword is a decoding instrument. It guides the reading, protects the text against non-understanding or false interpretation."[25] In this fashion, the Prologue begins to shape readerly expectations and competences regarding the narrative to follow.[26] By noting

---

22. M. A. Caws, *Reading Frames in Modern Fiction* (Princeton, NJ: Princeton University Press, 1985) xi.

23. Ibid., 117–18.

24. F. Hallyn and G. Jacques, "Aspects du Paratexte," quoted in Zumstein, *Intratextuality*, 123.

25. Ibid.

26. In saying this, we would locate ourselves in agreement with a moderate, reader-oriented frameworks (e.g., those of U. Eco in *The Role of the Reader: Explorations in the Semiotics of Texts* [Bloomington: Indiana University Press, 1979] and *Semiotics and The Philosophy of Language* [Bloomington: Indiana University Press, 1984] as well as Iser, *Implied Reader*) that posits a degree of cooperation on the part of readers. "The reader as an active principal of interpretation is a part of the picture of the generative process of the text" (Eco, *Semiotics*, 4). Such a framework takes into account the influence of the text on the "model reader" in any reading transaction. "Thus it seems that a well-organized text, on the one hand, presupposes a model of competence coming,

at the outset the shaping role the Prologue plays, we will be able to better account for its implication for a reading of John's gospel.

PARATEXT, ALLUSION, AND INTERTEXTUAL CONCEPTIONS

From the very first verse of John's gospel, we are aware of his poetic genius for structure as well as his predilection to communicate through allusion and intertextual associations. The Fourth Gospel says more than its words express. In this fashion, John is able to distill complex and comprehensive ideas in a single gesture. For example, "In the beginning" evokes the Genesis creation account and anticipation of "God" as subject. Despite such anticipation, or because of it, John gracefully introduces the presence and agency of "the Word." With a handful of carefully structured poetic phrases, John proceeds both to invoke the familiar Genesis account and to infuse it with an alternative yet complementary storyline. It is astounding all that John achieves in a brief, layered, and allusive span of text, not least the closest of conceivable connections between the Word and God. John's minimal quotations and allusions are a kind of shorthand that draws upon other texts to provide greater context and depth for his own statements. By introducing themes concisely through the paratextual device of framing, John effectively creates expectation in readers and sets the stage for how he will flesh out this theme over the course of his gospel.

Hence, from the outset, John signals to his audience an essential mode of his narrative, a mode that is characterized by 1) careful attention to structure, 2) a propensity toward intertextual layering, and 3) a surprising replacement or juxtaposition of expected themes and traditions. For example, vv. 1 and 2 together form a precise chiasm, as does each verse separately.[27] Moreover, there is an interweaving of the Genesis creation account with the career of the Word, a surprising yet illuminating exchange of the Word where one would expect God as subject.

We may notice that this careful narrative strategy is also prominent at the center of the Prologue in vv. 11–13. Indeed, at the center of the Prologue we find a similar strategy to the opening. Like the convergence of structure and intertextuality that subverts anticipation of God as subject and exchanges it with the complementary narrative of the Word, so the center of the Prologue

so to speak, from outside the text, but, on the other hand, works to build up, by merely textual means, such a competence" (Eco, *Semiotics*, 7–8).

27. Here it may be observed that John paratextually signifies on a small scale the larger contours of the Prologue.

deploys a comparable tactic. Both vv. 9 and 11 buildup anticipation by speaking of the Word "coming into the world" and "coming to his own."[28] According to the emerging Christian *traditium*, readers may reasonably anticipate some manner of *birth announcement*. Against the earlier backdrop of the Prologue's multivalent and timeless images, the current of the narrative flows toward an explicit, overt, and unambiguous *delivery* of the Word into the human realm. However, at the very crux of the Prologue one encounters a birth narrative of a different kind—an extraordinary parturition of the believer by God. Just as John 1.1–5 weaves together the intimate associations between the Word and God, so John 1.12–13 weaves together close associations between the new birth of believers in vv. 12–13 and the incarnation of the Word in v. 14. Moreover, by means of his chiastic structure and intertextual allusion, the Prologue reinforces the closest of relationships between the divine origin of believers and Jesus' own virgin birth.

Hoskyns is one of the few interpreters in the modern era that captures both the allusion to the virgin birth and this close connection between incarnation and believers as born of God.

> It is at this point, however, that the connection of thought between v. 13 and v. 14 emerges as a problem. The Evangelist did not write simply *The Word became flesh*, as though he were beginning a new topic. He wrote *And the Word became flesh*. That is to say, he links v. 14 closely to v. 13 . . . To the Evangelist the thought of the regeneration of the believers at once suggests the thought of the Son of God who for their salvation became flesh and was born. Therefore in the perspective of the Johannine Writings, this would seem to be the connection between v. 13 and v.14 in the prologue. If then, the spiritual regeneration of the believers and the incarnation of the Word of God are closely related and mutually suggested in the connection between vv. 12 and 14, the question arises whether not only the fact of the incarnation, but also its mode does not determine the form in which the description of the spiritual birth of the Christians is described in v. 13. The question arises whether the language does not presuppose the Virgin Birth.[29]

---

28. Because of John's multivalent nature, some have underscored the difficulty of discerning the timing and sphere of vv. 9–11. There is a tension between the timeless ministry of the Word and his entry into history. John is fond of such ambivalences. However, "coming into the world" world would seem to indicate the advent of the Word anticipating incarnation rather than the Word's timeless and eternal witness. "His own" no doubt refers to Israel and the Jewish people (Exod 9.5).

29. Hoskyns, *Gospel*, 164.

John communicates the connection of thought between Jesus' incarnation and the new birth of believers by the mutually suggestive image of the virgin birth. Allusion to Jesus' mode of incarnation is employed to lend significance and specificity to the astounding character of this event for believers.

EXPECTANT READERS

Given the key role that allusion to the virgin birth plays in characterizing those "born of God" at the pivot of John's Prologue, we may ask, what might John's readers have been expected to have known concerning the virgin birth? What might have comprised their shared presuppositions? What would a Johannine reader have inferred from such a provocative allusion? In considering these questions we are less concerned with identifying each distinctive source than with what constituted the core theological ideas and central christological concepts associated with the virgin birth.[30] What was the essential meaning and significance of the event in the Christian *traditium* that John engaged?

In a broad sense, the accounts of the virgin birth in Matthew and Luke share an emphasis on the in breaking of the supernatural into the natural and an emphatic declaration of divine sonship.[31] Each in their own way evokes God's creative act, heralding a new and singular work of the divine and a new era in God's saving initiative. The virgin birth discloses God's desire and ability to enter into human life and history. The event is profoundly christological and theological in focus rather than mariological.

Virgin birth is a potent symbol for new life through the power of the Spirit. As a unique, creative work of God, it provides an appropriate image for the Prologue's thoroughgoing Genesis allusions.[32] As such, this unique and unprecedented union of God and humanity signified by Jesus' virgin birth is an apt and fitting symbol for the divine begetting of believers. To

---

30. Within the canon itself, there appear to be at least two independent witnesses to the tradition represented by Matthew and Luke. Moreover, Luke's preface indicates that he has drawn upon previous narratives and tradition. Luke 1.1–2 may indicate that Christian tradition, such as the material relevant to the infancy narratives, was already available. Other texts may reflect some nuance of meaning regarding the miraculous or unusual birth of Jesus as well, e.g., Paul's use of verbal forms in Rom 1.3 and statements in other texts (Gal 4.4; Phil 2.7) or the reference to Jesus as the "son of Mary" (Mark 6.3) a phrase not without significance in a patriarchal culture. However, the meaning of all of these are open to debate.

31. At this level of generality, the same may be said for Mark's introduction (Mark 1.1–15).

32. Even in the Lukan infancy narrative, allusion to the Genesis creation account and the activity of God's Spirit are not lacking (Luke 1.35).

Born of God

draw upon the language of Matthew, Jesus' virgin birth signifies "God with us," the realization and fulfillment of what was promised in the old covenant.

The incarnation is also an eschatological sign that foreshadows the ultimate reconciliation of God and humanity. As Otto Piper suggests, "By making the birth of Jesus the starting point of God's good news, Matthew and Luke indicate that the virgin birth is an eschatological occurrence; that is to say, it is not just the rising of the curtain or the first of a series of historical events in the life of Jesus; it is the originating impulse by means of which all subsequent events in holy history have been rendered possible . . ."[33]

At its core, the virgin birth communicates a miraculous new birth by the power of God's Spirit apart from human initiative. It speaks to the uniqueness of Jesus' human yet divine nature and origin, foreshadowing the new relationship with God in which Christians participate. The "virgin birth" of believers, then, is a particularly appropriate allusion at this point, an apposite representation because the concomitant reality of the incarnation is the power to become children of God. It is a fitting metaphor for the union of God and humanity, for the divine filiation that believers now experience as born of God. The correlation can now be affirmed because the vast gulf between God and humanity has been spanned by the incarnation. "The narrative's logic implies a transferal: the Word that had been forever 'with God' (1:1–2) became 'flesh' (1:14) so others could be born not from flesh but from God (1:13; cf. 3:6)."[34] In this sense we can recognize the measure of truth in St. Athanasius' statement that God became man so that men might become gods.

Since this is a point of transformation, a pivot, we may also note several developments in the balance of the Prologue (vv. 14–18). According to Culpepper, vv. 9–10 represent the response of the world to the incarnation, while v. 14 represents the response of the community of believers. Hence, if vv. 11–13 form a transition and if v. 12 is its pivot, what indications are found in the balance of the Prologue that a transition has taken place? To begin, now that the Word has been received, we note the presence of the community of believers and the initial occurrences of first person language in vv. 14 and 16. A *witnessing* community is now present. It hardly needs to be said that this community was constituted by the act of divine begetting in vv. 12–13. These are those among whom the Word has come to dwell, those who behold his glory in v. 14, those who have received from his fullness in v. 16. Now that light has been "received" (ἔλαβον, v. 12; ἐλάβομεν v. 16);

---

33. O. A. Piper, "The Virgin Birth: The Meaning of the Gospel Accounts," *Int* 18 (1964) 145.

34. C. S. Keener, *The Gospel of John: A Commentary* (Peabody, MA: Hendrickson, 2003) 1:405.

light language yields to the vocabulary of revelation. A community *sees* (v. 14) *beholds glory* (v. 14) and is the recipient of *revelation made fully known* (v. 18). In addition to the first person testimony, we find language of family and relationship. The complement of "the Word was with God" (v. 1) yields to "God the beloved Son who is close to the Father's heart" (v. 18) with intimations of the incorporation of the "children of God" as well (v. 12).

If by an allusion to the virgin birth the center of John's Prologue underscores the astounding new birth of believers, those "born of God," how does it affect a reading of John? In what way might it contribute to the framing or paratextual nature of the Prologue? Having explored some of the implications of the center of John's Prologue, let us briefly consider how it creates readerly expectations and narrative competencies. As a paratext or framing device for the subsequent narrative, the Prologue aids readers in establishing central themes, oppositions, and the norms of the narrative. "The norms of the implied author are ostensibly drawn from Jesus and revealed by him. The Prologue, as we have seen, serves the crucial function of elevating the reader to the implied authors Apollonian vantage point before the spectacle begins."[35] Jesus' identity and the semantic emphases of the Prologue, not least that of new birth from God, serve as a helpful guide for readers to negotiate the distinctive, multileveled nature of John's narrative and provide insight on John's ironic mode in the episodes and encounters that follow.

As Culpepper notes, "by showing Jesus confronting a wide variety of individuals in everyday situations, the Gospel dramatizes the message that the Word has become flesh and dwelt among us."[36] Indeed, the episodic nature of John's gospel slows down the dynamic of the narrative that typically propels plot forward. Though undermining continuity of plot, this narrative characteristic enables readers to better assimilate the narrative thematically. "John's pervasive thematic integration allows, furthermore, for readers who know the story to see its end and its meaning in each of the familiar episodes . . . The effect of this narrative structure, with its prologue followed by episodic repetition of the conflict between belief and unbelief, is to enclose the reader in the company of faith."[37]

Though throughout the entire narrative the range of responses to the Word made flesh is rather broad, within the Prologue itself the responses have been narrowed down to those who receive the Word and believe and those who do not. Hence, in conclusion, let us briefly consider the episodes of Nicodemus and the man born blind, two significant encounters that

---

35. Culpepper, *Anatomy*, 168.
36. Ibid., 97.
37. Ibid., 97–98

Born of God

embody these central oppositions of belief and evince thematic connections to the theme of the new birth of believers in John 1.12–13.

NICODEMUS' MISCONCEPTION

As John's narrative progresses, readers will note there is a movement from unopposed ministry to heightened conflict. Early on, the disciples model a positive response to the ministry of Jesus, yet after John 5 a very clear division takes place between those who receive the light and those who do not. However, in John 3 Nicodemus is encountered as a multifaceted character that we may not immediately know how to assess. He is a complicated figure partly because he embodies so many of the thematic oppositions of John's Prologue.

Arriving early in the narrative before the rising conflict, Nicodemus may be encountered as a sympathetic character that has responded to Jesus' signs in Jerusalem. Nevertheless, he comes to Jesus by night, or by darkness (3.2). He is a member of the religious establishment that has failed to respond to John the Baptist or Jesus, and may represent the immediate and concrete example of those to whom Jesus has not trusted himself after performing signs in Jerusalem (2.24). Is he one who is open to the light or, as one who seeks Jesus by night, is he one who should be identified with the darkness that has not understood or overcome the light (1.5)?

As the discussion turns to the necessity of being born from above (vv. 3–10) readers, who have encountered this theme in the Prologue, already share the privileged point of view of the implied author and adopt an insider's perspective on Jesus' ironies. Nicodemus, however, appears to rapidly move from one who appears to understand, "Rabbi, we know that you are sent from God" (v. 2) to one who is reduced to groping after Jesus' dark and enigmatic statements. He is on the losing end of each exchange as he personifies that which is human and not from God, that which is of the flesh and not of the Spirit, that which is from below and not born from above.[38]

When Nicodemus appears again in 7.50–52, he exemplifies the division that has now occurred between the authorities and other Jews.[39] The irony is that Nicodemus, as a Jewish authority, embodies this division within himself—he has not made the transition to belief. He is a character that is

---

38. We may note that, like the relationship between the birth of believers and Jesus' incarnation, there is a close connection drawn between Jesus' origins here and that of the believer. Like Jesus, who is also from above, the believer who is born of the Spirit is also mysterious like the wind. Both their origin and destination remains a mystery to those from below, like Nicodemus (vv. 8–10).

39. See also, Culpepper, *Anatomy*, 134–36.

betwixt and between. In Luke's gospel the character of Zechariah, another unbelieving religious leader, also initially embodies a divided people. However, Zechariah eventually makes a transition to belief (Luke 1.5–23, 57–79) yet we are left to wonder whether Nicodemus will be successful. Are we to think of him as one who has experienced new life and new birth? Should we identify him now with light or does he remain in darkness? Nicodemus quintessentially remains an unresolved character through much of the narrative. Yet, his fading into the darkness during his first encounter with Jesus may foreshadow his ultimate unbelief. Later, he provides a kingly amount of spices for Jesus' burial, but even in his close association with Jesus' death and "lifting up" he lacks a revelatory, life-giving moment (3.14–15; 19.39–42). By all the standards of the Prologue, though he is one of the Jesus "own" (1.11) he has not understood or received the light but remains in darkness (1.5, 11). By the themes and oppositions of the Prologue that have established the norms of the narrative, he has not been born of God and has not been empowered to be a child of God.[40]

THE MAN BORN BLIND'S QUESTIONABLE PARENTAGE

The man born blind in John 9 presents a more positive and less ambiguous figure for readers than Nicodemus. Whereas Nicodemus is one of the most complex, conflicted, and ultimately disappointing characters by the standards of John's narrative, the man born blind is one of its most robust—fully embodying Johannine norms established for readers in the Prologue. Indeed, it is significant the degree to which the man born blind exemplifies themes and emphases of the Prologue and personifies what it means to become a child of God. The birth imagery shared by the Prologue and Nicodemus has frequently been noted in Johannine scholarship, but connections between the Prologue and the defining nature of the blind man's birth and transformation (vv. 1, 2, 19, 20, 32; cf. 1.12–13; 3.3–8) or the deficient role of his parents (vv. 18–25) have been less frequent.

Nicodemus and the man born blind are contrasting characters in numerous ways. Nicodemus has credentials as a member of the religious establishment, whereas the man born blind is accursed in the eyes of such leaders (v. 34). Nicodemus is introduced prior to the rising conflict in John's narrative, while the man born blind is encountered at the conflict's height, is immediately drawn into it, and is put on trial. Nicodemus continually gropes for comprehension, while the man born blind rapidly matures in

---

40. For a range of possible assessments of Nicodemus, see Beasley-Murray, *John*, 47; Culpepper, *Anatomy*, 136.

understanding and insight. Nicodemus is on the losing end of each exchange, while the increasingly plucky man born blind holds his own in the debate. Finally, Nicodemus fades into the darkness, while the man born blind crosses over from darkness to light.

Several scholars have noted the chiastic structure of ch. 9. Though there is minor variation in detail, there is significant agreement that the interrogation of the parents of the man born blind is located at the center of the structure.[41] Nevertheless, the testimony of the blind man's parents, or failure thereof, seems like a peculiar emphasis. Both in terms of plot and structure, the parent's inaction and ultimate abandonment of their child is strikingly anticlimactic. Yet, it is not without significance that the structural centrality and thematic emphasis of this scene parallel that of the center of the Prologue and underscore the contrast between human and divine parentage. At the crux of this scene, the man born blind is suspended between God's activity and his parents' inactivity. As a character he is defined both by a creative act of God, which transforms his birth condition, and by his parents' formal abdication of human responsibility. He is one who is no longer determined by his human parentage, but stands wholly determined by God's revelatory action.[42] Because of a unilateral, creative act of the divine, he now epitomizes one who has been born of God. Like the community that gives witness to glory in John 1.14–18, he gives true testimony to that which he has seen and experienced.

It has been common since J. Louis Martyn's *History and Theology in the Fourth Gospel* to highlight how the experience of the man born blind

---

41. E.g., P. Ellis and A. Culpepper maintain slightly different divisions, yet both concur that vv. 18–23 are central. Ellis outlines ch. 9 as (a) Jesus gives sight to the man born blind (9.1–7); (b) The Pharisees reject the man's testimony (9.8–17); (c) The Pharisees reject the parents' testimony (9.18–23); (b) The Pharisees again reject the man's testimony (9.24–34); (a) Jesus gives spiritual sight to the man born blind (9.35–38) (P. F. Ellis, *The Genius of John: A Composition-Critical Commentary on the Gospel of John* [Collegeville, MN: Liturgical, 1984] 158). Culpepper outlines the chapter as, Scene 1: The Healing of the Blind Man (9.1–7); Scene 2: The Neighbors and the Blind Man (9.8–12); Scene 3: The Pharisees Question the Blind Man (9.13–17); Scene 4: The Pharisees Question the Blind Man's Parents (9.18–23); Scene 5: The Pharisees Question the Blind Man a Second Time (9.24–34); Scene 6: Jesus Questions the Blind Man (9.35–39); Scene 7: Jesus Responds to the Pharisees (9.40–41) (Culpepper, *Gospel and Letters*, 174).

42. Prominent themes such as darkness and light, day and night, work and Sabbath, and the making of clay underscore God's present creative activity through Jesus. Jesus is not on trial in absentia merely for failing to observe the Sabbath, but for doing the works of God. The man born blind exemplifies the human condition, representing unfinished creation in need of a final creative act. He is paradigmatic of all humans born into this world who need to receive the light that enlightens all humanity (1.4, 5, 9).

personifies the Johannine community.[43] Nevertheless, the man born blind also functions paradigmatically, signifying a more universal experience of all believers central to John's Prologue. Based on a reader's appropriation of the Prologue's norms and emphases, he embodies, not only the historic community, but also the wider witnessing community of believers who, in all times and places, give first-person testimony to God's gracious activity (John 1.14–18; cf. 1 John 1.1–4). He provides eyewitness testimony to his experience of receiving the light. The injunction by the Pharisees to "give glory to God" is especially ironic as that is precisely what he has done from the beginning. Given that bearing witness to glory is the first act of those born of God (1.14) he is a quintessential expression of the Johannine theme of witness. Indeed, as in the Prologue, his testimony is added to that of John the Baptist, both in the Prologue and narrative proper (1.6–8, 15, 19–34; 3.25–36). As John's readers know, to receive the light is to become "a child of God," to be "born of God" (1.12, 13).

---

43. J. L. Martyn, *History and Theology in the Fourth Gospel* (Nashville: Abingdon, 1979).

10

Seeking Peace with Justice
Toward a Christomorphic Pneumatology[1]

PAUL ALEXANDER

I TOOK EVERY CLASS that I could with Benny Aker. It amounted to more than one-third of my Master of Divinity Degree. I even audited extra classes because I wanted to hear him teach. He challenged me and interrogated my assumptions. He reformulated my theology and reframed my perspectives of Scripture. He closed the door and talked with the class about how long it would take for things to change for the better. He taught me Greek, more Greek, and then more Greek. I eventually used the notes I wrote in my books from his classes as I taught Greek every semester for eight years. I learned much from his pedagogical style as well, and I know that it has helped me to engage my students in healthy ways. He was certainly the most influential professor in my seminary studies, and he helped me appreciate narrative in ways that opened me up to later receive Stanley Hauerwas and

---

1. I first presented this chapter as a paper, then entitled "Toward a Pentecostal Theology of Peacemaking," at SPS in March 2002, one year before the official U.S. invasion of Iraq. I edited it only slightly for this volume, but it contains the seeds of the concept of christomorphic pneumatology that I am developing more fully in another book. I had not arrived at the term until 2008, although the motto for Pentecostals and Charismatics for Peace and Justice (PCPJ) has been "Jesus-Shaped Spirit-Empowered Peace with Justice" for several years. Christomorphic pneumatology is simply a theologically technical way of saying Jesus-shaped and Spirit-empowered. Another way I like to think of incarnational theological ethics is "Dios con carne"—God with meat.

But These are Written . . .

Hans Frei and John Howard Yoder with gratitude. I felt grateful for Dr. Aker the entire time I was in seminary, and I missed him when I graduated. This *Festschrift* is a small gesture of gratitude for the life that Dr. Aker poured into us, and my chapter reflects not his emphases but my own. I cannot blame him for the path I am on, but I certainly thank him for reinforcing in me a concern to take Scripture and theology seriously. As I learned from him, when we take it seriously it can cost us our lives. For better or worse, I am a beneficiary of Dr. Aker's wisdom, scholarship, and twinkly smile, and I dedicate this essay to him.

INTRODUCTION

Many early Pentecostals believed that participation in the destruction of human life, even in warfare for one's own nation, was not congruent with a fully Pentecostal understanding of the "gospel" (εὐαγγέλιον). This biblically and theologically informed peace witness of our ancestors has been excavated, examined, and discussed for several years now by a number of scholars and pastors.[2] This historical and theological research has been appropriate and has challenged those who would privatize their Pentecostalism at the expense of social concerns.[3] However, simply echoing the passionate professions of the past, as significant and necessary as that endeavor is, will not sufficiently enable contemporary pentecostals to fully live into Spirit-baptized discipleship in the kingdom of God at this time. For that to happen, we must reexamine the Scriptures together with our heritage to see whether early claims for nonviolence and peacemaking can once again be supported as a faithful testimony to the story of Israel, Jesus, and the church. This conversation has already begun in Joel Shuman's 1996 article entitled "Pentecost and the End of Patriotism: A Call for the Restoration of Pacifism Among Pentecostal Christians."[4] This paper is meant to continue that discussion as a response to his call.

My objective is to show that a pentecostal theology well-grounded in the Scriptures will recognize that peacemaking should be a fundamental

---

2. A detailed account of the American Assemblies of God story can be found in P. Alexander, *Peace to War: Shifting Allegiances in the Assemblies of God* (Telford, PA: Cascadia, 2009).

3. From this point forward I will use the term "pentecostal" to refer to both Pentecostals and Charismatics as those who trust the power and gifts of the Spirit and the authority of Scripture to help them follow Jesus. This is similar to the way J. W. McClendon Jr. uses the term "baptist" to refer to those who recognize the authority of Scripture and their continuity with it. See *Doctrine* (Nashville: Abingdon, 1994) 5.

4. *JPT* 9 (1996) 70–96.

characteristic of Spirit-filled communities. This is quite a claim when we consider that many pentecostals have advocated the opposite for much of the twentieth century and even into the first decade of the twenty-first. We have fought for many nations, for many causes, and we have shed much blood. Nevertheless, I believe that if we take the time to examine who we say we are, and if we allow ourselves to be God's vessels, then we will conclude that peacemaking should characterize our Christian faith.

I believe God is calling the church to be faithful to the way of Christ in all things, and to therefore be a peacemaking church. This peacemaking encompasses seeking justice for the poor, promoting reconciliation between divided brothers and sisters in the faith, and reserving ultimate allegiance for God above all sectarian and Constantinian boundaries erected by nations, classes, genders, ethnicities, and geography. It addresses economic and social issues such as consumerism and globalization; it inspires our speaking truth and witnessing authentically to the way and life of Christ in everything. The call to make peace is not an invention; it does not impose a foreign substance on the gospel. To make peace means to unleash and take seriously the very heart of God as revealed in the incarnation. It is to accept and submit to the truth that "the wisdom that comes from heaven is first of all pure; then peace loving, considerate, submissive, full of mercy and good fruit, impartial and sincere." It is to believe that "peacemakers who sow in peace raise a harvest of righteousness" (Jas 3.17–18).[5] This is public and social, private and individual. It encompasses everything because it is based in the faith that Jesus Christ is actually Lord.

Where does one begin in this endeavor to help the church once again realize that violence and division, retaliation and enmity are not appropriate for those empowered by the Spirit of God? How does one show that love for all is included in Jesus' words in the Gospel of John, "Peace I give to you, my peace I leave with you" (14.27). The Assemblies of God began with evangelism as the basis for their pacifism during World War I: "From its very inception, the Pentecostal movement has been a movement of evangelism, studiously avoiding any principles or actions which would thwart it in its great purpose."[6] They believed that telling the story of Jesus to someone,

---

5. All English Scripture quotations are from the NIV.

6. "The Pentecostal Movement and the Conscription Law," *The Weekly Evangel* (Aug 4, 1917) 6. This introduction was followed with "The laws of the kingdom, laid down by our elder brother Jesus Christ, in His Sermon on the Mount, have been unqualifiedly adopted, consequently the movement has found itself opposed to the spilling of the blood of any man, or of offering resistance to any aggression. Every branch of the movement, whether in the United States, Canada, Great Britain or Germany, has held to this principle."

only later to kill that same person in combat, amounted to blatant hypocrisy. Evangelism is a fine place to examine peacemaking and war, and elsewhere I examine peacemaking as the opportunity for evangelical integrity, but here I will begin where the identity of the *Christ*-ian might begin, with Jesus Christ himself.[7]

CHRISTOLOGY AS THE *SOURCE* OF PENTECOSTAL PEACEMAKING[8]

My father always told me to "seek Jesus." Little did he or I know that this would lead me to advocate peacemaking as an integral part of the gospel. This priority of place for the Messiah is certainly appropriate when addressing anything, but especially peacemaking. Jesus is the one who said, "blessed are the peacemakers" (Matt 5.9a) and "love your enemies, do good to them" (Luke 6.35a). When Jesus' life, death, and resurrection are joined with his words, it reveals a peacemaking way of life that becomes the imperative model for the children of God. Simply put, joint-heirs with Jesus will share in his sufferings as well as his glory. Pentecostals especially should be appalled at the marginalization of Jesus when it comes to discussions of ethics. We should start and end with Jesus, the author and finisher of our faithfulness, who revealed to us the way of God. It is by him that we have been redeemed and for him that we seek the redemption of the world. Oppression, exploitation, greed, nationalism, and violence are difficult to justify without moving Jesus to the side, and this should not be acceptable for pentecostals. Jesus was faced with real options and temptations in his life that were not the Way, yet he was obediently faithful to God, and we must follow his example.

Getting to know the Jesus of the Christian Scriptures is a wonderful adventure, but it is also a continual challenge. Jesus himself said, "blessed is the [one] who does not fall away on account of me" (Luke 7.23) and Peter confirmed this later by calling Jesus the stumbling block that makes people fall (1 Pet 2.8). We must be sure that we identify the correct reasons why

---

7. P. Alexander, ed., *Pentecostals and Peacemaking: Heritage, Theology, and the 21st Century*, foreword by S. Hauerwas (Eugene, OR: Pickwick, 2012).

8. I would like to thank Craig Carter for allowing me to use his analysis of Yoder's thought in *The Politics of the Cross: The Theology and Social Ethics of John Howard Yoder* (Grand Rapids: Brazos, 2001) as the basis for the titles in this paper. More development along these lines will be done with ecclesiology as the shape and perhaps eschatology as the context of pentecostal peacemaking. I highly recommend Carter's book as an excellent introduction to the work of Yoder and his relationship to Karl Barth and Reinhold Niebuhr.

Jesus is a stumbling block to following God, for our description of the Messiah will determine our understanding of who we are to be. So, I will attempt the all-important task of interpreting the revelation of Jesus' life, murder, and resurrection. I will then apply it to contemporary pentecostals in a way that is faithful to the NT. If it challenges us to change our self-understanding, loyalties, and actions, then may the Holy Spirit empower us to be faithful.

In facing temptations, Jesus rejected the use of economics to avoid the cross and become king, and he rejected the authority and wealth of the kingdoms of the world because hunger for power and nationalism were not the ways that God would redeem the world.[9] Jesus rejected safety, security, control, and coercion even though they were real options. Instead, Jesus allowed himself to be rejected, and thus challenged economic power, nationalism, and violence. He consistently taught and demonstrated that "servant-hood replaces domination."[10]

As much as we may try to avoid it, the human who Christians claim was the incarnate God created a new social reality of people who are supposed to live like he did. Wealth, defense, and control are temptations that our generous, nonviolent, and submissive (though not always obedient to the powers) Messiah rejected. Jesus generously fed the hungry, but not for status, recognition, or power; we should do the same. Jesus accepted his own death at the hands of his enemies, and when we do the same we are taking up the cross and following Christ. God allowed his own son, and many others, to die while forgiving and seeking reconciliation with their attackers. Jesus did not force the cross on others, but he lived his life in such a way that challenged the status quo and forced them to deal with him, thus offering them an alternative way of dealing with conflict and hostility. He issued open invitations to participate with God in redeeming the world through aggressive love—a love obedient to God but submissive to those who stone the prophets.

Jesus even told his hometown that he was there not only for them but also for the outsiders, the poor, prisoners, the blind, and the oppressed. He made this so clear to them that they attempted to murder him because they did not want peace with their enemies. From Jesus' life we learn that making peace creates both friends and enemies—just like switching on a light in a dark room where oppression is taking place makes some rejoice and others angry. The oppressed rejoice but the oppressors are threatened. When we do not support the establishments that others around us worship, or at

---

9. J. H. Yoder, *The Politics of Jesus* (Grand Rapids: Eerdmans, 1972) 26. Carter notes the point of the biblical story is that the idolatry of nationalism is on the same moral level as Satan worship. See *Politics of the Cross*, 96.

10. Carter, *Politics of the Cross*, 97.

least highly admire, we are at odds with those who hold the (alleged) power. Valuing immigrants because we realize that this is not our land anyway, it is God's, and it used to belong to somebody other than us, is similar to when Jesus told the people of Nazareth that Elijah and Elisha could have healed the Israelites but ministered to foreigners instead. Siding with the poor, hungry, weeping ones, while also being foolish enough to say "watch out" to the rich, well-fed, laughing ones will bring hatred and exclusion. However, Jesus called into being a "community of voluntary commitment, willing for the sake of its calling to take upon itself the hostility of the given society."[11] Peacemaking admits that there is hostility and confronts it, it does not lie passively by. It attempts to destroy enmity by turning enemies into friends.

When Peter confessed Jesus as the Messiah, Jesus immediately told his disciples that he would suffer, be rejected, be killed, and be raised to life. He also did not hesitate to tell them that they themselves would also die. "Taking up the cross" was not a symbolic or figurative idea as Jesus taught it. It was true that, each day, following Jesus could get one killed. His call to imitate himself, both as a servant and as a murder/execution victim, was a call that the NT church understood very clearly. It took the resurrection and Pentecost to get them back to the Way, but even Peter went from denying Christ with the sword to exhorting the church: "When they hurled their insults at him he did not retaliate; when he suffered, he made no threats. Instead, he entrusted himself to him who judges justly . . . Do not repay evil with evil or insult with insult, but with blessing, because to this you were called . . ." (1 Pet 2.23; 3.9).

Jesus renounced the Zealot option numerous times during his ministry. It is possible that several of his disciples were Zealots who desired a violent revolution that would establish God's rule and reign on earth after the pagans were driven out of the land.[12] He rejected insurrection as an option after feeding the multitudes, after cleansing the temple, and for the third time, in the garden. Instead, he drank from the cup that the Father presented him. The temptation to take over and bring about peace and justice with force is a serious enticement; it is usually presented as the responsible or realistic way. But Jesus knew that the way of God is to bring conciliation through sacrificial love, not through force, for a coerced love is not love at all. Pentecostals today must also resist the temptation to take matters into our own hands through force. We must not think ourselves powerful enough to make things turn out right. A healthy Christology allows plenty

---

11. Yoder, *Politics*, 37.
12. Ibid., 47.

of room for action but no room for violence, regardless of the alleged good that could come from it.

Jesus, the Christ who makes peace, must be seen as a real threat to the status quo, to establishments, and to powers. There are those with vested interests who gain position, power, and wealth through division and enmity. This is true both in religious institutions and in nations. We should avoid so overly spiritualizing the life of Jesus that we make the mistake of thinking that the Jews and Romans misinterpreted Jesus when they thought they had to kill him to keep their order.

> Both Jewish and Roman authorities were defending themselves against a *real* threat. That the threat was not one of *armed*, violent revolt, and that it nonetheless bothered them to the point of their resorting to irregular procedures to counter it, is a proof of the political relevance of nonviolent tactics, not a proof that Pilate and Caiaphas were exceptionally dull or dishonorable men . . . Jesus' public career had been such as to make it quite thinkable that he would pose to the Roman Empire an apparent threat serious enough to justify his execution.[13]

People really hoped he would redeem Israel and they were rightly expecting a kingdom of God since that is what Jesus consistently talked about. The misunderstanding was that the life that leads to the cross, the faithfulness of the Messiah, was the inauguration of the kingdom. This is the way it happens. "Here at the cross is the man who loves his enemies, the man whose righteousness is greater than that of the Pharisees, who being rich became poor, who gives his robe to those who took his cloak, who prays for those who despitefully use him. The cross is not a detour or a hurdle on the way to the kingdom, nor is it even the way to the kingdom; it is the kingdom come."[14]

It is to this moment that pentecostals are called to be faithful witnesses. We should be able to look at the power structures in this world and speak the truth to them, calling out the injustice and oppression that promotes greed and holds itself above moral reproach. Nations that train their people in materialism and consumerism must be offered an alternative, a better way that is the way of God. I believe that God revealed to us in Jesus "an ethic marked by the cross, a cross identified as the punishment of a man who threatens society by creating a new kind of community leading a radically new kind of life."[15] Radical Christianity is supposed to be the hallmark

13. Ibid., 49–50.
14. Ibid., 51.
15. Ibid., 53.

of pentecostals, and it is appropriate to recognize that this involves living in communities (churches) that are threats to injustice and social/structural evil around us. Jesus' death is integrally related to his life; for he was killed because of the life he lived.

I am convinced that if we live as faithful witnesses to Jesus we very well may endanger ourselves and our families. There is always the hope that the offender will be won over by our love, but there is no guarantee. The calculating link between faithfulness to God and its efficacy has been broken by the cross; while we offer reconciliation we may be rejected and killed just like Jesus was. Indeed, by aggressively addressing racial and ethnic tensions, we will cause those benefiting from the conflict to demand silence, even by force. In addressing economic or gender issues, we hope that there will be confession, repentance, and restoration, but there may be retaliation instead. God has known this risk from the beginning. The faithful prophets in the Hebrew Scriptures received their punishment for speaking the truth; the faithful Son and children of God in the NT were prepared for it as well. This is why we are told to submit to the authorities in the context of enemy feeding and love as the fulfillment of the law (Rom 12–13).[16] If you feed the state's enemies, you may be sentenced to hang for treason. You then submit to the state when you accept this consequence. In doing so, you must never underestimate or overlook the exact way that Jesus responded to his executioners, "Father, forgive them" (Luke 23.34). Stephen took this so seriously that he almost quoted his Messiah as he was being executed, and we too are to face our deaths with this compassion and forgiveness. This is not an unreachable ideal of perfection that is only futuristic—that response simply avoids the real lordship of the Messiah in our lives. This way of sacrificial and suffering love is the way things really are if we believe that the God of Abraham, Isaac, and Jacob came in the flesh in Jesus of Nazareth.

Just as Jesus' death resulted from the life he lived and the truth he spoke, so his resurrection was God's vindication that this is God's way. Jesus trusted the Father to raise him from the dead, and was thus obedient even to a shameful death on a cross. Jesus, knowing that peace is made only by unselfishness and sacrifice, poured himself out in suffering and his glory came later. We who claim to be his followers can expect no easier road; we cannot claim to bring about peace, justice, or joy through the suffering of others, for our God demonstrates otherwise. In suffering with and for others, we ultimately, and without reservation, place our hope in God and God alone because we know that only God can raise us from the dead after we

---

16. Christians are not to suspend moral judgment and obey the state if it commands something that is against the way of God. See J. H. Yoder, *The Original Revolution* (Eugene, OR: Wipf & Stock, 1998).

are killed. If Jesus was not raised, then all the beatings, imprisonments, and testimonial deaths are truly crazy and we are to be pitied for our foolishness. But, if Jesus really is the Son of God, then we can make peace with our enemies just like Christ did, even when it costs us our lives, because we believe that God himself will vindicate our faithfulness. We trust God to judge justly. Christ's death falls between his life and resurrection. This sequence should be taken seriously in order to have a healthy Christology: Christ's sacrificial death is the result of his peacemaking life, it is in itself our peace exemplified, and his resurrection is the hope that we who make peace have in God. If we share in his suffering, we do so with the faith that we will share in his glory.

Thus far, I have focused mainly on the actual life of Jesus as presented in the biblical narratives. But the epistles also identify reconciliation and peacemaking as the very essence of the good news, for it is *good* because it is a non-coercive invitation to be united in God, and it is *news* because if it were not for Jesus the way would not be fully known. I do not here have the space to present how prevalent this unforced, yet proactive peacemaking centered in Christ is throughout the NT, so I will discuss only a couple of passages and note how we are by no means exempt from the call. Jesus as a maker of peace is stated explicitly in Eph 2:

> For he himself is our peace, who has made the two one and has destroyed the barrier, the dividing wall of hostility, by abolishing in his flesh the law with its commandments and regulations. His purpose was to create in himself one new person out of the two, thus making peace, and in this one body to reconcile both of them to God through the cross, by which he put to death their hostility. He came and preached peace to you who were far away and peace to those who were near.

Paul saw Jesus creating a unified body out of divided peoples, specifically Gentiles (the ethnicities/nations) and Jews. This peace and reconciliation came through real, material sacrifice and suffering. This is why Paul repeatedly mentions participating in Christ's suffering, which is so small compared to Christ's glory (the reconciliation of divided peoples). Christians are told to imitate God, not abstractly but in a concrete and particular way, "just as Christ loved us and gave himself up for us as a fragrant offering and sacrifice to God" (Eph 5.2b). Paul calls the faithful disciples "letters from Christ" who have the ministry and message of reconciliation (2 Cor 3–5) and who suffer terribly because of it (2 Cor 6).

Reference to Johannine literature must also be made in talking about Christology and peacemaking. The sectarian nature of the Fourth Gospel baffles many scholars today. How do we view the church's call to peacemaking in light of Johannine dualities?[17] How does the Johannine corpus relate to love of neighbor? Johannine literature calls the Christian community to be a witness of peace to a world that rejects them. This vocation includes missional peacemaking that is "cross-cultural and breaks racial boundaries."[18]

Many scholars focus on the sectarian nature of John's gospel, and even use the dualities—light versus darkness and child of God versus child of the devil—as support for the abolishing of Jesus' call to peace. To some, the vitriolic language used in reference to the Jews is evidence to a community where love of neighbor applies only to the Christian community, and therefore hatred of the enemy. Willard Swartley eloquently argues the opposite: "John's pervasive emphasis on love for one another becomes the means of appeal to outsiders, an essential form of encounter with the world. Love for one another is the *mark* of the community (13:34–35; 1 John 4:21) *the characteristic that draws people toward Jesus, as Jesus spoke about his own mission*—'I will draw all people to myself'" (12:32; cf. 3:14–16).[19]

The text of John makes explicit that the world may hate followers of Christ just as they hated Christ (John 3.20; 15.18; 17.14–16; 1 John 3.13) but Jesus never insists on reciprocal treatment. In fact, the passages of the upper room discourse and John 3 point to the love of the Christian community as its prophetic gift to the world:

> We may conclude from these considerations that the love commandment passages in John 13 and 15 are at home both theologically and socially in the context of the Johannine community's conflict with the synagogue authorities. The community's mutual love served as part of its testimony to the divinity of Jesus and also as an essential factor against the hatred it perceived itself as experiencing as a consequence of that testimony.[20]

---

17. I use duality here instead of dualism, which is in many cases preferred, in order to assert that the exclusivity of dualism paints a contradictory view of God and the world. Dualities, however point out a fundamental difference between God and the world, but still something that God can transcend and transform. All of the "dualities" talked about in John are still under the sovereignty of God. For a more in depth analysis of this topic, see M. Volf, "Johannine Dualism and Contemporary Pluralism," *Mod. Theol.* 21 (2005) 191–92.

18. W. M. Swartley, *Covenant of Peace* (Grand Rapids: Eerdmans, 2006) 314.

19. Ibid., 296.

20. D. Rensberger, "Love for One Another and Love for Enemies in the Gospel of John," in *The Love of Enemy and Nonretaliation in the New Testament*, ed. W. M. Swartley (Louisville, KY: WJKP, 1992) 301. For a more detailed analysis of the historical framework of the Johannine corpus, see D. Rensberger, *Johannine Faith and Liberating Community* (Philadelphia: Westminster, 1988) 15–36.

The Christian community, therefore, though much more sectarian in John's gospel, still has the ability and commission to be a community that witnesses to the transformative power of Jesus' message and to welcome *all* into the community who reflect that call.

This leads to a significant example of peacemaking in John's gospel: the encounter between Jesus and the Samaritan woman in John 4. This passage and John 20.19–23 speak to Christ's missional call to be peacemakers.[21] The encounter "is the foundation and possibility for peacemaking between alienated peoples, Jews and Samaritans."[22] In order to understand the nature of peacemaking in John, the context of this story must be understood as the disciples may have understood it. Jesus does not merely go to the "bad part of town," but rather engages with a people—specifically a woman—whom Jews hated dating back to the exile. For this reason, Jesus' offer of peace in John 20.21 should not be considered an offer of peace of mind, but rather a call to make peace. In both passages Jesus includes a commission, "I sent you to reap for that which you did not labor" (4.38) and "As the father has sent me, even so I send you" (20.21). Jesus does not send the disciples into the community of his followers, but rather into the world: "Within the fabric of the Gospel as a whole, together with her community and the community empowered by the commission represent the light of salvation, transformation, peace, and reconciliation in a world of hate, blindness, and persecution. Peacemaking is the mission; the mission is peacemaking—through the transforming power of the one who is the savior of the world."[23]

The Gospel of John then develops a new order for peacemaking where the example of peacemaking transforms into worship. Jesus defines a coming time when the worship barriers between even the most hated enemies will be broken down and worship will, "mediate the worship and peacemaking themes in that the alienating ideologies of cult are transcended by 'spirit and truth' that knows no worship wars, specifically none of geography or edifice."[24] In the same way Christian community must be an embodiment of Christ's mission, which extends beyond gender, racial, religious, and social divides and into enemy territory. Taking Christology seriously means seeing the prophetic witness of the Johannine community as a call to love in the midst of hate.[25]

---

21. Swartley, *Covenant of Peace*, 312–16.

22. Ibid., 304.

23. Ibid., 316.

24. Ibid., 307.

25. Special thanks to Jake Goertz for assisting me in the research and writing of this section on Johannine literature.

But These are Written . . .

Peacemaking is an essential Christian practice because it is the essence of Jesus the Christ, the precise Jesus of Nazareth presented in the Scriptures that made peace between peoples and with God. This Jesus is portrayed as the fulfillment of the hope of the Hebrew Scriptures and the call to Israel to be the prophet, priest, and witness to the world. This is a new covenant that reads the old covenant through the revelation in Jesus and calls the obedient to follow in his way. But love of enemies and forgiveness for one's murderer, hospitality for strangers and speaking truth to those with the power to kill, attempting to unite factions and divided people, these things seem quite difficult and almost impossible. How can this happen? What makes this a possibility for us rather than just a foolish dream? The answer to this question has been supplied by pentecostals for years, but it is time to link our fascination with the Holy Spirit to a Christology that is faithful to Jesus and his invitation to us.

PNEUMATOLOGY AS THE *MEANS* OF PENTECOSTAL PEACEMAKING

It has been shown that Luke's pneumatology continually empowers people to turn to God's way (seen best in Jesus) both in actions and speaking.[26] From Elizabeth, Mary, Zechariah, and John to the disciples after Pentecost, the Holy Spirit is crucial to the embodiment and declaration of what God is doing through Jesus and his followers. Jesus himself is also described as being "full of the Holy Spirit," "led by the Spirit," and "in the power of the Spirit" (Luke 4.1, 14). This is necessary because the path of reconciliation which involves healing demon-possessed outcasts at the expense of thousands of dollars worth of livestock is dangerous (Luke 8).[27] The call to sacrifice and suffering in order to bring peace is made possible only through God's gift of the Holy Spirit. We are not called to be superhuman—we are not expected to simply will ourselves into loving our enemies with some

---

26. J. B. Shelton, *Mighty in Word and Deed: The Role of the Holy Spirit in Luke-Acts* (Peabody, MA: Hendrickson, 1991); R. Stronstad, *The Charismatic Theology of St. Luke* (Peabody, MA: Hendrickson, 1985). By calling the Holy Spirit a means to an end is immediately to risk objectifying the Spirit rather than respecting the Spirit as a person of the Trinity. However, I view the Spirit this way based on the biblical presentation of the goal of Spirit-baptism/filling as particularly described in Luke-Acts. Specifically in Acts 1.8, "you will receive power when the Holy Spirit comes on you, and you will be my witnesses (martyrs) . . ."

27. Valuing people above stock (corporations, returns, dividends, etc.) today can have the same effects: healing for the dispossessed and anger accompanied by invitations to leave from the stockholders.

sentimental affection. Instead, we are called to be filled with the Spirit and imitate Christ. Jesus was empowered to love and value the rejected (women, lepers, thieves, foreigners, etc.) as a Spirit-filled human. The Lukan narrative recounts Jesus introducing his first public proclamation of good news to the poor, imprisoned, blind, and oppressed with his declaration, "the Spirit of the Lord is upon me." Christology shows us how to live and die while making peace; pneumatology enables it. This is a christomorphic pneumatology.[28] Luke makes a special point to show that Jesus relied on the Holy Spirit to help him through the temptations. "The way Jesus overcame temptation is a paradigm for the way his followers would overcome temptation . . . the temptations of Jesus are real . . . he overcomes the evil as God expects all people to triumph—through the power of the Holy Spirit."[29] I agree and would like to move past an abstract concept of overcoming of "temptations" to discuss the exact ones with which Jesus dealt. Jesus was offered many opportunities to use force or coercion to bring about the kingdom of God, but he prayed and trusted in the empowerment of the Spirit each time to reject this realistic and truly tempting option. He rejected the use of evil means to obtain a righteous end, but instead entrusted himself to God. It is no accident that he instructed his disciples to pray that they would not fall into temptation in the garden, and then told them to receive the power of the Spirit from on high so that they could disciple the nations. Making disciples requires an empowerment greater than can come from within oneself. Reconciling with enemies, loving outcasts, and challenging the status quo all necessitate the same empowering that the prophets of old and the Messiah himself were described as having.

Acts also portrays the relationship between the Holy Spirit and imitating Christ in reconciliation. The "witness" (μάρτυριός) or martyr, was for the entire world and crossed all linguistic and ethnic boundaries. The sixteen nations represented in Acts 2 all came together and formed Christ's body of which he is the head, with even Gentiles being brought in later. However, pentecostal pneumatology has only recently been linked with the biblical witness to christocentric peacemaking, and this needs continued attention.

A pentecostal pneumatology will remind us that we have God's empowering presence to realistically live lives that imitate Christ's forgiveness of enemies and sacrifice for reconciliation.[30] To be the unified yet broken

---

28. I am exploring christomorphic pneumatology more fully in a theological ethics book I am currently writing.

29. Shelton, *Word and Deed*, 58–60. He lists the temptations that bothered Jesus during his life as popular views of righteousness, taking short cuts, and condoning evil to do good.

30. This is a reference to G. Fee, *God's Empowering Presence: The Holy Spirit in the*

body of Christ in the world, to practice the transforming initiatives of peacemaking given by Jesus, and to truly be ministers of reconciliation is to fully depend on the empowerment of the Holy Spirit.[31] The Spirit was the enabling means for Jesus to live in tension with his enemies while inviting them to repent. The Spirit is God's gift to empower the church to be what we claim to be: the people of God who hope to glorify God as we daily pick up our instruments of execution and follow Christ.

I have briefly tried to show that Jesus is the source for our commitment to making peace between divided people. The parameters of this peace initiative extend as far as our worst enemy and as close as the people in our own homes, recognizing that our efforts will sometimes bring a sword, instead of peace, upon ourselves. Any disagreement about the primacy of peacemaking will have to be a discussion about how seriously we are to take Jesus as the Messiah, as our Lord, and as our example.

I have also attempted to show that Christology as a source for peacemaking is not sufficient because we cannot do it on our own. Just as we need God to show us the way in Jesus Christ, we need God to enable us to walk in it and follow. Thankfully, God has done this in Pentecost when he created a Spirit-empowered people who rely on and trust that this really is the way of redemption. Baptism in the Holy Spirit is the means by which we are enabled to be faithful even when it hurts, and to remember that peace and patience go together.

I am overjoyed and overwhelmed by the possibilities that Christ-centered, Spirit-empowered peacemaking presents to pentecostals. At the beginning of this twenty-first century, we number six hundred million that God has empowered to follow Christ as peacemakers who sow in peace. It must not be efficacy that determines our witness, but faithfulness to Christ alone. We may not always transform our enemies, but we can be faithful and seek their friendship by offering forgiveness and love. May the Spirit who led Israel, Jesus, and our ancestors in the faith lead us as well.

Letters of Paul (Peabody, MA: Hendrickson, 1994).

31. G. Stassen, *Just Peacemaking: Transforming Initiatives for Justice and Peace* (Louisville, KY: WJKP, 1992). 1) Acknowledge your alienation and God's grace realistically; 2) Go, talk, welcome one another, and seek to be reconciled; 3) Do not resist revengefully, but take transforming initiatives for peace; 4) Invest in delivering justice; 5) Love your enemies with actions, affirm their valid interests; 6) Pray for your enemies and bless them; persevere in prayer; 7) Do not judge, but repent and forgive; 8) Do peacemaking in a church or a group of disciples.

11

The Love of God
An Interdisciplinary Approach to Developing and Measuring Spiritual Maturity Based on a Johannine Love Ethic

EDWARD W. WATSON AND ANGELA L. WATSON

WHEN CONTACTED ABOUT OUR participation in this *Festschrift* written to honor the career of Ben Aker, it seemed natural for us to use this opportunity to report on a study that we had recently conducted which centered on measuring spiritual development. Professor Aker's career-long emphasis upon a Johannine model of love provides the perfect opportunity for us to honor him with this study. As a tribute to Dr. Aker's esteemed career, the following essay will seek to do three things. First, we will survey the love ethic presented in John's gospel and developed further in John's epistles.[1] Second, we will connect this love ethic to the spiritual development model established in Bernard of Clairvaux's work, *On Loving God*.[2] Third, we will describe an interdisciplinary approach to constructing a new measure of spiritual development and re-

---

1. It is the opinion of the authors that the Gospel and Epistles of John represent a common stream of tradition and as such, arguments of authorship lie outside the scope of this study.

2. Bernard of Clairvaux, *Bernard of Clairvaux: Selected Works*, trans. G. R. Evans (San Francisco: HarperSanFrancisco, 2005) 47–93.

port the empirical results of the instrument administered to college students, both theology and non-theology majors, based upon the Johannine model conceptualized through the lens of Clairvaux.

THE JOHANNINE LOVE ETHIC

The Gospel of John

Scholars have long debated whether or not John's gospel contains an actual moral ethic. In John's gospel, Jesus offers no real instruction to his disciples about the conduct of life until after he withdraws from his public ministry. Then, in John 13.34, he makes only one command to his disciples: "Love one another."[3] Although this command at first blush seems to lack specificity, in 15.12 Jesus goes on to expand the command with the qualifier "love one another *just as* I have loved you" (καθώς—cf.13.15; 15.9, 12; 17.11, 23). This addition to Jesus' earlier love command establishes a moral ethic where the perceived expected extent of love between Jesus' followers, as per his example, "is to be limitless in its self-giving."[4] The degree of love that is to exist between the followers of Jesus is to be measured against the magnitude of the love Jesus has for them. Jesus states that this "greater love" is ultimately gauged by the willingness "to lay down one's life for one's friends" (15.13).[5]

While some scholars maintain that John offers no real moral ethic at all and Jesus' command to love is unduly vague and overtly sectarian,[6] oth-

---

3. All Scripture translations are my own.

4. D. M. Smith, *Johannine Christianity: Essays on its Setting, Sources, and Theology* (Columbia: University of South Carolina Press, 1984) 178.

5. Jesus provides his disciples an example of self-denying love in the footwashing pericope which offers an emblematic sign of Jesus' self-sacrificing love ethic where the more powerful serve the weaker (John 13). Jesus states that the act is "an example that you should do as I have done for you" (John 13.15). That the episode points to a willingness to offer the ultimate self-sacrifice as expressed in the cross is found in Jesus' statement following the footwashing episode in 15.13: "Greater love has no one than this: to lay down one's life for one's friends." In the same way that Jesus was willing to humbly offer his life for others, so believers are to demonstrate this same type of love toward others. Richard Hays writes: "Jesus' death is depicted by John . . . as an act of self-sacrificial love that establishes the cruciform life as the norm for discipleship" (*The Moral Vision of the New Testament* [San Francisco: Harper, 1996] 145).

6. See W. Meeks, "Ethics of the Fourth Evangelist," in *Exploring the Gospel of John: In Honor of D. Moody Smith*, eds. R. A. Culpepper and C. C. Black (Louisville, KY: WJKP, 1996) 317. Meeks goes on to argue that the "love one another" rule creates a sectarianism that is "limited solely to those who are firmly within the Johannine circle" (318). Yet, while the community's primary responsibility is to love one another, the idea of world mission is not absent from the tradition as some would argue. In fact, the whole

ers like Andreas Köstenberger have done a good job refuting this argument by making the case that contained within Jesus' love command in John is a "deliberate focalization of all of Jesus' ethical demands" presented in the entirety of the canonical gospels and squarely established in the OT commands to love God and one's neighbor (Matt 22.37-40; cf. Deut 6.5; Lev 19.18).[7] This rationale acknowledges that, chronologically, the "new command" of love in John 13.34 is not new at all since in the heart of the Torah we find the commands to "love your neighbor as yourself" (Lev 19.18) and also to love the foreigner who resides among you (Lev 19.34). Further, the connection of the command to love one's neighbors (later extended to the love of enemies; Matt 5.43-48) with the command to love God formulates the center of Jesus' ethical teachings in the Synoptic Gospels (Mark 12.30-31). Yet, the Johannine love ethic, rather than betraying these traditions in order to create a reclusive and sectarian environment, actually builds upon these traditional aspects of moral conduct to provide a more intensive command centered upon the *new measure of love required* of the believer.[8] It is no longer simply a command to love others "as yourself," but rather believers are commanded to love according to the self-sacrificial measure of the love that Jesus has for them.

Moreover, the OT command to love God is also echoed throughout the story-world of John's narrative since obedience to this command in Johannine thought means to love and accept the one sent from God (John 3.31-36; 6.32-33, 35; 8.27-29; 10.30).[9] By loving and receiving Jesus, one is loving and receiving God, for "anyone who does not honor the Son does not honor the Father who sent him" (John 5.23). John claims that those who love God and are fathered by God will love and accept the Son of God sent

---

of the gospel is centered upon God's love for the world (cf. John 1.29; 3.16; 8.12; 9.5; 12.46-47). Moreover, John 13.34 shows that it is the love within the community that serves as testimony to the world. It is to this world mission that the disciples have been commanded to embark (John 17.18; 20.21). So, while it does seem that ethics takes a back seat to Christology in John's gospel, John cannot be restricted merely to its didactic content, but rather requires a fuller reading of the story to grasp the implications for the life of the community, cf. Hays, *Moral Vision*, 140. See also A. Köstenberger, "The Moral Vision of John," *MidJT* 4/2 (Spring 2006) 3-23. See also H. Boersma, "A New Age Love Story: Worldview and Ethics in the Gospel of John," *CTJ* 38/1 (Apr 2003) 116-17.

7. A. Köstenberger, "The Johannine Love Ethic," in *A Theology of John's Gospel and Letters* (Grand Rapids: Zondervan, 2009) 511.

8. See J. Bolyki, "Ethics in the Gospel of John," *CV* 45/3(2003) 204.

9. John claims that whoever accepts the son accepts the Father who sent him (14.6-9) receives the light that God sent into the world (1.3-5; 8.12) abides in God (15.4-9) is fathered by God (1.11-12) and as a result will have eternal life (3.16). Yet, those who reject the Son of God are condemned because they love the darkness rather than the light (3.18-21) and as a result are condemned to blindness (John 9.39-41).

into the world (John 8.42). If one does not receive the one sent from God, then one's claim to know and love God is deficient (John 5.37, 42; 8.15–19, 38–44, 53–55; 10.25–26).

So, although the decrees to love God and to love one's neighbor are easily established in the OT and the Synoptic traditions, echoes of these same mandates are contained in the Johannine tradition as well. Captured within John's gospel is a strong moral ethic founded upon the Torah, enhanced by the entirety of the moral teachings of Jesus centered upon loving God and loving others, and brought to final completion by the measure of Jesus' own love for his followers and the reception of the light that God sent into the world. According to the Johannine tradition, although one can make the claim that he or she loves God and loves others, if one is not willing to accept the Son sent from God or willing to lay down one's life for a friend, then one's claims of loving God and loving others are defective. Thus, rather than being a text that subverts the commands of the Torah and the Synoptic moral ethic, Johannine tradition actually intensifies these moral directives.

In the Johannine Epistles

First John 3.23 goes on to conceptualize these foundational commands into two basic complementary trajectories: Believers are "to believe in the name of his Son Jesus Christ" (i.e., love for God as shown in one's acceptance of God's self-sacrificial love for the world in Christ; 1 John 3.16; 4.9; 5.1–5); and to "love one another" (cf. 1 John 3.11, 14, 18; 4.7–8, 19–21). Interestingly, in 1 John, as in John's gospel, one's love for God and one's love for others are inextricably tied together. First John 4.21 states that "the commandment we have from him is this: those who love God must love their brothers and sisters also." The reason that the attribute of love is certain to be found in the children of God (who have expressed their love of God by their faith in Jesus Christ) is that doing so is consistent with the character of their father. That is, "God is love" (1 John 4.16b). In fact, the outgrowth of one's love for God as expressed in one's love for God's people is to serve as an assurance for believers that they are truly born of God: "We know that we have passed from death to life *because* we love one another" (1 John 3.14; emphasis mine). Conversely, John states that the opponents of 1 John who refuse to love their brothers and sisters do not love God (1 John 4.20–21) and "do not have eternal life abiding in them" (1 John 3.15). So, when believers "love one another," they exhibit their Father's character and have assurance that they have been "born of God and know God" (1 John 4.7).

The Love of God

Moreover, this presence of love in the believer's life is to generate boldness even for the Day of Judgment (1 John 4.17). The assurance that comes from the Father's character in the earthly lives of believers is culminated in the declaration, "As he is, so are we in this world" (1 John 4.17). This assertion is explained in 4.16b (and earlier in 4.8) when the Apostle reveals that "God is love." If God is love in this world, then his children who harbor his character within them are also to be love to those around them in need. The epistle expounds upon Jesus' love ethic found in the gospel not only by reiterating the imperative that members of the community are to love one another, but also by providing a practical implication. That is, Christians prove their godly love by adhering to the example of Christ and sacrificing their own interests in service of others (1 John 3.16; John 15.12–15) especially those with fewer resources from whom Christians have nothing to gain (1 John 3.17–18).[10] Moreover, John adds that this kind of self-denying love is to be the distinguishing mark of God's children (1 John 3.10). By fulfilling this love command, proof is given that a person is truly a disciple of Jesus (1 John 2.7–11; cf. 3.23; 4.19–21; 5.2–3). As believers emulate Jesus' love by putting others first, by denying self, and by enacting sacrificial service, the world will come to know God's love (John 13.34–35; 15.10–17; 17.20–25) because "through our acts of love, the invisible God is made visible—palpable—among us."[11]

If the Johannine love ethic mandates that self-sacrificial love is a trait that God's children have inherited from God, then it is impossible for the sons and daughters of God to turn away and refuse to love, in that love is ontologically and divinely embedded within their very beings.[12] So, in John's

---

10. Sharing the world's goods is but one example of practicing one's love towards another. The pragmatic example of economic justice should invite the community to consider other possible ways they can show love towards others.

11. Hays, *Moral Vision*, 375. See also J. G. van der Watt, "Ethics and Ethos in the Gospel according to John," *ZNW* 97 (2006) 147–76.

12. This point is strengthened by the rhetorical argument found in 1 John 2.29—3.10 where John contends that the children of God will look like the father, who begat them. John notes in this section that whereas the children of the devil look like their father (3.8) the children of God will look like their father by displaying his characteristics as well (3.9–10). For further information on how the children of God cannot refuse to follow God's command of love, see my article entitled "The Litmus Test of God's Children: Solving a Johannine Contradiction by Rereading 1 John 3:9–10 in Light of an Epexegetical Rendering of KAI," *Pax Pneuma* (2012) 31–41. As I argued there, it is my belief that the key to understanding how believers cannot sin (a shocking inclusion by John in 3.9) is found in 1 John 3.10 if translated correctly. Not only does 3.10 provide the explanation to the "cannot sin" statement in 3.9, it also contains the solution to the apparent inconsistency about sin in the life of the believer that plagues 1 John as a whole (compare 1 John 1.8, 10 with 1 John 3.6, 8–9). When 1 John 3.9–10 is translated

epistles, the Johannine love ethic is reflected in one's love for God resulting in the acceptance of his provision "that we should believe in the name of his Son Jesus Christ" and one's love for each another (3.23). In the end, whereas the opponents in 1 John failed in both of these commands, the true church simply cannot fail in them and still be the church because love is the distinguishing characteristic of the one who has been born of God.

JOHN'S LOVE ETHIC, BERNARD OF CLAIRVAUX, AND THE STAIRCASE OF CHRISTIAN MATURITY

Given that John's writings indicate that love is the marker of those who are born of God, it logically follows that as one grows more mature in Christ, one's love for God and for others will also continue to increase. This point was developed by the twelfth-century abbot St. Bernard of Clairvaux (1090–1153) in his letter entitled *On Loving God*, written for the cardinal deacon and chancellor of the Roman church. Clairvaux articulated a spiritual development process consistent with the Johannine love ethic by describing the changes that take place in believers' hearts as they are transformed into the image of Christ. Interestingly, as with John's writings, Clairvaux does not separate love of God from love of others, but rather sees the love for others as a natural outgrowth of one's love for God. He writes "How can you love your neighbor with purity if you do not love him in God? But he who does not love God cannot love in God. You must first love God, so that in him you can love your neighbor too."[13]

Clairvaux based his conceptualization upon five biblical assumptions: 1) God is love; 2) God created people in his image; 3) God desires the love of people; 4) with God's help, people can progressively learn to reciprocate God's love; and 5) God rewards the love of his people. Thus, God created people out of his nature, which is love, and he desires their reciprocal affection. People, however, are not innately equipped to reciprocate God's love. Rather, they are innately equipped to *develop the ability* to reciprocate God's

---

by allowing the καὶ in v. 10 to function epexegetically, the text ultimately and, in my opinion, correctly argues that children of God who have God's seed within them, cannot sin by refusing to love their brothers and sisters. Moreover, it is consistent with the author's arguments elsewhere since the specific sins that the opponents are accused of in the Johannine letters are essentially twofold: failing to love others (2.9; 3.11–12; 3.14–15; 3.17–18; 4.8; 4.20) and denying that Jesus is the Christ (2.22; 4.3; 2 John 7). Further, this reading also solves the apparent inconsistency between 1 John 3.6, 9 and 1.6–2.1 in that Christians do commit sin according to 1.6—2.9; yet, with regard to their confession of faith in Christ and their love for one another they cannot waiver.

13. Clairvaux, *On Loving God*, 75.

love. God subsequently meets each person at his or her present point of development and nurtures the developing capacity to love. As people begin to reciprocate God's love, they are consequently rewarded with the person of God (i.e., the object of their love).[14]

The Staircase of Christian Maturity Defined

Clarvaux's process through which people learn to experience and reciprocate God's love can be conceptualized as a staircase of Christian maturity. The staircase contains four steps:

> *Step One: The Love of Self for Self's Sake:* On this step, egocentric individuals enjoy God's love without being aware of God as the source of this love.
>
> *Step Two: The Love of God for Self's Sake:* On this step, individuals become aware that God is the source of love and thus begin to value God for the sake of that love, which they enjoy.
>
> *Step Three: The Love of God for God's Sake:* On this step, individuals begin to love God as their appreciation for him grows and they recognize God as an entity worthy of love even apart from the love that he provides for the individuals.
>
> *Step Four: The Love of Self for God's Sake:* On step four, individuals have grown to love God so completely that they take on God's love for his creation and love self for God's sake (with the self being redefined as the community of creation). On this step, individuals' appreciation for God has grown to the extent that they identify with God's own love for the whole of creation, even loving the redefined self for God's sake.

All people originate on the lowest step of this staircase and progressively move upward with God's help. Consistent with Object Relations Development Theory, however, each successive step would be theoretically based upon the growth that occurred on the preceding step(s).[15] Just as a child who grows up to share a mutually loving relationship with a par-

---

14. Ibid., 72–73.
15. For more on Object Relations Development Theory and potential spiritual applications, see T. Hall and K. Edwards, "The Spiritual Assessment Inventory: A Theistic Model and Measure for Assessing Spiritual Development," *JSSR* 41/2 (2002) 341–57. Also, see C. A. Meier, "Projection, Transference, and the Subject-Object Relation in Psychology," *JAP* 4 (1959) 21–34.

ent presumably developed into a reciprocating partner from a position of gratified dependence, so a Christian grows to reciprocate God's love after first moving through an immature focus upon the gratification of being in relationship with God. Thus, a person's development on the staircase reflects the natural maturation process, not a superior or inferior position in Christ. That is, Clairvaux's model presupposes that love for God derives from grace.

The Process of Growth Between the Steps

The individual initially meets God upon the first, foundational step. Clairvaux posits that non-Christians perceive that God, the creator, is responsible for their existence and the world in which they live (e.g., Rom 1.18–25). Consequently, even people who do not know him are able to respond to the God who created them with an immature kind of love. With reference to the first commandment to love God, Clairvaux explains that "because nature has become rather frail and weak, man is driven by necessity to serve nature first."[16] This attention to nature results in one's love for the body, given that the person "does not yet know anything but himself, as it is written, 'first came what is animal, then what is spiritual' (1 Cor. 15:46) and 'No man ever yet hated his own flesh' (Eph. 5:29)."[17] Axiomatically, according to Clairvaux, this human love for itself leads to love for God, from whom not only people but also the created things that gratify them have been derived.

Along a similar line of reasoning, together with created humankind's love for God, the creator, there exists a complementary human love one for another, the objects of creation. Clairvaux maintains that this love for others is inherent in the created person as a regulatory safeguard against humanity's self-love to grow "headstrong, as often happens, and it ceases to be satisfied to run in the narrow channel of its needs, but floods out on all sides into the fields of pleasure."[18] The second commandment, then, stops the overflow at once: "Thou shalt love thy neighbor as thyself." Clairvaux states: "This is wholly right that he who is your fellow in nature should not be cut off from you in grace, especially in the grace that is innate in nature."[19] Clairvaux surmises that Christ's two greatest commandments can be obeyed on the first step of spiritual maturity through the pro-social expression of our selfish love when it "is shared, when it is extended to the community."[20]

16. Clairvaux, *On Loving God*, 73.
17. Ibid., 73.
18. Ibid., 74.
19. Ibid.
20. Ibid.

As people grow more self-aware at this stage of development, they begin to perceive that they need God to facilitate their love for one another, in that it is God who provides them both love for themselves as well as the capacity to love others. Clairvaux compares this person to a wise man, "who is a bodily animal and does not know how to love anything" but who realizes that an alliance with God can lead to "everything that is good" and that, independent of God, he or she "can do nothing."[21] Loving self for self's sake is defined here as loving self because that is the natural response of the created person. People instinctively nurture themselves to ensure their survival. Moreover, they are able to recognize that this survival is further enhanced by relationships with other people. A person at this stage might be motivated by the thought, *"I want to be happy."* Another salient motivation at this stage might be, *"I want relationships with others that make me happy."* Hence, the focus at this stage is upon the drive to satisfy the individual's needs.

As noted, progression to the second step is precipitated by the development that takes place on the first step. Clairvaux expounds that while those on the first step are taught to attribute to God the gratification of their needs, on the second step their hearts become "softened toward the generosity of the redeemer."[22] They perceive through their own experience that the creator is a good God (Ps 34.8). At this stage of development, people realize that the God they met on the first step as the source of their fulfillment is unfailingly faithful and unselfish, consequently deserving of love in his own right. At this second step, obedience to love one another becomes even more natural as this developing individual "truly loves God, and therefore he loves what is God's."[23]

Loving God for self's sake is defined here as loving God as a result of what God has done on behalf of people. The origin of this embryonic, reciprocal love is described in the Johannine explanation that people love God because he loved them first (1 John 4.19). A person at this stage of development might be motivated by the thought, *"Everything good in my life comes from God. Nothing good in my life has been given to me apart from God."* Another motivating thought at this stage might be, *"God has shown me how to love. I would not be able to love others except that God has taught me how."* Hence, the developmental focus is the broadening perception of the multifaceted ways in which God is able to improve the individual's life. This increasing appreciation for the person of God results in a growing

---

21. Ibid., 76.
22. Ibid.
23. Ibid., 77.

recognition that God, as the source of these meaningful and important contributions, also deserves to be loved.

Again, progression to the third step was necessarily preceded by growth on the second step. Similarly, the development that occurred on the second step was engendered by the development that took place on the first. Thus, progression to the third step does not render the development that occurred on the preceding steps unimportant. Rather, the development of the third step should theoretically reorient the relevance of growth that took place at lower levels within a broadening perspective. This reorientation should occur naturally as a result of the individual's developing ability to appreciate and return God's love.

Individuals at the third developmental step have known the goodness of God in their lives. They have discerned God's worthy character. Moreover, they have grown to realize that the gracious and infallible nature of God entitles him to adoration regardless of the benefits the individual has derived from his or her relationship with God. According to Clairvaux, "He who trusts in the Lord not because he is good to him but simply because he is good truly loves God for God's sake and not for his own."[24]

Loving God for God's sake is defined here as loving God because of who God is. Clairvaux points to the psalmist as someone on this step when he proclaimed, "'We trust in the Lord, for he is good' (Ps. 118.1)."[25] A person at this stage of development might be motivated by the thought, *"I love God because of his essential goodness."* Another motivating thought on this step might be, *"God alone is worthy of adoration."* Hence, the focus at this stage is the celebration of God's irresistible and praiseworthy character.

Clairvaux asserts that the fourth step is probably not realized in this life, given that people appear unable to firmly grasp more than a momentary hold on the insight required to sustain one's position at this level. At the fourth step, even the love for self is filtered through one's identity in God.[26] Clairvaux posits that people are not really capable of perfect obedience to the first command in this incarnation because of the constant need to attend to the needs of the created body.[27] Subsequently, "as long as the care of the weak and miserable body demands one's attention"[28] people are incapable of fully abandoning themselves to love God, regardless of their sincere desire to do so.

24. Ibid.
25. Ibid.
26. Ibid., 78.
27. Ibid., 80.
28. Ibid.

Clairvaux allows, however, that a person would be truly "blessed and holy" if, while still in this body of flesh, he or she gained "even for a single instant something that is rare indeed in this life. To lose yourself as though you did not exist and to have no sense of yourself, to be emptied out of yourself and almost annihilated," wholly integrated as one whose identity was only in God.[29] Clairvaux argues that because everything has been created for God's glory (Isa 43.7) everything in creation should rightly conform to God's will. The complete abdication of self-service to utterly submit to God's interests would result in a transcendent ecstasy in which the individual were set free from weights that otherwise distract him or her from this glorious obedience. Clairvaux explains: "If indeed any mortal is rapt for a moment or is, so to speak admitted for a moment to this union, at once the world presses itself on him, the day's wickedness troubles him, the mortal body weighs him down, bodily needs distract him, he fails because of the weakness of his corruption, and—more powerfully than these—brotherly love calls him back."[30]

This internal conflict is reminiscent of the apostle Paul's struggle between leaving this life to be present with Christ versus remaining for the benefit to his fellow Christians (Phil 1.21–24). Clairvaux speculates that until the eschaton when people are given new celestial bodies, one's position at this step cannot be sustained. Nevertheless, he encourages his readers. Recalling Rom 8.28, Clairvaux expounds that the, "weak body helps the soul to love God; it helps it when it is dead; it helps it when it is resurrected, first in producing fruits of patience, second in bringing peace, third in bringing completeness. Truly the soul does not want to be perfected without what it feels has served it well in every condition. It is clear that the flesh is a good and faithful companion to the good spirit."[31]

Loving self for God's sake is defined here as loving the self as a member of God's beloved creation, reflective of God's glory, a unique expression of God's will. Clairvaux postulates, "The fourth degree of love is attained for ever [sic] when we love God only and supremely, when we do not even love ourselves except for God's sake."[32] A person at this stage of development might be motivated by the thought, *"My purpose is to live in perfect and uninterrupted union with God."* Another motivating thought might be, *"God is now in all and nothing merely human remains in his people."* Hence, the focus on this step is upon the complete integration of one's identity with God, in

29. Ibid., 78.
30. Ibid., 78–79.
31. Ibid., 82.
32. Ibid., 84.

perfect uninterrupted communion and without worldly distractions. As a result of this divine union, the sense of self is redefined and the individual is perceived as part of the created community, made one with its creator. It is interesting to note that, according to Scripture, people appear to be capable of attaining this level of development for only short periods of time before they are returned to the work left to do at the third step (Rom 8.22–23; 2 Cor 5.1–5). Preoccupation with the fourth step, then, may actually be indicative of a developmental problem. That is, the striving to achieve union with God should not express itself in a desire to avoid the hard work of development by escaping into a projection of God. This immature urge would not lead to the authentic attainment of the fourth level of development, but instead would distract the individual from developing authentic love for God and others.[33]

MEASURING SPIRITUAL MATURITY BASED ON A JOHANNINE LOVE ETHIC

Clairvaux's staircase of Christian maturity builds upon the Johannine love ethic by revealing that as believers mature in their love for God (for God's sake) those believers will also mature in their love for others. To this end, one of the authors has developed a measure of spiritual maturity based on the writings of St. Bernard of Clairvaux utilizing the Johannine love ethic as a guide.[34] The purpose of our study was to conceptualize and operationalize a model of spiritual development that accurately approximates Christian spiritual maturity as expressed through the ability to love as God loves, according to a Johannine framework. Our study conceptualized spiritual maturity in terms of epigenetic stage development defined by an individual's faith and love for God and the individual's love for humanity (1 John 3.23; cf. Matt 22.37–39; Mark 12.30–31) that is consistent with current developmental theories. In other words, development is expected to progress along a generally linear continuum but would also be expected to include fluctuations. That is, authentic movement forward would occasionally necessitate revisiting earlier points of development to reframe prior understandings and beliefs in light of increasingly mature insight into the self and relationships with others.

---

33. See Hall and Edwards, "The Spiritual Assessment Inventory," 341–57. Also, see C. A. Meier, "Projection, Transference," 21–34.

34. See A. Watson, *A Developmental Approach to Measuring Spiritual Maturity from a Christian Perspective* (Ann Arbor, MI: UMI Dissertation Publishing, 2011).

The new measure of Christian spiritual maturity consists of two subscales that have been designed to differentiate between stages two and three of Clairvaux's stages of Christian maturity. While loving self for self's sake is a step that does not require a Christian understanding of God and loving self for God's sake is a step that few if any Christians are able to realize, loving God for self's sake and loving God for God's sake are experiences familiar to many Christians. Thus, these two middle steps are the focus of this study.

Differences between loving God for self's sake and loving God for God's sake are focused upon two distinct kinds of reasons motivating love. One identifies with loving God for self's sake when recognizing the personal benefits derived from God. Conversely, one identifies with loving God for God's sake when recognizing that God deserves devotion regardless of any blessings derived from sharing a relationship with him. From an object relations developmental perspective, a healthy relationship should include both of these motivations. Just as wholesome relationships with other people should include elements of both personal gratification and a more selfless appreciation, one's relationship with God should also make room for both kinds of motivation. On the other hand, it seems tenable to propose that depending upon one's current point of development, one individual might be more motivated to love God out of gratification for the blessings derived from him while another individual might be more motivated to love God out of devotion for the inherently worthy nature of God's person. Scripture teaches that Christians imitate God in learning how to love as God loves. They love God because he first loved them (1 John 4.19). Moreover, Christians believe that as they grow in their relationship with God, they are transformed to be more like Christ, taking on his loving nature and expressing love toward the whole of creation (2 Cor 3.18).[35]

Although there is an abundance of biblical support for constructing a model of Christian spiritual maturity, this study employed a Johannine perspective of love to simplify our developmental framework. This conceptualization presumes first of all that people who share healthy relationships with God have been spiritually changed and thus partake of the nature of Christ (1 John 3.1-2; 4.17). Therefore, they have assistance from God to realize this new and developing nature as it is unfolding in their day-to-day

---

35. Jesus frequently complained about the disingenuous quality of devotion belied by external religious acts purported to honor God (e.g., John 5.8-18; 9.1-41; see also Matt 23.23-39). Therefore, this study follows the logic of P. Benson, M. Donahue, and J. Erickson that true faith maturity should find expression in Christian values that are manifested through attitudes and behaviors in agreement with the teachings of Christ ("The Faith Maturity Scale: Conceptualization, Measurement, and Empirical Validation," in *Research in the Social Scientific Study of Religion*, eds. M. L. Lynn and D. O. Moberg. 23 vols. [Greenwich, CT: JAI, 1993] 5:1-26).

lives (1 John 1.8–9). Consequently, Christians experience confidence in the presence of God, assured that their relationship with him is secure, easing concerns that they have fallen short of Christ's perfection (1 John 3.18–22).

Second, Christlike love is this framework's primary evidence to indicate Christian spiritual maturity. That is, given that God is love and Christ is love incarnate, people who claim to follow God must necessarily evidence godly love (1 John 4.7–8; 4.16). Christians have been admonished that it is impossible to love God, whom they cannot see, if this love is not also accompanied by love for the people whom God has brought into their lives (1 John 4.20–21). Moreover, genuine godly love is proven "not in word or speech, but in truth and action" (1 John 3.18). Christ demonstrated his godly love when he took on the form of lowly humanity and made their concerns his own rather than remaining in a divine form above human suffering (John 1.14; 3.16–17). In the same way, Christians who manifest genuine godly love cannot separate themselves and their interests from the interests of God and other people. Like Christ, they must demonstrate their love to others in measurable ways (1 John 3.17)

Constructing the Measure

The new scales of Christian maturity were used to measure spiritual development according to the scriptural tenet that believers should be identifiable by their love for God and humanity (e.g., John 13.35). Borrowing from the conceptual framework outlined by St. Barnard of Clairvaux's staircase of Christian love, sample statements were written to reflect each of the four levels of love development. Next, the authors discussed Clairvaux's theory with subject matter experts including five graduate theology students and two professors with graduate degrees in theology. These experts were then provided with brief descriptions of Clairvaux's four steps along with the sample items and asked to help construct additional items appropriate to the proposed developmental framework. The authors then examined these statements and revised them to improve clarity. A second panel of subject matter experts was recruited to further refine the new items. These experts included a professor with a PhD degree in Biblical Literature, a professor with a doctorate in Missiology, and a professor with a graduate degree in Christian Education. The subject matter experts evaluated the developing statements that reflected the second and third steps of Christian love by examining the revised items in light of brief statements describing the second and third steps of maturing Christian love. The experts then identified each statement by indicating whether or not it most accurately reflected either the second step, loving God for self's sake, or the third step, loving God for God's sake. Only the forty-two statements that were correctly identified by each expert were retained for further analysis.

Testing the Model: Summary of Findings

Although generating a logical theory of Christian spiritual maturity with exegetical support is important, empirically testing that model of Christian maturity in a sample of actual participants is equally important for validating the developing theory. Thus, the authors surveyed 541 students enrolled in a private Christian Midwestern university to learn more about their self-reported perceptions of spiritual and behavioral health. Both sexes were equally represented in this study. The majority of the students queried were between the ages of eighteen to twenty-five (87 percent). Moreover, most of the participants identified themselves as being Assembly of God, non-denominational, or Pentecostal (74 percent) having parents who were married (69 percent) being enrolled in their first or second year of university study (66 percent) being White (61 percent) and having been converted for eight years or longer (61 percent).

Consistent with Clairvaux's model, the less mature developmental stage, loving God for self's sake, was associated with poorer psychological and spiritual health. For example, this step was related to lower levels of object relations development with God, suggesting these participants suffered more instability in their relationships with God. This step was also associated with depression and with an identity status known as foreclosure, in which individuals make strong commitments to beliefs without actually exploring these beliefs and the personal reasons that motivate their convictions.

Also in keeping with Clairvaux's developmental framework, the more mature developmental stage, loving God for God's sake, was associated with psychological and spiritual health. An example was this step's relationship with a sense of awareness of God's presence in one's daily affairs. Similarly, this step was correlated with mature Christian beliefs, attitudes, and behaviors, including a desire to grow in one's relationship with God and to serve others in order to make the world a better place for everyone. This step was also associated with life satisfaction and a fulfilling sense of meaning and purpose.

An interesting finding revealed, however, that despite our hypothesis that development toward a more mature step would grow from foundational understandings built upon lower steps, the second and third steps were not correlated. That is to say, we postulated that either high scores on one step would indicate low scores on the other or that participants scoring either high (i.e., loved God) or low (i.e., did not love God) would yield similar patterns on both steps. What we found instead was that scores on one step were not associated with scores on the other in any substantive way. This lack of relationship suggested that the steps measured two very different and unrelated aspects of godly love. Further, while arguably more mature people tended to be less likely to identify with loving God for self's sake, all of the people surveyed both identified equally with loving God for God's sake and identified more with loving God for God's sake than with loving God for self's sake. That is, regardless of one's status on indicators such as choice of theology as a major, everyone was more likely to report mature reasons for their love of God, although theology majors reported substantially less agreement with immature reasons motivating their love for God than did their non-major counterparts. That scores on the two different steps were virtually unrelated suggested that loving God for self's sake and loving God for God's sake represent two different and discrete aspects of Christian spiritual development that are not affected by one another. This result could be interpreted in more than one way.

One possible explanation might be that Clairvaux's model is not best conceptualized by a staircase upon which development occurs by moving up toward a Christlike love (on the higher steps) while simultaneously moving away from a more egocentric love (on the lower steps). Development occurring on a symbolic staircase would presumably require an inverse relationship between steps in that the positive position on one step would presuppose a correspondingly negative position on the other step (i.e., a high score on step two would indicate a low score on step three or vice versa). Instead, Clairvaux's framework might suggest an orientation, or point of view, that could cause one to identify more strongly with one set of motivators for love of God than with another set, even if the sets of motivators themselves were not related to one another in an obviously hierarchical manner. In other words, even though all participants scored the same on the higher developmental step, indicating agreement with selfless reasons motivating godly love, theology majors indicated less agreement than did their counterparts in also identifying with self-serving reasons motivating love for God. It would be interesting to know how these same people might have scored on a measure assessing Clairvaux's fourth step, loving self for God's sake. Would more mature people have identified more reasons for loving self for God's sake than their less mature counterparts? Would the fourth step have also been unrelated to the second and third steps?

An alternative interpretation of the finding that the steps were not related might suggest support for the epigenetic nature of Christian spiritual development. Epigenetic development would allow for fluctuations difficult

The Love of God

to capture in one cross-sectional test administration. In other words, if Clairvaux's stage development is epigenetic in nature then individuals might identify more strongly with one step at one point in time than they might at another point in time, depending upon how they perceived themselves and God at the time of the different test administrations. In this case, a lower score at a later time would not necessarily indicate regression; rather, linear development forward might be accompanied by periodic movement backward to revisit earlier perceptions and understandings in need of re-negotiation before authentic growth could be realized.

A common example of this kind of epigenetic development might be the questioning of young adolescents when, for the first time, they confront doubts about the religious commitments that their families and faith communities have taught them to honor. For many such adolescents, authentic spiritual development would require them to question these commitments and to explore their convictions in terms of their true beliefs as opposed to merely accepting the beliefs of others because they have been instructed to do so. Thus, these adolescents might appear to be more mature in their spiritual maturity at one point in time, only to appear to have regressed in maturity at a later time, although a test administration that occurred later still might reflect that the intermediate appearance of regression actually yielded more maturity in the long term, if the testing of faith were successfully negotiated.

A test-retest study lends some credibility to the possibility of this latter interpretation. Given that theology majors identified substantially fewer selfish reasons motivating their love for God than did their counterparts, fifty theology majors who shared similar demographic characteristics with the first sample described were surveyed six weeks apart to determine whether or not their motivating reasons for loving God remained stable over time. These first year theology students had declared their majors but had not yet been exposed to critical study within their field. At the time of the test and retest administrations, these first semester students were enrolled in an introductory theology course designed to introduce them to a myriad of theological debates. Despite the first study's high internal consistency coefficients (N=541; $\geq.86$) the test-retest coefficients were much lower (Step 2=.77 and Step 3=.56). Taken together, these statistics suggest that Clairvaux's spiritual development was reliably measured, and that the variable being measured—presumably godly love—was somewhat unstable. Just as psychological states such as depression and anxiety change according to changing situations, reasons motivating love for God appeared to change as well. That the lower developmental step, loving God for self's sake, was more stable than the higher developmental step, loving God for

God's sake, gives further credence to this epigenetic notion of development. That is, a higher developmental level would presumably be less stable than would a lower developmental level. A longer period of time between test administrations might yield an interesting finding: Would godly love appear to be more or less stable over a longer period of time and, perhaps more importantly, do people report more selfless reasons motivating love for God at later test administrations? Are people developing godly love as they grow in their relationships with God?

CONCLUSIONS

The Johannine moral directive established upon an intensified love command evidenced in believers' acceptance of the one sent from above and their willingness to self-sacrificially lay their lives down for others has been connected by the authors to Bernard of Clairvaux's framework of spiritual maturity postulating that as Christians mature, their ability to love God and others continues to develop as well. The new measure of Christian maturity designed by one of the authors to empirically test the validity of Clairvaux's model of spiritual development, has revealed some interesting results. For example, Clairvaux's second and third steps appear to reflect two very distinct motivations for love of God. While the instrument demonstrated internal consistency, variability in test-retest scores suggested this sample of young Christian adults was still exploring their commitments motivating godly love. Even so, theology students did demonstrate substantially less agreement with loving God for self's sake.

Future studies sampling Christians who are older and have been converted longer could shed light on whether or not reasons motivating godly love remain stable over time. Additionally, a wider range in maturity as well as denominational affiliation could prove useful in investigating whether or not Clairvaux's second and third steps are more related than was evidenced in this young sample. While the theoretical model has good biblical and theological support, continued testing of the developing theory with human participants should reveal more about the way that actual Christian spiritual maturity unfolds.

12

The "Antichrists" Speak
A Message to the Community of 1 John

ROBERT A. BERG

I HAVE NEVER HAD the pleasure of taking a class taught by Ben Aker in an academic setting, but for many years I have been his student. I have learned from conference presentations and from church sermons. Since we have been members of the same congregation for many years, I get to hear him teach Sunday School classes and pick his brain in the hallway. And since his dear wife Barb has been an office colleague, there have been many occasions for informal conversation. Ben reflects the love of Jesus and the fire of the Holy Spirit. His students know how much he cares about the gospel and about them personally. I am so pleased to contribute to a collection in honor of a man I respect and value so highly.

First John was written in the wake of what could be called a church split. The author or "elder" refers to those who left the community (2.19) and much of what is said is driven by the threat posed to his readers by the defectors. He finds them critically at fault in both what they believe and in how they conduct their lives. They are so dangerous and contrary to the faith that the elder refers to them as "antichrists" (2.18, 22; 4.3; cf. 2 John 7).[1]

---

1. All Scripture translations are my own.

But These are Written . . .

Commentators universally point this out to their readers.[2] Some of what the elder writes only makes sense when we understand the severity of the situation. Our distance from the events, of course, guarantees that some of what we find in 1 John will always remain a puzzle. We can, however, infer a certain amount about the opponents from the text of 1 John. But what exactly did they believe about Jesus that the elder found so deficient? And how exactly did they fail his tests of acceptable behavior? And, given our experience with the animosity that often follows church splits, we must wonder: how accurately is the "other side" portrayed?

These questions are particularly appropriate to Pentecostals. One of the primary points of contention is what we might call the "discernment of spirits." The issue is reflected most visibly in 2.18–27 and 4.1–6. Feelings are intense because the basic issues are so central to the faith that it is a matter of spiritual life and death. Who was Jesus? How do we understand the working of the Spirit-*Paraclete*? How do we know who speaks for God and who speaks for the Devil? With their emphasis on the Holy Spirit's ongoing work of revelation and guidance, Pentecostals have always been open to "new" things from God. In the period before the establishment of an authoritative canon of Scripture, then, it is no surprise that enthusiasts would at times fail to maintain a balance between the Jesus tradition and claims of newer, deeper insights from the Spirit. How else can we imagine Paul using the example of someone claiming that the Spirit inspired the utterance, "Jesus is cursed" (1 Cor 12.3)?

The elder who authors 1 John strives to hold experience of the Spirit within the confines of traditional beliefs, especially those about Jesus. To do so, however, he must confront an interpretation of the Johannine tradition regarding the Spirit that threatens to undermine the community's doctrinal foundations. He dials back the expectation of new and deeper truths based on Jesus' words found in John 14–16, even to the extent of assigning the distinctive name given to the Spirit in the Gospel of John, the *Paraclete*, to Jesus (2.1). Commentators have failed to give enough attention to this reassignment of such a distinctive title for the Spirit. Given what and how the elder in 1 John writes, his "opponents" may resemble later problematic expressions of the Spirit such as Montanism and various sects within the modern Pentecostal movement.[3]

2. E.g., R. E. Brown, *The Epistles of John* (Garden City, NY: Doubleday, 1982); S. S. Smalley, *1, 2, 3 John* (Waco, TX: Word, 1984); G. Strecker, *The Johannine Letters* (Minneapolis: Fortress, 1996).

3. R. Brown is best known for his reconstructions of the history of the Johannine community in his *Epistles*, 49–68 and in *The Community of the Beloved Disciple: The Life, Loves, and Hates of an Individual Church in New Testament Times* (Mahwah, NJ:

The "Antichrists" Speak

What follows in this essay, unfortunately, is not a recent archaeological find. It is only a hermeneutical exercise. It is intended to reflect the time when 1 John was written; but we leave open its relation in time to any of the Johannine writings in the NT. How might a representative of "the antichrists" appeal to the same readers as those addressed in 1 John? If this exercise fosters thought about the nature of the issues involved in the conflict reflected in 1 John, it serves its purpose.

> The words of warning given by the *Paraclete* to his messenger for the ears of the faithless. Though you began with a knowledge of the Spirit of truth, you have failed to keep step with what the Spirit is saying. Unless you receive the new light of the *Paraclete*, you will suffer the same fate as the pagans. As he himself has recently told us, the coming of the Lord is near. Only those who have given heed to the messages spoken through the prophets of the *Paraclete* may have confidence on that day. Those who fail to follow the directions of the Spirit will face the same fearful judgment as those in the world.
>
> My former brothers, I only desire your good. So I write with the hope that you will hear my warning. We shared fellowship in our dedication to the teaching of the beloved disciple. Some of us suffered being expelled from the synagogue. We understand now that it was necessary for this to happen. God was showing us that we must not remain settled when the Spirit is calling us to move on to new and better things. Israel was once God's people, and Jerusalem was once where God chose to dwell, in his holy temple. But, as Jesus himself told the woman, the time came when all inhabitants of the earth were called to worship God in the Spirit and in truth.[4]
>
> So in this last day, we live in the age of the *Paraclete*. It is only through the *Paraclete* that we can worship in the Spirit and in truth. Do not follow the example of disobedient Israel, whose eyes were darkened by the Devil. In their hardness of heart, they rejected the light of revelation sent through our Forerunner.[5] In-

---

Paulist, 1979). Others give particular attention to the role of the Holy Spirit in the conflict between the communities involved. See G. M. Burge, *The Anointed Community: The Holy Spirit in the Johannine Tradition* (Grand Rapids: Eerdmans, 1987); J. C. Thomas, *1 John, 2 John, 3 John* (London: T. & T. Clark, 2004); R. A. Berg, "1–3 John," in *Full Life Bible Commentary to the New Testament*, eds. F. L. Arrington and R. Stronstad (Grand Rapids: Zondervan, 1999).

4. As in John's gospel, this may be rendered as "spirit"; so also in references to the same text later in this writing.

5. This appears to be a title given to Jesus, so it is capitalized here and throughout. The Greek is πρόδρομος, found in the NT only in Heb 6.20.

stead of welcoming God's new truth, they killed the one chosen by God to bear the Spirit and announce things to come. Beware! You are in grave danger of ending up under the same judgment for failing to respond to the light of the Spirit. Recall that the darkness is passing away, and the true light is already shining.[6]

We understand from your witnesses that you are being misled by the one you call the elder and those with him. Make no mistake: they represent a spirit of deceit.[7] They do not speak for God, our Forerunner, or the disciple of love.[8] God's wrath on them will be great at the coming of the Lord, and on all those who believe their lies. It is they who are responsible for the break in our former fellowship. They have refused to hear the voice of the *Paraclete* as he continues to guide us into all truth. How can you not see that life dwells only with those who have the anointing?[9] This alone is what distinguishes the anointed ones[10] from the world. You once had the anointing, just as Israel once had the blessing of God. Remember how Saul, Israel's first king, once was blessed with God's Spirit. But because he was disobedient and did not listen to God's instructions, the Spirit was taken from him and he lost his divine standing. You are in danger of the same loss. Save yourselves from being condemned with hard hearted Israel! To reject the living voice of the *Paraclete* is to reject God and his life.

I do not speak on my own authority. What I write to you is the message of the *Paraclete*, the same Spirit who anointed our Forerunner and the disciple of love to declare God's message. As the Spirit says: "Obey the words of the prophets of the *Paraclete*. They have seen God. They have known God. To them has been given the authority to hold and release sins. Those who follow their words will not be in sin; the anointing that kept Jesus from sin will also keep them from sin."

How can you doubt which of our groups truly has the Spirit? You can easily see how many have joined us from those who at one time were in your darkness. They now enjoy the blessings of the indwelling anointing. The anointing shows that they truly have been born of God, and so are without sin. For

---

6. The wording is the same as that in 1 John 2.8b.

7. Or "Spirit."

8. This appears to be the author's version of the "disciple whom Jesus loved" in John 13.23; 19.26; 20.2; 21.7.

9. "Anointing" here, and throughout, is the translation of χρῖσμα.

10. This seems to be the best translation of χριστοί. But given the use of the term later in the text, one wonders whether it should be translated "christs" here.

we know: Everyone who has been born of God does not sin, because his seed dwells in him; he cannot sin because he has been born of God.[11] Can anyone find us guilty of sin?

Is it not *we* who show the signs of being born of God? Is it not *we* who bear much fruit? Is it not among *us* that the *Paraclete* speaks with such power? Is it not *we* who demonstrate the greater works than even our Forerunner prophesied?

Our witnesses tell us that we are accused of not showing love for the brothers. I assure you that this is also deception from your leaders. We do have love for the brothers, those who have been born of God and are indwelt by the anointing. When you join us, you will see not only the powerful ministry of the *Paraclete* but share in the love of our brotherly fellowship. Your elder is a hypocrite. He is the one who shows no love to our brothers; he is guilty of the very charge he makes against us! He tells his followers to deny hospitality to our witnesses. Every day I hear from our brothers of the shameful treatment from some of your friends. (Many others among your friends, of course, have been very receptive of our brothers—for this we rejoice!) Of what is your elder afraid? He claims that he is the protector of the truth, but he is only an old man clinging to his own deceptive ideas. He sees how many of his followers have joined our community of the *Paraclete*. His only hope is to keep you in ignorance. He knows that if you realized the truth of how God is working among us, he would be left without a flock to lead, or more accurately, a flock to mislead. So he makes false accusations against us. We do indeed love our brothers, those who hear the voice of the *Paraclete* and live in fellowship with his anointed ones. Those who refuse to hear the voice of the *Paraclete* are not our brothers just as they are not the brothers of our Forerunner. The anointing does not dwell in them, they have not been born of God; they are not our brothers.

You greatly err in not knowing the words of the *Paraclete*. Remember what was said by our Forerunner, Jesus, in the days of his flesh: "I have many things to tell you, but you are not able to receive them now."[12] His disciples were not ready to hear the deeper truths at that time. But Jesus promised that what could not be spoken then would be spoken later. When the *Paraclete* comes, the Spirit of the truth, he will guide into all the truth.[13] This truth has been revealed to the prophets of the *Paraclete* in these days.

11. The wording is the same as that in 1 John 3.9 except that we find here the verb "dwells" instead of "remains."

12. Cf. John 16.12.

13. Cf. John 16.13.

But These are Written . . .

    Because you do not know the words of the *Paraclete*, you are ignorant. In your ignorance, you submit to teaching that has been left behind. Even in your ignorance you know the teaching of Jesus: "Truly I tell you that unless a man is born of water and Spirit, he cannot enter the kingdom of heaven. What is born of the flesh is flesh but what is born of the Spirit is spirit."[14]

    Jesus, you remember, also spoke of the living water of the Spirit that would be given to all those who are born of God. The anointing in us is the same anointing that came to Jesus in the water of his baptism. Just as the dove descended upon Jesus, the dove has descended upon all of us who have been born of God. Just as Jesus demonstrated that his work was the work of God by the power of the Spirit, so we who have the seed of God demonstrate that our work is the work of God by the power of the Spirit. And just as Jesus was raised in glory to a place of honor in heaven, so shall we who continue his ministry.

    Had you been obedient to the work of the *Paraclete*, you would know the new revelation that those of us in the community of the born of God already know. The *Paraclete* has said: "No longer think of Jesus as *the* Christ. For all those born of the Spirit are christs[15]—you are all marked by the same anointing. Like Jesus, you have all been born of water and Spirit. So do not call Jesus "the Christ" because he is only the first of many christs. In this last hour, the *Paraclete* will show you greater things than did your Forerunner."

    Can you see how great is your loss? By clinging to the authority of your elder, you have shut yourselves out from eternal life. The *Paraclete* also says: "Life is in the water, not the blood." This means that life from God comes not in blood, but water. Not in the shedding of blood but in the pouring of water. It is in the water that we are born of God and receive the Spirit. How could the blood of any fleshly being, animal or human, bring life of the Spirit? What is born of the flesh is flesh. It cannot affect what is of the Spirit. Jesus our Forerunner received the life-giving Spirit by water just as we did—we, that is, who have truly been born of God and share in the community of the *Paraclete*.

    The flesh can be of no help in the realm of the Spirit. Some among you believe that life comes from eating the bread and wine of the meal of remembrance. How can such a thing be? How can you be so foolish? When Jesus spoke of his flesh and

---

14. Cf. John 3.5.

15. See n. 9 above; "christs" here for χριστοὶ seems to fit the context better than "anointed ones."

The "Antichrists" Speak

blood, he meant these things in a spiritual sense. Things of the Spirit cannot be transmitted by things of the flesh: What is born of the flesh is flesh and what is born of the Spirit is spirit. Eternal life is of the Spirit, not of the flesh. Using the flesh to achieve things in the Spirit is futile. It is like Jesus himself said, "The one who strives to see God by deeds in the flesh is like those who built the tower in Babel. A tower of stone, no matter how high, can never gain entrance to the realm of God." God is spirit, and only those who worship in the Spirit and in truth will find him. God can no longer be found in Jerusalem or any other place of this world of flesh. God can now only be found through the operation of the *Paraclete*. Whoever has the *Paraclete* has life, and whoever does not have the *Paraclete* does not have life.

Listen to the witness of those who once were in your error and have joined the community of the *Paraclete*. Titus, who once served with your elder, has in recent days become one with us. He sends his greetings, but more importantly his appeal: "Escape the spirit of deceit that binds you. Truly the *Paraclete* has set his mark of approval on this community by his repeated visitations and prophetic words. The anointing has taken up residence in the members of this community, the true people of God. The time is late."

Another brother of ours, and former brothers of yours, is Phillip. He sends you this message: "What joy it is to be free of the yoke of the elder! To be free from the oppressive commandments reminiscent of the laws of the Jews! The truth has set us free, indeed. I urge you to join me and so many others who have found spiritual life in the community of the *Paraclete*. At each meeting we hear new words of the Spirit, of the new truth, and of the things to come promised by our Forerunner. You escaped the bondage of the synagogue; now escape the bondage of the elder and his cohorts. We await you!"

Do you need more to see that we speak for God and that your elder speaks only in deceitful selfishness? You have lost the enthusiasm you once had in the Spirit. By rejecting the ongoing witness of the *Paraclete*, you have removed yourselves from eternal life and you have placed yourselves in danger of suffering the judgment of God on unbelief.

But it is not too late. The *Paraclete* says, "Come! Drink of the living water that the Spirit pours out. Come! Drink of the new wine of the Age of the *Paraclete*. Come! Drink of the nectar of the coming things. Come! Learn of things you have not known and behold things you have not seen. Amen."

13

Choose Your Own Adventure
Teaching, Participatory Hermeneutics, and the Book of Revelation

BY ROBBY WADDELL

The book of Revelation remains for many Christians a book with "seven seals," seldom read and often relegated to a curiosity in the Bible. For others is has become *the* book of the New Testament, full of predictions for the future and revelations about the present.[1]

TEACHING THE BOOK OF REVELATION

FOR A LITTLE OVER a decade I have been teaching a course on the book of Revelation. My experience has been exclusively in the context of confessional institutions, and for the last nine years I have taught in a Christian liberal arts university affiliated with the A/G.[2] When my students arrive in

---

1. E. Schüssler Fiorenza, *The Book of Revelation: Justice and Judgment* (Philadelphia: Fortress, 1985) 1.

2. It is a pleasure for me to contribute to this collection in honor of Professor Ben Aker. Ben is a true pioneer biblical scholar within the Pentecostal tradition, and like many others of my generation I will be forever grateful for his example. I have been indirectly tutored by Ben through a number of his publications, which I have used as required reading in my classes. I have also benefitted from Ben's academic ministry through close friendships with his former students who serve as invaluable dialogue partners and colleagues.

class they already have a deep appreciation for the Bible even though their commitment to its value is not always matched by their familiarity with its contents. The disparity between doctrinal commitment and actual Bible knowledge notwithstanding, they all seem to share a participatory hermeneutic that is rooted in a belief that the Bible is the Word of God and has been written for them—both to read and to apply to their lives. So for example, "I know the plans I have for you," declares the Lord, "plans to prosper you and not to harm you, plans to give you hope and a future" (Jer 29.11).[3] Despite the fact that it clearly states in Jeremiah that God is speaking to the Jews who are in exile in Babylon, this passage is readily cited—with chapter and verse—by students seeking to comfort one another when facing the dilemma of having to declare a major or worse, facing another Spring semester without any romantic prospects. The historical context of this passage is less comforting than most of my students are prepared to learn. Not only have the Israelites lost their homes and their country, but they are told to build houses and settle down in Babylon because deliverance is not coming anytime soon. The generation that experienced the exile will not live to see freedom. The exile, however, is not the end of story. God's faithfulness will be demonstrated by delivering a future generation.

On the one hand, I encourage my students to avoid randomly selecting verses out of context. Nevertheless, I also encourage them on the other hand to maintain their participatory hermeneutic as long as it is informed by the historical context of the book and takes into account the literary conventions within the passage. When I teach on the gospels or the letters of Paul, the students adjust to the intended learning outcomes fairly easily. They are ready and willing to learn about the historical background of the book and engage in literary analyses of selected passages. However, when it comes to the book of Revelation, it is as if they have not only forgotten what I have taught them about reading with an awareness of context but also abandoned their own commitment to applying the text to how they live their lives. Not only are they less interested in the traditional historical-critical questions, they have forsaken altogether the participatory reading. The students do not read Revelation in the same devotional or theological way that they read the prophets or the gospels.

Although my students come from a wide array of denominational affiliations, the vast majority of them appear to fit into one of the following categories: either they are completely perplexed by the book and know little of its contents—except for a few vague ideas about the mark of the beast

---

3. All English quotations from the Bible are taken from the NIV unless stated otherwise.

and the end of world—or they have read every volume of the Left Behind series and are masters of the Dispensational interpretation.[4] All of the students, however, share a common assumption that the book deals exclusively with eschatological issues and therefore has relatively little to contribute to other theological topics and basically nothing to do with the practice of the Christian faith. Most of their initial questions have to do with the timing of the rapture, the identity of the antichrist, or the meaning of the mark and number of the beast. Always to their surprise (and sometimes to the chagrin of a few) we spend very little class time addressing these queries, rather I introduce the students to the historical scholarship on the book, giving special attention to the issues of genre, composition and structure, historical background, history of interpretation, literary analysis, and theological interpretation. I also attempt to teach my students sound hermeneutical strategies that will help them appreciate the symbolism in the book and comprehend its theological themes in such a way that they may hear what the Spirit is saying to the church today.[5]

According to the course evaluations, the majority of students by the end of the semester—despite their initial dismay—find the class to be beneficial. Many of them testify that not only has their understanding of Revelation increased but that the book has become much more applicable in their lives. For the first time they start to read Revelation not unlike the way they read the rest of Bible—as if it was written to them and can contribute to their theological understanding of Christ, the Holy Spirit, the church, worship and hymns, and so on.

One of the most enlightening aspects of the course is the time spent on the book's composition and structure. Revelation is extremely complex, evidenced by a lack of scholarly consensus regarding its structure. Part of the challenge is that its temporal sequence is often interrupted, which confuses the sense of time and development. Furthermore, the text is replete with doublets and repetitions. As a possible solution to this conundrum,

---

4. For a critical assessment of the Left Behind series and its effects on Pentecostalism, see P. Althouse, "'Left Behind'—Fact or Fiction: Ecumenical Dilemmas of the Fundamentalist Millenarian Tensions within Pentecostalism," *JPT* 13/2 (2005) 187–207; D. M. Coulter, "Pentecostal Visions of The End: Eschatology, Ecclesiology and the Fascination of the Left Behind Series," *JPT* 14/1 (2005) 81–98; and P. van der Laan, "What is Left Behind? A Pentecostal Response to Eschatological Fiction," *JEPTA* 24 (2004) 49–70.

5. See M. Levering, *Participatory Biblical Exegesis: A Theology of Biblical Interpretation* (Notre Dame, IN: University of Notre Dame Press, 2008) 1–16. Without discounting the value of traditional historical-critical approach, Levering's work focuses on the model of patristic-medieval biblical scholarship, which emphasizes the role of faith and the necessity of a confessional perspective.

a number of source-critical theories have been proposed, including (1) compilation theories which suppose that Revelation is a combination of earlier Jewish and/or Christian apocalypses, (2) theories of revision which argue that a single apocalyptic work evolved through various stages, and (3) theories which assume that fragments of Jewish apocalypses were incorporated into the original text.[6] Despite the possibility of such source-critical theories, many recent commentators have written with the assumption that the text contains a high level of literary unity.[7] Although the redactional theories which have been applied to the text are helpful to a certain degree,[8] I agree with those who see the text as a unified whole. There are simply too many possible ways of structuring the book that make sense of its complexities without having to develop elaborate theories of editorial activity.

In order to create an outline of the book commentators are forced to focus on a limited number of compositional elements. Proposed outlines have been based on the pattern of seven,[9] the concept of recapitulation,[10] repetitive phrases such as "I was in the Spirit,"[11] the use of chiasms,[12] or the book's similarity to a Greek play.[13] Presented with so many options it is inevitable that a student will ask, "Which outline is right?" There is not a simple answer to this question because all of these proposals have merit. "Studying the structure of Revelation," I tell my students, "is not unlike peering through the eyehole of a kaleidoscope." At first a pattern is in view containing specific colors and shapes that have clearly defined borders. However, the pattern is not as stable as it first appears. When the kaleidoscope is

---

6. For a brief discussion of the different types of source-critical theories, see G. R. Osborne, *Revelation* (Grand Rapids: Baker Academic, 2002) 27–28.

7. E.g., R. W. Wall, *Revelation* (Grand Rapids: Baker, 1991) 12–25; R. Bauckham, *The Climax of Prophecy: Studies on the Book of Revelation* (London: T. & T. Clark, 1993) 1–37, and G. K. Beale, *The Book of Revelation: A Commentary on the Greek Text* (Grand Rapids: Eerdmans, 1998) 108–51.

8. There are certain red flags which may signal redactional activity. For a discussion of these signals, see Schüssler Fiorenza, *The Book of Revelation*, 160–64.

9. A. Yarbro Collins, *Crisis and Catharsis: The Power of the Apocalypse* (Philadelphia: Westminster, 1984) 111–16.

10. C. H. Giblin, "Recapitulation and the Literary Coherence of John's Apocalypse," *CBQ* 56/1 (1994) 94–95.

11. Bauckham, *Climax*, 1–37; R. Waddell, *The Spirit of the Book of Revelation* (Blandford Forum, UK: Deo, 2006) 138–50.

12. Schüssler Fiorenza, *The Book of Revelation*, 159–80.

13. R. R. Brewer, "The Influence of Greek Drama on the Apocalypse of John," *AThR* 18 (1936) 74–92; J. B. Bowman, "The Revelation to John: Its Dramatic Structure and Message," *Int* 9 (1955) 436–53. For a structure devised as a three-act play, see D. L. Barr, "The Apocalypse of John as Oral Enactment," *Int* 40 (1986) 243–56.

But These are Written . . .

turned the colors and shapes are reconfigured to form a new design. Focusing on a particular pattern draws attention to both the formal construction of the book and highlights theological emphases which might otherwise go unnoticed. It should be noted that this metaphor is not intended to suggest that each compositional element is of equal importance to the book's structure or that there is an endless possibility of outlines. As a heuristic tool, the kaleidoscope is very helpful in introducing the students to the concept that Revelation is too intricate to be easily reduced to only one possible outline. Despite the usefulness of the kaleidoscope, when it comes to discussing specifics of the book's structure I prefer a different metaphor—the children's genre known as "Choose Your Own Adventure" (CYOA).[14]

CHOOSE YOUR OWN ADVENTURE

CYOA is a creative series of interactive children's books, originally published by Bantam Books from 1979 to 1999. The stories are written in the second person, resulting in a reading experience where "you" (the reader) are placed in the role of the protagonist. After the introduction to the story, "you" are asked to choose the next course of action. For example, in *The Lost Jewels of Nabooti* the first set of choices pose the following options: "If you agree to go on tomorrow's plane for Paris turn to page 4" or "If you demand more time, information, and extra help, turn to page 7." Once the reader makes the initial choice, a plot begins to develop leading to more choices and ultimately numerous potential endings. CYOA experienced phenomenal success. The original series contained 184 titles written by thirty different authors. Various spin offs followed adding nearly 100 additional titles. Translated into thirty-eight languages and with over 250 million books in print, CYOA is the fourth best-selling children's series of all time, behind *Harry Potter,* Enid Blyton, and *Goosebumps.* As a pedagogical device, I have found that CYOA serves as a helpful metaphor. By identifying common characteristics shared by both CYOA novels and apocalyptic literature, I am able to minimize the strangeness of Revelation and provide my students with a reading strategy that can help make sense of this peculiar ancient text. The features of CYOA that I highlight for comparison with Revelation include the second person point-of-view, the nonlinear reading experience, looping, multiple paths, and alternative endings.

---

14. The following history and description of CYOA comes from the series' official website, www.cyoa.com.

Second Person Point-of-View

The second person point-of-view of a CYOA begs comparison with the participatory hermeneutic that my students often use when they read the Bible. The closest biblical parallel to this phenomenon is in the Markan apocalypse when the writer breaks from the third person and addresses the reader directly with the caveat, "let the reader understand" (13.14). John uses a similar construction in Rev 13.18, "This calls for wisdom. Let the person who has insight calculate the number of the beast, for it is the number of a man. That number is 666." By directly addressing the reader, John encourages a participatory hermeneutic. I encourage my students to respond to the invitation to calculate the number of the beast. In order for them to make an informed interpretation, I introduce the phenomenon of *gematria*, a system of assigning numerical value to a word or phrase. Although this system has been used to try and identify many historical figures as the Antichrist, I advocate for a less complicated interpretation. In its lexical form the Greek word for "beast" (*therion*) is valued at 666, which means that John may simply be equating his animal metaphor—the beast, which he uses for an ungodly ruler—for a numerical metaphor: 666, the number of the beast. This interpretative option is strengthened by the fact that a common textual variant calculates the number of the beast as 616, which is the value of *theriou*, the spelling of "beast" used in this sentence. Other interpretative choices lead down endless rabbit trails.

In addition to the call for wisdom, the first beatitude in Revelation announces a blessing on "the one who reads and those who hear the words of the prophecy and keep what is written in it" (1.3). I encourage my students to hear this blessing as a personal invitation to read and obey the teachings in the book. On multiple occasions John uses a hearing formula, i.e., "whoever has an ear . . . hear." While this formation is not technically in the second person, it does invite the reader to participate. The hearing formula is used in each of the letters to the seven churches of Asia. These letters are not directed at the reader, though they are written in the second person—a formulation that is not used again until the judgment pronounced on Babylon in Rev 18.

Finally, John uses a number of imperatives, which may be read as a direct address to the reader. For example in Rev 22.17, "The Spirit and the Bride say, 'Come!' And let him who hears say, 'Come.' And let him who is thirsty come, let him who desires take the water of life without price." Most commentators see the first two imperatives in 22.17 as being directed toward Jesus, first with the Spirit and the Bride prayerfully petitioning Jesus to return followed by an invitation for the one who hears to join in the same prayer. Members of the present church, at least those who have ears to hear are given the opportunity to participate in the eschatological prayer of the Spirit and the Bride. The Spirit-inspired hope associated with the *parousia* is integral to Christian theology and necessary for the church which must wait patiently for that day. The third and fourth imperatives in 22.17 are most certainly not directed toward Jesus but rather are invitations for the thirsty to come and to take the water of life. The shift in audience, first addressing Jesus and then addressing the world, may seem sudden and unexpected. On the contrary, as Bauckham writes, "It is, in fact, a natural progression of thought. People who join the Spirit's prayer for the *parousia* are directing their lives in faith towards that promise. The invitation to the thirsty is also a call towards the eschatological future."[15] Indeed, this closing invitation given by the Spiritually inspired church reinforces the central message of the book that the people of God are to be a prophetic witness to the world (cf. Rev 11.1–13).

Nonlinear Reading Experience

The nonlinear narrative format of CYOA serves as second helpful analogy for reading Revelation. Attempting to read a CYOA novel straight through from cover to cover would result in complete and utter confusion. In fact CYOA books contain a warning that alerts the reader to this potential danger. In *The Lost Jewels of Nabooti*, the first page contains such a proviso:

> Do not read this book straight through from beginning to end! These pages contain many different adventures in your search. From time to time as you read along, you will be asked to make a choice. Your choice may lead to success or failure . . . Remember—think carefully before you make a move! Danger lurks at every turn.

In order for the story to make sense it is imperative that the reader follow the reading cues by choosing from the possible scenarios. The reader of Revelation faces similar challenges. The narrative is full of interruptions, repetitions, and recapitulations. Would it not it have been interesting if John would have included some of his own reading instructions? Not unlike the cross references listed in the margins of a Bible, CYOA-type questions could guide a reader through the maze of the text. I give my students the following illustration.

---

15. Bauckham, *Climax*, 168.

At the end of the each of the seven messages there is a promise for the one who conquers. If you conqueror then you will receive a prize. However, there are no instructions about how to conquer. For example, in Rev 3.5 you are promised to receive a white robe if you conquer. If John had been writing a CYOA then the promise to the conqueror would have been followed by a set of questions. "If you want to know how to conquer turn to Rev 12.11" or "If you want to know more about your reward turn to Rev 6.9–11." If you chose to learn how to conquer then you discovered in Rev 12.11 that conquering is only possible by the blood of the lamb, the word of your testimony, and not loving your life so much as to shrink from death. You might wonder whether the final part of this verse is an exaggeration. Do you really have to be willing to die, or is this simply a hyperbole for boldness of witness? If you had chosen the second option and turned to Rev 6.9–11 you would have discovered that the possibility of your death was not an overstatement.

> When he opened the fifth seal, I saw under the altar the souls of those who had been slain because of the word of God and the testimony they had maintained. They called out in a loud voice, "How long, Sovereign Lord, holy and true, until you judge the inhabitants of the earth and avenge our blood?" Then each of them was given a *white robe*, and they were told to wait a little longer, until the full number of their fellow servants, their brothers and sisters, were killed just as they had been.

I am guessing that your own death was not exactly your first thought when you were told that you would be getting a reward for conquering! At this point you are offered a new selection of options. "If you are very scared and would like to know how the story ends turn to Rev 7.14," or "If you are feeling brave and you would like to see what role you will play before the end turn to Rev 19.14." In the first scenario you learn that apparently the final number of witnesses is eventually complete and it is actually an innumerable multitude. Although the whole group is described as having survived the great tribulation, they have not washed their robes and made them white in their own blood but rather in the blood of the lamb. If you had been feeling brave, then you would have discovered in Rev 19.14 that white robes are the standard uniform for those who are in the army of heaven, and you have been drafted for the final eschatological battle.

But These are Written . . .

Given the complexity of Revelation, this illustration could go on and on, which is a testimony to another commonly shared principle of my students, namely that Scripture is so rich that a new lesson can be learned with every (re)reading. I give this example to my students and ask them to write their own CYOA adaptation of Revelation. The exercise requires them to observe the cues in the text that create cross references, which I believe enrich the reading experience of the book.

Looping

When reading a CYOA, it is possible that a particular set of choices may trap you in a loop, directing you back to the same page over and over—normally with an allusion to the situation looking familiar. The only option in such a case is for you to return to the beginning and restart the adventure. Although the reader of Revelation never becomes completely trapped in a recurring sequence of events, this feature of CYOA does provide an analogous comparison to the recapitulation that often occurs in the book. The best example of this phenomenon is the series of seven seals, seven trumpets, and seven bowls, which share in common a number of characteristics. The seals and the trumpets both contain an interlude between the sixth and seventh item (7.1–17 and 10.1—11.13, respectively). All three series follow a pattern where the elements are organized in a 4 + 3 pattern. The first four seals refer to a horse and a rider, dividing the series into four horsemen and three other judgments. In the second series, the first four trumpets result in judgments while the final three trumpets serve as warnings. Finally, the first four bowls in the third series parallel the first four trumpets in the second series, regarding their objects of judgment (i.e., earth, sea, rivers, and sun) thus creating another 4 + 3 pattern.[16]

In addition to these characteristics, each of the three series ends with a similar yet expanded assortment of sound effects that serve as a soundtrack for the judgments. This multimedia show—which appears to be a remake of an earlier recording made of a theophany at Mount Sinai (cf. Exod 19.16)—is first heard in the throne room with flashes of lightning, voices, and thunders (4.5). With each subsequent occurrence the phrase expands either by adding an extra item or in the case of 16.18–21 lengthening the description of the final two sounds effects. Not unlike the customary "The End" at the close of a movie, the final bowl judgment concludes with a single word, γέγονεν, followed by the music and lightshow finale:[17]

16. Ibid., 10–15.
17. Ibid., 202–4.

4.5: flashes of lightning, voices, and thunders

8.5: thunders, voices, flashes of lightning, and an earthquake

11.19: flashes of lightning, voices, thunders, an earthquake, and great hail

16.18–21: flashes of lightning, voices, thunders; and there was a great earthquake, such as was not since there were men upon the earth, so great an earthquake, so mighty . . . and great hail, every stone about the weight of a talent.

John's use of repetition may be the result of a rabbinical exegetical method known as equivalence of expression (גזירה שוה).[18] The method was a form of elaborate cross-referencing where the use of a term or phrase in two separate texts was considered to be sufficient reason that the texts should be used to interpret each other. In any case, the repetition of these sights and sounds adds support to the idea that the judgments first mentioned in the series of seven seals are later recapitulated by the trumpets and bowls.[19] Getting caught in an endless loop in a CYOA may not have a direct parallel with Revelation, though the similarity between looping and recapitulation is helpful for my students because it enables them to see the text as something other than a simple linear unveiling of sequential events.

Multiple Paths

Both CYOA and Revelation offer multiple paths through the text, and consequently multiple reading experiences. The paths in a CYOA are determined by readers' choices—the decisions they make. In Revelation the paths are also determined by readers' choices such as what compositional elements they decide to emphasize and how they decide to understand the structure of the book. The paths do not necessarily determine the ending (sometimes in a CYOA they do; in Revelation they do not) but they do determine the

---

18. גזירה שוה is a form of Peshat perhaps best represented by Hillel. For a summary of this form of exegesis, see B. Rosenzswig, "The Hermeneutic Principles and Their Application," *Tradition* 13 (1972) 49–76.

19. In addition to the repetition of the Sinai language, the seventh trumpet and the series of bowls is further connected by the first part of 11.19 (And there was opened the temple of God that is in heaven; and there was seen in his temple the ark of his covenant) being echoed in 15.5–6 (And after these things I saw, and the temple of the tabernacle of the testimony in heaven was opened). "Thus, despite the intervention of chapters 12–14," according to Bauckham, "the whole sequence of bowls is clearly marked as a development of the seventh trumpet" (Bauckham, *Climax*, 9).

scenes and experiences along the way. Scholars of Revelation have identified many possible structures.

In regards to the macrostructure of Revelation, one of the most influential compositional elements is John's repetitive phrase, "I was in the Spirit" (1.10; 4.2; 17.3; 21.10). Based on this repetition, the text can be divided into six major sections:

1. Prologue (1.1–8)
2. Vision of Christ and the letters to the seven churches in Asia (1.9—3.22)
3. The Lamb and the opening of the seven-sealed scroll (4.1—16.21)
4. The judgment of the harlot/Babylon (17.1—21.8)
5. The description of the bride/New Jerusalem (21.9—22.9)
6. Epilogue (22.10–21)

This outline has several things to commend it. The Prologue and Epilogue are easily identifiable,[20] and it is generally agreed that the vision of Christ and the letters to the seven churches form the next segment of the book. The following section is not as easy to defend given the length of the section and the variety of topics that are covered in it. When John repeats that he was in the Spirit (4.2) he introduces a long and complex portion of the vision (4.1–16.21). John's adventure begins with a worship service in the throne room of heaven where he eventually notices the seven-sealed scroll in the hand of God.[21] John learns that only the Lion/Lamb is capable of breaking the seals and opening the scroll.

Chapter 6 records the opening of the first six seals which increase in length and escalate with intensity. Before the seventh seal is opened, however, John includes a description of those sealed by God (7.1–17). After this interlude, the seventh seal is opened, resulting in a time of silence during which the prayers of the saints from under the altar are heard. The prayers of the saints serve as a pause in the action between the announcement of the seven trumpets in 8.2 and the description of the trumpets in 8.6—9.21, forming an ABA' pattern. The descriptions of the trumpet blasts increase

---

20. Compare the parallel phrases in the Prologue and the Epilogue (cf. 1.1; 22.6).

21. Especially within the futurist camp, chs. 4–5 serve as an introduction to the rest of the book. This is one of the structural systems that is based on 1.19 where "what you have seen" refers to 1.9–18, "what is" refers to 2.1—3.22, and "what must happen after these things" refers to 4.1—22.5. See J. F. Walvoord, *The Revelation of Jesus Christ: A Commentary* (Chicago: Moody, 1989) 47–49; R. T. Thomas, "John's Apocalyptic Outline," *BSac* 123 (1966) 334–41.

Choose Your Own Adventure

in length as the judgments intensify much like the progression of the seals. The series of trumpets follows the same pattern as the series of seals with a break (or literary pause) between the sixth and seventh element. The interlude separating the sixth and seventh trumpets serves a similar role to the interlude separating the sixth and seventh seals. Both passages create a literary delay postponing—at least in the narrative—the final judgment in the series. Thematically, the interludes are also linked together because they both provide information concerning the protection and activity of the people of God in relation to the judgments.[22]

In the second interlude, John sees "another mighty angel" who is holding in his hand a little scroll. The angel speaks, resulting in another series of seven—the seven thunders.[23] In this case, John is told that time is running out and there will not be time for him to record the events related with the seven thunders, which expedites the time of the seventh trumpet. The mighty angel instructs John to take a scroll from its hand and eat it (an allusion to Ezek 3.1–3). Eating the scroll implies the seer's consumption of the revelation. Following the digestion of the scroll, the angel commands John to prophesy. John's subsequent prophecy is the vision of the temple and the two witnesses in Rev 11. In other words, Rev 11.1–13 is the content of the scroll which John received from the angel. Although later chapters of Revelation will greatly expand on it, according to Bauckham, "the central and essential message of the scroll is given most clearly here (11.1–13)."[24] The end of this longer interlude is clearly marked by 11.14 which announces that the second woe has passed but the third woe is soon to come.

The sound of the seventh and final trumpet appears to be an announcement of the end of the world as we know it and the beginning of the kingdom of God on earth.

> The seventh angel sounded his trumpet, and there were loud voices in heaven, which said: "The kingdom of the world has become the kingdom of our Lord and of his Messiah, and he

---

22. Contra Michaels, who identifies the sealing of the people of God in ch. 7 as part of the sixth seal and likewise he identifies the eating of the scroll and the prophecy concerning the two witnesses in 10.1—11.14 as part of the sixth trumpet (J. R. Michaels, *Interpreting the Book of Revelation* [Grand Rapids: Baker, 1998] 55–60).

23. If the series of seven thunders is included in the numbering of the series of sevens in this section then the total comes to four (i.e., seals, trumpets, thunders, and bowls). Noticing the seals affected a quarter of the earth and the trumpets affected a third of the earth, one might expect the thunders to affect still a larger percentage—perhaps one half (A. M. Farrer, *The Revelation of St. John the Divine* [London: Clarendon, 1964] 125). The seven thunders most likely are an allusion to Ps 29 where the voice of the Lord, which is depicted as thunder, is mentioned seven times.

24. Bauckham, *Climax*, 266.

> will reign for ever and ever." And the twenty-four elders, who were seated on their thrones before God, fell on their faces and worshiped God, saying: "We give thanks to you, Lord God Almighty, the One who is and who was, because you have taken your great power and have begun to reign (Rev 11.15–17).

It is noteworthy that the threefold temporal description of God has now been reduced to a twofold description. God is no longer designated as the one who is and was and is to come, but rather as the one who is and was. John's shorten designation is appropriate because the seventh trumpet has announced the coming of God. This is the end of the story. The cat is out of the proverbial bag. In the end, God is king. The wicked are judged, and the saints are rewarded (11.18). This abbreviated version of end is followed by a self-contained, albeit integrated, story of the woman clothed in the sun, the red dragon, and the two beasts.

It is possible that the throne room vision and the three recapitulating series of seals, trumpets, and bowls—along with their perspective interludes and looping soundtracks—provide a literary structure for the second major division in the Apocalypse (4.1—16.21).[25] However, unlike the interlocking chiasm that links the seals to the trumpets, the series of trumpets and bowls are separated by a substantial story, which stands at the center of the book. Having announced the end with the sound of the seventh trumpet, John recaps the gospel story in Rev 12.1–17. A woman is going to give birth to a child who will rule the earth. Satan, the red dragon, wants to kill the child but fails because the child is taken to heaven and will not return until much later. (If you want to learn about that story turn to Rev 19.) Given that the dragon cannot destroy the child or his mother, he turns over his power to the beasts, which torment the other children of the women—those who keep God's commands and hold fast their testimony about Jesus (i.e., Christians). When teaching my class on Revelation, I refer to this section of the book as a Jumbotron, an oversized screen used at sporting events to replay the action in the game and advertise future events. Not unlike John who saw a sign in heaven, your adventure through Revelation has brought you to this central point. You can pause in your journey, look up in the sky, and watch a replay of the plan of salvation.

The centrality of this story is less pronounced in the outline that I have been following up to this point. As opposed to abandoning that structure based on the phrase "I was in the Spirit," I offer the following chiasm as an alternative plotline (or to mix my metaphors, as a different design in the kaleidoscope).

---

25. Waddell, *Revelation*, 138–46.

Choose Your Own Adventure

    A. Prologue and greeting (1.1–8)

      B. Seven churches [1st "in the Spirit"] (1.9—3.21)

        C. Seven seals [2nd "in the Spirit"] (4.1—8.5)

          D. Seven Trumpets (8.2—9.20; 11.14–19)

            E. The Two Witnesses (11.1–13)

              F. The Woman and the Dragon (12.1–18)

            E.' The Two Beasts (13.1—15.8)

          D.' The Seven Bowls (16.1–21)

        C.' The harlot/Babylon [3rd "in the Spirit"] (17.1—19.10)

      B.' The bride/Jerusalem [4th "in the Spirit"] (19.11—22.5)

    A.' Epilogue (22.6–21)[26]

As much as I like both outlines described thus far, neither structure does justice to the complexity of the final chapters of Revelation.[27]

Alternative Endings

As a pedagogical metaphor, CYOA provides no better comparison with Revelation than our last category—the alternative endings. One of the most empowering things about reading a CYOA is that your choices really do matter, determining the outcome of the story. If you choose to do so, you may backtrack in the story and make other decisions and thereby produce a different end result. The primary difference between CYOA and Revelation is that in a CYOA you may have many possible outcomes while in Revelation you only have two—either your adventure ends in Babylon or it ends in the New Jerusalem. In classical apocalyptic duality, there are only two options. From a third person point-of-view, a reader will learn about both Babylon and the New Jerusalem; however, a participatory hermeneutic requires a choice.

Doublets in the text suggest that the vision of the harlot/Babylon (17.1—19.10) and the vision of the bride/New Jerusalem (21.9—22.9) form parallel scenes which are connected by a transitional passage (19.11—21.8).[28]

---

26. Many commentators have produced outlines of Revelation based on the theory of chiasms. This particular outline is slightly adapted from M. Wilson, "Review Article of R. Waddell's The Spirit of the Book of Revelation," *Pneuma* 29/2 (2007) 158.

27. An abundance of possible outlines exist for these final chapters. For a representative list see Beale, *Revelation*, 109.

28. C. H. Giblin, "Structural and Thematic Correlations in the Theology of Revelation 16–22," *Bib* 55/4 (1974) 433–59.

But These are Written . . .

The final two visions contain significant verbal parallels. They both begin with an expanded form of the literary marker, "he carried me away in the Spirit" (17.3 and 21.10, respectively). In addition to the expanded literary marker, both visions share broader parallel introductions and conclusions:

> 17.1a: Then came one of the seven angels who had the seven bowls and it spoke with me, saying, "Come, I will show you . . ."
>
> 21.9a: Then came one of the seven angels who had the seven bowls . . . and it spoke with me, saying, "Come, I will show you . . ."
>
> 19.10: I fell down before his feet to worship him, but he said to me, "Do not do that, I am a fellow servant of you and your brothers . . . Worship God."
>
> 22.8b–9: I fell down to worship before the feet of the angel who showed to me these things, and he said to me, "Do not do that, I am a fellow servant of you and your brothers . . . Worship God."

Furthermore, the conclusion to each vision includes a beatitude (cf. 19.9b; 22.7b). Each of the final visions also contains thematic parallels contrasting the dual images of a woman and a city (i.e., the harlot/Babylon vs. the bride/New Jerusalem).

The section between the final two visions provides far more than a simple transition. Indeed, 19.11—21.8 contains the penultimate tale of all time, namely the apocalypse of Jesus Christ [i.e., the second coming (19.11–21) the millennium (20.1–10) the final judgment (20.11–15) and the new creation (21.1–8)]. The final eschatological judgment alluded to in 6.17 though previously delayed is narrated at last (19.11–20). Likewise, the depiction of final judgment in 14.14–20 points forward to 19.15. Numerous other descriptions of Jesus exist that link ch. 19 to earlier portions of the text.[29]

Employing a participatory hermeneutic requires the reader to either identify as a citizen of Babylon or as a citizen of the New Jerusalem. I tell my students that they have a choice to make. Are they going to be unfaithful, like a harlot, and be committed to a beastly system or are they going to be faithful, like a bride, and be committed to the Lamb that was slain? The challenge in teaching Revelation is that the predominant theological perspective in Pentecostal/Charismatic/Evangelical circles reduces the eschatology within the text to a thin prediction of the future. It fails to appreciate that the eschatology of the text includes an inaugurated understanding of the

---

29. Cf. 19.11//3.14: he is faithful and true; 19.12//1.14; 2.18: eyes like a flame of fire; 19.15//1.16; 2.12, 16: sharp sword from his mouth; 19.15//2.26–27; 12.5: rule all the nations with a rod of iron: 19.16//17.14: king of kings and lord of lords.

kingdom. The Lamb of God is already on the throne. My real concern is for the current status of the church which has been duped into believing that she is safe because a popular interpretation of the book has convinced her that if she is not presently suffering—physically, socially, economically, or politically—that she is not in any imminent danger of being destroyed by the beast. In fact, the danger of the church—especially in North America and Europe—assimilating into the beastly systems of the world has never been more prevalent (cf. the messages to the churches in Ephesus and Laodicea, Rev 2.1–7 and 3.14–22 respectively).

CONCLUSION

CYOA novels and apocalyptic literature share in common a number of motifs, including adventure, travel, mystery, world culture, ancient civilizations, scary creatures, and outer space. Revelation contains many of these same themes. John makes several references to mysteries in Revelation, one being Babylon, a civilization that was ancient even in John's day. John also travels to a high mountain, carried by an angel who shows him the New Jerusalem descending from outer space. As for the scary creatures, you can have your pick from either the good guy (i.e., a seven-eyed, seven-horned formerly slain lamb) or the bad guys, (i.e., the red dragon, the beast from the sea, and beast from the earth). Lastly, implicit references to Rome—the primary world culture of the era—fill every section of Revelation. Identifying the similarities between CYOA and Revelation allows me to highlight for my students the literariness of Revelation. Rather than simply being an impenetrable book full of cryptic symbols, they get a glimpse of the multilayered meanings, and they start to appreciate the book in ways they have heretofore been unable to do.

14

Will The Real Church Please Stand Up?
An Exegetical Examination of Revelation 11.1–13
By Jeremy S. Crenshaw

I AM ESPECIALLY PRIVILEGED to be a part of this *Festschrift* and to provide a contribution in honor of my friend and mentor Ben Aker. I first encountered Ben in a course at AGTS. I remember that students feared taking his courses because he was known for challenging both their presuppositions and their scholarship. After all, he could read his Greek Bible faster than we could read our English versions! I soon learned that the fears were warranted and yet misleading. Ben expected top notch scholarship, but he also showed a love for his students and a passion for the word of God that drew me in and made me want to "sit at his feet." Whether it was listening to him exegete the Bible at AGTS, watching him worship or teach Sunday school at Evangel Temple, sitting with him and Barb next to the water in Branson, or dialoguing with him by phone on one of our routine calls, I was glad to have him teach me.

What Ben really gave to me was an even greater passion for Scripture and Jesus. He taught me that love for God and study of his word goes hand in hand. Ben gave me a hunger for knowledge that encouraged me to continue my studies. He introduced me to critical methods of Bible study while nurturing balance in the way that I used them. He challenged me to grow as a scholar and as a Christian. One of his sayings was "you must have a relationship with Christ in order to properly interpret Scripture." Unfortunately,

Will The Real Church Please Stand Up?

I cannot include all that this great man of God means to me in such a short section, but I can say that I would not be the person that I am today had I not been influenced by Ben Aker.

In fact, it is because of Ben's teaching that I decided to work with Rev 11 as my contribution to this *Festschrift*. His class on Revelation gave me the desire to understand the message of the Apocalypse and its meaning for the church. I chose the title that I did because I believe that an exegetical examination of this passage can help to answer multiple problems that plague the church today. On the one hand, much of the church still denies that the Spirit operates in the same manner that he did during the time of Jesus and the Twelve. On the other hand, Pentecostals and Charismatics believe in the continuance of the power of the Spirit in the same manner as recorded in the book of Acts, but many prefer eschatological systems of interpretation, specifically dispensationalism, that weakens their ecclesiology. While Rev 11 has been studied at length by scholars in the past, with the exception of a few,[1] elements have often been ignored that can help the church develop a greater understanding of its identity and function. Therefore, what follows is an exegetical examination of Rev 11 that remains in dialogue with scholars from various positions but seeks to answer the aforementioned questions concerning the nature of the church and the empowerment of the Spirit.

THE TEMPLE

The temple, along with the two witnesses, is probably the most controversial symbolism used within the interlude of Rev 10.1—11.13. Those who lean toward the preterist group tend to view the temple as the literal Jerusalem temple that was destroyed in 70 C.E.[2] This, in turn, means that they usually try to date the writing of the Apocalypse at around the same time. In addition, the outer court refers to the actual court of the Gentiles that was present in Herod's temple. Those in the dispensational group see this as the literal rebuilt temple of the tribulation period. Thus the image is that of the 144,000 Jewish "worshipers"[3] from 7.1–8 being persecuted by the followers of the Antichrist for "forty-two months."[4]

---

1. See e.g., R. Waddell, *The Spirit of the Book of Revelation* (Blandford Forum, UK: Deo, 2006); and C. S. Keener, *Revelation* (Grand Rapids: Zondervan, 1999).

2. See e.g., D. Chilton, *The Days of Vengeance: An Exposition of the Book of Revelation* (Fort Worth, TX: Dominion, 1987); and J. Roloff, *The Revelation of John*, trans. J. E. Alsup (Minneapolis: Fortress, 1993).

3. All translations are my own unless indicated otherwise.

4. See e.g., J. F. Walvoord, *The Revelation of Jesus Christ* (Chicago: Moody, 1966).

A modified dispensational view holds that the temple represents a remnant of believing Jews.[5] Still, others hold that the temple and outer court represent either a mixture of believers and unbelieving Jews (Swete) or the world in conflict with the church (Beale). Some even see the outer court as those who have left the church and are now standing in opposition (Hendriksen).[6] Aune purports that the inner court is representative of the wilderness of protection where the remnant is saved from the tribulation.[7] The most common view today is that the temple somehow represents God's spiritual protection of the church.[8] In any event, it is easy to see the vast amount of theories that revolve around the temple of this passage.

John is given a measuring rod or stick and told to measure "the temple of God, the altar, and those who worship in it" (11.1).[9] This is very similar to the experience of Ezekiel in which he saw a heavenly figure with a measuring rod in his hand (Ezek 40.1–5). Zechariah also experienced a similar occurrence, as a man with a measuring line went out to measure the city of Jerusalem (Zech 2.1–5). John is most likely drawing from the imagery of Ezek 40–48 and Zech 2.1–5 combined with Dan 8.11–13 and 12.7. The measuring is a symbolic action that reveals that God will protect his people spiritually, but they will go through physical persecution. However, the prominence of the prophetic element linking this action with Zechariah should not be understated due to John's emphasis upon prophecy throughout the entire interlude of Rev 10.1—11.13. Therefore, for John, the picture is one of duality; his message is meant to convey both its prophetic nature and God's protection of his people.

Beale points out that this rendering of the measurement is consistent with the fulfillment pattern in Ezek 40–42.[10] The measuring in Ezekiel symbolically protected the temple from idolatry within its vicinity. In turn, John uses it to show that God would protect his people from being affected by

---

5. G. E. Ladd, *A Commentary on the Revelation of John* (Grand Rapids: Eerdmans, 1972) 149–50.

6. A great synopsis of various positions concerning the temple can be found in G. R. Osborne, *Revelation* (Grand Rapids: Baker, 2002) 408–9.

7. D. E. Aune, *Revelation* (Dallas: Word, 1997) 2:598.

8. See e.g., R. H. Mounce, *The Book of Revelation* (Grand Rapids: Eerdmans, 1977) 213.

9. It is the opinion of this author that the disciple John wrote the book of Revelation. Arguments against John's authorship have thus far been unconvincing. However, it is not the purpose of this article to rehash all of the arguments pertaining to authorship. Therefore, John is referred to in this article as the author primarily for the sake of convenience.

10. G. K. Beale, *The Book of Revelation: A Commentary on the Greek Text* (Grand Rapids: Eerdmans, 1998) 561.

idolatrous influences (cf. Rev 2.2; 6; 14–15; 20–24). However, the meaning of this message from John seems to be deeper than just spiritual protection, especially when combined with his emphasis upon prophetic witness and the close connection of this interlude with Zech 2–4.[11] Although the church will undergo persecution and even death at the hands of the wicked, due to their prophetic witness, they will come forward victoriously through "the blood of the Lamb and the word of their testimony" (Rev 12.11). The victory of the saints can be seen in parallel with 21.15–21, where an angel measures the city, gates, and walls of the New Jerusalem. The New Jerusalem has no outer court because God has come to victoriously live in the midst of his people where there is no more persecution. Therefore, as Osborne states, "the measuring of the sanctuary here (in Rev 11) is a 'prophetic anticipation' of the final victory of the church."[12] It would also seem to convey a message concerning the church and its identity and function in the world.

The fact that the temple in Rev 11 is measured, and that it is an allusion to the temple of Ezek 40–48 and the city of Jerusalem in Zech 2.1–5, does not seem to indicate a literal temple structure. As aforementioned, these measurements convey the idea of divine protection and presence. Indeed, the biblical model of the temple is clearly not about a physical structure that houses God, but the presence of God among his people (Gen 1–3; Exod 25.8; Num 2.2; Ezek 43.7; John 1; 2.19–21; Acts 2; Rev 1; 11.19; 21.22; 22.4). The corpus of Johannine writing also suggests a more symbolic reading based upon the presence of God. In John 1, Jesus is called "the word" (λόγος) that became flesh and "dwelt or took up residence" (ἐσκήνωσεν) among humanity. John even places this idea on the lips of Jesus when he states "destroy this temple, and in three days I will raise it up" (John 2.19). He is then able to tell the Samaritan woman at the well that the time has now arrived in which people will worship God in spirit instead of in temples such as the one in Jerusalem (John 4.20–24).

Furthermore, the context surrounding the temple of the Apocalypse would suggest a symbolic reading. For instance, Rev 1 records Jesus as the high priest who walks among the candlesticks that are representative of the seven churches of Asia to which John is writing. It is obvious that Jesus is

---

11. Cf. Waddell, *The Spirit*, 165, notes that "Zech 2.1–5 conceivably vies with Ezekiel to be the most resonant intertextual echo in v. 1. Unlike the vision of Ezekiel, both Zechariah and John omit the actual description of the measuring. Furthermore, the vision of Ezekiel is followed much more closely by John in Rev 21.10–17 . . . Nevertheless, defining the intertextual echo need not mean an exclusive decision . . . For John, the prominence of Zechariah is carried through to 11.4, where echoes of Zech 4 resound in the description of the two witnesses."

12. Osborne, *Revelation*, 412.

not walking through a literal temple with candlesticks but that his presence is with the churches. Revelation 11.19 records John having a vision of God's temple in heaven that contains the Ark of the Covenant. Clearly, this is a reference to the presence of God and a worship ceremony, not of a literal building that contains his presence.

Ironically, the temple in Ezek 40–48 finds its ultimate fulfillment in the city of Rev 20–22 where there is no temple because the Father and Jesus are present. Like Ezekiel, John places great emphasis on his description of the holy city. There can be little doubt that John deliberately uses his description to parallel Ezekiel's temple. For instance, the flow of water, life-giving trees, and the direction that the structure faces all serve as indicators. In addition, Ezekiel describes the name of the city as being "the Lord is there" (Ezek 48.35). In turn, John, in his description of the new heaven and new earth, notes that God dwells with humanity. The ultimate expression of the glory of God among his people is seen in Rev 22.4 in which the New Jerusalem is revealed as the place Ezekiel describes of God in unimpeded relationship with his people.[13]

The word used for temple in Rev 11 is ναὸν. This seems to indicate that John is specifically alluding to the inner temple structure because ναός is not generally used when referring to the courts outside of the temple building. Therefore, "the court outside of the temple" is not likely referring to the outer court of Herod's temple. The outer court of Herod's temple is called the court of the Gentiles in modern literature, but it was not known as such during the time of the NT. It is also not one of the outer courts of either Solomon's or Ezekiel's temple. This means that this court must be the one mentioned as the court of the priests in NT times.[14] Consequently, the altar of Rev 11 is likely the altar of incense and the outer court would be the one containing the altar of burnt offering. In addition, the worshippers must be priests who are allowed to enter and give an offering of incense within the holy place. Since both locations represent parts of the temple, and John is alluding in part to Dan 8–12 and the "shattering of the power of the holy people," it would seem that the symbolism reveals the church under God's spiritual protection while being persecuted by the world.

John is told not to measure the outer court because "it has been given to the nations" that "will tread underfoot the holy city for forty-two months" (Rev 11.2). Interestingly, many in the dispensational and preterist groups

---

13. The close relation of John's prophetic calling in Rev 10 with Ezekiel's call narrative further connects the temple of Rev 11 with Ezekiel's temple and also John's emphasis upon prophetic witness and Spirit empowerment.

14. R. Bauckham, *The Climax of Prophecy: Studies on the Book of Revelation* (Edinburgh: T. & T. Clark, 1993) 268.

would prefer the translation "Gentiles" for (ἔθνεσιν) instead of "nations" because they either see the temple as symbolic of national Israel, a literal rebuilt temple in Jerusalem, or the Jerusalem temple that was destroyed in 70 C.E. However, the better translation according to the context of Revelation and the entire NT seems to be "nations." As Bauckham so aptly states, "it is highly unlikely that in Rev 11.1–2 John intends to speak literally of the temple which had been destroyed in 70 CE and the earthly Jerusalem, in which he nowhere else shows any interest. He understands the temple and the city as symbols of the people of God."[15]

Furthermore, Beale points out that a literal reading is implausible because of its misunderstanding of John's visions, "which contain heavenly symbols and not photographic images with a one-to-one identity to earthly realities."[16] For instance, many have used the reference to "the holy city" (πόλιν τὴν ἁγίαν) in connection with OT and NT passages to substantiate their claim for the literal city of Jerusalem. However, John uses "city" (πόλις) in the Apocalypse to refer to the future city of God that is inhabited by believers from every tribe, tongue, and nation (3.12; 21.2, 10). Therefore, in the context of Revelation, 11.2 must be referring to a portion of the heavenly city or community of God that is represented by believers on earth.[17]

In 11.1, John has already suggested that the "trampling of the holy place" in Dan 8.11–13 is a symbolic reference to the "shattering of the power of the holy people" in Dan 12.7. "This shattering which is therefore also the trampling of the holy place (Dan 8.13) and city, John, of course, understands as the great persecution of Christians, which Rev 7 has already foreseen."[18] It is also unnecessary to hold that this passage reproduces an older prophecy, from before 70 C.E., that has not been fulfilled (since in 70 C.E. the sanctuary itself was destroyed by the nations).[19]

The NT evidence is astounding regarding the temple. First, as previously mentioned, Jesus establishes himself as the temple by saying "destroy this temple, and in three days I will raise it up" (John 2.19). Second, the NT records that the presence of God in the Holy Spirit now lives within the church and each believer, signifying the temple (Matt 3.11; 27.51; Luke 3.16; 11.10; John 14.16; 16; 20; Acts 2). In fact, the NT makes clear that there is no distinction between Jew and Gentile in this regard (Acts 15.8–9). Third, Paul elaborates further on believers as the temple of God (Rom 5; 8) and

---

15. Ibid., 272.
16. Beale, *A Commentary on the Greek Text*, 568.
17. Ibid.
18. Bauckham, *Climax of Prophecy*, 268.
19. Ibid., 271–72.

says that "they are not all Israel who are descended from Israel" (Rom 9.6). He then goes on to say that "you (believers) are the temple of God and the Spirit of God dwells in you." Furthermore, "if any man destroys the temple of God, God will destroy him, for the temple of God is holy, and that is what you are" (1 Cor 3.16–17).

Fourth, Paul goes on to specifically mention the Gentiles as part of this temple of the Holy Spirit (Eph 3.1–21) and the one body of Christ which represents the temple (4.4–6). Indeed, the people of God are those, who like Abraham, have come to belief in the Lord (Gal 3). He purports that what Christ enacted by his sacrifice was more perfect than the "mere copy" made by human hands, alluding to the man made temple (Heb 9.23–25). Through these examples it is clear that God's new covenant temple is only to be associated with the church and his presence (Heb 9; Rev 3; 7; 14; 15; 16). It is unanimously agreed upon that the temple in Rev 11 is referring at least in part to God's people, and the NT is clear that God's people are only those who have faith in Christ. In addition, the new covenant temple is always referred to as the dwelling place of God with his people the church, or the individual believer. Therefore, it would seem that any attempt to claim that the temple of Rev 11 is a literal structure, exclusively Jewish, or a return to Israel as God's people is out of line with Scripture and against the testimony of Christ and his work, which is the central theme of the Apocalypse.

THE TWO WITNESSES

The identity, function, and events surrounding the two witnesses in the interlude of Rev 10.1—11.13 may make this the most hotly debated passage in the book of Revelation. Many in the dispensationalist camp would prefer to identify the witnesses as a combination of Enoch, Elijah, Moses, or two other specific people that are discovered by using a literal interpretation of the text. According to Seiss, the two witnesses cannot be the saints seen in heaven because they have already died once, "and these two witnesses die subsequent to their prophesying, (thus) we are driven to search for some saints in heaven who never have died."[20] Still, many historicists hold that the two witnesses are a combination of the old and new covenant church and the Bible.[21] This belief stems from interpreting the candlesticks as the old and new covenant church and the olive trees as the prophets and the

---

20. J. A. Seiss, *The Apocalypse: Lectures on the Book of Revelation* (Grand Rapids: Zondervan, 1964) 244.

21. See e.g., R. Caringola, *The Present Reign of Jesus Christ: A Historical Interpretation of the Book of Revelation* (Springfield, MO: Reformed, 1995).

apostles. The reality is that presuppositions in the process of interpretation have led to almost too many speculations than can be counted regarding the identity of the two witnesses.

The message that John conveys continues in 11.3 with, "And I will give power/authority to my two witnesses, and they will prophesy for 1,260 days, clothed in sackcloth." The text does not specify what exactly it is that God "will give" (δώσω) his "witnesses" (μάρτυσίν). However, the ministry of the witnesses that follows their arrival suggests that God has given them the power of the Spirit in order to be effective in their mission.[22] In addition, it seems as though the future tenses "will give" (δώσω) and "will prophesy" (προφητεύσουσιν) should not be seen as determining a future time that this will take place: "The tense by itself cannot determine the time because the tenses and moods alternate from future to present and from indicative to subjunctive in this passage. The future tense verbs probably emphasize divine determination rather than future time, just as aorist passive ἐδόθη in v 2 has the same sense and does not refer primarily to past time."[23]

It is the context that must determine the time, and it seems clear that in Rev 11 John is referring to the church in the past, present, and future. Interestingly, Osborne points out the contrasting uses of the word "give" in 11.2, 3. In 11.2 the church is "given" over to the nations to be trampled, and in 11.3 God "gives" the church the power to be victorious by witnessing through its persecution.[24] When questioned about the time of the end, Jesus stated that "you (the church or individual believers) will receive power when the Holy Spirit has come upon you; and you shall be my witnesses both in Jerusalem, and in all Judea and Samaria, and even to the remotest part of the earth" (Acts 1.8). Peter then connects Joel's prophecy concerning the pouring out of the Spirit (giving of power for witness) in the last days to the filling of the Spirit on Pentecost (Acts 2.17–21). The importance of the eschatological church being Spirit-filled can hardly be missed when combined with the prophetic emphasis of both John's calling and the two witnesses.[25]

22. Waddell, *The Spirit*, 171.
23. Beale, *A Commentary on the Greek Text*, 572.
24. Osborne, *Revelation*, 419.
25. For further study into the role of the Spirit in Rev 11, see e.g., Waddell, *The Spirit*, and J. C. Thomas, "Toward a Pentecostal Theology of Prophetic Witness: The Testimony of the Apocalypse (Revelation 11.3–14)" paper at an SPS meeting, 2007. For some great sources concerning the biblical model of Spirit empowerment, see e.g., R. Stronstad, *The Charismatic Theology of St. Luke: Trajectories from the Old Testament to Luke-Acts*; B. Aker, "New Directions in Lukan Theology: Reflections on Luke 3.21–22 and Some Implications," in *Faces of Renewal: Studies in Honor of Stanley M. Horton*, ed. P. Elbert (Peabody, MA: Hendrickson, 1988) 108–27; B. Aker, "Acts 2 as a Paradigmatic

But These are Written . . .

The time frame for the witnesses prophesying is set at 1,260 days or roughly three and a half years. Although many have interpreted this time frame to be literal, Krodel and others have argued that John is again alluding to Daniel (7.25; 9.27; 12.7) and the well known events surrounding the Maccabean Revolt.[26] John connects the witnesses to the temple and the woman in Rev 12 by repeating the time frame allusion of three and a half years from Daniel in a different way each time (Rev 11.1–2, 3; 12.14). One reason for this is because the temple, witnesses, and woman are all symbols that represent the same thing—the church. In any case, the time frame is not meant to be taken as a literal period of time.

The symbolism that Daniel, and in turn John, uses to describe a short time of persecution comes from the period of Antiochus Epiphanes IV. Antiochus ruled the Seleucid Empire from 175 B.C.E. until his death in 164 B.C.E. In the biblical world he is most noted for his treatment of the Jews that is mentioned in the Maccabean writings. Second Maccabees records that Antiochus returned from a failed campaign in Egypt and found that Menelaus, his appointed high priest in Jerusalem, had been deposed. Antiochus assumed the Jews had revolted and either imprisoned or killed 80,000 men, women, and children within a three day span. In addition, he looted the temple, instituted the worship of Zeus, set up "abominable offerings" on the altar, and outlawed Jewish religious practices.

> Harsh and utterly grievous was the onslaught of evil. For the temple was filled with debauchery and reveling by the Gentiles, who dallied with prostitutes and had intercourse with women within the sacred precincts, and besides brought in things for sacrifice that were unfit. The altar was covered with abominable offerings that were forbidden by the laws. People could neither keep the sabbath, nor observe the festivals of their ancestors, nor so much as confess themselves to be Jews (2 Macc 6.3–6 NRSV).

Narrative for Luke's Theology of the Spirit," paper presented at the Annual Meeting of the ETS, 1998; B. Aker, "'Breathed' A Study on the Biblical Distinction Between Regeneration and Spirit Baptism," *Paraclete* (Summer 1983) 13–16; B. Aker and G. B. McGee, *Signs and Wonders in Ministry Today* (Springfield, MO: GPH, 1996); P. Grabe, "Hermeneutical Reflections on the Interpretation of the New Testament with Special Reference to the Holy Spirit and Faith," in *The Reality of the Holy Spirit in the Church: In Honour of F P Möller*, ed. Willem Johannes Hattingh (Pretoria: J. L. van Schaik, 1997); S. Horton, *Acts* (Springfield, MO: Logion, 1981); G. D. Fee, *God's Empowering Presence: The Holy Spirit in the Letters of Paul* (Peabody, MA: Hendrickson, 1994); W. W. Menzies and R. P. Menzies, *Spirit and Power: Foundations of Pentecostal Experience* (Grand Rapids: Zondervan, 2000); W. Atkinson, "Pentecostal Responses to Dunn's Baptism in the Holy Spirit: Luke-Acts," *JPT* 6 (Apr 1995) 87–131.

26. G. A. Krodel, *Revelation* (Minneapolis: Augsburg Fortress, 1989) 220.

This period of three and a half years was the time from Antiochus' persecution and abomination that made desolate in 167 B.C.E. until the rededication of the temple in 164 B.C.E.[27] It would thus seem probable, when combined with the temple symbolism of 11.1–2, that John makes use of the pattern of three and a half years to symbolize a short time of persecution. While the time frame in this passage is primarily symbolism conveying a prophecy concerning the period of Antiochus Epiphanes and the "abomination which caused desolation," the destruction of Jerusalem (Mark 13.4; Matt 24.15) through the Jewish war against Rome from 67 to 70 C.E., also brought fulfillment as a "proleptic anticipation of the last days."[28]

As aforementioned, the temple and the witnesses seem to be grammatically connected by John in this passage. While the holy place within the temple is protected from pollution through idolatrous influences (Rev 11.1–2) the witnesses are protected from harm during their mission (11.3, 5). Furthermore, both the trampling of a portion of the temple and the witnesses mission carry a time frame of three and a half years. The forty-two months in which the nations will trample part of the temple most likely comes from John's extensive use of his new exodus motif within Revelation. In fact, it is likely that John patterns the entire Apocalypse after the theme of the new exodus (see 12.6, 14).[29] Therefore, the forty-two months correspond to the forty-two years that the Israelites spent in the wilderness before entering the promised land. Two years come from the time the Israelites spent moving from the Red Sea to Mt. Sinai and from Mt. Sinai to Kadesh in the Desert of Paran (Exod 19.1; Num 1.1; 10.11; 13.26). The Israelites spent another forty years between Kadesh and their entrance into the promised land (Num 14.33–34).

The period of 1,260 days likely comes from an allusion to Dan 7.25 and 12.7, where "time, times, and half a time" is used as an apocalyptic time frame. As previously mentioned, John borrows from the imagery of the OT so that he can convey the message that has been given to him. When compiled with the witnesses' power to "shut up the sky," it also seems as though John is alluding to 1 Kgs 17–18, in which Elijah prevented rain from falling

---

27. Krodel, *Revelation*, 220.

28. Osborne, *Revelation*, 414.

29. In Exodus, the children of Israel remain in the land while Moses, God's witness, prophesies before Pharaoh. In turn, God punishes the Egyptians for not listening to his witness through plagues similar to those in Revelation. Instead of heeding the word of God, Pharaoh and the Egyptians punish the Hebrews who they blame for God's wrath. The exodus finally takes place after God's most severe judgment upon the Egyptians occurs. Interestingly, John uses the same pattern of prophetic witness, rejection of the prophetic message, and resulting judgment throughout Revelation.

for less than three years. Jewish tradition and the NT put the drought at three and a half years (Luke 4.25; Jas 5.17). John must have this in mind "when he says that the two witnesses can prevent rain from falling 'during the days of their prophesying' (11.6), i.e., during the 1,260 days (11.3) or three and a half years of their prophetic ministry."[30] The time frame of the witnesses, together with that of the temple, shows that John sees these two events as occurring simultaneously.

God's two witnesses are described as being clothed in sackcloth. Sackcloth is a garment of mourning woven together from either camel or goat hair. The witnesses dress matches that of prominent biblical prophets, including John the Baptist (2 Kgs 1.8; Isa 20.2; Zech 13.4; Mark 1.6). The word "sackcloth" (σάκκους) appears one other time in the Apocalypse (6.12), where it is used to describe the darkness of the sun after one of the signs of judgment. Bratcher says that "this detail shows that the message of the two prophets was to be one of imminent doom and destruction, and a call for people to repent while there was still time."[31] Still, Brighton purports that the dress of the two witnesses suggests that they will have "a 'penitential' attitude of humble and sacrificial service."[32] It seems likely that both of these assessments are correct based upon the context of the passage. For the prophet, the wearing of sackcloth often carried the dual meaning of sorrow and humbleness over sin, and judgment (Isa 3.24; 58.5; Jer 4.8; Matt 11.21). In addition, the ministry of the witnesses brings both judgment (Rev 11.13a) and repentance (11.13b).

The prophetic witnesses are further described as "the two olive trees and two lampstands that stand before the Lord of the earth" (11.4). The allusion in this passage is clearly to Zech 4.1–14 and his seven-branched lampstand and olive trees. The images in Zechariah refer to Zerrubabel the king and Joshua the high priest who were anointed by the Spirit to accomplish God's purpose. "Strikingly, in Revelation the redeemed of the Lord are called a kingdom of priests, or even kings and priests."[33] Furthermore, John has already used lampstands to symbolically speak of the church (Rev 1.12, 20; 2.1). If the seven churches of Asia, and therefore the church universal, is referred to as seven lampstands in the beginning of the Apocalypse, then why should the two lampstands in Rev 11 refer to anything else? Therefore, the context of the passage within Revelation suggests that John has the church in view. Bauck-

---

30. Bauckham, *Climax of Prophecy*, 275.

31. R. G. Bratcher, *A Translator's Guide to The Revelation to John* (New York: UBS, 1984) 88.

32. L. A. Brighton, *Revelation* (St. Louis: Concordia, 2009) 291.

33. D. E. Holwerda, "Suffering Witnesses—To What End?" *CTJ* 41/1 (Apr 2006) 128.

ham rightly reports that the seven lampstands represent the whole church, since seven is the number of completeness. In addition, the two lampstands are symbolic of the church's role of Spirit-filled witness. The reason for this is because of the well known biblical requirement that evidence be acceptable only on the testimony of two witnesses (Num 35.30; Deut 17.6; cf. Matt 18.16; John 5.31; 8.17; 15.26–27; Acts 5.32; 2 Cor 13.1; Heb 10.28; 1 Tim 5.19) and the connection of this passage with Zech 4.[34]

Interestingly, the entire community of believers are repeatedly referred to as those who give testimony concerning Jesus (Rev 6.9; 12.11; 17; 19.10; 20.4). An important point to stress is that the appearance of two lampstands as opposed to seven does not mean that John has only a partial group of the church in view. As aforementioned, the two lampstands are symbolic of a complete legal witness. Beale argues that this "legal atmosphere" is made more prominent by John's use of "witnesses" (μάρτυσίν) that refers to legal witness. "This nuance is borne out by observing that in at least six of the nine uses of the word in the Apocalypse it refers to a witness that is rejected by the world's legal system and that results in penal consequences (so 1.9; 6.9; 12.11, 17; 20.4)."[35] Beale's argument seems foolproof considering the fact that the rejection of the witnesses' message in Rev 11 leads to judgment from God.

Like the lampstands, the olive trees are also given as a symbol of the two witnesses. The olive trees were to represent Zerrubabel and Joshua as well (Zech 4). The point of the symbolism in Zechariah was that God was in charge of their mission, and he would make sure that they completed their task. In fact, God gave them the message that it was "not by might nor by power, but by my Spirit, says the Lord of hosts" (Zech 4.6). Consequently, John uses the symbolism of Zech 4 to show the church that God, through the power of his Holy Spirit, is protecting them and will destroy their enemies. Through this symbolism, John confirms the presence of the Spirit in their mission (see Acts 2). It is therefore clear in this passage that John has in view the church of the *eschaton*; the eschatological church is marked by the power of the Spirit working fully in her midst to empower her to preach the good news of Jesus Christ to the world (Acts 1.8; 2.4; 2.16–21). This is not a future church, but rather Rev 11.1–13 serves as a prophetic call to the people of God to be faithful witnesses empowered by the Spirit.[36]

The expectation that the Spirit of prophecy would be made available to God's people during the last days can be traced throughout the OT. Numbers 11.29 alludes to this when Moses expresses his desire that "all the Lord's

---

34. See Bauckham, *Climax of Prophecy*, 274; Waddell, *The Spirit*, 172.
35. Beale, *A Commentary on the Greek Text*, 575.
36. Waddell, *The Spirit*, 174.

people were prophets, [and] that the Lord would put his Spirit upon them." Joel prophesied that the Holy Spirit would be poured out on all flesh (2.28). In turn, Peter proclaimed the events of Pentecost as the fulfillment of this OT expectation (Acts 2). Thus, in Rev 11, "John is calling the church to engage in its prophetic role by bearing witness to Jesus via the power of the Spirit."[37]

The two witnesses of Rev 11 are further identified as having the power of "fire" that "flows out of their mouth to devour their enemies," to "shut up the sky so that rain will not fall during the days of their prophesying," to "turn the waters to blood," and "to strike the earth with every plague, as long as they desire" (11.5–6). Due to the obvious allusions to Elijah and Moses, many have used these verses as proof texts for the belief in two literal OT prophets coming down from heaven during the end times. However, there are other key indicators, besides the ones already mentioned, that contradict that position. For instance, in no place in Rev 11 is there any mention of the two witnesses coming down from heaven. In fact, the dialog to John in v. 2 suggests that the two witnesses are already on earth at that time. In addition, John never records Elijah and Moses, or any other prophetic character, descending from heaven to prophesy against the nations.

As previously mentioned, the power to "shut up the sky" for three and a half years is a clear reference to the drought that Elijah brought about in 1 Kgs 17–18. The powers to "turn the waters to blood" and "strike the earth with every plague" are a clear reference to Moses and the events surrounding the exodus (Exod 7–12; 1 Sam 4–8). However, it is important to note that "the powers of each of the OT prophets are attributed to both of the two witnesses, not divided between them."[38] This fact also seems to destroy the theory that John has the literal individual prophets in view. After all, if the argument is that the powers given indicate the two individual identities of Elijah and Moses, then it could only be expected that each would perform those specific powers delegated to them individually. However, these witnesses use their powers corporately and in unison. Additionally, the beast from the abyss is said to "make war with them" (Rev 11.7). It is hard to imagine how the beast could "make war" against only two people.[39]

The communication that the two witnesses "stand before the Lord of the earth" indicates that the witnesses are under the protection of God during the time of their mission. In fact, Rev 11 indicates that they are not able to be harmed during their time of witnessing (11.5; cf. John 7.30; 8.20). Indeed, "to kill God's witnesses is impossible, so long as their witness is

---

37. Ibid., 175.
38. Bauckham, *Climax of Prophecy*, 276.
39. Ibid.

unfulfilled."[40] The fire that comes out of their mouth to destroy their enemies is reminiscent of Elijah calling fire down from heaven (2 Kgs 1.9–12). However, in Rev 11 the witnesses do not call down fire from heaven; it comes from their mouths (11.5). By using this imagery, John indicates that the power of the witnesses is in the words of their testimony (cf. 12.11). Truly, the testimony of the witnesses is so powerful that "the gates of Hades will not overpower it" (Matt 16.18). In fact, Jer 5.14 says that the word of God, spoken by the prophet, consumes ungodly people like fire consumes wood (cf. Rev 1.16; 2.12, 16; 9.17–19; 12.15–16; 16.13; 19.15, 21).[41]

The power of the witnesses to turn the water to blood and bring plagues upon the earth reveals John's new exodus theme that runs throughout the Apocalypse. The symbolism is that the witnesses, who are on earth, are delivering the word of God to the nations. The nations continue to ignore the testimony of the witnesses (9.20–21; 11.9–10; 16.11). In turn, God pours out his judgment upon the wicked until the witnesses are finally victoriously removed from the scene. The key difference in John's version is that the church is able to gain victory over the nations by reaching some through the power of their witness in conjunction with God's judgment (Rev 11.13). The witnesses' powers over the plagues seem to refer to their ability to give signs of divine judgment, corresponding with their preaching of repentance, which is symbolized by the sackcloth that they wear.[42] Therefore, the judgments in the Apocalypse serve to warn sinners of their need to repent based upon the witnesses' testimony to Jesus (6.9–11; 12.11; 17; 19.10; 20.4).

When the testimony of the two witnesses is complete, the beast of the abyss overcomes and kills them. The dead bodies of the witnesses "lie in the street of the great city which mystically is called Sodom and Egypt, where also their Lord was crucified" (11.7–8). Once again, it is important to note here that the future tense "will make" (ποιήσει) does not determine the time. The fact that the witnesses testimony is said to be complete refers back to the martyrs (the church) who have lost their lives due to "the testimony which they had maintained" (6.9). As mentioned earlier, the testimony of the witnesses is what has brought judgment upon the wicked (cf. John 12.48). Moreover, God does not allow the beast to have his temporary victory until after the testimony of the witnesses is finished. This directly connects to God's message to the martyred saints that "they should rest for a little while longer, until the number of their fellow servants and their brethren who were to be killed even as they had been, would be completed"

---

40. H. B. Swete, *The Apocalypse of St. John* (New York: Macmillan, 1907) 132.
41. Brighton, *Revelation*, 296.
42. Bauckham, *Climax of Prophecy*, 277.

But These are Written . . .

(Rev 6.11). Therefore, the task of the church is once again seen as perseverance and witness even in the face of death, which is part of the theme of the entire Apocalypse (2.3, 9–10, 13, 19; 3.8; 6.9–11; 12.11; 13.10; 14.12–13; 15.2; 17.14; 19.7–10; 20.4–5; 21–22).

The beast that comes from the abyss to make war against God's witnesses is clearly connected with Satan. Some theologians take the beast to be the antichrist figure that is expected to come during the *eschaton*. Still, others simply see the beast as a direct representation of Satan. John's use of the definite article may suggest that the identity of the beast is well known. John has already seen a demonic army and their leader Abaddon/Apollyon, "the (destroyer) angel of the abyss," emerge to attack humanity (9.1–11). John also reports seeing two beasts in Rev 13, one from the sea and one from the earth, which are controlled by the dragon. The dragon's identity is revealed as Satan in 12.9. "In 9.1–11 the demonic hosts (under their leader) afflict the unbelieving portion of the human race, in Rev 12 and 13 they afflict the church—the woman who bore the Son."[43]

The context of the beast in Rev 11 suggests that he should be viewed as Satan. The reason for this is because Rev 10, 11, and 12 are all functioning to tie the first part of the Apocalypse together with the last. In Rev 10, John is given a scroll by a divine messenger (Holy Spirit?)[44] and told to prophecy (cf. Rev 5). The result comes in Rev 11 as the Spirit-filled church is shown to be involved in mission even during persecution and death (cf. Rev 6.10–11; 12.11; 13–15; 17; 19–22). Moreover, Rev 12 gives the overall story of God's people, from the beginning until their victory, while leading into the final stage of the *eschaton* and the final elaboration cycle of John's vision. Due to the fact that Rev 12 is so closely connected with the interlude of 10 and 11, it is much more likely that the beast mentioned here is the same as the dragon.

As a consequence of the statement "where also their Lord was crucified," many have speculated that the "the great city" where the witnesses lay dead for three days is the literal city of Jerusalem. However, in Revelation, "the great city" always refers to Babylon and Rome (14.8; 16.19; 17.18; 18.2, 10, 16, 18–19, 21) or Sodom and Egypt (11.8). Sodom was a place of sexual immorality that refused to follow God's commandments and was therefore punished by God's judgment (Isa 1.16; Jer 23.24). Egypt was the land of the exodus and the plagues, where God's people were oppressed (Exod 7–12).

---

43. Brighton, *Revelation*, 297.

44. Waddell, *The Spirit*, 150–64, forcefully argues that the messenger of Rev 10 is none other than a theophany of the Holy Spirit. In fact, the Spirit is the one that commissions John in Rev 10 and is the narrator of Rev 11. If true, this would solve issues involved with the change in speaker from Rev 10 to 11 (angel to divine) and serve to accentuate further John's message concerning the Spirit-filled church.

Will The Real Church Please Stand Up?

In essence, John combines the symbolism of Jerusalem, "where also their Lord was crucified," with Babylon, Rome, and Egypt in order to give his audience the picture of a sexually perverse, idolatrous, and oppressive world that he calls "the great city."[45]

That John has witnesses throughout the entire world in mind is exemplified in Rev 11.9 where "those from the peoples and tribes and tongues and nations will look at their dead bodies." Indeed, it is hard to imagine how John, or his first-century audience, could anticipate everyone being able to see the witnesses if they were two individuals in the literal city of Jerusalem. Furthermore, the Greek word used for their bodies is actually "body" (πτῶμα). The reason for this is that John has a corporate entity in mind. It is important to note here that although both witnesses, or the church, are purported to die, this does not mean that John foresees the death of all Christians through martyrdom. As previously mentioned, John is symbolically viewing the entire history of the witnessing church in which martyrdom has been a major part. In addition, John's message to the first-century church is to persevere in the face of persecution and death brought on by Satan. The description of v. 9 is a clear reference to those whom Jesus purchased with his blood (5.9) and to John's command to prophesy (10.11). In other words, John clearly has in view witnesses from around the world who are giving testimony to Jesus.

The death, resurrection, and ascension of the witnesses is patterned after the events surrounding Jesus' death, resurrection, and ascension. The "three and a half days" are linked with the forty-two months, 1,260 days (11.2–3) and the resurrection of Jesus "after" three days (Mark 8.31; 9.31; 10.34). It seems likely that John also has Ezek 37.1–14 in mind. Ezekiel saw an army of dry bones that was brought to their feet by "the breath of life." It is apparent that John has the same theme of resurrection in view for the church. However, the most prominent allusion by John is the connection between the witnesses and Christ. Jesus ascended into heaven with a cloud (Acts 1.9; cf. 1 Thess 4.17). In the end, Jesus will "come on the clouds" when he returns in judgment (Dan 7.13; Matt 24.30; Mark 13.26; Luke 21.27). In any event, John begins to attach great significance to the resurrection of the witnesses. "Our author distinguishes between 'the first resurrection' of the faithful (Rev 20.4–6) and the resurrection of the rest of humanity (20.11–15). The resurrection/ascension of the witnesses in 11.12 introduces the notion of the 'first resurrection' which is unfolded in 20.4–6. John never tells all at once but presents different aspects in succeeding cycles."[46]

---

45. Krodel, *Revelation*, 226.
46. Ibid., 227.

But These are Written . . .

It is important to note here that the resurrection of the witnesses and their ascension to heaven (11.11–12) does not indicate that the *parousia* has yet taken place. The *parousia* would at this point seem premature considering that many spectators are apparently converted in 11.13. Additionally, 19.11–12 seems to make the clear indication that the *parousia* will take place at the end of history. John has not yet reached the point in his cycles of elaboration in which the *parousia* takes place. However, he is clearly alluding to it in this passage. We also know that the resurrection occurs at the return of Christ, which Mark places after the great tribulation.

> For in those days there will be such tribulation as has not been from the beginning of the creation that God created until now, and never will be . . . But in those days, *after that tribulation*, the sun will be darkened and the moon will not give its light, and the stars will be falling from heaven, and the powers that are in the heavens will be shaken. *Then* they will see the Son of Man coming in clouds with great power and glory. And *then* He will send forth the angels, and will gather together His elect from the four winds, from the farthest end of the earth to the farthest end of heaven (Mark 13.19, 24–27).[47]

The message is that although the witnesses suffer death and humiliation at the hands of the wicked for a time, God will raise them up into a cloud as they ascend victoriously (Rev 11.12; cf. 1 Thess 4.17). The article with "cloud" is probably functioning in an anaphoric manner. This means that the cloud is either pointing back to the cloud that covered the mighty angel of 10.1, or to the cloud with which Christ will soon return (1.7). While Rev 10 is the closer antecedent, the cloud of 1.7, which is also an articular prepositional phrase, supplies the better conceptual parallel.[48] Interestingly, the cloud can also be connected to John's theme of exodus/new exodus (Exod 13.21; 14.19–20; 24.15–18; Num 9.17–21; Deut 31.15–16; Matt 24.30; Mark 14.62; Acts 1.9). After dealing with the death, resurrection, and ascension of the witnesses, John focuses on the joyful reaction of the world that had shown hostility toward God's people. By doing this, John further connects the interlude with the preceding six trumpets and with their climax in the seventh trumpet.

---

47. Italics are used for emphasis.
48. Osborne, *Revelation*, 431.

THE GREAT EARTHQUAKE

The Greek word used for the earthquake in Rev 11.13 is σεισμὸς. This is referred to seven different times in the Apocalypse (Rev 6.12; 8.5; 11.13; 11.19; 16.18). In 8.5 and 11.19, the earthquake is used to refer to the awesomeness of God's majesty. The earthquake also appears in the events surrounding the end of history (6.12; 16.18). In 11.13, John uses the earthquake in connection with the resurrection and ascension of the witnesses. Although the earthquake is certainly symbolic of the majestic and awesome glory surrounding the church as God raises her up, it seems clear that its point is one of judgment. It is for this time that the martyred saints in heaven have been praying (6.9–11). In addition, this connects directly to the messenger of Rev 10 and his announcement that "there will be delay no longer" (10.6) and with John's further explanation of the destroyed city in 16.18–19.

Still, the emphasis appears to be on a partial judgment rather than complete destruction for the wicked. This seems to match the one-fourth killed in the seals and the one-third killed in the trumpets. The reason for this is that the judgments of God in the Apocalypse have been patterned closely after the plagues of the first exodus and are therefore a call to repentance.[49] This call for repentance can be seen in the statements at the end of each cycle of judgments (9.20–21; 11.13; 16.9–10).

Although there has been much debate concerning the repentance of the remnant in Rev 11, the elements of fear and giving glory to God indicate their authenticity. The angel with the "eternal gospel" in 14.6–7 calls out to "those who live on the earth, and to every nation, and tribe, and tongue, and people" to "fear God and give Him glory" and to "worship Him." Furthermore, Osborne makes a good argument for 15.4 and 16.9 indicating that an offer of salvation has been given based upon the context of the call to repentance that is inherent in all of the judgments in the Apocalypse.[50] The OT contains many instances where a call to repentance was exemplified by the statement "give glory to God" (1 Sam 6.5; Isa 42.12; Jer 13.16). In the Apocalypse, God's "bond-servants" are said to be "those who fear him" (Rev 19.5) and the multitude in heaven sings "Let us rejoice and be glad and give the glory to Him" (19.7). Due to John's emphasis on the church and her mission to give testimony to the nations concerning Jesus throughout the interlude of 10.1—11.13, it is much more prudent to see true repentance taking place in 11.13.

---

49. Ibid., 339.
50. Ibid., 434.

But These are Written . . .

THE WHOLE ENCHILADA

Revelation 11.1–13 is the story of God's church in mission. John's use of Daniel's prophecies concerning the "shattering of the power of the holy people" (12.7), the trampling of the holy place and the host (8.13; cf. Rev 11.2), and the defeat of the saints at the hands of Satan (Dan 7.21; cf. Rev 11.7) all point to the manner in which God is using the church to bring both judgment and salvation. Much like the story of the exodus, the church will witness to the world and in turn bring judgment upon the nations for their unbelief and antagonism against God. However, the power of the gospel through the witnessing church is so effective that many will be saved due to their testimony.

Through the power of his Holy Spirit, God has already equipped the church for the task of witnessing (Acts 2.4, 16–21). He has assured the church that her mission will be accomplished "not by might nor by power, but by my Spirit, says the Lord of hosts" (Zech 4.6). The Spirit-filled church of today is the church of the *eschaton* that is marked by the Spirit working fully in her midst to empower her to preach the good news of Jesus Christ to the world (Acts 1.8; 2.4; 2.16–21). The Spirit also empowers the church to be bold in her witness (Acts 4.31; 9.27–28; 13.46; 14.3). Through the Spirit, the church will be able to endure the persecution and hardship that Satan and his forces bring to bear upon her. The church will emerge victoriously in the sight of wicked people from all nations who have helped to "make war" on her.

Those that read the interlude of Rev 10.1—11.13 as either a return to national Israel, or simply a historical episode, miss the glory and majesty of the high christological message that John intends. John is telling the church that Christ has already won the victory at the cross and has saved and delivered believers "from many peoples, and nations, and tongues, and kings" (1.5; 10.11). He will deliver the church in the new exodus from Satan and the evil world just as he did the Hebrews from Egypt. Christ has equipped the church with the power and authority to witness through his Spirit. In turn, he has commissioned the church to give testimony to him even to the point of death. However, he has promised the church that she will be victorious in her mission and that he is protecting her spiritually for that victory.

The church is not meant to be caught sign watching, as was Jewish expectation (Matt 24.3) but simply faithful in the work that they have been called to do (24.44–51). In fact, the church needs to throw away any form of dispensationalism and Jewish nationalism in favor of a theology that is thoroughly based upon the work of Christ. We should not attempt to read the OT into the NT, but the NT into the OT, as John and all of the other NT writers do. We are to operate and function in the light of Christ. We are the

Will The Real Church Please Stand Up?

chosen people of God, "a royal priesthood, a holy nation," and "a people for God's own possession" (1 Pet 2.9; cf. Rev 5.10). We have been measured out and protected (11.1–2), not to testify to the validity of national Israel, or simply a historical episode, but to the power of Christ's victory. Therefore, the message of Rev 11 is that God has called and empowered us by his Spirit to persevere in the face of evil as we witness during this time of the end; it is a powerful message of ultimate victory through Jesus Christ.

15

The Spirit of the Lamb
A Reflection on the Pneumatology of Revelation
Frank D. Macchia

The pneumatology of the book of Revelation is a fascinating topic of study, in part because of the rich imagery regarding the Spirit offered in the book. The overall emphasis on discernment in the Spirit in Revelation makes the topic relevant for a postmodern era in desperate need of spiritual guidance. I offer this essay in honor of a friend, teacher, and scholar who has taught me much over the years, not only about theological scholarship but also about the Christian life. I wish Ben Aker God's richest blessings as he continues to give to many that which he has given to me.

THE SEVEN SPIRITS

The reference to the "seven spirits" of Rev 1.4 is one of the intriguing symbolic expressions of the book. There are four lines of argument that may be used to support the contention that these "seven spirits" are actually a rich reference to the Holy Spirit. First, the seven spirits are part of a triadic greeting typical of the NT. The seven spirits occur in this greeting where the Holy Spirit belongs. The greeting offers grace and peace "from him who is, and who was, and who is to come, and from the seven spirits before his throne, and from Jesus Christ, who is the faithful witness, the firstborn from the dead, and the ruler of the kings of the earth" (1.4-5).[1] Such greetings form the liturgical foundation for later trinitarian theology. It is fully understandable that the church has tended to view these seven spirits as a sevenfold Spirit, the Holy Spirit of God.

Second, the seven spirits and their work are described in ways typical of the Holy Spirit. If the Father is Creator (4.11) and the Son is Redeemer (5.9) then the spirits go out from the Lamb throughout all the earth to enable discernment of the Lamb's words and works (5.6). This is precisely what one would expect of the economy of the Spirit. The Spirit is the sevenfold Spirit because the Spirit is the "fullness and wholeness of God's work" in the world.[2] The Spirit is the Spirit of prophecy (19.10). There is also an implicit connection with the seven churches as possibly symbolic of the whole church empowered in its witness throughout the world. Implied is the Pentecostal truth that the fullness of the Spirit is meant to propel the church into the world to bear witness to the Lamb. This sevenfold Spirit as described in 5.6 is possibly a cryptic reference to Pentecost.

Third, the Spirit is at the throne in proximity to the place where the Father and the Lamb are seated. The seven spirits do not participate with the creaturely host in worshipping the Lamb in ch. 5. In fact, the seven spirits are inseparable from the Lamb as his "eyes," attached to the one who is receiving praise, implicitly identified on the side of the one worshipped rather than on the side of the worshippers (5.6f). Revelation 4 and 5 are quite clear that there is a sharp divide between the creaturely realm that has no access to the revelation of the scroll and the Lamb who is worthy to have such access because he occupies the throne with the Father and has redeemed creation (a work only God can accomplish). Revelation 5 is clear that "no one in heaven or on earth or under the earth could open the scroll or even look inside it" (5.3). No creature is excluded from this helpless alienation from the sacred scroll. Interestingly, the seven spirits do not sit helplessly by as do the creatures, unable to discern the scroll. The spirits are rather the very power of discernment, the seven eyes of the Lamb that discern all things! If the Lamb is worthy to transcend the creatures to discern the scroll, so are the seven spirits. If the Lamb is worshipped for being able to discern as only God can, so are the spirits who are identified as the Lamb's eyes. The seven spirits are identified with God and not the creatures. They receive praise; they do not give it. This text is perhaps the only place in the NT where the Spirit is on the side of receiving praise.

---

1. All English quotations from the Bible are taken from the NIV unless stated otherwise.

2. U. Schnelle, *Theology of the New Testament*, trans. M. E. Boring (Grand Rapids: Baker, 2007) 760.

But These are Written . . .

WIDER REFERENCES TO THE SPIRIT

There are a number of references to the Spirit in Revelation that may be added to the above insights to provide us with rich resources for contemporary pneumatology. As noted above, the deity of the Spirit is clearly implied in Revelation. Such is also the case because the Spirit is designated as the Spirit *of God* (3.1; 4.5; 5.6) more specifically, of the Creator who imparts the "breath of life" (11.11, echoes here perhaps of Gen 2.7 and Job 33.4). The Spirit in Revelation is also intimately connected to Jesus. The Spirit speaks the words of Jesus and provides the wisdom for discerning these words in life. Not only does the Spirit speak the words of Jesus but these words are discerned (understood, contextualized) in the Spirit (2.7, 11, 17, 29; 3.6, 13, 22). The discernment is not only conceptual but involves wisdom for life. It involves repentance, patient endurance, and faithful living. The discernment of the words of Christ in the Spirit among the faithful is part of their consecration unto God as the lampstands of the temple. The Spirit implicitly consecrates the people of God, making them living witnesses to Christ in the world. An argument can be made that the phrase "in the Spirit" occurs at key places in Revelation, serving to introduce each new act in the enfolding revelatory drama (1.10; 4.2; 17.3; 21.10).[3]

Yet the Spirit is not just the impersonal power that enables discernment of Christ. Note 22.17: "The Spirit and the bride say, 'Come!' And let the one who hears say, 'Come!' Let the one who is thirsty come; and let the one who wishes take the free gift of the water of life." Notice that the Spirit is the principle speaker who seems to invite Christ to come in the larger context of 22.16–20 (Christ seems to answer in v. 20: "Yes, I am coming soon") an invitation given in response to Christ's statement in 22.16. Those who discern in the Spirit join their voices to the Spirit's in yearning for and inviting Christ to come, but they also extend an invitation to those who are thirsty to come in order to drink from the free gift of the water of life (implicitly from the Spirit of God, 22.17). The Spirit speaks, in harmony with Christ to be sure, but the Spirit still speaks. There is implied here a distinct personal agency involved in the work of the Spirit in Revelation.

The Spirit is also the means by which the churches will convert the nations to the Lamb. Richard Bauckham has shown that the witness to the nations by the Spirit of prophecy through the church is at the core of the message of Revelation.[4] The two witnesses of ch. 11 who play such a pivotal role in

---

3. See R. Bauckham, *The Climax of Prophecy: Studies on the Book of Revelation* (New York: T. & T. Clark, 2000) 150–73.

4. Ibid., 150–73. Cf. also R. Waddell, *The Spirit of the Book of Revelation* (Blandford Forum, UK: Deo, 2007).

bearing witness to Jesus during the time of trial are connected to Zech 4 in their description as the two olive trees and lampstands (11.4). Zechariah 4 promises that the two anointed trees are servants who will serve the Lord of all the earth in the Spirit (Zech 4.6, 14). The two witnesses are thus implicitly symbolic for John of the prophetic people who will go forth in the Spirit of the Lamb into all the earth to testify to Jesus and to the truth of God that Christ represents. They do so in truth and with signs and wonders of God's power. When slain at the conclusion of their witness, they are vindicated by being raised up and by ascending to the throne. The Spirit is thus the Spirit of prophecy who testifies of Jesus and who vindicates the witness of the faithful to Jesus. As Christ was parodied by the dragon and the beast, so also the prophetic witness of the Spirit through the faithful is set in stark contrast to the forces of darkness who seek to parody them. Evil spirits pour forth from the mouths of the dragon, the beast, and the false prophet to perform signs and to go out to the kings of the whole earth in order to gather them for battle against God (16.13–14). There is in the world a spirit of anti-Lamb, or, if you will, an anti-Spirit. As the Spirit speaks in testimony to Christ through the witness of the faithful throughout the earth, so the evil spirits go out from the dragon, the beast, and the false prophet to the whole earth in service to them in order to foment rebellion against God. The evil spirits seek to inspire a world movement in fulfillment of the mission of the forces of darkness but there is no discernment in their work. They are not the eyes of the Lamb; they do not discern the truth of God, nor do they bear witness as the true Spirit of prophecy. They spread only darkness and deception, words without insight or truth. They proceed only from the mouth and not from the eyes for they are blind to the truth of genuine wisdom. They are bound to be exposed by the light of the Spirit of Truth. Their mission will never find fulfillment. When they are crushed, they will not rise again; their witness will not be vindicated nor will they have the final word.

In addition, the Spirit of prophecy in Revelation has implications for the church's worship. John was in the Spirit on the Lord's Day, implying that the Spirit was important as the means of worship. Notice that the text concerning the role of the Spirit of prophecy in testifying of Jesus (19.10) is given in the words of the fellow servant who had just rejected John's worship and had instructed John to worship God instead: "At this I fell at his feet to worship him. But he said to me, 'Do not do that! I am a fellow servant with you and with your brothers and sisters who hold to the testimony of Jesus. Worship God! For it is the Spirit of prophecy who bears testimony to Jesus'" (19.10). Recall that John had also fallen prostrate before the risen Christ in ch. 1 but without any such correction. Evidently, worshipping a servant of God contradicts the Spirit's prophetic testimony to Jesus but not worshipping Christ. One worships God and Christ in "Spirit and Truth" for Revelation. The Spirit of prophecy directs the congregation to exalt Christ and to worship God. Moreover, the Spirit's invocation with the bride for Christ to "come" in 22.17 implies an invitation for Christ to reign on the earth as the Lord (11.15). The Spirit is enabling the people of God to exalt Jesus as Lord. The worship inspired among the people of God brought together by the Spirit of prophecy involves every nation, tribe, and language (7.9–10). The unity in the Spirit of truth and worship never dissolves the colorful diversity of God's creation.

Moreover, the Spirit is the Spirit of life that raises the dead (11.11) and sustains the faithful in their eternal life with God (22.17). The Spirit of prophecy is more deeply the Spirit of life, the Spirit who gives rise to life, sustains it, and renews it in the image of the Lamb. This is the Spirit who eternally sustains the faithful in the heavenly city and does so in a way that causes life to flourish way beyond that which existed in the original garden of Eden. In the heavenly city, the waters of the Spirit take the creation beyond that early beginning to the fulfillment that God had always intended for creation.

APPLICATION

The pneumatology of Revelation offers us resources for a contemporary pneumatology. The Spirit in Revelation is the Spirit of prophecy (19.10) and discernment. This statement is powerful in its brevity and is relevant to pneumatology in a world of an ever-expansive and possibly chaotic cacophony of voices calling out for our attention. Michael Welker notes that the term "Spirit" is notoriously vague and susceptible to being high-jacked in the contemporary context by self-serving and destructive forces. Every movement or institution can boast of having a noble or virtuous "spirit." Indeed, these sources of massive influence in our world do seem to exercise a spiritual influence of sorts, but how truly virtuous is it? The mass media tends to create the illusion that social processes are under the control of common sense and tried and true moralities. Beneath the veneer of this imagined morality are deeply entrenched and competing public interests that often discriminate and oppress. Discernment becomes difficult due to the tendency in the West to see the Spirit as a non-material and detached phantom or ghostly figure, which is easily discredited in the modern world (most everyone knows that there is no such thing as ghosts).[5] Meanwhile, spiritualities abound that are harnessed to vague goals revolving around self-discovery or personal health, wealth, and the "good life." It has be-

5. M. Welker, *God the Spirit* (Minneapolis: Fortress, 1992) 5–7.

come customary to deal with a plethora of problems within the context of personal "spirituality." While the term sounds meaningful on the surface (and can become genuinely meaningful) we struggle to know what it means.

The image of the Spirit as nebulous in meaning is strengthened by theologies that have stressed the Spirit's transcendence and otherworldliness, as mysterious and numinous, beyond finding out. Welker notes that discernment has thus become urgent to pneumatology in the contemporary context. It is not that the Spirit is not free and mysterious, but Revelation informs us that the Spirit's freedom is defined in specific ways that resist human idolatry and that follow in the path of freedom opened up for us in the story of Jesus as the risen Lamb. That in which the Spirit's transcendent mystery and supernatural quality consists must become clear through discernment into the Spirit's intervention in the story of Jesus as the crucified and risen Lamb. "The Holy Spirit makes God's power and God's righteousness knowable."[6] The Spirit of prophecy, of truth, is involved in discernment and interpretation. There is a great need for a discernment of the truth that genuinely sets free and makes whole. There is at base a need to recognize the role of the Holy Spirit *of God* and *of Christ* as the Spirit of Truth or of prophecy, as stressed in Revelation (19.10). The Spirit in Revelation is the Spirit of prophecy because the discernment that the Spirit offers does not arise fundamentally from human goals or competing interests but from the reign of God and the story of the Lamb's self-sacrificial life for the redemption of humanity and the power of his victory over that darkness that opposes the Lamb. The Spirit discerns the words of this crucified Lamb spoken to us in the churches today.

Before Christians can clearly discern the implications of Christ for their world, they must first understand the words of Christ for themselves. The Spirit of prophetic discernment begins at home. The story of the risen Lamb must fundamentally shape their corporate life and worship before they can properly discern with prophetic insight the conflict between prophetic truth and corporate deception in the world. The challenge is to note the difference between the Spirit that goes out into the world in witness to the Lamb of God and the deceptive spirits that go out from the mouths of the dragon, the beast, and the false prophet. Notice that the Spirit goes out from the eyes of the Lamb (with discernment) while the evil spirits only go out from the mouths of the dragon, the beast, and the false prophet (16.13). There is no sight, no discernment in the spirits that go out from the forces of darkness. One cannot see this difference in the world unless one also sees the difference at home within the community gathered around Jesus and dedicated in the Spirit to his truth. One is struck in chs. 2 and 3 by

---

6. Ibid., 21, 30–31.

the repetitiveness of the phrase "let them hear what the Spirit says to the churches" (2.7, 11, 17, 29; 3.6, 13, 22). It is spoken over and over for emphasis. It is mentioned seven times. The sevenfold Spirit thoroughly penetrates the world of the seven churches with a sevenfold call for discernment. No stone is meant to be left unturned. Every church is addressed in particular and every aspect of the life of the churches is to be placed under the glaring light of prophetic truth. The goal is to help the churches to see the world through the discerning eyes of the Lamb, the discernment of the Spirit. Before they can do that, they must first see themselves clearly. Their own eyes must first be cleared of any and all sources of blindness. This is not a rigid perfectionism that tolerates no weakness. They are still regarded as lamps surrounding Christ, even in their weakness, though the church of Ephesus is threatened with removal if it does not repent (2.5). This is rather a call for clarity and focus, for repentance and discipline, as an ongoing way of life for the community of faith in the world. Prophetic discernment does not just involve intellectual insight but more broadly a wisdom that penetrates thought and life. Life is restructured in a way that is fitting to its role as witness to the life and truth of the Lamb of God.

16

Was John the Revelator Pentecostal?
Robert P. Menzies

I COUNT IT A great privilege to be able to contribute this essay to a work honoring Ben Aker, a passionate Pentecostal scholar who has encouraged many students through the years to read the NT with fresh eyes.

Was John the Revelator Pentecostal? The question may sound anachronistic given the fact that the modern Pentecostal movement was birthed little more than a century ago. Nevertheless, if we define a Pentecostal as a follower of Jesus who believes that every believer can experience a baptism in the Spirit, understood in the light of the Pentecostal experience of the early church (Acts 2) to be a prophetic enabling, distinct from regeneration, that empowers its recipient to bear bold witness for Christ in the face of persecution, then I would argue that there are strong reasons to answer this question with an unequivocal "yes." In fact, in the following essay, this is precisely what I plan to do. I will argue that the author of the Apocalypse was indeed, in the sense noted above, Pentecostal. I will do so first, by looking at the role of the *Paraclete* in the Gospel of John; then, by examining John's use of the term "spirit of prophecy" in Rev 19.10; and finally, by analyzing John's description of the "two witnesses" in Rev 11.3–13.[1]

---

1. All English quotations from the Bible are taken from the NIV unless stated otherwise.

But These are Written . . .

THE *PARACLETE*

The nature of the relationship between the author of the Gospel of John and John the Revelator is widely debated. Many scholars suggest they are one and the same, the apostle John;[2] others, while disputing this claim, speak of a Johannine school.[3] Fortunately, for our purposes it will be sufficient to recognize that both works come from the same theological milieu or school of thought. Thus, it is entirely appropriate, regardless of one's view of authorship, to suggest that John's gospel can shed light on the theological perspective of John the Revelator. With this in view, we shall begin our inquiry into the pneumatological orientation of John the Revelator by examining the role of the *Paraclete* in John's gospel.

The Functions of the *Paraclete*

In the latter part of John's gospel, in the midst of Jesus' farewell discourse, we find three texts that speak of the Holy Spirit as the *Paraclete* (14.16-26; 15.26-27; 16.7-15). The term *Paraclete*, introduced here in the gospel for the first time and applied consistently to the Spirit in each of these texts (14.16, 26; 15.26; 16.7), suggests that John has something special in mind. Clearly here the Spirit is described in a unique way.

A review of the Greek literature reveals that the term παράκλητος refers to "one called alongside," an advocate, who offers counsel and assistance in a court or dispute.[4] This meaning accords well with the manner in which the term is used in 1 John 2.1, the only other place the term occurs in the NT outside of John's gospel. In spite of this evidence, many have felt that the functions attributed to the *Paraclete* in John 14–16 are not consistent with this forensic setting and the associated sense of "advocate." Other explana-

---

2. G. R. Osborne, *Revelation* (Grand Rapids: Baker, 2002) 5-6; R. H. Mounce, *The Book of Revelation* (Grand Rapids: Eerdmans, 1997) 31; G. E. Ladd tentatively suggests the apostle John authored both the Gospel of John and Revelation, but in the latter case utilized a scribe (*A Commentary on the Revelation of John* [Grand Rapids: Eerdmans, 1972] 8).

3. G. R. Beasley-Murray notes that "scholars are increasingly inclined to" view both authors as the disciple of the same master (*The Book of Revelation* [Grand Rapids: Eerdmans, 1972] 36); B. Witherington suggests the author of Revelation is a "prophet from the Johannine community" (*Revelation* [Cambridge: Cambridge University Press, 2003] 3).

4. J. Behm, in his study of the term παράκλητος, concludes: "Thus the history of the term in the whole sphere of known Greek and Hellenistic usage outside the NT yields the clear picture of a legal advisor or helper or advocate in the relevant court" (Behm, "παράκλητος," *TDNT* 5.803).

tions of the term have been put forward, including "comforter," "exhorter," and "helper." Yet, as Anthony Billington observes, "the vast majority of the studies drive us back to a primary forensic context" for the term.[5]

Billington, citing several recent studies, notes that throughout his gospel, John features a trial motif. This motif is accentuated by the use of courtroom terminology, especially the term "witness."[6] It is also advanced by the discourses within the gospel, where various parties question and interrogate one another and their explanations. The trial motif carries over into Jesus' farewell discourse, which forms the context for the *Paraclete* sayings. In John 14–16, then, Jesus reassures the disciples that, in spite of his imminent departure, they will not be left alone. Jesus will send the *Paraclete*, another advocate, who will aid them in the cosmic trial already underway between Jesus and the unbelieving world.[7] Let us examine how the *Paraclete* functions as an advocate in this cosmic trial.

The forensic functions of the *Paraclete* are clearly evident in John 15.26–27 and 16.5–16. In John 15.26–27, we read: "When the [*Paraclete*] comes, whom I will send to you from the Father, the Spirit of truth who goes out from the Father, he will testify about me; but you also must testify, for you have been with me from the beginning."

This passage appears in a setting that highlights the world's rejection of Jesus and his disciples: "If they persecuted me, they will persecute you also" (15.21). The world's rejection of Christ, even in the face of his words (15.22) and deeds (15.24), establishes its guilt. The repeated references to conflict, guilt, and witness establish the forensic character of the passage.

The specific function ascribed to the *Paraclete* is that of a witness. He will testify concerning Christ (15.26).[8] This can only mean that he will seek to persuade the world that it unjustly rejected and crucified Jesus, who is in reality the Son of God, God's agent of salvation. This theme is developed

---

5. A. Billington, "The Paraclete and Mission in the Fourth Gospel," in *Mission and Meaning: Essays Presented to Peter Cotterell*, eds. A. Billington et al. (Carlisle, PA: Paternoster, 1995) 94. Note also the conclusion of Gary Burge: "This context of juridical trial and persecution presents us with the most likely catalyst for John's introduction of the term ὁ παράκλητος" (*The Anointed Community: The Holy Spirit in the Johannine Community* [Grand Rapids: Eerdmans, 1987] 205).

6. Of the over two hundred occurrences in the NT of μάρτυς ("witness") and its cognates, approximately forty percent are found in the Johannine literature (John, 1–3 John, and Rev). More specifically, μαρτυρέω ("testify") occurs seventy-six times in the NT and thirty-three times in the Gospel of John. The term μαρτυρία ("testimony") occurs thirty-seven times in the NT and fourteen times in the Gospel of John.

7. Billington, "Paraclete and Mission," 100; for the trial motif, see 95–101.

8. Rev 19.10, "For the testimony of Jesus is the spirit of prophecy," forms a striking parallel to John 15.26.

more fully in John 16.8–11: "When he comes, he will convict the world of guilt in regard to sin and righteousness and judgment: in regard to sin, because men do not believe in me; in regard to righteousness, because I am going to the Father, where you can see me no longer; and in regard to judgment, because the prince of this world now stands condemned."

Although this passage contains numerous exegetical difficulties, the essential meaning is relatively clear. The *Paraclete* will press home his case against the world: first, that its rejection (unbelief) of Christ is the essence of its sin; second, that although the world crucified Jesus as a criminal, his death, resurrection, and exaltation vindicate him as the Righteous One; third, Jesus' vindication establishes that those who oppose him already stand condemned.[9] The *Paraclete*, then, will bear witness against the world.

It is important to note, however, that the Spirit as the *Paraclete* will do this, "not by some inward testimony in the hearts of the people of the world, but by the outward testimony of words spoken by Jesus' disciples in the course of their mission."[10] The *Paraclete* is given to the disciples to be *their* advocate — that is, to support *their* witness to the world.[11] This is also the point of John 15.26–27: "He [the *Paraclete*] will testify about me; but you [the disciples] also must testify."[12] Note the following verses, John 16.1–4, which emphasize that the *Paraclete's* role is to enable the disciples to stand firm in the face of persecution and, in this setting, to testify boldly about Jesus.[13]

The fact that the *Paraclete* comes to encourage and enable the witness of the disciples is further highlighted in John 14.16–26 and 16.12–15. In John 14.16, we read that Jesus will send "another *Paraclete*" to assist the disciples. This indicates that Jesus during his earthly ministry has served as a *Paraclete*. In view of the trial motif running throughout John's gospel, Billington correctly stresses that the work of the Spirit and Jesus at this point are one and the same: to confront a hostile world.[14] This is precisely why the disciples will not be orphans (14.18). Left on their own, they would be helpless, unable to prosecute their case against the world. But with the Spirit as their advocate, they will not be alone. Indeed, the Spirit as *Paraclete* will teach them "all things" and remind them of everything Jesus had said (14.26). So

---

9. Cf. John 12.30–32. See M. Turner, *The Holy Spirit and Spiritual Gifts: Then and Now* (Carlisle, PA: Paternoster, 1996) 87.

10. J. R. Michaels, *John* (Peabody, MA: Hendrickson, 1989) 282.

11. See also Turner, *Holy Spirit and Spiritual Gifts*, 87.

12. Billington, "Paraclete and Mission," 109: "The Paraclete's work is not independent of their witness. John does not teach a witness by the Spirit that is not also a witness through the believing community."

13. Michaels, *John*, 277.

14. Billington, "Paraclete and Mission," 109–10.

also John 16.12–15 declares that the *Paraclete* will guide the disciples "into all truth."[15] In this forensic context, these words take on a specific meaning. The Spirit will help the disciples recall and understand important aspects of Jesus' teaching so that they may press home their case against the world (i.e., witness effectively).[16]

It is important at this juncture to note the similarities and differences between the functions of the Spirit as *Paraclete* in John 14–16 and the functions attributed to the Spirit in John 3–7. In John 3–7, we are introduced to a series of passages that describe the life-giving function of the Spirit. In John 3.5 ("born of water and the Spirit") John, drawing upon Ezek 36.25–27, presents the Spirit as a soteriological agent. John 6.63, "the Spirit gives life," and John 7.37–39, which identifies "living water" with the Spirit, both describe the Spirit as the source of spiritual life. John 4.23–24 again presents the Spirit as a soteriological agent. The collocation of Spirit and truth in this specific text ("true worshippers will worship . . . in spirit and truth") identifies the Spirit as the agent who reveals Jesus' true identity and the significance of the cross to the "true worshipers." Thus, in each of these passages, John emphasizes the Spirit's role as the source of spiritual life. As is the case in John 4.23–24, this is generally accomplished through the revelation of wisdom (i.e., revealing Jesus' true identity).

We have noted that the *Paraclete* also imparts wisdom. Yet the difference at this point should not be missed. Although both the *Paraclete* and the life-giving Spirit convey wisdom, the nature and purpose of this wisdom is quite distinct. The life-giving Spirit enables its recipients to grasp the significance of the cross and Jesus' true identity. The *Paraclete*, on the other hand, given to disciples *in order to assist their witness*, offers charismatic wisdom by enabling the disciples to recall and understand the teaching of Jesus. The purpose of the *Paraclete* is not to grant the disciples that wisdom which is essential for right relationship with God (i.e., spiritual life). Rather, the *Paraclete* grants a special kind of wisdom; it is wisdom that is directed toward the unbelieving world in the form of witness.

In short, I am suggesting that the trial context of John's gospel in general and, more specifically, the forensic terminology in the *Paraclete* passages, call us to recognize the *Paraclete's* distinctive role and function. He comes to the disciples as their advocate, one who assists them in presenting

---

15. John 16.13–15 also suggests that the *Paraclete* will guide the church in its mission ("tell you what is yet to come"). The stress on the authority of Jesus is very similar to what we find in Matt 28.18.

16. In view of the forensic setting, "all things" (14.26) and "all truth" (16.13) probably refer to all that the disciples will need to know in order to prosecute their case against the world. The conceptual parallels with Luke 12.11–12 are striking.

But These are Written . . .

the case of Christ against the world. He accomplishes this task by encouraging and enabling bold witness in the face of opposition and persecution. Although the *Paraclete* grants wisdom—he helps the disciples recall and understand the teaching of Jesus—this wisdom is ultimately directed toward the world. Thus, it is charismatic rather than soteriological (i.e., essential for right relationship with God) in nature and should be distinguished from the life-giving wisdom imparted by the Spirit in John 3–7.

The *Paraclete* and John 20.22

All of this becomes doubly interesting when we remember that John describes a pre-ascension bestowal of the Spirit with these words: "And with that he breathed on them and said, 'Receive the Holy Spirit'" (20.22). There are good reasons to view this event as the fulfillment of the promise of the life-giving Spirit in John 7.38–39 ("'Whoever believes in me . . . streams of living water will flow from within him.' By this he meant the Spirit, whom those who believed in him were later to receive. Up to that time the Spirit had not been given, since Jesus had not yet been glorified") and not the fulfillment of the promise of the *Paraclete*.

First, this judgment is supported by the distinctive functions attributed to the life-giving Spirit of John 3–7 and the *Paraclete* of John 14–16. We have already noted that the Spirit in John 3–7 comes as the source of regeneration. Similarly, John 20.22 clearly describes the disciples' reception of the life-giving Spirit. The verb John uses, ἐνεφύσησεν, which is translated "he breathed," is exceptionally rare. This verb, however, is found in Gen 2.7 where it describes God's breathing into Adam the breath of life.[17] This careful use of language would undoubtedly remind John's readers of the creation account. The point of the parallel could not be missed. Just as God breathed into Adam the breath of life, so also Jesus now breathes into the disciples the Spirit of new creation.[18] By way of contrast, the *Paraclete* comes to the disciples in order to enable their testimony for Jesus.

Second, and equally telling, is the matter of timing. John 7.39 states that the life-giving Spirit "had not been given, since Jesus had not yet been glorified." Since for John Jesus' glorification generally refers to the death and

---

17. The verb is also found in Wis 15.11, which is essentially a citation of Gen 2.7, and in Ezek 37.9, which refers to God's breathing into the dry bones of Israel the breath of life. The Ezek 37.9 reference is important in that here, too, we see the verb associated with the creation of new life.

18. The imperative, "Receive the Holy Spirit," in this context would naturally be understood to signify that the life-giving Spirit was actually imparted.

the resurrection of Jesus,[19] this promise accords well with the post-resurrection (pre-ascension) fulfillment in John 20.22. The *Paraclete* promises, however, indicate that the *Paraclete* will come, indeed can come, only after Jesus has ascended to the Father. This is stated most clearly in John 16.7: "But I tell you the truth: It is for your good that I am going away. Unless I go away, the [*Paraclete*] will not come to you; but if I go, I will send him to you" (cf. John 14.18–19; 16.7). These temporal markers indicate that in John's view, the life-giving Spirit is received by the disciples in John 20.22 and that this bestowal of the Spirit cannot be equated with the sending of the *Paraclete*. The *Paraclete* can come only after Jesus ascends to the Father. The inescapable conclusion is that the *Paraclete* promises anticipate a fulfillment at Pentecost.

John's Theological Synthesis

The judgment that the John 20.22 bestowal of the Spirit should be distinguished from the promise of the *Paraclete*, which is fulfilled at Pentecost, is shared by numerous scholars, including James Dunn and Max Turner.[20] Nevertheless, both Dunn and Turner stress the theological unity of these bestowals of the Spirit, suggesting that both bestowals are of the same character.[21] Yet this understanding of John raises a number of questions. Why would John speak of two experiences of regeneration by the Spirit? Put another way, if the Pentecostal gift is indeed the climax of conversion-initiation, why detail *another* bestowal of the Spirit that functions in essentially the same way?

This question becomes all the more acute when we remember that John did not have to record the John 20.22 bestowal of the Spirit; none of the other gospel writers do, why does he? Surely John, writing in the 90s, would have recognized the confusion an account of a pre-Pentecostal bestowal of the life-giving Spirit would cause. It is evident that traditional accounts of the development of early Christian pneumatology, particularly those that

---

19. The term δοξάζω occurs twenty-three times in John's gospel. When John speaks of the glorification of Jesus, he often has in mind Jesus' death on the cross (12.23; 12.27–28; 13.31–32; 17.1). In John 12.16, Jesus' glorification most likely refers to the death and resurrection of Jesus, and this is probably the case in John 7.39 as well. For a similar assessment of John 7.39, see G. R. Beasley-Murray, *John* (Waco, TX: Word, 1987) 1:117.

20. J. D. G. Dunn, *Baptism in the Holy Spirit: A Re-examination of the New Testament Teaching on the Gift of the Spirit in Relation to Pentecostalism Today* (London: SCM, 1970) 176–82; Turner, *Holy Spirit and Spiritual Gifts*, 97–100.

21. Dunn, *Baptism*, 181–82; Turner, *Holy Spirit and Spiritual Gifts*, 99–100.

stress the homogeneity of Luke and Paul, are simply unable to explain in an intelligible manner John's narrative.[22]

The answer to this riddle is, however, easily explained if we place John within the process of the development of early Christian pneumatology. If, as I have argued elsewhere,[23] Paul was indeed the first Christian to articulate the soteriological aspects of the Spirit's work and his broader perspective did not impact the more limited, prophetic pneumatology of the non-Pauline church until after the writing of the Synoptic Gospels and Acts, then we can see John as providing a later synthesis of these two pneumatological strands. Clearly John is aware of Paul's larger perspective, as is obvious by John's references to the life-giving Spirit (John 3–7). This being the case, it is only natural that John would seek to answer a question not addressed in the Synoptic Gospels: When did the disciples receive the Spirit as a regenerating force (the Pauline gift of the Spirit)? Since the Synoptic Gospels and Acts represent an early stage in the early church's developing awareness of the Spirit's work and know the Spirit only as the source of prophetic inspiration (e.g., the Pentecostal gift of Acts 2) they would not have pondered this question. But after Paul's insights have become more widely known, then the question and the need to address it would have arisen. In the 90s, John writes his gospel from this larger pneumatological perspective, and so he seeks to answer this critical question. His answer is straightforward: John 20.22 marks the moment when the disciples received the life-giving Spirit; this experience is theologically distinct from the later bestowal of the *Paraclete* (i.e., the Pentecostal gift) which enables the disciples to bear witness for Christ.

Particularly significant for our study is the recognition that the *Paraclete* promises: (1) are directed to every believer; (2) anticipate (and thus, from John's perspective, are shaped by) the Pentecostal gift of the Spirit; (3) distinguish this gift from the moment of regeneration; (4) portray the Spirit in prophetic terms as the source of charismatic wisdom; and (5) the power that will animate the disciples' bold witness for Christ, especially in the face of opposition and persecution. As we shall see, virtually all of these points are echoed in the Apocalypse.

---

22. The typical response that these events are shaped by their unique position in salvation-history misses two critical points: first, John attributes different functions to these bestowals of the Spirit; second, John is writing in the 90s with the needs of his churches in view.

23. See R. P. Menzies, *Empowered for Witness: The Spirit in Luke-Acts* (Sheffield: Sheffield Academic, 1994); and *The Development of Early Christian Pneumatology with Special Reference to Luke-Acts* (Sheffield: Sheffield Academic, 1991).

THE SPIRIT OF PROPHECY

In the book of Revelation, the Holy Spirit is, above all, the source of prophetic inspiration. John the Revelator frequently refers to being "in the Spirit" (1.10; 4.2; 17.3; 21.10) when he receives charismatic revelation. In numerous instances, he also encourages his churches to "hear what the Spirit says" (2.7, 11, 17, 29; 3.6, 13, 22). However, the most striking reference is found in Rev 19.10: "For the testimony of Jesus is the spirit of prophecy" (ἡ γὰρ μαρτυρία Ἰησοῦ ἐστιν τὸ πνεῦμα τῆς προφητείας).

Several exegetical issues confront one seeking to interpret this important passage. First, how shall we understand the phrase, "the testimony of Jesus"? If we read it as a subjective genitive, then the phrase refers to the "testimony borne by Jesus." If we see the phrase as an objective genitive, then it speaks of "the testimony about Jesus" borne by others. Commentators divide over which interpretation is most fitting, but many recognize that we need not restrict the meaning of the phrase to only one of the options listed above. Indeed, as Stephen Smalley notes, the phrase very likely includes both elements, "the testimony was given by Jesus to believers, who then handed it on to others."[24] Nevertheless, in view of the usage of this phrase elsewhere in the Apocalypse (1.2, 9; 12.17; 19.10a) the phrase should be seen as "primarily an objective genitive, referring to the church's testimony to Jesus."[25] The immediate context also supports this reading. The striking statement, "the testimony of Jesus is the spirit of prophecy," is uttered by an angel as he urges John the Revelator not to worship him, not to submit to idolatry (Rev 19.9–10a). Of course, the pressures to submit to false worship that confronted John's churches were great and included overt persecution. In this context, the phrase in question refers to "testimony about Jesus uttered in the face of opposition and persecution."

A second question centers on the meaning of the phrase, "the spirit of prophecy." Some, such as the translators of the NIV, understand πνεῦμα here to mean "essence" rather than as a reference to the Spirit of God. Thus, the NIV does not capitalize "spirit" and renders that passage with this force: "the testimony of Jesus is the spirit [or essence] of prophecy." Yet this reading of the text is almost certainly wrong. The literature of intertestamental Judaism routinely portrays the Holy Spirit as the source of prophetic inspiration. The association between the Spirit and prophecy was so strong that the Targums frequently translate references to the Spirit of God with the

---

24. S. S. Smalley, *The Revelation to John: A Commentary on the Greek Text of the Apocalypse* (Downers Grove, IL: IVP, 2005) 487.

25. Osborne, *Revelation*, 677.

phrase "the Spirit of prophecy."[26] Additionally, we have already seen that Luke's emphasis on the Spirit as the source of prophetic inspiration (e.g., Acts 2.17–18) is echoed in John's *Paraclete* promises and elsewhere in the Apocalypse (e.g., "in the spirit"). There can be little doubt, then, that with this phrase John the Revelator refers to "Spirit-inspired prophecy." Thus, the full sentence should be rendered: "Testimony about Jesus in the face of opposition and persecution, this is Spirit-inspired prophecy."

One final question pertaining to this passage must be addressed. Who does John see as uttering this Spirit-inspired testimony? Is this prophetic witness confined to a select group of prophets within the community? Or, does John view every believer as potentially testifying by the Spirit of prophecy? The angel's declaration, "I am a fellow servant with you and with our brothers who hold to the testimony of Jesus" (19.10), suggests that John has, at least potentially, every believer in mind at this point. This angelic pronouncement is echoed in a parallel statement recorded in Rev 22.9, "I am a fellow servant with you and with your brothers the prophets and of all who keep the words of the book." This parallel statement highlights the broad nature of this band of fellow servants.[27] This band of Spirit-inspired witnesses includes "all who keep the words of the book," although here a specific group of prophets is also mentioned. It would appear that John the Revelator's perspective on prophecy is similar to that of Luke and Paul: In one sense, every believer is potentially a prophet; nevertheless, there are also some, perhaps due to the frequent and powerful manner in which the gift is exercised, that are specifically designated "prophets." In short, I have argued that, according to John the Revelator, all of God's people may be empowered by the Spirit, through a prophetic enabling, to bear bold witness to Jesus. This conclusion is strengthened by John's description of the "two witnesses" in Rev 11.3–13.

THE TWO WITNESSES

In Rev 11.3–13, we are introduced to "two witnesses" who prophesy with great power for a period of time. When their testimony is finished, the two witnesses are attacked and killed by the beast. Yet, after a short period of time, God's breath reanimates them and the resurrected witnesses ascend into heaven, vindicated and victorious. The vindication and victory of the witnesses is marked by the judgment on earth that immediately follows their ascension to heaven.

26. See the texts cited in Menzies, *Development*, 99–104.
27. So also Smalley, *Revelation*, 568–69.

Was John the Revelator Pentecostal?

Prophecy plays a dominant role in this brief narrative.[28] The two witnesses prophesy and the miracles they perform are modeled after two of the greatest prophets in Israel's history, Moses and Elijah. The two witnesses suffer the fate of the prophets: they are rejected and killed. Yet, in terms reminiscent of the ultimate prophet, Jesus, they are resurrected by God and ascend into heaven.

Who are these two witnesses? This passage has a long history of interpretation and numerous identities have been proposed for the two witnesses.[29] Nevertheless, the majority of scholars today identify the two witnesses as symbols representing the church. There are good reasons to read the text in this way.

The structure of Revelation suggests that the church is the focus of this passage. The interludes that appear between the sixth and seventh seal in Rev 7.1–17 (the 144,000 and the Great Multitude) parallel the interludes that appear between the sounding of the sixth and seventh trumpets in Rev 10.1—11.13 (the Bitter Scroll and the Two Witnesses). As Robby Waddell notes, these interludes highlight a recurring theme, "namely the people of God and their polemical relationship with evil."[30] Whereas the interludes in Rev 7 focus on the security of the church as the people of God—they are now sealed so they will not experience God's wrath and their eternal destiny as members of a transnational worshipping community is assured—so also the interludes in Rev 10.1—11.13 feature the church, although now the focus is the church's ministry in the world.

John the Revelator also explicitly identifies the two witnesses as "the two olive trees and the two lampstands that stand before the Lord of the earth" (11.4). John's imagery has been influenced by Zech 4.1–14, which records Zechariah's vision of a golden lampstand and two olive trees. In Zechariah's vision, the lampstand symbolizes the temple and the two olive trees represent Joshua the high priest and Zerubbabel the governor. The vision centers around the angelic declaration: "'Not by might nor by power, but by my Spirit,' says the Lord Almighty. What are you, O mighty mountain? Before Zerubbabel you will become level ground. Then he will bring out the capstone to shouts of 'God bless it! God bless it!'" (Zech 4.6–7). This message indicates that, in spite of opposition, Zerubbabel will complete the rebuilding of the temple (cf. Zech 4.9).

---

28. R. Waddell, *Spirit of the Book of Revelation* (Blandford Forum, UK: Deo, 2006) 171.

29. For a survey of these identifications, see D. E. Aune, *Revelation 6–16* (Nashville: Thomas Nelson, 1998) 599–603.

30. Waddell, *Revelation*, 150.

But These are Written . . .

In John the Revelator's vision, the single lampstand has been transformed into two, and the two olive trees are interpreted as these two lampstands. Since John elsewhere uses lampstands to represent churches (1.12) and he specifically states that "the golden lampstands" are "the seven churches" (1.20), it seems clear that here also John has the church in view. Although John speaks of two rather than seven lampstands, the number is probably due to the fact that valid testimony requires two witnesses (Deut 19.15). It is evident, then, that the two witnesses represent the church as a whole.[31] Just as the lampstand symbolized the entire temple in Zechariah's prophecy, so here the two witnesses symbolize the entire church.[32]

The two witnesses are described as powerful prophets who boldly prophesy in the face of opposition. Initially, they destroy their antagonists with fire from their mouths, reminiscent of Elijah's destruction of the soldiers of King Ahaziah (2 Kgs 1.10). They also have power "to shut up the sky" and "to turn the waters into blood" (11.6). The former judgment is an allusion to the drought induced by Elijah in 1 Kgs 17.1, the latter to the plague Moses inflicted upon the Egyptians in Exod 7.14-24. After the two prophets complete their task of bearing witness, the demonic beast from the Abyss kills them. The inhabitants of the earth gloat over their corpses, which are left unburied in the streets. But, as we have noted, God vindicates the prophets. They are brought back to life, and as their persecutors watch in terror, they ascend into heaven. The allusions to the death, resurrection, and ascension of Christ should not be missed (cf. Rev 11.8).[33]

John the Revelator's message now comes into focus. In Rev 11.1-13, he issues "a prophetic call to the people of God to be faithful witnesses."[34] In the midst of opposition and persecution, John urges the church to rely on the Holy Spirit who, through a prophetic enabling, will grant them strength to faithfully bear witness to God and the Lamb. In the end, they will be vindicated and victorious. John the Revelator understands that this witness must and will be carried out: "'not by might nor by power, but by my Spirit,' says the Lord" (Zech 4.6).

---

31. Beasely-Murray, *Revelation*, 184.

32. Waddell, *Revelation*, 174.

33. Waddell aptly states, "The entire ministry of the witnesses can now be seen as a replica of the ministry of Christ" (ibid., 181).

34. Ibid., 174.

CONCLUSION

Was John the Revelator Pentecostal? The evidence suggests that he was. His vision of the future includes a church that, in the midst of intense persecution, is powerful and bold in its witness that Jesus is Lord. Although the church will be despised and battered, it will be vindicated and ultimately victorious. Furthermore, its witness will have a powerful impact, for it will gather together people from every tribe and nation to worship the Lamb. Yet John the Revelator recognizes that the church can stand against the demonic forces allied against it and remain faithful to its calling to be witnesses of the Lamb only as it is empowered by the Holy Spirit. So he calls the church to rely on the power of the Spirit to carry out its mission in the world. John sees the Spirit's power as being available to every believer in the form of a prophetic enabling. The witness of the church to the lordship of the Lamb is nothing less than Spirit-inspired prophecy.

John the Revelator's vision of the church then is very similar to the picture of it offered by Luke in the book of Acts. Both Luke and John affirm that the church is a community of prophets, called and empowered to bear witness for Jesus. And, if the *Paraclete* promises reflect the Revelator's perspective (as most would affirm), then John the Revelator also viewed this prophetic community as being shaped by a specific, prophetic anointing distinct from regeneration. Since the Gospel of John distinguishes between the moment and functions ascribed to the coming of the *Paraclete* and those ascribed to the reception of the life-giving Spirit, it is reasonable to suggest that John the Revelator also shares this perspective. Indeed, the *Paraclete* promises appear to be another way of speaking about the prophetic anointing received by the disciples of Jesus at Pentecost.

These conclusions are significant for current attempts to articulate a Pentecostal theology that is both faithful to the Scriptures and relevant to the life of the contemporary church. A number of the finest scholars in Pentecostal and Charismatic circles have recently sought to connect the Pentecostal gift (i.e., Spirit-baptism in Luke-Acts) to Christian initiation.[35] Thus, they have also rejected attempts to view Spirit-baptism as logically distinct from conversion and focused on empowerment for witness. Underlying this trend appears to be the assumption that this approach allows us to integrate more fully Luke's prophetic pneumatology with Paul's broader,

---

35. See Turner, *Holy Spirit and Spiritual Gifts*; S. Chan, *Pentecostal Theology and the Christian Spiritual Tradition* (Sheffield: Sheffield Academic, 2003); F. D. Macchia, *Baptized in the Spirit: A Global Pentecostal Theology* (Grand Rapids: Zondervan, 2006); A. Yong, T*he Spirit Poured Out: Pentecostalism and the Possibility of Global Theology* (Grand Rapids: Baker, 2005).

soteriological perspective. Yet I would argue that in the only NT writings that clearly seek to do this very thing, the Johannine writings, which stem from the 90s and reflect an awareness of both pneumatological strands, this is precisely what they do not do. Rather, the Gospel of John and the book of Revelation emphasize the church's need to experience a prophetic anointing distinct from regeneration if it is to fulfill its calling in the world. This is the case because "the testimony of Jesus is the Spirit of prophecy" (Rev 19.10).

17

One Thousand Two Hundred Sixty Days
A Charismatic-Prophetic Empowerment Reading of Time and God's People in the Book of Revelation

By Craig S. Keener

It is a special privilege for me to dedicate this essay to my mentor Ben Aker. It was his personal example that led me into biblical scholarship, modeling for me how I could fulfill my calling to teach Scripture most effectively in this area. As a recent convert from heady atheism, I had probably reacted against scholarship more than most young Pentecostals even in that era, but when I felt the Spirit in Ben's Greek exegesis course, I began to pay attention. Ben would say things in class that I had felt in prayer just a week or two before, and I gradually realized that exegesis was quite compatible with Pentecostal experience. He mentored me in a fatherly way. It was he who first directed me toward ancient Jewish sources and later to the social historical approach. I had initially tried to resist admitting that background information was necessary for understanding the Bible, but as reading the Bible itself began breaking down that prejudice, Ben's teaching whetted my appetite insatiably for more information.

Because of space constraints in this essay, I have merely summarized some of Ben's impact on me, but suffice it to say, I would not have gone into biblical scholarship without his example. Ben has not become known for publishing books as widely as some scholars, including some others who influenced me early on. This was, however, because he was investing his time in students like me; our literary productivity is indebted to his ministry of teaching and his devotion to both Scripture and his students.

Because I learned so much from Ben, however, I have encountered the difficulty of trying to narrow down the subject on which to write. I first considered writing about the voice of the Spirit in John 16 (the subject of my third-year Greek paper for Ben) and the Johannine theme of knowing God (the subject of my Johannine theology paper for Ben and later of my master's thesis)[1] but most of this information is already incorporated in my John commentary.[2] I considered the relation between the Gospel and Epistles of John, but this subject is too well-worn. I considered the water motif in John, where my work developed one of his most profound lectures in Johannine theology, but I incorporated that material into my master's thesis, dissertation, commentary, and a chapter in a monograph.[3] I finally settled on a different area where Ben impacted my thinking: chronology in the Book of Revelation. Although I treated the subject in my Revelation commentary,[4] I will highlight here more distinctively its connection with Spirit-empowered witness.

THE END TIME IN REVELATION 12 AND EARLY CHRISTIANITY

Peter's adaptation of Joel 2.28-29 in Acts 2.17-18 has long served as a thesis statement for what Pentecostalism is about: Spirit-empowered proclamation. Many early Pentecostals, under the influence of end-time ideas then current, believed that their movement would quickly usher in the end of the age. As that generation drew to a close, some leaders, like Smith Wigglesworth, came to believe that in the future another revival would succeed

---

1. "Studies in the Knowledge of God in the Fourth Gospel in Light of its Historical Context" (MDiv thesis, AGTS, 1987).

2. *The Gospel of John: A Commentary*, 2 vols. (Peabody, MA: Hendrickson, 2003).

3. Others have since published on the topic. My thesis was in 1987; the dissertation ("The Function of Johannine Pneumatology in the Context of Late First-Century Judaism" [PhD diss., Duke University, 1991]) a few years later; the monograph on the Spirit (*The Spirit in the Gospels and Acts* [Peabody, MA: Hendrickson, 1997]) later still and the John commentary in 2003.

4. *Revelation* (Grand Rapids: Zondervan, 1999) 289-93, 318-25.

where early Pentecostalism had failed. It is said that Wigglesworth believed that this movement would bring together word and Spirit.[5]

Undoubtedly, the final revival (defined as the last one retroactively by its proximity to Jesus' return) will bring together word and Spirit; the prophetic witnesses of Revelation are Spirit-empowered proclaimers of God's message.[6] But whether a revival turns out to be the final one or not, Spirit-empowered witness ideally characterizes all the work of the church in this age; what we call "revival" is simply recovering what we were meant to be.

Peter interprets the eschatological context of Joel's "afterward" as "in the last days," a familiar enough expression for a future era (e.g., Isa 2.2; Ezek 38.16; Mic 4.1).[7] What is significant is that Peter construes his own time, when the Spirit was being poured out, as fulfilling these days, a pattern consistent with early Christian use of this and similar phrases[8] and even of something like the Jewish expectation of the "birth pangs" preceding the end (Rom 8.22).[9] In an early Jewish setting, the early Christian use of "last days" unmistakably indicates a claim that they were already in the end time,[10] already experiencing or at least on the verge of some of the future era. The Spirit is an eschatological gift (e.g., Isa 44.3; Ezek 36.27; 37.14; 39.29; Joel 2.28–29) so those who receive the Spirit have begun to experience the life of the future age.[11] If Jesus is king and Messiah, and if he has both come yet will come again, then the expected kingdom is "already" as well as "not yet."

We should not be surprised if Revelation, which participates in a distinctive way in the matrix of early Christian thought, offers a similar conception. In Revelation, as in Acts, Spirit-empowered witnesses become harbingers of the coming era.

---

5. G. Stormont, *Wigglesworth: A Man Who Walked with God* (Tulsa: Harrison, 1989) 114. Stormont knew Wigglesworth personally.

6. Rev 19.10; cf. prophets in 11.18; 16.6; 18.20, 24; 22.6, 9; John's experience of the Spirit in Rev 1.10; 2.7, 11, 17, 29; 3.6, 13, 22; 4.2; 17.3; 21.10; and probably 14.13; possibly 22.17.

7. All translations are my own.

8. In their respective contexts, 1 Tim 4.1; 2 Tim 3.1; Heb 1.2; Jas 5.3; 1 Pet 1.20; 2 Pet 3.3; Ign. *Eph.* 11.1; *2 Clem.* 14.2; *Barn.* 4.9; 16.5.

9. Cf. Isa 26.17–19; *1 En.* 62.4; *b. Sanh.* 98b; *b. Šabb.* 118a; perhaps *1QH* 3.7–12.

10. See Isa 2.2; Hos 3.5; Mic 4.1; Dan 2.28; *11Q13* 2.4; *1 En.* 27.3–4; cf. *4Q509* 2.19; *2 Bar.* 76.5; *T. Zeb.* 8.2; 9.5; *T. Iss.* 6.1. See more fully comment in my *Acts: An Exegetical Commentary*, 4 vols. (Grand Rapids: Baker Academic, 2012) esp. 1:877–78.

11. Cf. Rom 8.23; 2 Cor 1.22; 5.5; Eph 1.13–14; Heb 6.4–5. I address this concept in Acts 2 more fully in my *Acts*, 1:673, 783–84.

But These are Written . . .

PROPHETIC WITNESS IN THE END TIME

A reliable character in Revelation explains that the "testimony of Jesus" emphasized throughout the rest of the book is the Spirit of prophecy (19.10).[12] This declaration is again consistent with early Christian teaching, where the prophetic "word of the Lord" was the testimony about Jesus (Acts 1.8; 8.25; and passim) and speaking the gospel was speaking God's own message (1 Thess 2.13). Of course, as elsewhere in early Christianity, there were prophets in a narrower, more specific sense (e.g., Acts 11.27; 13.1; 21.9, 10); John's own prophecy is extensive (Rev 1.3; 10.11; 22.7, 10, 18–19). Yet the Spirit inspired all genuine testifying for Christ, whether detailed or not. This broader definition of inspired speech would therefore encompass not only prophecies in gathered assemblies of believers but also bold personal evangelism, from its most basic forms to what some now call "prophetic evangelism" (when it is genuinely Spirit-led).[13]

In Acts, this testimony was accompanied with "power" (1.8) which Luke-Acts frequently associates with healings and exorcisms (Luke 4.36; 5.17; 6.19; 8.46; 9.1; Acts 3.12; 4.7; 10.38; probably 6.8). Miraculous signs evoking earlier biblical prophets also accompany prophetic witness in a symbolic narrative in Revelation (11.5–6).[14] In Acts, to be sure, the "witnesses" are in first measure the Eleven (1.8) but their mission serves as paradigmatic for the mission of the continuing church as a whole, which receives the same empowerment for the same purpose (cf. e.g., 22.15, 20).[15] In Acts, the entire community is empowered to speak for God by the inspiration of his Spirit (2.17–18, 38–39); the same is no less true in Revelation, on the usual reading of ch. 11 (see discussion below).[16]

---

12. "Testimony of Jesus" probably functions as an objective genitive (F. F. Bruce, "The Spirit in the Apocalypse," in *Christ and Spirit in the New Testament: Studies in Honour of C. F. D. Moule*, eds. B. Lindars and S. S. Smalley [Cambridge: Cambridge University Press, 1973] 338) hence "testimony about Jesus", but the subjective element is not necessarily incompatible here (M. E. Boring, *Sayings of the Risen Jesus: Christian Prophecy in the Synoptic Tradition* [Cambridge: Cambridge University Press, 1982] 106; cf. Rev 1.1–2).

13. On prophetic evangelism, see e.g., M. Stibbe, *Prophetic Evangelism: When God Speaks to Those Who Do not Know Him* (Milton Keynes, UK: Authentic Media, 2004); for some elementary examples, see C. S. Keener, *Gift & Giver: The Holy Spirit for Today* (Grand Rapids: Baker, 2001) 51, 57–58.

14. John's usual terminology, however, differs; Luke's favorite term for "sign" appears with false prophets in Revelation (13.13–14; 16.14; 19.20).

15. See again fuller discussion in my Acts commentary.

16. Probably also 11.18 (where "saints" and "those who fear your name" are presumably identical, hence also "prophets"; all fit as "servants"); possibly also some other texts, such as 22.9, though the relation between "saints" and "prophets" is ambiguous in

This emphasis, though not unique in every respect, is distinctive to and characteristic of early Christianity. Some Jewish circles believed that the Spirit was no longer active in their day, certainly on the level found in earlier biblical times;[17] yet the biblical prophets had promised an outpouring of the Spirit for the eschatological time, as noted above. The pervasiveness of Christian prophets in Revelation (see 11.18; 16.6; 18.20, 24; 19.10; 22.9) reinforces that it involves the end-time period—the period in which John himself was bearing witness. The activity of the Spirit thus also attests that the community in which the Spirit is active, the community proclaiming Jesus, is God's own community.[18]

Granted, the early Christian conception was not completely unique. The Qumran community, for example, believed that the Spirit was active among them; but even in their case, this activity signaled their place on the edge of the end time.[19] Qumran texts associated the Spirit both with purification and with prophecy, but we do not find the pervasive flourishing of inspired prophecy (perhaps excepting communal exegesis)[20] or prophetic engagement of the larger world found in early Christianity.[21] Of course, spirits and prophecies had to be tested (cf. 1 John 4.1); John accepted only prophecy associated with Jesus, and specifically the true Jesus. Against false prophecy (Rev 2.14, 20) true prophecy was connected with Jesus (Rev 19.10; cf. 1 John 4.2–3; John 14.26; 15.26–27; 16.13–14).

PROPHETIC WITNESS AND TIME IN REVELATION 11

Johannine theology recognizes that believers are already in the eschatological time, for many antichrists already exist (1 John 2.18; cf. 2 Thess 2.7a). Although Revelation emphasizes future eschatology much more than John's

---

some passages (cf. 16.6; 18.20, 24). On all believers as potential prophets in Revelation, see e.g., D. Hill, "Prophecy and Prophets in the Revelation of St. John," *NTS* 18 (July 4, 1972) 401–18, here 414.

17. See e.g., Keener, *Spirit*, 13–16.

18. Cf. also J. M. Ford, "'For the Testimony of Jesus is the Spirit of Prophecy' (Rev 19.10)," *ITQ* 42 (1975) 284–91.

19. See D. E. Aune, *The Cultic Setting of Realized Eschatology in Early Christianity* (Leiden: Brill, 1972).

20. Josephus does mention prophecy among the Essenes, but it does not appear as pervasively as in early Christianity. Its occurrence among Essenes might be related to some of the parabiblical literature found in those circles, perhaps including apocalypses like most of *1 Enoch*.

21. This is especially the case for those of us who continue to understand the Qumran community as a sectarian community largely withdrawn from the world into the wilderness. Revelation embraces that image (12.6) alongside that of prophets (11.3).

gospel does, its portrayal of the present era is consistent with the realized eschatology dominant in the gospel.[22] Depending on the identity of the two witnesses in Rev 11, the eschatological time period during which they minister could also represent the current time.

Recent Pentecostal interpreters often view the two witnesses as the church, and not without good reason.[23] I offered the following arguments for this position, which is also the most common view among scholars generally,[24] in my Revelation commentary:[25]

1. They appear as lampstands—a symbol that Revelation elsewhere applies to churches (1.20).[26]

2. The olive tree imagery refers to Zech 4.11–14, which in turn referred to the high priest Joshua and the king Zerubbabel, who sought to restore the holy city; in Revelation, it is Christ's followers who are a kingdom and priests (1.6; 5.10).[27]

3. Like John himself (10.11), these witnesses prophesy (11.3, 6), a mission that elsewhere in Revelation belongs to all servants of Christ (cf. 19.10).

---

22. See discussion in Keener, *Gospel of John*, 124, 137–38, 320–23.

23. See e.g., R. Waddell, *The Spirit of the Book of Revelation* (Blandford Forum, UK: Deo, 2006) 174. For their paradigmatic role regarding Spirit-inspired prophetic witness, see ibid., 170–91; J. C. Thomas, "Toward a Pentecostal Theology of Prophetic Witness: The Testimony of the Apocalypse (Revelation 11.3–14)" paper at the SPS meeting, 2007 (brought to my attention by R. Waddell).

24. E.g., J. W. Bowman, *The First Christian Drama: The Book of Revelation* (Philadelphia: Westminster, 1968) 71; D. Hill, *New Testament Prophecy* (Atlanta: John Knox, 1979) 89; R. Bauckham, *The Climax of Prophecy: Studies on the Book of Revelation* (Edinburgh: T. & T. Clark, 1993) 166, 273–75; J. R. Michaels, *Revelation* (Downers Grove, IL: IVP, 1997) 138–39; C. H. Talbert, *The Apocalypse: A Reading of the Revelation of John* (Louisville, KY: WJKP, 1994) 45–46; D. E. Aune, *Revelation*, 3 vols. (Dallas: Word, 1997) 631; G. K. Beale, *The Book of Revelation: A Commentary on the Greek Text* (Grand Rapids: Eerdmans, 1999) 572–75; M. G. Reddish, *Revelation* (Macon, GA: Smyth & Helwys, 2001) 211–12; G. D. Fee, *Revelation* (Eugene, OR: Cascade, 2011) 150; cf. R. H. Mounce, *The Book of Revelation* (Grand Rapids: Eerdmans, 1977) 218 (the end-time church); I. Newton, *Observations upon the Prophecies of Daniel and the Apocalypse of St. John: In Two Parts* (London: J. Darby and T. Browne, 1733) 286.

25. Keener, *Revelation*, 289–93.

26. Two lampstands can represent all the church just as seven do (Rev 1.20; G. R. Beasley-Murray, *The Book of Revelation* [Greenwood, SC: Attic, 1974] 184); they are probably doubled as witnesses (Num 35.30; Deut 17.6; Bauckham, *Climax*, 274).

27. Here in the midst of a ruined and desecrated city (11.2) a spiritual Sodom and Egypt (11.8, the recipient of fiery judgment and plagues elsewhere in Revelation) as they await the New Jerusalem (14.1; 21.2).

4. The narrative's blending and adaptation of various biblical prophetic motifs, for example fire coming from the witnesses' mouths rather than from heaven, suggests that we understand it symbolically.[28]

When we ask how to apply the text, the answer is the same whether the witnesses represent the church or simply prophetic models for the church: prophetically empowered witness. The Reformers, for example, applied the prophecy of the two witnesses to a revival of prophecy in their own day.[29] But symbolism is pervasive in Revelation (sometimes explained, as in 1.20, and sometimes obvious in a first-century setting, as in 17.9) and the witnesses may represent the church itself.

If, as most scholars think, the witnesses represent the church, the 1,260 days might represent the church age. If so, the period would designate not the literal length of time, but rather the *kind* of time—a time of great tribulation (cf. the similar figure in Dan 12.1, 11). This would probably not be John's first figurative reapplication of time in Daniel: believers in Smyrna would, like Daniel and his friends, be "tested" for "ten days" (Rev 2.10; Dan 1.12–15).

The figure of 1,260 days represents forty-two months or three and a half 360 day years, figures that appear in Daniel (7.25; 9.27; 12.7). Some think that the slight adjustment to Daniel's figure (12.11–12) would have appealed to those interested in symbolic numbers in John's day.[30] In any case, there are reasons to doubt that Revelation intends the figure literally:

1. Revelation rarely uses Jewish symbols, even from Scripture, without reapplying them christologically (e.g., the messianic lion is now the lamb; 5.5–6).

2. Daniel's own figure reapplies and extends a period in an earlier prophecy (Jer 29.10; Dan 9.2, 24).

3. The gospels interpret Daniel's tribulation as fulfilled in the events of 66–70 C.E., before Revelation was likely written.[31]

---

28. Cf. Thomas, "Theology," 4, noting the accumulation of previous biblical prophets' power and arguing that in these witnesses "the prophetic anointing by the Spirit seems to be complete."

29. R. L. Petersen, *Preaching in the Last Days: The Theme of "Two Witnesses" in the Sixteenth and Seventeenth Centuries* (New York: Oxford University Press, 1993) 59–87.

30. Bauckham, *Climax*, 401–3, explores these numbers: e.g., 1,260 is the sum of even numbers up to seventy, and forty-two of even numbers up to twelve.

31. See C. S. Keener, *The Gospel of Matthew: A Socio-Rhetorical Commentary* (Grand Rapids: Eerdmans, 2009) 573–83. Some others may have also reapplied the tribulation period; cf. D. S. Russell, *The Method and Message of Jewish Apocalyptic* (Philadelphia: Westminster, 1964) 198–201.

But These are Written . . .

Arguments like these do not require us to suppose that Revelation applies the figure symbolically to a period of time different from the one envisioned by Daniel, but they do allow for the possibility. What raises the probability of this thesis significantly is the next mention of the 1,260 days, in 12.6.

TIME IN REVELATION 12

Most scholars agree that the ascension of the child in 12.5 refers to Jesus' exaltation. This agreement has implications for how we understand the tribulation period of 1,260 days, because in 12.6 this period seems to immediately follow Jesus' exaltation. During this period the woman is (like Israel in the exodus) nurtured in the wilderness. Other early Christian passages also compare the period between initial redemption and entering into one's inheritance to Israel's experience in the wilderness.[32] That is, the woman's experience easily enough depicts the experience of Christ's people between the already and the not yet.

Regardless of one's interpretation of the wilderness, however, if the 1,260 days immediately follows Christ's exaltation and stands for the tribulation that ends at his return, no author after the mid-30s of the first century could intend it literally. Instead, Revelation reframes the expected period of eschatological tribulation christocentrically: end-time believers are already experiencing that tribulation. This approach is analogous to pointing out that the expected eschatological antichrist is already present among those who deny Jesus (1 John 2.18). This is not to deny that there could be a final, intense period of tribulation or final opposition to Christ's kingdom; it is only to insist that, for Revelation, such tribulation characterizes the entire course of this age. After all, if Jesus himself did not know the time of his coming (Mark 13.32) Satan would not know it; spiritual conflict would normally be in effect until the end.

If Revelation depicts tribulation on earth, it offers also another side of the picture, portraying a heavenly war corresponding to these earthly events. In Rev 12, Jesus' exaltation is accompanied by heavenly combat, through which Satan and his angels are cast out. Jewish myths commonly associated the fall of angels with the events of Gen 6.[33] By contrast, Revela-

32. 1 Cor 10.1-11; Eph 1.14; Heb 3.8; 4.11; Jude 5; cf. John 1.23; cf. J. D. Hester, *Paul's Concept of Inheritance. A Contribution to the Understanding of Heilsgeschichte* (Edinburgh: Oliver & Boyd, 1968).

33. 1 Pet 3.19-20; 2 Pet 2.4; Jude 6; Philo, *Gig.* 16; *1 En.* 6.2; 19.1; 69.5; 106.13-15; *Jub.* 4.22; 5.1; 7.21; *2 Bar.* 56.13-15; *T. Sol.* 6.3; *2 En.* 18.5-6; probably CD 2.18; 1Qap Gen^{ar} 2.1; cf. D. S. Russell, *The Method and Message of Jewish Apocalyptic* (Philadelphia: Westminster, 1964) 249ff.; M. Barker, "Some Reflections upon the Enoch Myth," *JSOT*

tion's christocentric proclamation instead focuses theologically on the hostile angels' most grievous rebellion and humiliation, at the pivotal event in history, the Christ event.

If there is any doubt as to the time in which these events take place theologically, we should note Revelation's words: the accuser of believers can no longer accuse them (12.10). Elsewhere in early Christian theology, Christ's exaltation as believers' advocate silences any accusations against them (Rom 8.33-34). Revelation's portrayal here is consistent with this teaching.

Moreover, Revelation indicates the result of Satan, the dragon, no longer being able to accuse them: salvation and the kingdom have come. When do "salvation" and the "kingdom" come? Revelation associates the coming of these events with two moments. One is Christ's future return (11.15; 19.1) but this passage cannot refer to that event, which would not leave Satan even a "short" time (12.12). Moreover, Christ's exaltation should protect believers from Satan's accusations already, not merely at the second coming.

Revelation therefore refers here to the other possible moment: "salvation" and the "kingdom" came through Jesus' death, resurrection, and exaltation (1.9; 2.27; 7.10; cf. 1.6; 5.10).[34] Many Jewish people expected Satan's defeat in the future, but Christians recognize that the expected Messiah has already come. Christ has already defeated Satan, and by the standards of cosmic and even human history Satan has just a short time.[35] (The short period of 1,260 days can stand for a much longer time by human standards, just as the "one hour" of 17.12 does.) The shift from a future defeat of Satan to a past one corresponds to the shift in messianic expectation for those who acknowledge that Jesus the Messiah has come; for outsiders to the faith, this shift would have been dramatic.[36]

---

15 (1980) 7-29.

34. Jewish sources that expected the kingdom only in a future sense could apply such terms to the day of judgment (*1 En.* 60.6) but commentators usually recognize that Revelation looks to the cross and resurrection here (e.g., H. Schlier, *Principalities and Powers in the New Testament* [New York: Herder & Herder, 1961] 49).

35. With e.g., M. Rissi, *Time and History: A Study on the Revelation*, trans. G. C. Winsor (Richmond, VA: John Knox, 1966) 38, 117; Bowman, *Drama*, 78; Beale, *Revelation*, 646-47; cf. A. Kassing, "Das Weib das den Mann gebar (Apk 12,13)" *Benediktinische Monatschrift* 34 (Nov-Dec 1958) 427-33; for the figure in 12.14, see Rissi, *Time*, 112.

36. R. Bauckham views this reorientation of conventional Jewish expectations as "unprecedented" (*Climax*, 185).

But These are Written . . .

THE ONE HUNDRED FORTY-FOUR THOUSAND NEW JERUSALEMITES

In Rev 12.11, believers "overcome" Satan through the blood of the lamb and the word of their testimony. That is, even when facing death, they maintain their message about Christ, inspired by the prophetic Spirit (see 19.10). Satan persecutes them because they keep God's commands and maintain the testimony about Jesus (12.17). In the surrounding chapters, the world overcomes Jesus' witnesses, overpowering them in human terms (11.7; 13.7). By contrast, this passage offers a heavenly perspective: it is Christ's witnesses who overcome by refusing to be silenced about Jesus (see also 15.2). Like the seven churches with their diverse tests, believers are called to overcome (2.7, 11, 17, 26; 3.5, 12, 21; 21.7; cf. 1 John 2.13–14; 4.4; 5.4–5). In the language of another Johannine source, Jesus' followers have tribulation in this world, but through Jesus they have overcome the world (John 16.33).

John also portrays the overcomers who persevere through martyrdom as 144,000 chaste men (compare 14.1, 3, with 15.2–4). Some scholars view the listing of the twelve tribes that constitute the 144,000 believers (7.4–8) as evoking an OT military census, hence view these "overcomers" in military terms.[37] In any case, the battle in Revelation is a spiritual one; even in 19.11–16, Christ's followers accompany him but do not fight. Revelation depicts believers suffering, without retaliation, for proclaiming Christ, a situation familiar perhaps to the churches of Smyrna and Philadelphia but foreign to the compromised believers of Sardis, Laodicea, and some Western churches today.

Who are these overcomers? To be consistent, one should either take everything about these overcomers literally—144,000 Jewish male virgins from twelve tribes (minus Dan; and today most tribal ancestry has been forgotten)—or take it all symbolically. A symbolic approach would be more in keeping with the character of the rest of Revelation more generally. Indeed, the number can hardly be literal. The number of the 144,000 is the number of the saved, for these are God's "servants" (7.3) which elsewhere refers to believers (1.1; 2.20; 6.11; 19.10; 22.3, 6, 9).[38] Revelation elsewhere depicts believers as spiritually Jewish (2.9; 3.9) even using the most fundamental ancient symbol for Judaism, lampstands, to depict the churches (1.20). Thus the following vision may give a more literal interpretation of the first one:

---

37. Ibid., 216–19; idem, "The Book of Revelation as a Christian War Scroll," *Neot* 22 (1988) 17–40.

38. From the standpoint of global Christianity today, the number of God's servants here is very small, but in John's day the number may have seemed large, or at least not small.

the 144,000 Jewish warriors (7.4–8) are actually an innumerable multitude from all peoples (7.9–17).[39] In fact, the next passage plainly applies OT texts about Israel's restoration to all believers, including Gentile ones (7.9, 15–17, with Isa 25.8; 49.10). In Rev 5.5–6, John heard about a conquering lion yet saw a slain lamb; here he hears about what might be a Jewish end-time army but sees what may be a multicultural multitude of martyrs (cf. perhaps the white robes in 6.11; 7.9).

Later the 144,000 appear with the lamb on Mount Zion, bearing his name in contrast to the world that bears the beast's name instead (13.16—14.1). Presumably they are on Mount Zion because they are its people, the New Jerusalemites. This vision of hope contrasts with the fall of Babylon announced in 14.8, a contrast that Revelation soon develops more fully. The two cities appear in contrast more clearly later, when John is carried away in the Spirit to witness both Babylon (17.3) and the New Jerusalem (21.10). The former is portrayed as a prostitute, decked out with gold and pearls (17.3–5) the latter, as a bride, made of gold and with gates of pearls (21.10–14). The bride, a city incomprehensibly vast (21.16–17) is incomparably greater than the "great city" Babylon (17.18; 18.10, 16, 18–19, 21); those with faith to live for the promised future world can resist settling for the cheap gratification of the prostituted present one. The chaste bride is the feminine image that corresponds with the masculine image of the chaste 144,000.

John's symbolism clearly depicts the Babylon of his day as Rome, which (like Babylon of old) destroyed Jerusalem and enslaved God's people.[40] Nevertheless, his interest is not a particular empire, whether the earlier Babylon or the present Rome; his eschatological beast blends features of the four beasts of Daniel (7.3–8; Rev 13.2). Rome, like earlier Babylon, simply embodied the spirit of the oppressive evil empire, the world system hostile to God and God's people. Though part of a small, persecuted minority sect, and banished to the island of Patmos, John envisioned the collapse of mighty Babylon, just as the earlier Babylon had fallen. A few centuries after John, Rome fell, but, as Revelation anticipated, the church is now close to reflecting all peoples before God's throne.

---

39. A second revelation could confirm as well as supplement a first one; see e.g., Gen 37.6–9; 41.1–7.

40. The "seven mountains" of 17.9 are clear enough (see e.g., Varro, *Lang.* 5.7.41; Dionysius of Halicarnassus, *Ant. rom.* 4.13.2–3; Pliny, *Nat.* 3.5.66; Silius Italicus 10.586; 12.608; Statius, *Silvae* 2.3.21; 4.1.6–7; Suetonius, *Dom.* 4.5; Symmachus, *Ep.* 1.12.3; *Sib. Or.* 2.18; 11.116; and passim in ancient literature); cf. also the "city that rules the kings of the earth" (17.18); the cargoes lamented in 18.12–13; the treatment of Rome as a new Babylon in Jewish apocalyptic; and so forth. Most commentators view Rome as Babylon.

But These are Written . . .

But as Babylon seemed powerful only to the people of this age, the truly majestic New Jerusalem, the city to come, belonged to the oppressed servants of God, proclaiming Christ and a future hope in the face of opposition. The city of the coming world, the New Jerusalem, is shaped as a cube, like the biblical holy of holies (21.16; 1 Kgs 6.20). But the dimensions of the city do not easily fit the wall: twelve thousand stadia cubed for a wall of a mere 144 cubits (21.16–17). These dimensions are not meant literally, but instead are meant to recall Revelation's earlier use of twelve thousand and 144,000.[41] That is, the New Jerusalem is the city of God for the people of God, the New Jerusalemites. All the followers of the lamb have a part in that city. They are the 144,000, the two witnesses, and the prophetic saints who appear elsewhere in the book: those who proclaim Christ and therefore have a share in the promised future (cf. 11.18). The prophetic character of God's people is part of their identity in this age.

CONCLUSION

It seems likely that Revelation portrays the present period as eschatological, the period between the Lord's first and second comings. Revelation also portrays this period as one of intense prophetic witness, and through a variety of images, believers as God's witnesses. The ideal image of God's people in this age in Revelation is as Spirit-empowered witnesses for Jesus. May we act as the prophetic people that Revelation invites us to be.

---

41. With e.g., Bauckham, *Climax*, 399.

18

The Vocabulary and Phraseology of Revelation

TIMOTHY P. JENNEY

I HAVE HAD THE honor of knowing Benny Aker for more than thirty-eight years, first as an undergraduate professor, then a graduate professor, and finally as a colleague and friend. I first found him intimidating as an undergraduate. He was an intense man: tall, with dark hair, piercing eyes, and sunken cheeks. He also had little tolerance for those not prepared to give their best. I am chagrined to admit I fell into that category the first several years. After all, I intended to be a youth pastor—and what need does a pastor of youth have of Greek and Hebrew (or studies, for that matter)?

As I matured and grew in dedication to my studies, I found Dr. Aker to be a constant source of encouragement. He became a mentor, even taking me to one of his doctoral classes, so I could sit in and see what "real scholarship" looked like. He encouraged me to consider graduate work and, eventually, doctoral work. As a graduate professor, I found him to be among the most stimulating, out-of-the-box thinkers I have ever had (and I have sat at the feet of some great, great men). I also learned that his scholarship and service to the church had come at great personal cost, a cost that only seemed to humble him further and soften his heart even more toward God. I have since followed his path in more ways than one.

It is an honor to be able to contribute to this *Festschrift* for a beloved professor. Thank you, Benny, for all you have done.

But These are Written . . .

SCOPE OF THE STUDY

One of the most persistent questions in the study of Revelation is the source of its vocabulary and phraseology. In this article we will use one of the latest generation of Bible software programs to try to shed some light on this issue.[1]

Bible software was not generally available when I penned my 1993 dissertation on Revelation at the University of Michigan.[2] Though the dissertation contained a few statistical surveys, I had to do all the research by hand. I found it inefficient and time-consuming. I was able to use software in the research for my 1999 commentary on Revelation.[3] However, it lacked both the wealth of tagged texts now available and the most sophisticated of the four searches we will employ in this study. The current availability of both makes this reappraisal a timely one.

Our goal is to investigate the strength of the relationship between Revelation and five different corpora of Greek literature:

1. Greek New Testament (GNT)[4]

2. Septuagint (LXX)[5]

3. Pseudepigrapha[6]

4. Apocryphal Apocalypses[7]

5. Philo[8]

---

1. Accordance®10 Bible Software (www.accordancebible.com). Several of the other major Bible software programs are also capable of similar kinds of searches, including BibleWorks 9 (www.bibleworks.com) and Logos 4 (www.logos.com). The goal here is not to recommend a particular brand of Bible software, but to encourage the use of software for statistical studies of this kind—and to be transparent about the search engine and text databases upon which this study is founded.

2. "The Harvest of the Earth: The Feast of Sukkoth in the Book of Revelation" (PhD diss., University of Michigan, 1993).

3. "Revelation," in *The Full Life Bible Commentary*, eds. F. L. Arrington and R. Stronstad (Grand Rapids: Zondervan, 1999) 1535–1629; Reissued as *Life in the Spirit New Testament Commentary*, eds. F. L. Arrington and R. Stronstad (Grand Rapids: Zondervan, 2003).

4. Novum Testamentum Graece (Greek New Testament) (NA^{27}) (Altamonte Springs, FL: OakTree Software, Inc., 2009. Version 1.0).

5. Greek Septuagint (LXX1) (Altamonte Springs: OakTree Software, Inc., 2010. Version 4.5).

6. The Greek Pseudepigrapha (PSEUD-T) (Altamonte Springs, FL: OakTree Software, Inc., 2009. Version 4.5).

7. The Apocryphal Apocalypses (APOCAL-T) (Altamonte Springs, FL: OakTree Software, Inc., 2010. Version 1.1).

8. Works of Philo (PHILO-T) (Altamonte Springs, FL: OakTree Software, Inc., 2009. Version 2.7).

The Vocabulary and Phraseology of Revelation

The specific edition of each corpus is the latest version of the morphologically tagged text available.

The dating of many of these individual books is widely contested, and at times the dating of individual chapters within some of these books vary widely. Accordingly, this study makes no attempt to determine whether Revelation derived its vocabulary and phraseology from the books or the inverse—the books derived theirs from Revelation.

We will use four different lines of investigation. The first is a search for the *unusual* words in NA[27] (those appearing between one and ten times) that occur in Revelation. The second is a search for the *common* words in Revelation (those occurring eleven or more times in NA[27]), omitting common particles, prepositions, conjunctions, and pronouns. The third is simply a search for every noun and verb appearing in Revelation. The fourth search is unlike the first three, as it looks for *phrases* in Revelation, rather than individual words. In Accordance it is called an "infer" search.[9]

Infer is an excellent tool for researching intertextuality, which makes it perfect for our use. However, it is unusual enough that it deserves a bit of explanation. Infer finds every possible phrase of a specific length in the source text, ignoring only those where 50 percent or more of the words are the most common. The search engine then locates every occurrence of all of those phrases in another text. In addition, it permits users to specify a certain amount of "fuzziness" in the matches.

This study uses an "infer 3, ±1" search. The "±1" means that a single word may be added or subtracted. This is a very fine net to cast, and seems the best approach if this search is to catch very short phrases, like titles and appellations. However, it has the unfortunate side effect of producing a lot of "background noise," in that so many phrases contain the Greek verbs λέγω "to say" and εἰμί "to be."

Organization

The body of this article is organized into six sections: one for each of the five corpora and a concluding section that compares all five. Each of the five sections covers all four lines of investigation. The results are presented as a verbal summary, with supporting graphs and tables (which have been gathered together in the appendices). Each investigation's result is displayed as a graph and a table of the chapters in the corpus with the highest number of average hits and total hits. This provides an objective way to assess the individual chapters in each corpus with the closest relationships to Revelation.

9. To my knowledge, only Accordance currently features this specific type of search.

But These are Written . . .

Space constraints have generally limited tables to just the top twenty chapters in each corpus. This study also includes a table of summary statistics covering all five corpora, allowing us to compare them.

The conclusion is divided into two parts: a summary and a reflection. The summary offers some preliminary observations about the data, which is presented in the table of summary statistics and an aggregate table listing the highest chapters in all five corpora. However, this study is intended to be foundational, rather than conclusive. We invite readers to use this raw data to shape their own studies and draw their own conclusions. To advance this goal, full-sized graphs, a complete spreadsheet of every table, and working Accordance workspaces are available online.[10] The reflection evaluates the study itself and appraises the future of computer-assisted Bible research.

THE FIVE CORPORA

No one will dispute that Revelation's vocabulary is unusual. It consists of 911 different words (lemmas)[11] of which 128 are unique to that book within NA^{27}—47 of which are not even found in the LXX. The LXX does use 81 of the 128 (63.3 percent) which is the highest percentage of any of corpora within our consideration. Only 69 (52.9 percent) of them occur in the pseudepigrapha, 59 (46.1 percent) in Philo, and a mere 22 (17.2 percent) in the apocryphal apocalypses. The widely varying size of these different corpora (as illustrated by the total words of each in Table 1) does not allow for a one-for-one comparison, but the low number of these words that appear in the apocryphal apocalypses is remarkable nevertheless. Though small by the standards of the other corpora, the apocryphal apocalypses themselves are more than twice the size of Revelation.

Greek New Testament (NA^{27})

As part of the literature of the GNT, the most obvious comparison to Revelation is the rest of NA^{27}. This gives us a baseline against which to compare the other four bodies of literature in our investigation. The graphs display the search results for all four searches: Revelation's unusual words, common words, all nouns and verbs, and phrases. The scale is number of hits per

---

10. Access these resources here: http://accordancefiles1.com/revelation/Revelation.zip.

11. All statistics in this article were derived from Accordance and its tagged texts.

The Vocabulary and Phraseology of Revelation

one thousand words. The height of the graph automatically varies with the results, so one must be careful when comparing one graph to another.

Overall, the graphs are what one would expect. Revelation's unusual words (Fig. 1A) appear seldom in the rest of the GNT (save for a spike around Matt 25–26) while the common words (Fig. 1B) are frequent and fairly evenly distributed throughout the corpus. Figure 1C, "All Nouns and Verbs," is midway between the two. Figure 1D holds the biggest surprise. It reveals a strong similarity between the phrases in Revelation, the Gospel of John, and 1–3 John. In fact, it turns out that the phraseology of some of the [other] Johannine literature is more like Revelation than some chapters of Revelation!

These graphs are too coarse, especially at this size and resolution, to identify specific chapters with a strong relationship to Revelation. For this we must turn to Table 3. It displays the top thirty-two chapters in NA^{27}, sorted for both highest number of hits and highest average hits per one thousand words.

While tables do not give the bird's-eye view of a graph, they do provide excellent detail. Particularly intriguing are the ten chapters in NA^{27} that have the strongest relationship to Revelation's unusual vocabulary, by average hits (1 Cor 5; Rom 1; 1 Cor 8; Jude; Heb 9; 2 Pet 2; Matt 24; Col 4; Acts 21; Jas 5) or total number of hits (Luke 12; Matt 24; Rom 1; Acts 21; Luke 23; Mark 15; Luke 10; Mark 6; Luke 11; Jude). These statistics indicate a strong probability that additional work in these chapters would increase our understanding of Revelation and vice versa. In addition, Revelation's shared phraseology with the Johannine literature (John 1, 9, 15, 17; 1 John 1–4) lends support to the idea of shared authorship, an idea that has been (re)gaining acceptance in recent years.[12]

In this case, we will simply point out that the most dramatic difference between Revelation and the rest of the NT is found in its use of unusual words and phrasing. At the outset, these two (A and D) seem to be the best lines of investigation for our purposes. The other two lines of investigation (B and C) will serve as a control.

---

12. In the years immediately after (and for a long time following) the publication of R. H. Charles' watershed *A Critical and Exegetical Commentary on the Revelation of St. John* (Edinburgh: T. & T. Clark, 1920) it became academically untenable to maintain a Johannine authorship for the Apocalypse. His argument from the linguistic evidence against it was that overwhelming. Many scholars seemed to have overlooked the fact that Charles himself said, "We shall deal here only with the linguistic evidence on this question, which is in itself decisive. We shall, however, discover later that the two writers were related to each other, either as master and pupil, or as pupils of the same master, or as members of the same school" (1:xxix). Even this statement we consider too pessimistic in the light of this research, while we still want to acknowledge the weighty contribution Charles made to Revelation studies.

But These are Written . . .

Septuagint (LXX)

The vocabulary of Revelation is much closer to that of the LXX than it is to the rest of the GNT. Of the 382 unusual words in Revelation, the LXX has 315 (82.5 percent) while the rest of the GNT has but 256 (67 percent) (Table 2). The LXX also contains 81 (63.3 percent) of the 128 words unique to Revelation in the GNT (Table 1). However, the LXX is also more than four times the size of Matthew—Jude, so it is hard to make a firm judgment based upon just whether certain words appear.

An overall assessment is better based upon the graphs of the four searches (Figs. 2A–D), which plot every occurrence of the three sets of vocabulary words and Revelation's phrases. These graphs make it clear that the LXX has a much stronger relationship to Revelation in both its use of the Apocalypse's unusual words and its phrases. It is not as close to Revelation in its use of the GNT's common words.

The chapter-by-chapter breakout (Table 4) contains some surprising results. Consider the list of chapters with the highest average of unusual words. Revelation is most often linked to Daniel, less often to Zechariah or the Wisdom literature. Zechariah 8 and Daniel chs. 2 and 3 do appear, but chapters from other books predominate. The LXX books with the greatest use of Revelation's unusual words however, include descriptions of the wilderness tabernacle (Exod 26, 27, 37) Solomon's temple (1 Kgs 6–7; 2 Chr 3) Ezekiel's vision of God's throne (Ezek 1) the restored temple (40–43) and the inheritance of the tribes (48) the Mosaic sacrifices for the Temple and its various feasts (Num 28ff.) and the great culminating praises of the Psalter (Pss 147–50). They even include the story of Balaam and Balak (Num 22ff.).

There are other chapters in this table that offer equally intriguing possibilities for further research, especially among those identified as sharing Revelation's phraseology. Before we wander too far afield from our primary purpose though, it would be well to call attention to Table 2.

The LXX uses Revelation's unusual words more than twice as often as the GNT. It uses Revelation's phrases more than ten times as often. Its use of common words is slightly less, but its use of all nouns and verbs nearly identical. The conclusion is obvious: the relationship between the LXX and Revelation is much stronger than Revelation's relationship to the rest of the NT.

Pseudepigrapha

The Pseudepigrapha encompasses more books than LXX (seventy-four vs. fifty-one) but it only has 58.1 percent of its chapters, and 29.4 percent of its

The Vocabulary and Phraseology of Revelation

words (Table 1). Despite this difference in size, the corpus uses almost as many of the unique words in Revelation as the LXX (52.9 percent vs. 63.3 percent). Its verses also only average about three-fourths the length of those in the LXX. As a result of these differences, it is important that we focus on the number of average hits to compare it to other bodies of literature. These are the statistics least affected by the varying sizes of the books, chapters, and verses.

The Pseudepigrapha is also a very diverse body of literature—and Figure 3A shows an equally diverse use of Revelation's unique vocabulary. There are sharp peaks in the *Sibylline Oracles, Jubilees,* the *Testament of Judah,* and Demetrius. However, there is a dramatic difference between Figure 3A and Figure 3D. The latter shows very little relative use of Revelation's phrasing in the *Sibylline Oracles* for instance, but relatively high use elsewhere in the corpus.

The chapter-by-chapter breakout in Table 6 illustrates just how misleading statistics can be, at least when not balanced by other kinds of analysis. For instance, *Jubilees* 5 is the chapter with the highest average hits in unusual words (187.7 hits per one thousand words) but the chapter is only a single short verse with three hits. *Sibylline Oracles* 26, ranking fifth (76.7 hits per one thousand words) is just as bad: two fragmentary verses with but a single hit.

On the other hand, 179 hits in Aristeas the Exegete is impressive—until one realizes that this book has but a single chapter: 322 verses and 19,342 words in length! Clearly, the best solution is to keep an eye on both the number of hits and average hits in corpora with chapters of such wildly varying lengths.

With that fact in mind, there are several books with chapters here that do seem to warrant closer examination: the *Sibylline Oracles,* the *Ascension of Isaiah,* the *Testaments of the Twelve Patriarchs,* and 1 *Enoch.*

The Pseudepigrapha uses Revelation's unusual words almost exactly as much as the LXX (twenty-three hits per one thousand words vs. twenty-four hits per one thousand words). As we pointed out earlier, this is a much more accurate standard than comparing the number of hits per verse or hits per chapter, as the chapter length of the two bodies of literature is so different. However, the Pseudepigrapha overall does not show as close a relationship in its use of phrasing. It is only 68.2 percent as likely (7.4K hits per one thousand words vs. 10.9K hits per one thousand words) to use Revelation's phraseology.

But These are Written . . .

Apocryphal Apocalypses

If we had any expectations at all about this study, it was that the Apocryphal Apocalypses would shine as examples of Revelation's influence. We were wrong. Figure 4A shows some dramatic differences among these books, but relatively little overall use of Revelation's unusual words. This corpus also has the lowest number of Revelation's unique words (22 of 128 lemmas, or 17.2 percent—Table 1). This body of literature is the smallest of the five corpora we examined, only about 14 percent the size of the NT and just over 3 percent the size of the LXX. Nevertheless, we found the results disappointing. The results forced us to reassess our own opinion of what is unique and important in Revelation (a good thing, really).

The summary statistics in Table 2 show that the Apocryphal Apocalypses have about the same frequency of use of Revelation's unusual words as the LXX and the Pseudepigrapha, no more and no less. Their use of Revelation's phrases is significantly higher than the Pseudepigrapha's (10.21K average hits per one thousand words vs. 7.42 average hits per one thousand words) but not quite as high as the LXX's (10.88K avg. hits per one thousand words).

Within the corpus, there are individual chapters that warrant special attention. The number of chapters of the *Apocalypse of Moses* appearing in both unusual words and phrases is impressive, recommending study of the entire apocalypse. The single appearance of six *Esdras, Apocalypse of Paul, Apocalypse of John,* and *Apocalypse of John Chrysostom* in both lists is also noteworthy, as each of them has but a single chapter (so they each only appear once).

Philo

The final corpus we will consider is Philo. It is a large corpus and so it is not surprising that 59 (46.1 percent) of Revelation's unique words appear in it (Table 1). Yet the Pseudepigrapha's use is even higher (both in raw numbers and averages) though it is just over a third (39.4 percent) of its size.

There is another variable we must take into account when considering Philo. The corpus is 74.7 percent of the size of the LXX, but only has 38 books to the latter's 51—and only 52 chapters to the LXX's 1150. Philo's sentences tend to be long too, averaging 53 words to the LXX's 20. This wide disparity means that comparing total hits will be useless. It is important to focus on average hits instead.

The Vocabulary and Phraseology of Revelation

All this aside, Figure 5A shows some impressive spikes within the corpus, indicating Philo's use of Revelation's unusual words is not consistent, but localized in specific chapters. The other worthwhile graph is Figure 5D, which also shows some notable spikes.

Philo's *Quaestiones et solutiones in Genesin* 3 tops the chart of chapters with the average highest use of Revelation's unusual words (32.77 average hits per one thousand words; 41 total hits) (Table 7). The rest of the chapters range in the teens, against a background average for Philo of only 16 (in other words, there is little significant difference between them). This suggests that a different resolution for the graph in Figure 5A may have been more helpful than the current one.

Likewise, there is but a single standout chapter in the use of Revelation's phrases: *Hypothetica* 7. Its 5.5K average hits per one thousand words are dramatically higher than the rest of Philo, which declines from 4.8K rather steadily and predictably. Either of these chapters, *Quaestiones et solutiones in Genesin* 3 or *Hypothetica* 7 would seem good places for further research.

While Philo is rather disappointing after the last three corpora we have examined, it is dramatically closer to Revelation than is the rest of the GNT. Its average of 16 unusual words per thousand is more than twice what we find in Matthew—Jude. Its phrasing is also closer, four and one-half times closer: 3.99K average hits per one thousand words vs. Matthew—Jude's 0.86K. Its use of Revelation's common words is less frequent, as is its use of all of Revelation's complete list of nouns and verbs, but the first two statistics are fascinating nevertheless.

CONCLUSION

Summary

It is no exaggeration to say that Revelation is simply out of place in the GNT (Table 2). The rest of the corpus (Matthew through Jude) demonstrates the least relationship to Revelation in its vocabulary and phrasing of *any* of the five corpora we investigated.

The LXX, the Pseudepigrapha, and the Apocryphal Apocalypses all use Revelation's unusual words far more than the rest of the NT, though none of them has as high a use as Revelation itself. Even Philo uses these words more frequently. As for Revelation's phrases, they appear far more often in the literature outside the NT than they do in Revelation itself! The LXX and the Apocryphal Apocalypses are more than five times as likely to use Revelation's phrases as the book itself; the Pseudepigrapha uses them almost four times as often, while Philo places a distant fourth at twice as often. The rest of the NT, by contrast, uses Revelation's unusual words only one-tenth as often, while its phrasing appears less than half as frequently. It is no wonder that most readers of the GNT find themselves at a loss when interpreting the book!

Moving to the consideration of individual chapters, Table 8 shows the top thirty chapters from all five corpora with the highest average use of Revelation's vocabulary and phrasing. Notice that only four chapters from the NT appear on the chart. First Corinthians 12 appears at the bottom of the "Unusual" total hits column. Three chapters use Revelation's phrasing, all among the top ten for average hits per one thousand words: 1 Thess 1; 1 John 1; 1 Tim 2.

So, where are Revelation's "nearest neighbors"? They dwell among the books in the LXX and the Pseudepigrapha. These are also the corpora with the highest use of Revelation's unique words (Table 1—though Philo comes close to the Pseudepigrapha in this statistic). All of these chapters recommend themselves for further study; any one of them would make a fine paper for someone who wants to do comparative studies with Revelation (hint . . .).

Reflection

This research into Revelation's vocabulary and phraseology suggests that today's Bible software and tagged texts are well suited to such statistical analysis—and that such analysis will continue to offer important insights. The first line of investigation (Revelation's unusual vocabulary) and the fourth (Revelation's phrases) yielded the best results, easily identifying other corpora and specific chapters within them with the strongest relationships to Revelation.

The third line of investigation (all of Revelation's nouns and verbs) offered little. Upon reflection, that makes sense. After all, the 128 different lemmas unique to Revelation within the GNT is only 14 percent of its whole vocabulary—too little to be very helpful in highlighting other texts related to it. The second line of investigation (common words in NA[27]) was the least useful. This search demonstrated Revelation's uniqueness within the NT but proved to be of little use when comparing it with other corpora.

The Bible software used in this article was easily up to the tasks I asked of it. It generated accurate results to these very sophisticated linked searches surprisingly fast. In fact, it took more time to format the tables in this article than to run all the searches! Bible software is offering increasingly sophisticated searches to users. Perhaps more importantly, the number of morphologically and syntactically tagged texts available to these types of programs is increasing, as are the number of their features. These programs continue to evolve rapidly, to the overall good of our discipline. The future looks bright for computer-assisted Bible research.

Appendix 1

Tables

Corpus	Rev	Matt–Jude	NA²⁷	LXX	PSEUD	APOC	PHILO
Books	1	26	27	51	74	11	38
Chapters	22	238	260	1,150	668	61	52
Verses	405	7,536	7,941	28,971	11,684	600	8,278
Different Words (Lemmas)	911	5,292	5,420	13,773	10,659	1,999	12,772
Total Words	9,856	128,302	138,158	587,480	172,646	19,300	438,608
Average verses/ Chap	18.4	30.5	30.5	25.2	17.5	9.8	159.2
Average words/verse	24.3	17.4	17.4	20.3	14.8	32.2	53.0
Unique Revelation Words (in NA²⁷)							
Number of words appearing	128	0	128	81	69	22	59
Percentage	100%	0.0%	100.0%	63.3%	52.9%	17.2%	46.1%

Table 1: Revelation's Unique Vocabulary

Corpus	Rev	Matt–Jude	NA²⁷	LXX	PSEUD	APOC	PHILO
Books	1	26	27	51	74	11	38
Chaps	22	238	260	1,150	668	61	52
Verses	405	7,536	7,941	28,971	11,684	600	8,278
Words	9,856	128,302	138,158	587,480	172,646	19,300	438,608
Unusual Words							
Different lemmas	382	256	382	315	311	134	266
Total hits	727	914	1641	13,676	4,130	458	7,069
Highest hits/ Chap	80	15	80	115	179	101	321
Average hits/ Chap	33.05	3.84	6.31	11.89	6.18	7.51	135.94
Median hits/ Chap	28	3	3	9	3	4	141.5
Average hits/verse	1.8	0.12	0.21	0.43	0.35	0.76	0.85
Average hits/1000 words	74	7	12	23	24	24	16
Common Words							
Different lemmas	473	964	967	899	931	687	863
Total hits	4,229	53,568	57,797	193,412	57870	7,439	116,217
Highest hits/ Chap	263	582	582	633	3,847	1,996	5,083
Average hits/ Chap	192.23	225.08	222.30	168.18	86.83	121.95	2,234.94
Median hits/ Chap	191	200	198.5	153	52	41	2,341

Average hits/verse	10.44	7.11	7.28	6.68	4.953	12.40	14.039
Average hits/1000 words	429	418	418	329	335	385	265
All Nouns and Verbs							
Different lemmas	677	579	677	621	619	424	567
Total hits	3,906	33,192	34,859	136,340	38,499	5,400	62,384
Highest hits/ Chap	245	384	384	484	1,997	1,402	3,076
Average hits/ Chap	177.55	139.46	134.07	118.56	57.63	88.52	1,199.69
Median hits/ Chap	181.5	128.5	119	106	36	32	1,340
Average hits/verse	9.64	4.40	4.39	4.71	3.30	9.00	7.54
Average hits/1000 words	369	259	252	232	223	280	142
Phrases							
Total hits	19,068	99,472	118,540	6,394,203	1,280,787	197,075	1,749,502
Highest hits/ Chap	1,287	1,410	1,410	24,256	63,605	48,727	92,870
Average hits/ Chap	866.73	417.95	455.92	5560.18	1,917.35	3,230.74	33,644.27
Median hits/ Chap	845.5	328	350.50	4737.5	1,351.5	1,364	37,858.5
Average hits/verse	47.08	13.20	14.93	220.71	109.62	328.49	211.34
Average hits/1000 words	1.94K	0.76K	0.86K	10.88K	7.42K	10.21K	3.99K

Table 2: Summary Statistics

Unusual Words				Common Words			Nouns and Verbs			Phrases			
Ave	Chap	Hits	Chap	Ave	Chap	Ave	Chap	Hits	Ave	Chap	Hits	Chap	Ave
92.9	Rev 21	76	Rev 18	86.2	Acts 11	380.7	1 John 1	88	2.08K	Rev 7	1140	John 6	.852K
88.5	Rev 9	59	Rev 21	92.9	1 Cor 12	378.8	1 Thess 1	90	1.75K	Rev 13	1079	Rev 18	1.39K
86.2	Rev 18	80	Rev 9	88.5	Matt 2	376.1	1 Tim 2	77	1.68K	Rev 9	1118	Rev 2	1.50K
63.4	Rev 14	47	Rev 14	63.4	Rom 5	374.1	1 Thess 3	86	1.65K	John 17	1099	John 8	.834K
61.0	Rev 8	25	Rev 2	50.7	Rev 17	371.5	Heb 5	82	1.53K	Rev 3	1066	Acts 7	.836K
58.4	Rev 15	18	Rev 19	48.1	Matt 4	364.3	1 John 4	157	1.52K	Rev 19	1138	Mark 14	.725K
56.5	Rev 4	23	Rev 1	51.5	Matt 25	364.0	1 John 5	147	1.51K	Rev 14	1118	Luke 22	.778K
55.9	Rev 6	32	Rev 6	55.9	Matt 28	362.8	John 3	224	1.49K	Rev 2	1241	Mark 6	.895K
51.5	Rev 1	33	Rev 3	45.9	Rev 5	360.9	1 Tim 3	73	1.47K	Rev 10	573	Luke 1	.747K
50.7	Rev 2	42	Rev 12	47.0	Acts 1	358.5	John 1	288	1.46K	Rev 6	839	Rev 7	2.08K
49.4	Rev 7	27	Rev 22	46.1	John 3	358.4	1 Cor 8	78	1.44K	Rev 17	819	Rev 19	1.52K
48.1	Rev 19	36	Rev 16	43.3	Rom 6	357.5	1 Tim 4	73	1.40K	Rev 20	760	Matt 26	.688K
47.0	Rev 12	28	Rev 11	40.2	Matt 19	355.2	1 Cor 13	72	1.39K	Rev 18	1287	Rev 9	1.68K
46.1	Rev 22	28	Rev 7	49.4	Matt 27	355.2	John 4	306	1.38K	Rev 1	884	Rev 14	1.51K
45.9	Rev 3	32	Rev 8	61.0	John 4	354.1	2 Cor 13	78	1.35K	Rev 21	1100	Rev 21	1.35K
43.3	Rev 16	28	Rev 4	56.5	Rev 8	353.7	1 Cor 2	93	1.32K	Rev 16	852	John 17	1.65K
40.2	Rev 11	28	Rev 17	38.7	Matt 26	352.9	John 5	253	1.28K	Rev 5	589	Mark 9	.961K

38.7	Rev 17	22	18	Rev 15	58.4	352.6	Rom 4	177	242.3	1 John 3	150	1.24K	1 John 1	327	1079	Rev 13	1.75K
38.5	Rev 10	15	17	Rev 20	31.3	351.4	Rev 4	143	242.3	Gal 6	86	1.20K	Rev 12	716	1078	John 4	.896K
32.6	Rev 5	15	16	Rev 13	26.0	349.6	John 1	387	238.6	Rom 13	89	1.19K	Rev 11	826	1071	John 1	.968K
31.3	Rev 20	17	15	Rev 10	38.5	349.2	Matt 22	301	237.5	3 John	76	1.18K	Rev 22	719	1066	Rev 3	1.53K
26.0	Rev 13	16	15	Rev 5	32.6	349.0	Matt 17	230	237.4	2 Thess 1	66	1.12K	Rev 8	458	1049	Luke 9	.685K
21.0	1 Cor 5	6	15	Luke 12	10.4	347.7	Acts 9	348	236.2	John 10	223	1.11K	Rev 15	341	983	Luke 8	.681K
19.2	Rom 1	13	14	Matt 24	13.3	347.5	John 5	361	233.2	John 8	339	1.09K	1 John 3	676	942	Luke 24	.846K
16.7	1 Cor 8	5	13	Rom 1	19.2	347.4	Rev 7	190	232.7	John 9	218	1.06K	1 John 2	819	934	John 9	.997K
14.9	Jude	10	13	Acts 21	12.8	346.6	Acts 4	305	232.5	Rom 6	106	1.01K	1John 4	596	919	John 7	.789K
14.3	Heb 9	9	12	Luke 23	10.2	346.5	Matt 9	299	231.9	2 John	77	.999K	John 9	934	890	John 11	.703K
13.6	2 Pet 2	7	11	Mark 15	11.5	346.4	1 Cor 13	97	231.9	John 6	384	.995K	Rev 4	405	884	Rev 1	1.38K
13.3	Matt 24	14	11	Luke 10	10.2	346.4	1 Cor 14	283	230.8	1 Cor 5	66	.967K	John 1	1071	878	Matt 27	.654K
13.2	Col 4	5	11	Mark 6	8.5	345.9	1 John 5	193	230.7	Acts 7	325	.961K	Mark 9	1093	878	Matt 13	.642K
12.8	Acts 21	13	11	Luke 11	8.2	344.1	1 Tim 3	96	229.4	1 John 2	178	.955K	Eph 1	468	852	Rev 16	1.32K
12.4	Jas 5	6	10	Jude	14.9	343.4	1 Tim 5	148	228.5	Matt 22	197	.942K	John 15	620	848	Matt 12	.729K

Table 3: Revelation's Vocabulary and Phraseology in NA[27]

Unusual Words				Common Words				Nouns and Verbs				Phrases				
Ave	Chap	Hits	Chap	Ave	Ave	Chap	Hits	Ave	Chap	#	Ave	Chap	Hits	Hits	Chap	Ave
150.5	Ps 150	14	Ezek 40	86.3	396.0	Jer 35	137	336.9	Ps 28	63	18.6K	Num 30	9.5K	24.3K	1 Kgs 8	12.4K
108.5	2 Chr 3	46	Num 7	51.1	386.8	2 Chr 19	123	312.1	Jer 35	108	16.8K	Ezek 31	9.3K	23.9K	Dan 3	9.8K
96.7	Exod 27	50	1 Kgs 7	63.0	386.2	Jer 42	190	309.2	Ezek 30	171	16.6K	Ps 105	13.3K	22.5K	Ps 118	7.8K
93.0	Exod 41	61	Exod 26	82.7	380.2	Jer 33	246	307.6	Bar 1	171	16.6K	Zech 13	4.7K	22.2K	Deut 28	11.5K
89.5	Exod 37	40	Num 22	61.9	379.3	Zech 8	223	297.6	Zech 8	175	16.5K	Hos 2	11.6K	20.9K	1 Macc 10	10.5K
86.3	Ezek 40	115	Ezek 41	93.0	378.6	Jer 41	223	289.5	Isa 4	44	16.4K	Ps 149	2.4K	20.8K	1 Esd 8	9.7K
82.7	Exod 26	70	Ezek 48	62.3	377.8	Isa 52	133	288.5	Odes 13	15	16.3K	Deut 30	10.7K	20.5K	Ps 77	16.2K
74.8	Ezek 1	48	Dan 3	23.9	375.6	Ezek 18	314	287.7	Ezek 38	183	16.3K	Ps 104	11.1K	20.4K	1 Kgs 2	9.7K
71.7	Ps 148	18	Num 29	61.5	374.3	2 Kgs 24	192	284.6	2 Kgs 24	146	16.2K	Ps 77	20.5K	20.2K	Gen 24	11.8K
71.1	Num 23	51	Num 23	71.1	372.3	Bar 1	207	283.0	2 Chr 19	90	16.0K	Ps 99	1.7K	20.0K	1 Macc 9	12.1K
69.0	Ps 149	10	1 Kgs 6	65.7	371.5	Prov 29	159	282.5	Gen 1	235	15.8K	Hos 11	4.1K	20.0K	Lev 13	11.5K
67.0	Num 28	40	Ezek 43	63.9	371.4	Gen 1	309	280.3	Exod 19	176	15.4K	Lev 8	15.1K	19.4K	1 Macc 5	12.3K
65.7	1 Kgs 6	51	Exod 9	55.4	370.1	Hos 3	47	277.4	Hag 1	114	15.4K	1 Chr 10	5.9K	19.2K	Dan 4	12.6K
64.6	Zech 8	38	Exod 27	96.7	366.9	Isa 33	204	277.0	Zech 6	100	15.4K	2 Sam 4	6.3K	19.2K	1 Macc 11	11.4K
63.9	Ezek 43	51	Exod 1	74.8	366.7	Dan 7	293	276.7	Isa 18	57	15.3K	Jdt 13	10.3K	19.0K	Ezek 16	11.7K
63.0	1 Kgs 7	80	1 Macc 4	39.6	366.0	2 Chr 27	71	274.8	Exod 40	158	15.3K	Jdt 6	9.6K	19.0K	Ezek 20	14.7K
62.3	Ezek 48	58	2 Chr 3	108.5	365.1	Ps 133	23	274.3	1 Kgs 13	277	15.3K	Ezek 14	10.6K	18.5K	2 Chr 6	13.6K
61.9	Num 22	66	Jer 28	33.5	365.0	1 Chr 22	192	273.9	Zech 1	126	15.2K	Josh 20	16.4K	17.8K	Neh 9	14.9K
61.5	Num 29	53	Lev 4	44.2	363.6	1 Kgs 14	108	273.0	Ezek 35	80	15.1K	Isa 34	6.0K	17.7K	Judg 9	11.6K
60.8	Ps 147	9	Dan 2	30.7	363.1	Exod 19	228	272.0	Jer 33	176	15.0K	Gen 39	9.5K	17.6K	Dan 11	14.9K

Table 4: Revelation's Vocabulary and Phraseology in the LXX

Unusual Words						Phrases					
Ave	Chap	Hits	Chap	Hits	Ave	Chap	Hits	Hits	Chap	Ave
187.5	Jub. 5	3	Aris. Ex.	179	12.0	Ascen. Isa. 29	18.8K	4992	63605	Aris. Ex.	4.3K
136.4	T. Adam B 2	9	Sib. Or. 3	169	25.8	T. Job 33	18.0K	3449	12760	Ps. Sol. 17	12.7K
100.0	T. Sol. A 21	11	Sib. Or. 5	101	23.8	T. Dan. 7	17.7K	1131	12275	Ord. Levi	8.4K
88.8	T. Jud. 25	19	Sib. Or. 8	100	25.3	Apoc. Sedr. 6	17.2K	2353	9072	4 Bar. 7	9.3K
76.9	Sib. Or. 26	1	Sib. Or. 1	76	24.5	Ascen. Isa. 18	16.8K	3063	8526	Ascen. Isa. A 3	11.9K
71.4	Liv. Pro. 13	2	Apocr. Ezek.	72	36.2	T. Naph. 9	16.6K	846	7967	Eup. 2	5.0K
71.4	T. Sim. 9	2	Eup. 2	71	44.3	Liv. Pro. 6	16.6K	695	7865	Ps. Sol. 2	11.3K
69.2	T. Naph. 5	13	Sib. Or. 2	67	24.1	Ascen. Isa. 26	16.5K	3968	7684	Ascen. Isa. 10	14.7K
69.0	T. Jud. 4	4	Sib. Or. 14	66	23.7	1 En. 11	16.4K	818	7642	Artap. 3	4.6K
66.7	Jub. 38	2	Dem. 2	64	52.9	1 En. 101	16.0K	3257	7174	Sib. Or. 3	1.1K
66.7	T. Reu. 7	3	Ps.-Phoc.	55	29.0	Liv. Pro. 7	16.0K	671	7111	Ascen. Isa. 4	15.7K
63.8	Dem. 4	6	Sib. Or. 11	51	20.3	L.A.E. 37	15.9K	2455	7022	4 Bar. 9	8.9K
63.6	T. Sol. B	7	T. Sol. A 18	44	34.2	Ascen. Isa. 4	15.7K	7111	6999	Ps. Sol. 8	11.4K
61.1	T. Jud. 5	8	Sib. Or. 12	42	18.5	Ps. Sol. 1	15.7K	1831	6900	4 Bar. 6	10.3K
60.2	Ascen. Isa. 29	16	Sib. Or. 4	41	27.1	L.A.E. 39	15.4K	1883	6687	1 En. 10	11.3K
60.0	T. Sim. 5	9	Sib. Or. 7	40	28.3	L.A.E. 32	15.4K	1971	6526	Dem. 2	5.4K
58.8	1 En. 26	8	Sib. Or. 13	37	27.9	Ascen. Isa. 5	15.4K	3936	6493	Ascen. Isa. 16	14.0K
57.9	4 Esd. 14	7	Ord. Levi	34	23.3	L.A.E. 42	15.3K	3446	6484	Ascen. Isa. A 1	12.4K
57.4	L.A.E. 22	7	Jub. 3	33	55.6	L.A.E. 41	14.9K	999	6450	1 En. 106	11.5K
56.6	Apoc. Ab. 12	21	3 Mac. 5	30	24.8	Liv. Pro. 5	14.9K	656	6429	Ascen. Isa. 23	11.9K

Table 5: Revelation's Vocabulary and Phraseology in the Pseudepigrapha

Unusual Words					Phrases				
Ave	Chap	Hits	Hits	Chap	Ave	Ave	Chap	Hits	Hits	Chap	Ave
65.57	6 Esd.	4	101	Apoc. Paul	17.12	15.8K	Apoc. Mos. 37	2455	48727	Apoc. Paul	8.3K
56.91	Apoc. Mos. 22	7	68	Apoc. John	20.01	15.3K	Apoc. Mos. 39	1883	26095	Apoc. John	8.0K
54.95	Apoc. Mos. 8	5	34	Gos. Bart. 4	29.69	15.3K	Apoc. Mos. 32	1971	13293	Apoc. John Chry.	6.9K
50.96	Apoc. Mos. 29	8	29	Apoc. John Chry.	15.11	15.2K	Apoc. Mos. 42	3446	9172	Gos. Bart. 4	8.0K
49.38	Apoc. Mos. 33	8	21	Apoc. Pet. (Akh.)	20.61	15.0K	6 Esd.	912	7767	Apoc. Pet. (Akh.)	7.6K
41.96	Apoc. Mos. 43	6	16	Apoc. Esd 5	31.07	14.7K	Apoc. Mos. 41	999	6456	Apoc. Esd. 4	9.7K
40.98	Apoc. Mos. 20	5	14	Apoc. Esd. 4	20.99	13.1K	Apoc. Mos. 33	2122	5908	Gos. Bart. 2	6.0K
40.00	Apoc. Mos. 26	5	9	Apoc. Esd. 2	19.07	12.9K	Apoc. Mos. 29	2030	3887	Apoc. Esd. 2	8.2K
40.00	Apoc. Mos. 6	4	9	Gos. Bart. 2	9.83	12.7K	Apoc. Pet. (Rain.)	1535	3868	Apoc. Esd. 5	7.5K
34.72	Apoc. Mos. 17	5	8	Apoc. Mos. 29	50.96	12.7K	Apoc. Mos. 36	874	3799	Apoc. Esd. 1	9.2K
32.71	Apoc. Mos. 40	7	8	Apoc. Mos. 33	49.38	12.2K	Apoc. Mos. 15	1334	3446	Apoc. Mos. 42	15.2K
32.26	Apoc. Mos. 37	5	7	Apoc. Mos. 22	56.91	12.2K	Apoc. Mos. 2	1404	3442	Apoc. Esd. 6	8.5K
31.07	Apoc. Esd. 5	16	7	Apoc. Mos. 40	32.71	12.1K	Apoc. Mos. 27	1409	2586	Apoc. Esd. 7	7.2K
30.93	Apoc. Mos. 1	3	7	Apoc. Pet. (Pat. Quo.)	25.55	11.8K	Apoc. Mos. 16	1729	2455	Apoc. Mos. 37	15.8K
29.69	Gos. Bart. 4	34	6	Apoc. Mos. 43	41.96	11.8K	Apoc. Mos. 12	741	2160	Apoc. Mos. 13	11.6K
28.17	Apoc. Mos. 9	4	6	Apoc. Esd. 6	14.81	11.6K	Apoc. Mos. 13	2160	2137	Apoc. Mos. 40	10.0K
27.27	Apoc. Mos. 10	3	5	Apoc. Mos. 8	54.95	11.4K	Apoc. Mos. 3	1201	2127	Apoc. Esd. 3	6.6K
27.21	Apoc. Mos. 16	4	5	Apoc. Mos. 20	40.98	11.4K	Apoc. Mos. 22	1396	2122	Apoc. Mos. 33	13.1K
25.55	Apoc. Pet. (Pat. Quo.)	7	5	Apoc. Mos. 26	40.00	10.7K	Apoc. Mos. 24	1227	2030	Apoc. Mos. 29	13.0K
24.79	Apoc. Mos. 38	3	5	Apoc. Mos. 17	34.72	10.3K	Apoc. Mos. 17	1484	1971	Apoc. Mos. 32	15.3K

Table 6: Revelation's Vocabulary and Phraseology in the Apocryphal Apocalypses

Unusual Words						Phrases					
Ave	Chap	Hits	Hits	Chap	Ave	Chap	Ave	Hits	Hits	Chap	Ave
32.77	QG 3	41	321	Spec. 1	15.39	Hypoth. 7	5.5K	5971	92870	Leg. 3	4.6K
19.01	Mos. 2	307	311	Her.	17.02	Leg. 2	4.8K	38690	71200	Spec. 1	3.4K
18.90	Leg. 1	165	307	Mos. 2	19.01	Hypoth. 11	4.6K	2292	64250	Her.	3.5K
18.46	Plant.	187	301	Mos. 1	15.74	Leg. 3	4.6K	92870	63953	Mos. 1	3.3K
17.99	Aet.	189	285	Leg. 3	14.20	Hypoth. 6	4.6K	4131	61361	Legat.	3.3K
17.60	QG 1, 2	54	244	Somn. 2	16.42	Leg. 1	4.4K	38231	57473	Somn. 1	3.8K
17.43	Congr.	179	243	Opif.	16.25	QG 1, 1	4.1K	10214	55872	Migr.	3.9K
17.02	Her.	311	241	Spec. 2	14.62	Gig.	3.9K	14471	54585	Mos. 2	3.4K
16.61	Sacr.	180	233	Legat.	12.52	Fug.	4.0K	49880	54460	Opif.	3.6K
16.42	Somn. 2	244	206	Somn. 1	13.74	Migr.	3.9K	55872	53464	Mut.	3.5K
16.33	Prov. 1	4	202	Ebr.	15.42	Somn. 1	3.8K	57473	52064	Abr.	3.5K
16.30	Hypoth. 7	21	189	Aet.	17.99	Conf.	3.8K	45283	51549	Somn. 2	3.5K
16.25	Opif.	243	187	Plant.	18.46	Deus.	3.8K	38571	50119	Spec. 2	3.0K
16.13	Prov. 2	77	185	Mut.	12.16	Ebr.	3.8K	49420	49880	Fug.	4.0K
15.74	Mos. 1	301	181	Abr.	12.09	Plant.	3.8K	38024	49420	Ebr.	3.8K
15.42	Ebr.	202	180	Sacr.	16.61	QG 1, 2	3.7K	11457	47231	Det.	3.7K
15.39	Spec. 1	321	179	Congr.	17.43	Post.	3.7K	46311	46311	Post.	3.7K
14.78	Decal.	141	176	Fug.	13.80	Det.	3.7K	47231	45283	Conf.	3.8K
14.62	Spec. 2	241	174	Spec. 3	13.82	Opif.	3.6K	54460	43800	Ios.	3.0K
14.34	Sobr.	59	165	Leg. 1	18.90	Cher.	3.6K	30817	43680	Virt.	3.2K

Table 7: Revelation's Vocabulary and Phraseology in Philo

Unusual Words					Phrases			
Ave	Chap	Hits	Chap	Hits	Ave	Chap	Hits	Chap	Ave
187.5	Jub. 5	3	Jub. 19	458.3	11	T. Sim. 9	11	Ascen. Isa. 29	18.8K	4992
150.5	Ps 150	14	Jub. 31	454.6	10	3 Bar. 14	15	Num 30	18.6K	9515
136.4	L.A.E. 2	9	Eup. 1	416.7	15	Ps 28	63	T. Job 33	18.0K	3449
108.5	2 Chr 3	46	T. Job 19	415.4	27	1 Thess 1	90	T. Dan 7	17.7K	1131
100.0	T. Sol. A 21	11	Sib. Or. 22	407.4	11	1 John 1	88	Apoc. Sedr. 6	17.2K	2353
96.7	Exod 27	50	Ps. Sol. 18	403.2	100	1 En. 18	112	Ascen. Isa. 18	16.8K	3063
93.0	Ezek 41	61	1 En. 25	402.8	85	3 Bar. 5	23	Ezek 31	16.8K	9246
89.5	Exod 37	40	Jub. 17	400.0	14	1 Tim 2	77	Ps 105	16.6K	13278
88.8	T. Jud. 25	19	Hist. Rech. 1	400.0	72	Jer 35	108	Zech 13	16.6K	4737
86.3	Ezek 40	115	Jub. 15	400.0	4	Ezek 30	171	T. Naph. 9	16.6K	846
82.7	Exod 26	70	Apoc. Sedr. 13	397.3	58	Sib. Or. 26	4	Liv. Pro. 6	16.6K	695
76.9	Sib. Or. 26	1	Jer 35	396.0	137	Bar. 1	171	Hos 2	16.5K	11577
74.8	Ezek 1	48	T. Sol. C	394.4	56	Ps. Sol. 11	52	Ascen. Isa. 26	16.5K	3968
71.7	Ps 148	18	T. Sim. 9	392.9	11	Apoc. Sedr. 3	39	Ps 149	16.4K	2375
71.4	Liv. Pro. 13	2	Hist. Rech. 6	392.6	64	Apoc. Sedr. 12	40	1 En. 11	16.4K	818
71.4	T. Sim. 9	2	T. Ash. 4	389.9	62	Zech 8	175	Deut 30	16.3K	10723
71.1	Num. 23	51	Hist. Rech. 23	389.4	44	Hist. Rech. 19	48	Ps 104	16.3K	11109

69.2	T. Naph. 5	13	387.0	2 Chr 19	123	296.3	Sib. Or. 22	8	16.2K	Ps 77	20452
69.0	Ps 149	10	386.0	Jer 42	190	295.1	L.A.E. 22	36	16.0K	1 En. 101	3257
69.0	T. Jud. 4	4	385.4	Liv. Pro. 10	79	295.1	6 Esd.	18	16.0K	Ps 99	1648
67.0	Num 28	40	385.2	Benj. 11	52	294.9	L.A.E. 29	46	16.0K	Liv. Pro. 7	671
66.7	T. Reu. 7	3	385.0	T. Job 23	72	293.0	Apoc. Mos. 29	46	15.9K	L.A.E. 37	2455
66.7	Jub. 38	2	384.6	Sib. Or. 26	5	292.7	Apoc. Mos. 22	36	15.8K	Apoc. Mos. 37	2455
65.7	1 Kgs 6	51	381.7	Ps. Sol. 6	50	292.6	T. Naph. 5	55	15.8K	Hos 11	4091
65.6	6 Esd.	4	381.0	T. Levi 19	48	291.7	Hist. Rech 13	28	15.7K	Asen. Isa. 4	7111
64.6	Zech 8	38	381.0	Acts 11	249	289.5	Isa 4	44	15.6K	Ps Sol. 1	1831
63.9	Ezek 43	51	380.0	Jer 33	246	289.2	Liv. Pro. 23	24	15.4K	L.A.E. 39	1883
63.8	Dem. 4	6	379.0	Zech 8	223	288.5	Odes Sol. 13	15	15.4K	L.A.E. 32	1971
63.6	T. Sol. B	7	379.0	1 En. 18	130	288.1	Zeph.	17	15.4K	Lev 8	15135
63.4	Rev 14	47	379.0	1 Cor 12	239	287.7	Ezek 38	183	15.4K	1 Chr 10	5875

Table 8: Revelation's Vocabulary and Phraseology in the Five Corpora

Appendix 2

Graphs

REVELATION'S VOCABULARY AND PHRASEOLOGY IN NA^{27}

Unusual Words

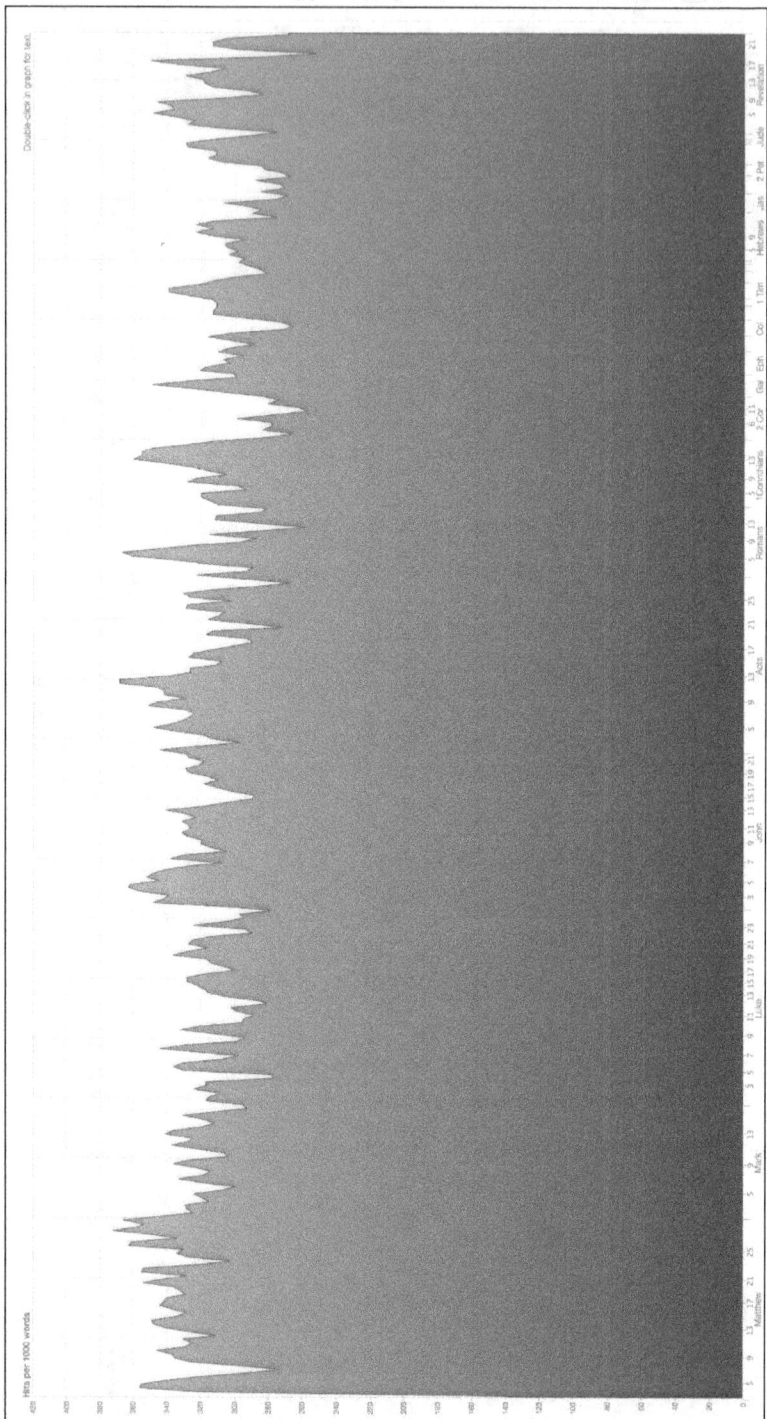

Common Words

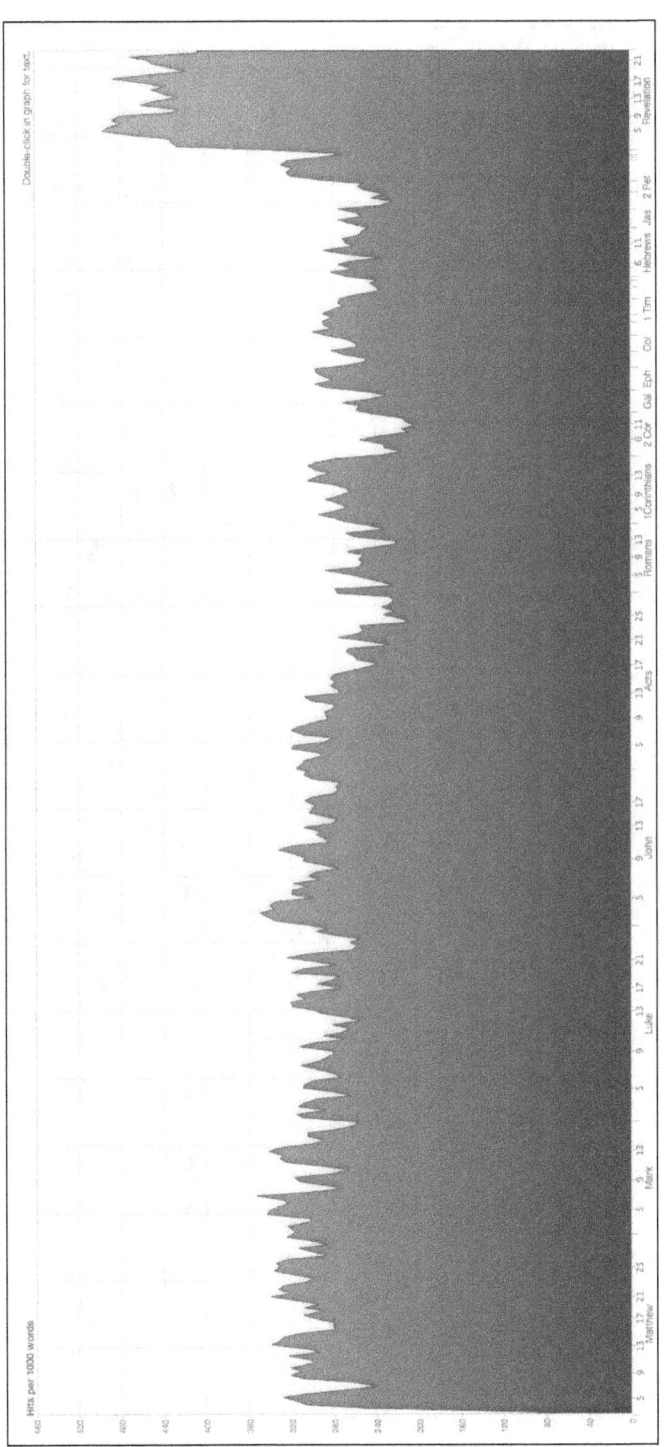

All Nouns and Verbs

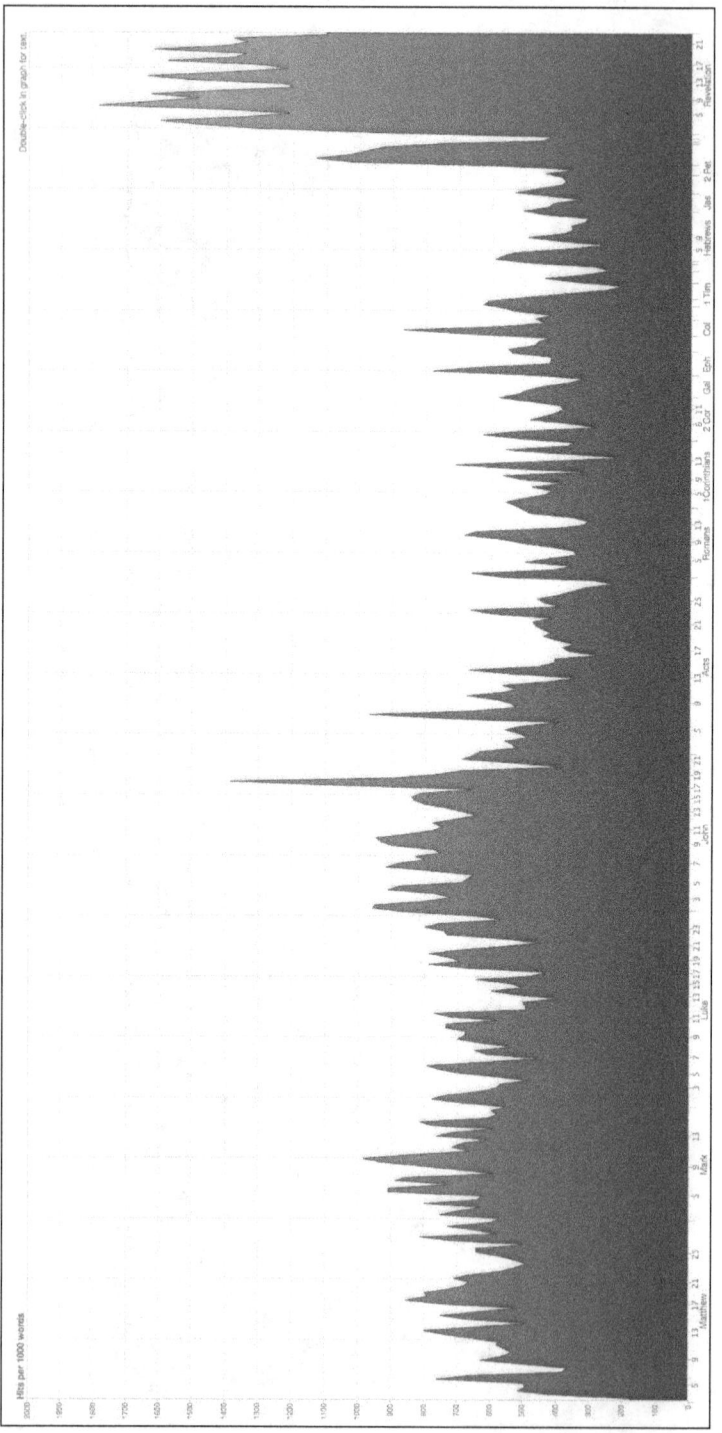

Phrases

**REVELATION'S VOCABULARY
AND PHRASEOLOGY IN LXX**

Unusual Words

Common Words

All Nouns and Verbs

Phrases

REVELATION'S VOCABULARY
AND PHRASEOLOGY IN PSEUDEPIGRAPHA

Unusual Words

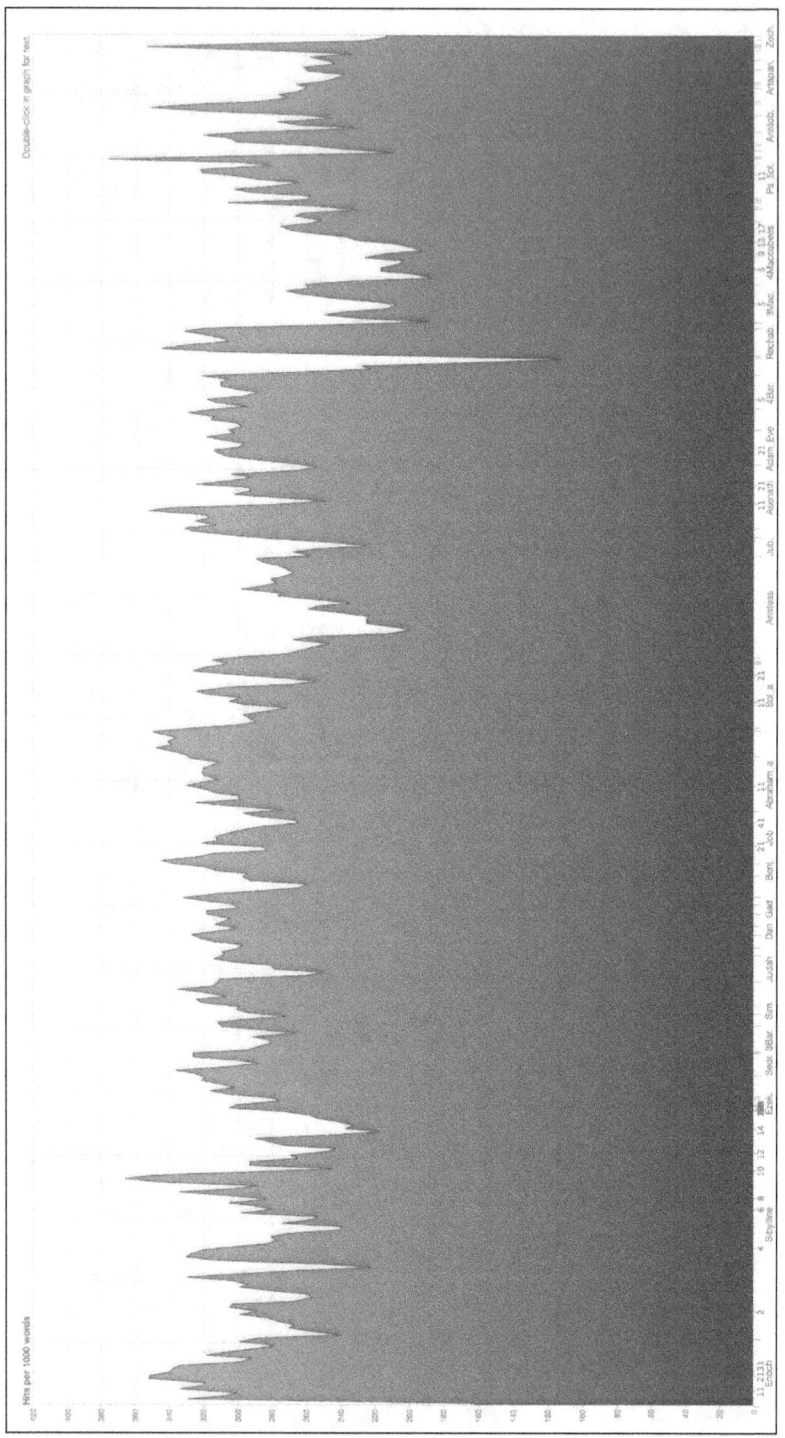

Common Words

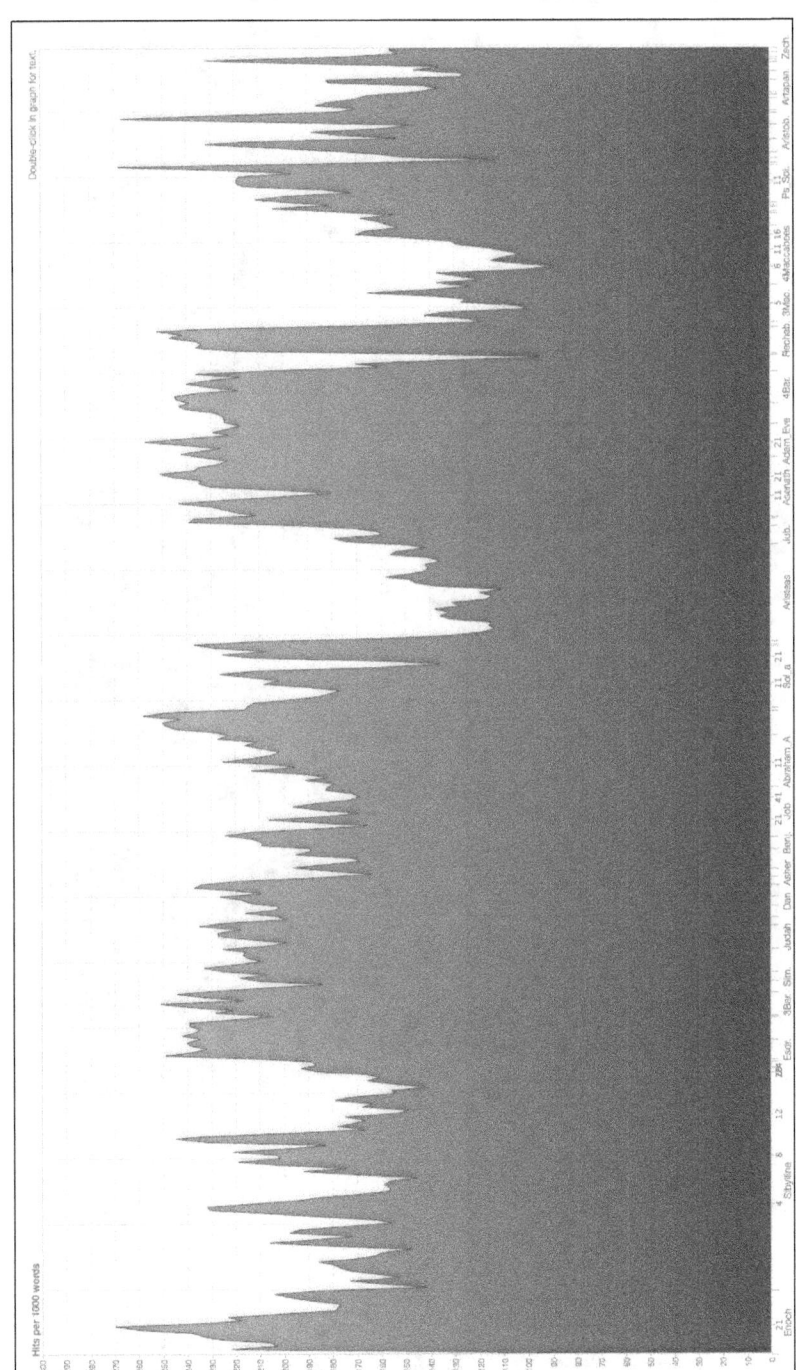

All Nouns and Verbs

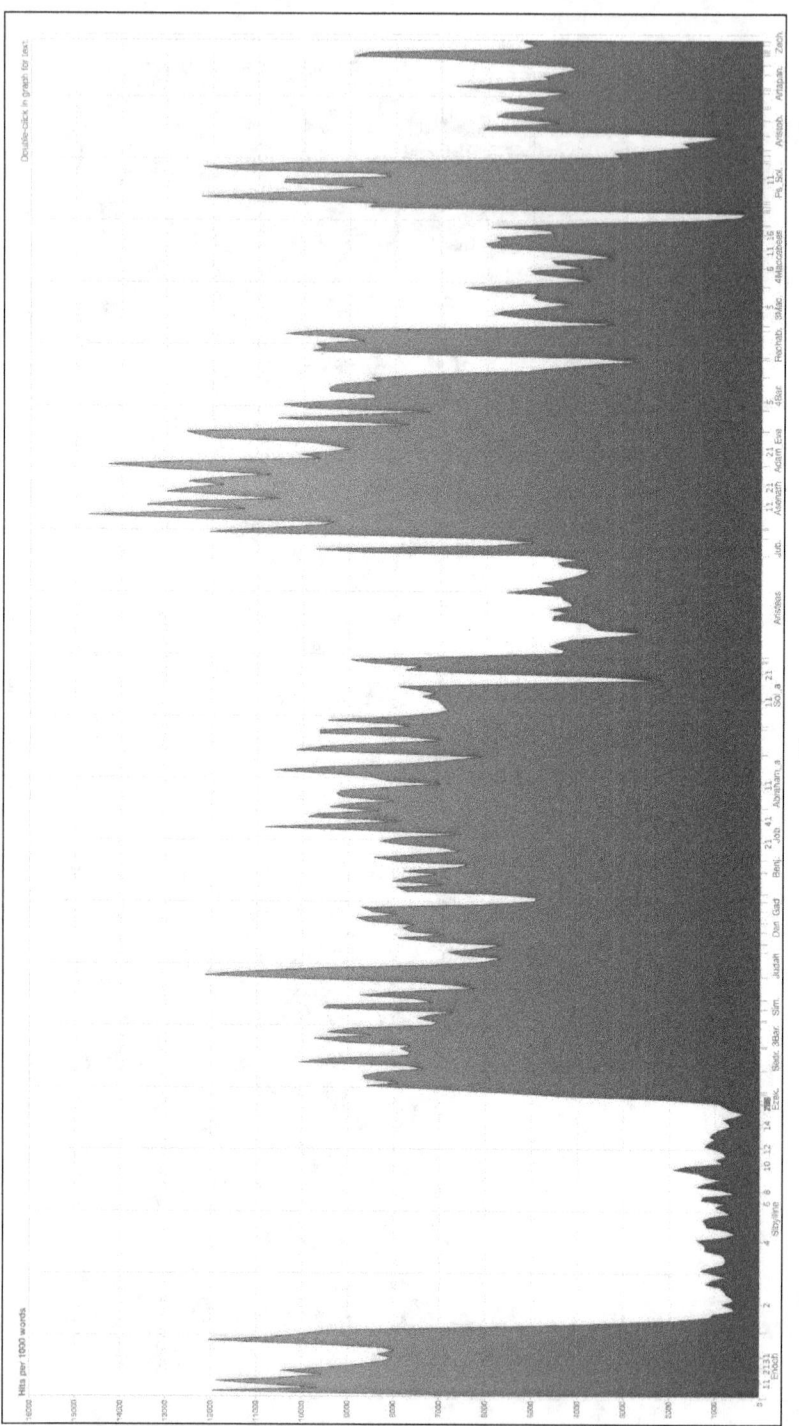

Phrases

**REVELATION'S VOCABULARY
AND PHRASEOLOGY IN APOCRYPHAL APOCALYPSES**

Unusual Words

Common Words

All Nouns and Verbs

4D. Phrases

REVELATION'S VOCABULARY AND PHRASEOLOGY IN PHILO

Unusual Words

Common Words

All Nouns and Verbs

Phrases

Select Author Index

Alexander, P., 140n2
Althouse, P., 180n4
Anderson, P. N., 92n12
Attridge, H. W., 126n15
Aune, D. E., 196, 231n29

Balfour, G., 104n9, 119–20
Barr, D. L., 181n13
Barrett, C. K., 49, 81n4, 101n1, 119–20
Barus, A., 100n28
Bauckham, R., 50n9, 126, 184, 187n19, 189, 199, 205n34, 216n3, 241n30, 243n36
Beale, G. K., 191n27, 196, 199, 205
Beasley-Murray, G. R., 61n9, 105n11, 126n13, 136n40, 222n3, 227n19, 240n26
Behm, J., 222n4
Belleville, L., 113n44
Benson, P., 165n35
Berg, R. A., 173n3
Bernard, C. K., 74n34
Billington, A., 223–24n12
Blenkinsopp, J., 109n27
Blinzler, J., 126n16
Boismard, M. E., 104n8, 125
Bolyki, J., 155n8
Borchert, G. L., 55
Boring, E., 75n39
Boyarin, D., 127n18
Boyd, G. A., 91n10
Bratcher, R. G., 204
Brighton, L. A., 204
Broadhead, E. K., 28–29,

Brodie, T. L., 126n15
Brown, P. E., 19–22
Brown, R. E., 50n8, 61n10, 62n14, 63, 75n37, 77n47, 172n3
Bruce, F. F., 93n14, 238n12
Bultmann, R. K., 105n12, 128
Burge, G. M., 54, 173n3, 223n5

Cadbury, H. J., 61n8
Caringola, R., 200n21
Carter, C., 142n8, 143n9
Caws, M. A., 129
Charles, R. H., 251n12
Chilton, D., 195n2
Cortés, J. B., 101n1
Coulter, D. M., 180n4
Crouch, D., 70n18
Crouch, P., 6
Culpepper, R. A., 102nn2 and 4, 105nn13–14, 106nn18–19, 112n39, 119n52, 122n4, 123, 125n12, 128n21, 133–34, 136n40, 137n41

Dodd, C. H., 108n23
Donahue, M., 165n35
Dunn, J. D. G., 227

Eco, U., 129n26
Edwards, K., 159n15, 164n33
Ellis, P. F., 137n41
Ensor, P., 50
Erickson, J., 165n35

Select Author Index

Fee, G. D., 15, 103n5, 104n9, 115n49, 151n30
Ford, J. M., 239n18
Friesen, S., 71n21

Galot, J., 60n4, 125, n4
Gardner-Smith, P., 125
Genette, G., 105n14,
Gruenler, R. G., 55n21
Guthrie, D., 81n3

Haenchen, E., 77n43
Hall, T., 159n15, 164n33
Hanson, K. C., 78
Harland, P., 68n10
Harrison, E. F., 61n7
Hasel, G., 18n7
Hays, R., 154n5, 155n6
Heil, J.-P., 74nn32, 36, 75
Hill, D., 239n16,
Horsley, G. H. R., 65, 66n5, 67n8, 71–72
Hoskyns, E., 124–25, 131

Iser, W., 127n19, 129n26

Jones, L. P., 117n50

Kautsky, J. H., 72
Keener, C. S., 48n2, 51, 53, 56, 74n34, 104n8, 109nn27–28, 120n54, 238n13, 240n22, 241n31
Köstenberger, A. J., 48–49, 155, n6
Kraybill, J. N., 68n10
Krieger, M., 102n2
Krodel, G. A., 202

Ladd, G. E., 24n3, 222n2
Lagrange, J. M., 60n3
Lenski, G., 72
Levering, M., 180n5
Lincoln, A. T., 35n13, 109n26
Lindars, B., 74n36
Louw, J. P., 38n17,

Macchia, F. D., 233n35
Madden, P. J., 74n32,
Manning, Jr., G. T., 113n44

Manolaraki, E., 74n30
Marlow, R., 93n14,
Marshall, I. H., 93n14
McClendon, Jr., J. W., 140n3
Meeks, W., 154n6
Meier, C. A., 159n15, 164n33
Menzies, R. P., 228n3, 230n26
Metzger, B. M., 86n1
Michaels, J. R., 61n9, 82, 189n22
Moloney, F. J., 61n7
Morris, L., 21–22, 81n4, 86n1
Mounce, R. H., 43n29, 196n8
Murray, P., 121n1

Nebeker, G. L., 23, 25
Neirynck, F. J., 125, 126n13
Nida, E. A., 38n17

O'Day, G. R., 105, n12
Oakman, D. E., 78
Osborne, G. R., 181n6, 196n6, 197, 201, 211

Pinnock, C. H., 15–17, 19, 21n14, 23
Piper, O. A., 133
Plumer, E., 29,
Pryor, J. W., 60n5, 125n12

Rensberger, D., 148n20
Rissi, M., 243n35
Rogers, G., 68, 69n15
Roloff, J., 195n2
Rosenszwig, B., 187n18,
Rubenstein, J. L., 110nn29 and 33, 111n35
Russell, D. S., 241n31

Scherrer, P., 69n15
Schnackenburg, R., 101n1, 103n7, 109, 118n51,
Schüssler Fiorenza, E., 181n8
Seiss, J. A., 200
Smalley, S. S., 229, 230n27,
Smith, D. M., 51n11, 126n15,
Stassen, G., 152n31,
Stibbe, M. W. G., 102n4, 112n38, 238n13,
Strobel, L., 91n9

Select Author Index

Stronstad, R., 201n25
Swartley, W. M., 148,
Swete, H. B., 196

Tenney, M. C., 22n17
Thomas, J. C., 28n1, 31nn7–8, 32n9, 35n14, 201n25, 240n23, 241n28
Thompson, M. M., 49
Turner, M., 224nn9, 11, 227, 233n35
Twelftree, G. H., 29–30

Unger, M. F., 80n2

van der Laan, P., 180n4
van der Watt, J. G., 157n11
van Tilborg, S., 69n15
Vellanickal, M., 60n4, 61n11, 62n13, 63n17

Volf, M., 148n17
Von Harnack, A., 60n4

Waddell, R., 191, 195n1, 197n11, 201n25, 208n44, 217n4, 232n33, 240n23
Wall, R. W., 127
Walvoord, J. F., 188n20, 195n4
Watson, A., 164n34
Welker, M., 218–19
Wilson, M., 19n26
Witherington III, B., 91n9, 222n3
Wyckoff, J. W., 20n12

Yoder, J. H., 140, 142n8, 146n16
Yong, A., 233n35

Zumstein, J., 127n19, 128n20